Myanmar Update Series

Debating Democratization

IN MYANMAR

EDITED BY

NICK CHEESMAN
NICHOLAS FARRELLY
TREVOR WILSON

LSEAS

INSTITUTE OF SOUTHEAST ASIAN STUDIES
Singapore

First published in Singapore in 2014 by
ISEAS Publishing
Institute of Southeast Asian Studies
30 Heng Mui Keng Terrace
Pasir Panjang
Singapore 119614

E-mail: publish@iseas.edu.sg
Website: http://bookshop.iseas.edu.sg

ISEAS Library Cataloguing-in-Publication Data

Debating democratization in Myanmar / edited by Nick Cheesman, Nicholas Farrelly and Trevor Wilson.
    Papers originally presented to 2013 Myanmar/Burma Update Conference held at the Australian National University, Canberra, from 15 to 16 May 2013.
1. Burma—Politics and government—21st century—Congresses.
2. Democratization—Burma—Congresses.
3. Burma—Economic policy—Congresses.
4. Burma—Armed Forces—Congresses.
5. Social conflict—Burma—Congresses.
I. Cheesman, Nick.
II. Farrelly, Nicholas.
III. Wilson, Trevor.
IV. Australian National University.
V. Myanmar/Burma Update Conference (2013 : Canberra, Australia)
DS530.4 B972 2013   2014

ISBN 978-981-4519-13-7 (soft cover)
ISBN 978-981-4519-14-4 (hard cover)
ISBN 978-981-4517-15-1 (e-book, PDF)

Cover photo: Yangon workers protesting for a minimum wage
Photograph by U Thike Tun (a.k.a. "Boothee"), Myanmar Times

Typeset by Allison Ley
Printed in Singapore by Markono Print Media Pte Ltd

CONTENTS

LIST OF TABLES

LIST OF FIGURES

LIST OF ILLUSTRATIONS

ACKNOWLEDGEMENTS

The March 2013 Myanmar/Burma Update conference was the biggest such conference since the Australian National University (ANU) held its first Burma Update in 1999. The conveners/editors are grateful to the Australian Agency for International Development (AusAID) for its generous financial support for the conference, for this publication of the conference papers, and for a follow-up policy workshop in 2014.

The Department of Political and Social Change, ANU College of Asia and the Pacific, has throughout shown unwavering support for the Update. We thank Andrew MacIntyre, the College Dean, Paul Hutchcroft, then Director of the School of International, Political and Strategic Studies, and Greg Fealy, the Head of the Department of Political and Social Change, for their encouragement and involvement. We especially appreciate the wise guidance of Ed Aspinall in organizing and running the conference, and in assisting the process of publication of the conference papers. Other staff at the College who deserve thanks for their assistance include Julie Fitzgibbon, Dan Striegl, and Allison Ley.

The editors wish to thank the Institute of Southeast Asian Studies (ISEAS) in Singapore for agreeing once again to publish the conference papers. The editors also wish to thank Christine Wilson for her dedicated copy-editing and indexing assistance, and the ANU Cartographic and GIS Services for their assistance with maps for this publication.

The 2013 Update was the first to have a Burmese-language session, and the postgraduate students who participated in that event and helped out in numerous other ways over the duration of the conference have our special appreciation. We look forward to their participation in future events by way of conference presentations and papers, and to their involvement in the process of democratization in Myanmar.

CONTRIBUTORS AND EDITORS

Nick Cheesman is a lecturer at the Department of Political and Social Change, ANU College of Asia and the Pacific, and co-convener 2013 ANU Myanmar/Burma Update Conference.

Kerstin Duell is an independent consultant and journalist based in Singapore.

Renaud Egreteau is Research Assistant Professor, University of Hong Kong.

Anders Engvall is a Research Fellow at the Southeast Asia Research Program, Stockholm School of Economics in Sweden.

David Ennis is an international electoral expert, with extensive experience in the management of elections in post-conflict and transitional societies.

Peter Erben is an international electoral expert based in Jakarta.

Nicholas Farrelly is a research fellow at the School of International, Political and Strategic Studies, ANU College of Asia and the Pacific, and co-convener of the 2013 ANU Myanmar/Burma Update Conference.

Thomas Kean is the editor of the English-language edition of *The Myanmar Times*.

Kyaw Soe Lwin is a PhD candidate at the City University of Hong Kong.

Kyaw Thu Aung is Director of Paung Ku, a consortium of humanitarian civil society groups based in Myanmar.

Kyle Lemargie is an international electoral expert working on projects in Southeast Asia.

Ma Khin Mar Mar Kyi is a Post-Doctoral Research Scholar at Oxford University.

Morten B. Pedersen is Senior Lecturer in International and Political Studies, School of Humanities and Social Sciences, University of New South Wales, Canberra.

Andrew Reynolds is Professor of Political Science Department, and Chair of Global Studies, University of North Carolina, Chapel Hill, and is an international electoral expert.

Andrew Selth is an Adjunct Associate Professor, Griffith Asia Institute, Griffith University, Brisbane.

Seng Maw Lahpai is an independent researcher based in Sydney, Australia.

Soe Nandar Linn is a Research Associate at the Myanmar Development Resources Institute (MDRI), Yangon.

Than Than Nu is Secretary General of the Democratic Party (Myanmar).

Sean Turnell is Associate Professor, Department of Economics, Macquarie University, Sydney; Founder of the Burma Economic Watch.

Tamas Wells is a PhD candidate in politics at the University of Melbourne, and an aid consultant.

Trevor Wilson is a Visiting Fellow at the Department of Political and Social Change, ANU College of Asia and the Pacific, and co-convener 2013 ANU Myanmar/Burma Update Conference.

Winston Set Aung is Deputy Governor of the Central Bank of Myanmar and former Deputy Minister of National Planning and Economic Development of Myanmar.

I
Foreword

1

MYANMAR
REFORMS GATHERING MOMENTUM

Winston Set Aung

Until 2011 Myanmar had been as if asleep for quite some time. When Myanmar woke up, it was abruptly faced with a world economy in crisis, including the sovereign debt crisis in the European Union and economic recession in the United States. While the economies of many countries in the Southeast Asian region (except, perhaps, for countries that had an adequate level of domestic consumption, such as Indonesia) suffered various impacts as a result of these developments, particularly because of their effect on international trade and investment, for Myanmar the blows were shattering.

In addition to these external factors, which have had both direct and indirect impacts on the national economy as well as on regional economies, Myanmar has been struggling to address internal multi-dimensional problems that had developed over past years. Myanmar was isolated for many decades, but despite this, the Myanmar government did try systematically to tackle development issues in various sectors. The quick fixes and short-term therapies that were practised in the past caused these inter-connected issues to become more complex, which means that now systematic multi-dimensional policies are needed to address them adequately. Aiming at developing a more systematic approach for resolving these issues, the Myanmar government has drafted a reform framework, under which sectoral priority areas for people-centered development have been identified through a multi-dimensional approach. Among these priority areas are some in which quick wins for the nation and the people have been further identified.

Among all the priority areas for development identified in Myanmar's overall reform framework, numerous measures were specified for early action, taking into account the proper sequencing for development. If you were to ask me whether or not this process has produced a perfect reform framework for Myanmar, I would have to say that that goal is still a long way off, and the framework far from perfect. However, with sustained commitment on the part of the government and others, tremendous efforts are being made to move things forward in every possible way.

Perceptions of Myanmar's reforms vary, and expectations for Myanmar's socio-economic development are great. There are many people, including the majority of the international community, who appreciate the significant progress in the area of political and economic reform that the government of Myanmar has already achieved, with the result that the majority of international sanctions against Myanmar have been either lifted totally or suspended. Many others, especially from international organizations, have been deeply concerned about the rapidity of Myanmar's development. A number of international organizations have suggested that it might be better to slow the current rapid pace of change, and to move forward more steadily and with more caution. At the same time, many people inside and outside the country are frustrated because they think that things are still moving very slowly.

Probably all are correct. People have different perceptions depending on where they are and how they see things. No doubt there has been progress but, inevitably, there will be mistakes in some areas while in others development may lag behind. It is most important to ensure that the political will and commitment to move things forward at a reasonable pace is sustained, that mistakes are promptly and efficiently corrected and lessons learned, and that progress brings significant benefits to the population at large, not just to the select few.

Myanmar has chosen the path to democracy because that is what is desired by its own people. Hence, Myanmar has to develop its economic and social development plans in line with democratic principles. In many areas, measures to increase transparency and accountability have been applied. Many ministries increasingly implement selection processes through international tenders and bidding, instead of simply granting concessions to businessmen or companies who have good connections with government agencies. The best example of this can be found in the selection process for two international mobile phone operators, which was conducted transparently and professionally, in line with international practice.[1]

Civil society groups and businesses in the private sector are increasingly involved in development planning through consultative meetings. They are also involved in the process of drafting laws. One example is the World Bank's Community Driven Development (CDD) programme, through which villagers are being empowered to choose, plan, build, monitor, and account for small infrastructure projects to improve their lives. Another example is the process of drafting the *Foreign Investment Law*, the *Myanmar Special Economic Zone Law*, and the Small and Medium Enterprises Law, in which civil society groups, private business associations, and international organizations are involved. In addition, the views of civil society groups and of the private sector were taken into account in developing the Framework for Economic and Social Reforms (FESR).[2] A similar process is also being followed in drafting the National Comprehensive Development Plan (NCDP).

Policy-makers are very concerned about the possible widening of inequity as a result of the process of development. Hence, a master plan for comprehensive rural development has been drawn up with the purpose of not only alleviating poverty but also reducing inequity and narrowing the rural-urban gap. In addition, attempts are being made to improve the rule of law, encourage fair competition, and increase economic freedom as part of the socio-economic development process in line with democratic practices.

For many stakeholders in Myanmar democratic practices are still very new, and as a result, there may be cases where some people cross the line of normally-accepted behaviour, act emotionally without taking into consideration hidden consequences, complain too easily and criticize each other without strong justification, or make mistakes. Of course, this kind of situation is not at all abnormal during a transition period such as Myanmar is undergoing, when, in many ways, everything is a learning process. However, if this situation were to persist for a long time, it could become a factor that discourages the development process, and could even have the potential to reverse the direction of reform, which would be one of the worst possible outcomes. The only way to avoid such situations is to enhance trust among all stakeholders through close collaboration, understanding, and friendship.

There is an invisible association between trust, patience, understanding, friendship, and socio-economic development. There is not much evidence to determine whether socio-economic development is an exogenous or endogenous variable in this relationship, but it is a variable without which the reforms may not happen and changes may not be sustained. Myanmar has achieved significant reform in the area of political development (although there still is a long way to go to reach perfection) and it is important that this political progress should influence and underpin socio-economic development. Many international organizations have been flocking into Myanmar with a large amount of assistance for socio-economic development; however, Myanmar understands that such assistance serves only for a short-term (or perhaps a medium-term) purpose. In the long term, Myanmar needs to stand on its own feet, and it needs to start preparing now for that time. Clearly, the investment and trade sectors will play a very important role in enabling Myanmar to achieve this independence in the long term.

One key aim of Myanmar's government is for equitable development in economic, social, and environmental spheres. A focus is on eight priority areas for rural development, while concurrently investment and trade are being liberalized and actively promoted. Attempts are being made to create a favourable investment climate for both foreign and domestic investment. However, as for a number of other countries in the Asian region that face various limitations in hard and soft infrastructure development, it is easier said than done to create such a climate in a short time. But time is a luxury Myanmar cannot afford. Hence, special economic zones are being developed where top-notch hard infrastructure can be developed in a very short time, and where streamlined, transparent, and predictable policies favourable to investment and trade can be adopted. It is hoped that this will lead to a situation where a level playing-field can be created and a positive investment climate can be ensured in a very short time.

In addition, the Small and Medium Enterprises Law is being drafted in collaboration with business associations and international organizations that include the German Society for International Cooperation (GIZ) , the United Nations Industrial Development Organization (UNIDO), the United Nations Economic and Social Commission for Asia and the Pacific (UNESCAP), Japan External Trade Organization (JETRO), and others. Its aim is to facilitate and support small and medium-sized enterprises in a holistic and comprehensive way, not only to grow but also to complement foreign investment.

Myanmar has been moving forward at a speed that many people could not have imagined even two years ago. In many areas, lessons gained from the experience of other countries in the region have been used effectively to move things forward with confidence; however, in some other areas, what is being done is not without risk. Myanmar is now very willing to learn from other countries in order to take advantage of being a latecomer to development. Many government ministries are working with international consultants provided by various international organizations in order to access information without which Myanmar cannot make the most of the latecomer's advantage—but there are many things that Myanmar still needs to learn and improve. Significant development has been achieved within just two years, but there is still a long way to go. Reform is not just a one-time effort; it is a process. More precisely, it is an evolutionary process. Hence, it needs some time to evolve.

In this evolutionary process of reform, the government cannot on its own achieve a good result without having a tremendous level of cooperation with civil society at various levels. It is time for all the stakeholders, including the government of Myanmar and civil society groups both inside and outside the country, to become more active friends of Myanmar. Donors and international organizations should collaborate closely, hand-in-hand with the Myanmar government, to pursue people-centered, equitable, inclusive, and sustainable development. The goal is to make Myanmar once again a responsible member of the global community.

Notes

1   The Myanmar Government's Information Team issued a press release on 27 June 2013 announcing that two foreign companies had been awarded mobile telephone licences, together with a detailed description of the tender process.

New Light of Myanmar, "Telecommunications Operator Tender Evaluation and Selection Committee issues press release", *New Light of Myanmar*, 28 June 2013, pp. 16, 5, 6 <http://www.burmalibrary.org/docs15/NLM-2013-06-28-red.pdf> (accessed 14 October 2013).

2   The Framework for Economic and Social Development was prepared for the government by the Myanmar Development Resources Institute in late 2012 as an attempt to ensure better integration of social and economic policies across government agencies. Its principles will be used by all government ministries as the basic guide for new projects.

II

Introduction

2

DEBATING DEMOCRATIZATION IN MYANMAR

Trevor Wilson

Myanmar is, at last, entering a period of democratization. However, a great deal of uncertainty remains, as the contents of this book reveal. What sort of democracy Myanmar might eventually become remains unclear, and we cannot make many assumptions about the intentions of many of the individuals and organizations central to the process of democratization. The reform process is neither smooth nor certain, and much uncertainty remains about the prospects for implementation of policies, even where the will for genuine change exists on the part of at least some in the national leadership.

Experts on democracy and democratization talk about the need both to enable and to consolidate democratic practices, so that new forms of social and political behaviour are "routinized" and become habitual (Linz and Stepan 1996). The democratization process in Myanmar has not yet had sufficient time for us to speak of democratic practices being habitual; nevertheless, participants at the 2013 Myanmar/Burma Update Conference, whose contributions comprise the contents of this book, have been keen to explore the extent to which the new government in Myanmar has so far succeeded in its pursuit of ambitious reforms.[1]

Key questions asked at the conference that have made their way into this volume address whether or not the government's reform agenda will fully embrace democratization, and if so, in what ways, or whether the government might attempt to push back against public aspirations for improvements and reforms. Some observers of the political changes that have occurred since the previous conference in May 2011, such as Morten Pedersen, were inclined to concur that the reform program was a calculated long-term strategy and seemed irreversible. They pointed to the many new policy initiatives from the centre, the apparent sincerity of elite actors about the need for consensus on democratic transition, and the growing popular sentiment for social and political change, as evidence that the country is firmly on a democratizing path. In holding this view, Pedersen is joined by other prominent Myanmar watchers (see, for instance, Callahan 2012; Emmerson 2012; Min Zin and Joseph 2012).

In his foreword to this volume, Deputy Minister of National Planning and Economic Development and former academic Winston Set Aung notes the complexity of reforms, and the potential for one reform or set of reforms to be derailed by set-backs in others, due to the interconnectedness of the overall agenda. He openly admits that the outcomes are not likely to be perfect and that some mistakes may be made. He also sets out how economic policy-making is expected to become more democratic and more connected to the interests of small entrepreneurs, which can only be good news for persons concerned to see Myanmar's economy develop after decades of false starts and extremely slow growth when compared to its counterparts in the region. Anders Engvall and Soe Nandar Linn for their part explain some of the progressive economic policy changes that have already been introduced. The holding of the 2013 World Economic Forum meeting in Naypyitaw in June 2013 was certainly a notable achievement for Myanmar, and the attendance of more than 1100 participants from 57 countries was testimony, if it was needed, to the level of interest in its economic future.

However, some other observers have been less confident, as various deep-seated problems have continued to confront Myanmar's leaders, distracting them from the reform agenda, posing worrying challenges for national development, and potentially denying people the better opportunities they want and deserve. These problems include the resurgent civil war in Kachin State, where there seems little prospect of an end to conflict or of a resolution of the underlying tensions that caused the fighting, about which Seng Maw Lahpai provides sharp insights in her chapter. Another cause for grave concern is the outbreak and spread of communal conflict, with disturbing undertones of racial and religious intolerance. Also of concern are constraints on the process of embedding and consolidating many of the liberalizing moves that have already been made, as well as constraints on the establishment of new arrangements to protect the important freedoms that underpin democracy anywhere.

Yet there is no doubt about the substantive policy changes that have already had discernible impacts on the lives of many people. Most important is the country's new-found freedom of expression, and with it, the great expansion of uncensored print media outlets. The liberalized print media are displaying surprising capacity to report and comment in a timely and accurate fashion on most of Myanmar's problems, providing a new space for reasonably substantial public policy debate. There has also been a noticeable widening of freedom in other areas—for example, the greatly enlarged freedom to dissent and to engage in public protest; freedom of assembly and of association, including allowing workers to organize trade unions; and freedom to travel around the country. The implementation of some of these reforms is still incomplete: Kyaw Soe Lwin offers a meticulous case study of the struggle by workers and their new trade unions for better working conditions; Tamas Wells and Kyaw Thu Aung provide a detailed description of the growth in farmers' efforts to function freely and without restrictions. They conclude hopefully "not only that some grassroots civil society networks are experiencing new freedoms, but also that they are actively pushing for further change", and "the impacts of recent political reforms in Myanmar are not confined only to elites, nor is it only elites who are capable of effecting change. Ordinary citizens and civil society networks may also be agents of democratization".

Against these grounds for optimism, the legacy of major problems that are not yet being adequately tackled suggests that we ought to exercise caution and remain firmly realistic in making assessments about the prospects for reform. For example, the goal of national reconciliation is frustrated by the impunity that the army enjoys. Politically, the National League for Democracy (NLD) has not yet been able to represent itself across the full range of government responsibilities as a viable alternative to the military-established Union Solidarity and Development Party, which currently holds an overwhelming number of seats in the national legislature. Ethnic groups have not yet been able to organize their own pathways towards greater responsibility and justice for their people. International capital is returning, but not at a pace or in a manner such as to satisfy demands for immediate improvement in living standards and employment opportunities. The gap between rich and poor is not narrowing.

One persistent problem for the Myanmar government is that it is taking a long time for the beneficial impact of many reforms to trickle down to ordinary people. As Sean Turnell discusses, farmers and the poor have yet to see much in the way of real improvement, and there are not yet significantly more employment opportunities for the young, the educated, and those who prefer not to enlist in the army or join the government. Women are not benefitting noticeably, as Khin Mar Mar Kyi outlines in her chapter, based on wide-ranging interviews where she finds "women continue to face structural inequality, violence, and discrimination". Some people in authority are not sufficiently convinced of the need for reform, the army is not noticeably adjusting its behaviour outside the major towns, and long-standing systemic failures such as corruption continue. While hope has been sparked, if the 2015 elections draw close and not enough reforms are solidly embedded for the future, the hope could give way to cynicism or anger.

Meanwhile, state institutions—including the bureaucracy, courts, and police—continue to function much as they have done for over two decades, although most are adapting, albeit slowly, to the many liberalization reforms. Measures to effect change originating from Naypyitaw have not yet, for most people, been tangibly realized. Hopes are high, but so too is scepticism born of half a century of military dictatorship and the memories of earlier, lost moments of promise. Thus, on the topic of policing, Andrew Selth judges that the Myanmar government recognizes that a change in approach and engagement with the public is needed, but points to the experiences of other countries where police reform took quite a long time. More broadly, observing that Myanmar's policy-making is likely to remain under military influence in the coming decade or so, Renaud Egreteau argues that "Post-SPDC politics in Myanmar offers a case study of an army carefully moving down the praetorian scale—but still not fully retreating to its barracks and disengaging from politics". He concludes with the observation that the outside world "has begun to recognize that beyond Aung San Suu Kyi's iconic figure it will have to deal with an enduring Burmese praetorian machine". Whether or not one is convinced by Egreteau's explanations of post-junta praetorianism, all agree that the military will remain central to the country's politics for some time to come—thus casting doubt on the extent, speed, and character of democratization.

One feature of the recent political developments in Myanmar is that they have brought to the table of scholarship on the country some researchers with no prior background in work in that country, who, like the rest of us, are intrigued by what is happening there and why (see, for instance, Diamond 2012). Many of these researchers come with extensive relevant experience elsewhere, and are bringing to their work on Myanmar invaluable comparative insights on questions ranging from the most suitable measures to ensure more inclusive and democratic decision-making, more equitable allocation of wealth and resources, and better access to opportunities and avenues for improvement. Kyle Lemargie and his colleagues offer some fascinating insights along these lines regarding electoral reform, pointing out how the right decisions on design of electoral systems to underpin democratization outcomes are vitally important to the strengthening of support for Myanmar's fledgling political institutions.

Among long-standing observers of Myanmar, as well as some newcomers, the rapid developments since early 2011 are, not surprisingly, prompting considerable "revisionism". Mostly this is revisionism in the best sense: many writers are looking anew at a familiar landscape and acknowledging unanticipated positive trends. Nor are they the only ones. As Kerstin Duell correctly notes, activists in exile are also in the business of revising expectations and explanations about what is happening and why, and while some have continued to make a "significant contribution" from abroad since 2011, others are now making their contributions inside Myanmar. Some exiles are returning to witness developments personally, and are staying in order to contribute or are pledging to visit again and get involved actively without fixed views of the past.

For countries undergoing political transition, the readiness of exiles to return and participate in the new political and social life is one important indicator of the sustainability of the transition process: the return of exiles ensures their full inclusion in the process, makes their technical skills and practical know-how available to inform and strengthen the new politics, and contributes visibly and symbolically to a sense that genuine nation-building is under way. Daw Than Than Nu, daughter of the former prime minister U Nu, was one of the first to return to Myanmar in the mid-2000s, initially for personal reasons. In her chapter, she explains how, ahead of the

2010 elections, she formed the Democratic Party (Myanmar), and reflects on the nature of political dialogue between her party and other parties, as well as with the government, in the subsequent years.

While the presence of the returnees broadens the base of support for Myanmar's reforms, their return has provoked some criticism amongst other exiled activists, some of whom remain vehemently opposed to living under the 2008 Constitution, which has been written so as to protect military interests and insulate military personnel from prosecution. So far these criticisms have not found much support, but have, rather, generated comments that those exiles are hankering after a lost dream and past failed policies. That the "official" government in exile—the National Coalition Government for the Union of Burma (NCGUB), for many years headed somewhat unconvincingly by Daw Aung San Suu Kyi's cousin, Dr Sein Win—disbanded itself on 14 September 2012 is in this respect a sign of the times.

Although "democratization" is the theme of this volume, and a key issue in the current period of politics in Myanmar, whether or not it will in the long run prove to be a relevant analytical lens through which to assess events remains to be seen. Aung San Suu Kyi has repeatedly made it clear that democracy is unquestionably her goal for Myanmar, and nobody has seriously challenged this. Moreover, as far as one can judge, the people of Myanmar who are her supporters are increasingly taking democracy as their guiding principle. So, too, are many of the country's newly-emergent institutions. As Thomas Kean documents, a multi-party parliament is starting to operate as a fledgling check-and-balance mechanism on the executive, although it is still a long way from being a truly effective institution. In her chapter, Khin Mar Mar Kyi argues that the treatment of groups such as women still has not improved markedly.

One collateral benefit of Myanmar's reforms is that it is already relatively easier to conduct certain kinds of research in the country. The full benefits of this are yet to be realized, but it appears that on-the-ground surveys are far easier to carry out than before (or can even be carried out without obtaining official approval), that ordinary people are more comfortable being interviewed for research, and, in some cases, that government data is more readily criticized by Myanmar officials. Whereas earlier research was usually the subject of polarized debate between those outside the country who could not do work on the ground and those who could and did but were forced to make compromises to get access, it is a very positive sign for scholarship on Myanmar that this period has come to an end and a new phase of research, by new and ambitious researchers, is under way.

Far from being the last word on Myanmar's democratization, the chapters in this publication consist, rather, of some of the first in-depth analyses of events in Myanmar in this remarkable period of excitement and change, a period that in the long run will prove critical to the country's prospects for lasting democracy. Just how "democratization with Myanmar characteristics" will develop remains, for the most part, to be seen. In any case, whatever form democratization takes, the real test will be whether or not it sufficiently meets the aspirations and needs of Myanmar's people.

Note

1   The Myanmar/Burma Update Conference is a periodic event held approximately every eighteen months at the Australian National University in Canberra, bringing together experts from Australia, Myanmar, and around the world to debate current trends in political, economic, and social affairs in Myanmar. For more details on the 2013 Update, and on the conference series, visit <http://asiapacific.anu.edu.au/myanmarburma-update>.

References

Callahan, Mary. "The Generals Loosen Their Grip". *Journal of Democracy* 23, no. 4 (2012): 120–31.

Diamond, Larry. "The Need for a Political Pact". *Journal of Democracy* 23, no. 4 (2012): 138–49.

Emmerson, Donald K. "Minding the Gap between Democracy and Governance". *Journal of Democracy* 23, no. 2 (2012): 62–73.

Linz, Juan L. and Alfred Stepan. *Problems of Democratic Transition and Consolidation: Southern Europe, South America and Post-Communist Europe*. Baltimore: Johns Hopkins University Press, 1996.

Min Zin and Brian Joseph. "The Democratic Opportunity". *Journal of Democracy* 23, no. 4 (2012): 104–19.

3

MYANMAR'S DEMOCRATIC OPENING
The Process and Prospect of Reform

Morten B. Pedersen

Myanmar is in the midst of momentous political changes. Over the past two years, the country's new quasi-civilian government has taken unprecedented steps to end half a century of military rule, economic stagnation, and international opprobrium. This chapter assesses the significance of the ongoing reform process, considers why the government is changing tack now, and identifies some of the main challenges and risks ahead. The analysis reveals a government that is defying conventional wisdom and low expectations, yet at the same time faces such major structural obstacles that one should be cautious about assuming that the end point of the transition will be democracy.

THE SIGNIFICANCE OF THE REFORM PROCESS

The conventional view leading into the 2010 elections was that this was purely a cosmetic move to shore up the existing regime and unlikely, therefore, to result in significant change (for example, Lintner 2011; Nyein 2009; for a dissenting view, see Pedersen 2011). Early developments seemed to support this pessimistic view. In its efforts to maintain control of the transition, the military government made a mockery of democratic elections and managed to secure, by hook *and* by crook, a landslide victory for its own party, the Union Solidarity and Development Party (USDP) (Englehart 2012). It subsequently appointed a new cabinet made up largely of former senior military officers, led by the prime minister of the previous regime, General Thein Sein, now President U Thein Sein. This, however, is when the expected story of continuity ended and real change began. Once in office, the new government proceeded in short order *not* to try to shore up the existing regime, but effectively to start unravelling it.

The reforms undertaken by the post-2011 government are well known, and a few highlights will suffice here (for more detail, see Holliday 2013; International Crisis Group 2012, 2011). Most of the country's 1000-plus political prisoners have been released; opposition leader Daw Aung San Suu Kyi has been elected to parliament, where she now chairs the Committee for the Rule of Law; a ceasefire has been reached with the Karen National Union (KNU), thus ending the world's longest-running armed insurgency; trade unions have been legalized; and the media has been freed to publish real news and honest criticism of the government. Also, governance has substantially improved. For the first time in fifty years, government officials are speaking openly about the country's problems; competent ministers have been brought in to take charge of key reform areas; new bills are being critically debated in parliament, often with input from civil society groups; and serious efforts are under way to combat corruption, liberalize the economy, and alleviate poverty, supported by international organizations and bilateral donors. As Human Rights Watch concludes, "a government that has long treated its people as enemies is beginning to treat them as citizens; a regime that thumbed its nose at the world is now extending a hand for assistance and advice" (Malinowski 2013, p. 1).

There are obvious limitations to the reform process. Constitutionally, Myanmar still contains strong elements of military rule (Bunte 2011), even if in practice the *Tatmadaw* (armed forces) plays a greatly diminished political role. While fighting has ceased in most areas, a brutal war has reignited in Kachin State, where serious human rights violations against civilian populations continue (Transnational Institute 2013*b*). Communal violence between Buddhists and Muslims has brought to the surface a deeply racist element in mainstream Myanmar Buddhist culture, including among members of the otherwise highly respected *Sangha* (Buddhist monastic order), who have been instigating violence against Muslims (Human Rights Watch 2013). Finally, despite the new government's efforts to reform the economy, millions of deeply impoverished households have yet to see significant material benefits from the new system. In some areas, reform, paradoxically, has created further problems, as bigots exploit the new media freedoms to spread hateful anti-Muslim propaganda, and vested interests expropriate land to position themselves for the expected influx of foreign investment (Transnational Institute 2013*a*).

Nonetheless, there can be no question that the changes over the past two years are extremely significant, and hold within them the seeds of an entirely new political system. To complain that Myanmar is not a democracy yet, as sceptics are still wont to do, or that some parts of the state continue to behave in repressive ways, is simply to state the obvious. Deep-rooted authoritarian structures cannot be reformed overnight. While it is, of course, important to be aware of the limitations and work to overcome them, the important markers at this early stage are the *direction* of change and the *commitment* to change—and neither of those should be in doubt. Neither growing political instability nor resistance from regime conservatives has become an excuse to back off from the reform process. On the contrary, President Thein Sein has gone all in, effectively staking the legacy of his presidency on successfully bringing peace and democracy to a long-suffering country (Thein Sein 2012). Importantly, he has the support of other key leaders, including Speaker of the lower house, U Shwe Mann (Lloyd-George 2012), and, to a degree at least, Commander-in Chief, Senior General Min Aung Hlaing (Callahan 2012, pp. 127–28).

THE ORIGINS AND PROCESSES OF CHANGE

Any attempt to explain the recent changes must start with the person, and the personality, of President Thein Sein, who has been a crucial catalyst for much of what has happened. But the president is, of course, not doing this in a vacuum, and he is not doing it alone. In order to get a fuller picture, we need to look also at the broader ideological, political, and economic context that has motivated not only Thein Sein and fellow reformers, but also other segments of the ruling elite, to embrace, or at least accept, reform. Four sets of issues, or incentives, would appear to be particularly relevant in this respect: the military's self-image, the improved national security situation, Myanmar's economic woes, and the positive response to the reforms by other groups, notably the National League for Democracy (NLD) and Western governments. Concern over the sustainability of military rule may have been a factor, too, but if so, it was one of a second order.

Leadership Change

The transfer of leadership from former Senior General Than Shwe to Thein Sein was a necessary condition for change. The ongoing transition, like Myanmar politics in general, is led from the top, and without a strong push from the new president it is inconceivable that the wheels of reform would have been put in motion. Thein Sein is a very different leader from Than Shwe. While his former boss had all the hallmarks of a dictator, Thein Sein has a much less autocratic leadership style. Already before he became president, those who knew him described him as a humble and decent man who treated others well and was genuinely concerned with the plight of the poor (interviews by author, Yangon, 2008–10).[1] Despite his advancement to the top of an often brutal and corrupt institution, there are no stories of personal brutality or corruption by the former general. Most importantly, as president, he has shown a genuine commitment to reach out to other groups to make them partners in a common effort to rebuild the country.

The Military's Self-Image

The new government, of course, could not have accomplished everything it has, had the broader environment not permitted. It is important, in this respect, to recognise that the Myanmar military, the *Tatmadaw*, has never seen itself as a ruling class. Rather, its self-image is that of "guardian" of the state, which steps in only at times of crisis to save the country (Pedersen 2008, pp. 96–99). In the 1970s, Ne Win voluntarily ended twelve years of direct military rule by establishing a socialist one-party system, similar to that practised by several of Myanmar's neighbours at the time. Yet, by the time of the 1988 uprising and the collapse of the Burma Socialist

Program Party (BSPP) government, which saw the military take direct power again, the world *zeitgeist* had changed and the only legitimate system of government was multi-party democracy. Thus, it has been the declared policy of the post-1988 military regime since the beginning to hand back power to a democratically-elected government. Although the first attempt to do so in 1990 was aborted after the democratic opposition won a landslide election victory, it was never really in doubt that direct military rule was a temporary situation.

The National Security Situation

For reform to occur, however, not only must those in power have good reasons to change, they must also lack strong reasons to resist it. For decades military conservatives in Myanmar have resisted reform, in part at least due to a concern that civilian politicians were incapable of handling the serious national security threats facing the country (Pedersen 2008, p. 99–100). While this belief in military supremacy no doubt remains, two developments meant that by 2010 concerns about civilian rule were significantly alleviated: first was the relative weakening over time of the military's main opponents; second was the adoption of the 2008 Constitution.

It is impossible to understand political developments in Myanmar without considering the question of national security, which goes to the core of the military's role in society. There are three aspects of this, encapsulated in the *Tatmadaw's* commitment to safeguard the "three national causes"—non-disintegration of the Union, non-disintegration of national solidarity, and perpetuation of sovereignty. These three causes have guided the military since the 1950s and are highlighted also in the preamble of the new constitution. Loosely translated, they refer to perceived threats arising from ethnic separatist groups, political opposition groups, and the outside world.

The military took power in 1962 to safeguard the integrity of the Union against perceived threats from ethno-nationalist groups as well as to end factional infighting within the ruling Anti-Fascist People's Freedom League (AFPFL), which had raised the spectre of state collapse. These domestic problems were seen also to increase the risk of international interference, and thus to constitute a threat to Myanmar's independence and national sovereignty, which had been won from Britain only fourteen years earlier and remained fragile in the face of Cold War superpower machinations in the region.

The return to direct military rule in 1988 happened in broadly similar circumstances. The popular uprising that summer caused the collapse of the BSPP government and brought the state apparatus to a near standstill. Chaos reigned in the streets and public services stopped functioning. To make matters worse, the Burma Communist Party (BCP), seeking to exploit the unrest in the cities, launched a new offensive from their headquarters near the Chinese border in north-eastern Shan State, while a fleet of American warships was sighted just outside Myanmar territorial waters, prompting concern about a foreign military intervention (Maung Aung Myoe 2007).

The post-1988 period has been defined in large part by the efforts by the new military regime, the State Law and Order Restoration Council (SLORC)—later renamed the State Peace and Development Council (SPDC)—to ensure that 1962 and 1988 would never be repeated, and the relative success of those efforts helped set the scene for the reforms now under way. During the 1990s, the *Tatmadaw* was able to dramatically strengthen its control of the previously ungoverned border areas. This was done through a combination of a massive military build-up in former conflict zones, the negotiation of ceasefires with most of the major insurgent groups, and a number of successful military campaigns against hold-out groups such as the KNU (Kivimäki and Pedersen 2008). In the cities, intense surveillance by military intelligence and unrelenting repression similarly reduced the democracy movement to a shadow of its late-1980s self. The NLD, in particular, suffered under the heavy pressure, and by the early 2000s was barely functioning as an opposition party (although it remained an important symbol of resistance to military rule). As the "Saffron Revolution" in 2007 showed, popular resentment of military rule remained high, yet in 2010 the military regime was more dominant and more firmly in control of the country than any previous Myanmar regime.

Another important development from a military security perspective was the finalization and adoption in 2008 of the new constitution (although through a rigged referendum). The SLORC/SPDC had been working on this new law since 1993, with the explicit purpose of ensuring that a strong government would emerge. Although the constitution formally establishes a multi-party democracy with regular elections and associated civil and political rights, it also sets up a strongly centralized government with a continued key role for the *Tatmadaw*, including strong representation on the powerful National Defence and Security Council, 25 percent of the seats in parliament, and control of all security-related ministries and committees. The military is also accorded full internal autonomy, subject to neither executive, nor legislative or judicial, civilian authority. Crucially, the criteria for amending the constitution effectively give the commander-in-chief veto power.

In sum, by the time of the transfer of power in 2011, the *Tatmadaw* would have felt relatively secure. Its major foes had been defeated or outmanoeuvred, and the 2008 Constitution built in a number of safeguards to ensure continued military control of key aspects of government. Against this background, the military leadership could finally afford to experiment with liberalization and even partial democratization.

The Economy

The military's self-confidence, coupled with the improved security situation, brought on not only the 2010 elections but also, helped by Senior General Than Shwe's advancing age, a new generation of top leaders. But there is nothing to indicate that the former strongman had planned for the extent of changes that have occurred over the past two years. On the contrary, both the new constitution and the conduct of the elections strongly suggested that Than Shwe had in mind a system that placed more emphasis on military control than on democratic government, although within a formally democratic frame. To fully understand the current reform process, we need therefore to look at additional factors that led the new government to break with this conservative agenda. The change of leadership, as already argued, was one; another was the deteriorating economic situation and an associated deepening sense of failure on the part of many in the military.

Although the main concern of successive military regimes in Myanmar has been to safeguard the state against perceived internal and external threats, there has always been a secondary concern with economic development, or *modernization*, generally expressed in terms of building "a modern and developed nation". The first military regime sought to jump-start the economy through a more effective implementation of socialism (but failed). The post-1988 regime also, initially, tried to turn the economy around, this time by undertaking a series of market-oriented economic reforms (but was defeated by its own incompetence and preoccupation with security, compounded by international sanctions and isolation). During the reign of Senior General Than Shwe, who took over in 1992, national economic goals were less prominent in government policy, probably because the commander-in-chief was preoccupied with a series of national security threats, including the "re-emergence" of the democracy movement after the release of Aung San Suu Kyi from house arrest in 1995, the Asian Economic Crisis in 1997, and the imposition of ever-tightening Western sanctions. This seeming disregard for developmental goals by the top levels of the regime was not, however, shared by the wider ranks of the military, who grew increasingly dissatisfied with the deteriorating economic situation and became concerned with finding solutions. Along with related concerns about Myanmar's growing dependence on China, the most common criticisms of regime policies heard from within the military in the decade leading up to the change of government in 2011 were concerned with economic mismanagement and corruption (interviews by author, Yangon, 2000–2010).

The fact is that, aside from a few hundred generals and crony businessmen, the SLORC/SPDC economic system served no one in the country. On the contrary, there was a growing sense that Myanmar was being left behind and exploited by its neighbours. This goes a long way towards explaining why there has apparently been significant support for reform, even among members of the traditional elite. For the great majority of people, including many in the military, regime change simply promises a better future.

Political Momentum

Compared to earlier periods, the situation at the start of 2011 was uniquely conducive to reform. The threat to national security had been minimized and concerns about economic development had moved to the forefront. The latter was certainly the case for Thein Sein and fellow reformers, and their agenda appears to be widely shared to have created the space for major reforms. To understand how far and quickly the political landscape has changed, we need to consider a final element: the decision made by the NLD, as well as most ethnic armed groups and, perhaps most importantly, Western governments, to cooperate with the new government.

It is instructive in this respect to compare the current situation with two previous windows of change in the late 1980s and the early 2000s. During the 1988 uprising, an opportunity for reform appeared to emerge when new President Maung Maung offered to hold multi-party elections within three months. The leaders of the embryonic democracy movement, however, rejected the president's offer, demanding that an interim government be installed to oversee the elections. With massive protests continuing in the streets, the state soon collapsed (Maung Maung 1999). Within weeks, the military reasserted control to stave off the chaos, thousands of protesters were killed or arrested, and the offer of quick elections was taken off the table. Although the new military regime did proceed to organize multi-party elections twenty months later, in May 1990, the NLD's landslide victory and demands for an immediate transfer of power again caused a heightened sense of threat on the part of the military leadership, which subsequently refused to step down.

The next window came about a decade later, in the years between 2001 and 2004, when then intelligence chief and prime minister General Khin Nyunt made an effort to co-opt the NLD and re-engage with the international community (Magnusson and Pedersen 2012, pp. 37–46). Much like in the present situation, Aung San Suu Kyi privately expressed confidence in Khin Nyunt and the possibility of reform. A secret deal was reached whereby Aung San Suu Kyi would be released from house arrest and the NLD would join the National Convention and work with the government to draw up a new constitution. Western countries at that time, however, showed little interest in a process of incremental reform, refusing to reconsider their existing approach, which was in effect a demand for immediate regime change. With nothing to show for his efforts, Khin Nyunt's reform gambit collapsed. The promise to release Aung San Suu Kyi was rescinded by Senior General Than Shwe, who was probably never enthusiastic about the deal in the first place; the NLD returned to a politics of confrontation; Khin Nyunt was purged, along with hundreds of other reformers and supporters; and the reform drive crumbled as hardliners reasserted control of regime policy.

On each occasion, military leaders judged that transferring power to an elected government (or to the NLD) constituted an unacceptable risk, and simply pulled the plug. In 1988 and 1990, the non-compromising position adopted by domestic opposition forces was the main factor, while in 2001–04 the lack of Western buy-in was a critical impediment.

By contrast, the present situation is characterized by a demonstrated willingness by both the NLD and Western governments, as well as key ethnic armed groups, to work, for the moment at least, with the sitting government within the framework of the 2008 Constitution. The deal reached by Thein Sein and Aung San Suu Kyi in August 2011, in particular, was a game-changer, paving the way for the re-registration of the NLD as a political party and for its subsequent entry into parliament after a mini-landslide victory in the 1 April 2012 by-elections. While the earlier releases of political prisoners and other liberalization measures by the government had been widely welcomed, they were essentially one-way measures. Yet to have members of the ruling military-affiliated party and the main opposition party working together in parliament—with the clear understanding that the NLD would be able to compete on fair terms in the next general elections in 2015—lifted public hope for the reform process to a whole new level. This political "ceasefire" between the two main Burman groups has helped create a sense among ethnic armed groups that it is imperative to be part of the reform process, and has kept them "on-side" despite serious misgivings, especially about the conflict in Kachin State. It has also provided cover for Western governments supportive of the reform process to throw aside any remaining hesitations and move rapidly toward a full normalization of relations with Myanmar. This rapprochement with former enemies of the state has, in turn, given Thein Sein's government both credibility and new motivation, and has infused the reform process with a political momentum that would otherwise have been lacking (Kyaw Yin Hlaing 2012, p. 210). The government has responded with even more in-depth reforms.

Alternative Explanations

In contrast to the explanation offered above, which places the initiative with the new government, democracy activists have been arguing that change was forced upon the military by Western sanctions or fear that the "Arab Spring" might spread to Myanmar. Neither of these lines of analysis is convincing, however.

Myanmar's military rulers have always taken pride in resisting external pressure, which has been a core element of their self-legitimation (Pedersen 2008, pp. 221–23). Twenty years of escalating Western sanctions served to rally the military behind hardline leaders, not to spur calls for reform.[2] In the early days of the sanctions regime it may have seemed theoretically possible that pride would eventually have to give in to economic necessity, but without the cooperation of Myanmar's neighbours, this was never a realistic scenario; and by the late 2000s the military regime was in a much stronger position, not only militarily and politically but also economically. Although the overall economy was in dire straits, gas exports and other natural resources kept the state solvent (and its top leaders comfortable), and several major new revenue-earners were set to go on stream, notably the new Shwe gas field off the Rakhine State coast and the associated Chinese gas and oil pipelines. Moreover, by this time, the momentum of the pro-sanctions movement had passed. The Obama administration had retreated from America's long-standing coercive strategy, and with Myanmar's neighbours praising the 2008 Constitution and 2010 elections as significant progress, there was no prospect of further serious sanctions. There is no doubt that the new government was keen to see sanctions lifted, but this is more persuasively explained by the obstacles international isolation posed to its new developmental agenda than as a reason for the adoption of that agenda in the first place. Tellingly, the government has been much more focused on securing the resumption of general trade, investment, and aid, which is critical to broad-based development and poverty alleviation, than on getting removed those sanctions that directly targeted members of the military regime.

The impact of any hypothetical fear on the part of Myanmar's military leaders that they might go the way of other dictators recently deposed in North Africa and the Middle East is harder to assess, but the timing of events does not support the claim that this was a crucial factor either. The "Arab Spring" began only in early 2011, when Myanmar's reform process was already under way. Also, the new government has much less reason to fear such a fate than the old one. Unlike former Senior General Than Shwe and Vice-Senior General Maung Aye, neither President Thein Sein nor any of his fellow reformers have ever been held publicly responsible for the repressive practices of the previous regime. On the contrary, they had a fairly good reputation among the Myanmar public even before the start of reforms (interviews by the author, Myanmar, 2000–2010).

Most tellingly, the recent reforms have gone much further than any defensive agenda would have warranted, and indeed have come to present a significant threat to vested elite interests. For the first time in fifty years, a government is challenging the *Tatmadaw's* political power and economic privileges on a broad, if still limited, scale. The military no longer makes policy outside of its core area of national security; regional commanders have lost their position as governors in their local areas; and the military holding companies have had several lucrative monopolies taken away. Even if practice halts behind legal developments, there is no question that the military's political and economic influence has been diluted. Moreover, things are set to change further. By legalizing the NLD and granting it a national political platform, the government has all but guaranteed that its own party, the USDP, will lose the 2015 elections. At the same time, broader society has been mobilized in unprecedented ways that significantly increase the risk of a popular backlash to any future regressive steps. The genie is out of the bottle, and the current leadership has released it both knowingly and willingly.

In sum, Myanmar's reform path has more in common with the top-down transition in the former Soviet Union than with the bottom-up transitions that occurred in Eastern Europe, or more recently in North Africa. Thein Sein and his fellow reformers are reforming because they want "more" for the country, not because they were forced to compromise to protect themselves.

THE CHALLENGES AHEAD

The reform process has gathered significant momentum. Reformers have consolidated their control over the executive (Jagan 2012) as well as over the legislature, and have moved decisively in many areas. This, in turn, has convinced most external groups that the new government is genuinely committed to reform, and their decision to back the process, as noted, has further added to the momentum. Every success for the government is making it harder to contemplate going back to the bad old days of repressive rule, economic stagnation, and international isolation, and is helping to create a bandwagon effect in the direction of reform.

There are some difficult political challenges ahead. In order to consolidate the reforms, the government will have to negotiate a series of "deals" with other political actors, in which the challenge will be to strike a balance between supporters of the old regime (notably the military) who have grown accustomed to power and privilege, and previously marginalized groups who are expecting to benefit from the new regime.

The current stage of the reform process is characterized by a unique style of "national politics" in which all sides are putting immediate party interests aside for the sake of long-term reform. Defying expectations, both the president and the chairman of the ruling party, lower house Speaker Shwe Mann, have proven to be effective coalition builders, often taking on board policy suggestions from opposition groups, rather than using their institutional power to push through a narrow party agenda (Nyein Nyein 2012).[3] This has facilitated an unusually non-confrontational style of parliamentary politics that puts some mature democracies to shame.[4] Aung San Suu Kyi, too, has reached out across party lines to build bonds with former enemies. Indeed, the opposition leader has favoured relationship- and trust-building to such an extent that she has come under fire from long-standing supporters for her perceived failure to challenge the government on human rights issues (Hindstrom 2012). Even the military appears to be taking a cooperative approach, at least away from the battlefield. While army leaders seemingly defied repeated presidential orders at the end of 2012 to halt the fighting in Kachin State, military ministers and members of parliament have generally played a constructive role in Naypyitaw, refraining from intervening in affairs outside of their mandate.[5]

Still, no fundamental redistribution of power has taken place yet, and the danger is that moderates on all sides could face rebellion from more hardline elements within their own groups. With the 2015 elections likely to encourage a return to more confrontational politics and patience wearing thin among some groups who feel that they have yet to benefit from the reform process, the potential for serious upheavals in the medium term, which could put the entire reform process at risk, should not be underestimated. The challenges Myanmar faces in this respect are common to many transitional countries and centre around the negotiation of three key socio-political relationships—between old and new elites, the Burman and ethnic minorities, and state and society.

Elite Relations

To continue to move forward, the *reformers* in the government will need to strike a balance between appeasing *hardliners* in the old authoritarian elite who could block their efforts, and accommodating *moderates* in the democratic opposition who might otherwise desert the reform coalition and join the *radicals* in rejecting compromise with members of the old regime.

The most immediate challenge in this respect is the relationship between the ruling USDP and the opposition NLD, which is widely expected to sweep the 2015 elections and thus displace the old political elite. However, the prospect of an NLD landslide victory has also raised serious concern in the ranks of ethnic groups and other opposition parties, which, equally, stand to lose representation in parliament (interviews by author, Yangon, December 2012). To ensure that critical relationships do not break down prior to, or as a result of, the 2015 elections, some kind of agreement that protects the core interests of both old and new elites will need to be reached. Yet the NLD is giving mixed signals about its willingness to consider political compromises with other groups. While Aung San Suu Kyi is clearly making efforts to build bridges to the USDP, as well as to the military, and has been careful to demonstrate that she is a "responsible" national leader,[6] the NLD has given little indication that it is willing to consider sharing power. Aung San Suu Kyi, who long projected an image of being unconcerned with power, now says openly that she has her eyes set on the presidency.[7] Moreover, the NLD seems intent on going for an all-out victory in 2015 (and thus erasing the injustice of the party being denied its first election victory in 1990). The party has refused, so far, to accept reform of the electoral system to introduce some form of proportional representation, which could produce a more equal distribution of seats in the next parliament. It has also rejected requests from ethnic parties to form a broad electoral alliance among opposition parties, insisting that it intends to run in all constituencies across the country (interviews by author, Yangon, December 2012). These are emotionally-charged issues for the NLD, which has suffered twenty years of intense repression after being denied power in 1990. However, it is hard to see how the party's aspirations for another landslide victory in 2015 can be reconciled with the need in a plural society for power-sharing, non-partisan politics and, not least, the imperative of ensuring continued military support for the reform process. Even the personal relationship between key government reformers and Aung San Suu Kyi, which is currently good, is bound to come under pressure as competition to become the next president heats up. While President Thein Sein may be content to retire, many believe that USDP Chairman Shwe Mann, like Aung San Suu Kyi, has ambitions to become president. And as a Myanmar saying goes, "There is not room for two lions in one cage".

It is not a given that a decisive (and very likely destabilizing) shift of power from the old to a new elite would result from free and fair elections in 2015. It is possible, for example, that key reformers will split from the USDP and set up a new party that will be more competitive in the next elections; or that they could reach a deal with the NLD to share the top posts in a new government. After all, the reformers are widely credited by the general public for their achievements (Ghosh 2012), and the NLD may see an advantage in keeping some of the most experienced and talented ministers in the current government on to strengthen the next administration. Failing that, the current 2008 Constitution still effectively constitutes a "pact" between the military and democratic elites (although one imposed by the military and only grudgingly tolerated by the NLD as a temporary basis for government), which may ease the fears of the military and other vested interests about a future NLD-led government and thus help pre-empt a backlash coup. However, it will be incumbent upon the NLD, as the likely winners in 2015, to take deliberate steps to end the long-standing zero-sum approach to politics in Myanmar. Unless, the party is prepared to share power and continue the current, essentially incremental, approach to change, turbulent waters ahead can be expected.

Majority-Minority Relations

A second set of critical negotiations is taking place between the Burman-dominated government and ethnic armed groups. Myanmar's long-standing civil war is the main reason why military rule has persisted for so long, and it is impossible to imagine democracy taking root in the country in the absence of peace. The traction that the new government has got on this issue is, arguably, its most important achievement to date, and also the main protection against military interference in government affairs and, potentially, another coup. If the peace talks break down and there is a return to significant fighting, it will be all but impossible to strengthen the authority of the civilian government. At best, the government's writ will extend only to the border of the conflict areas. At worst, the military may feel compelled to reject civilian authority altogether and re-establish military rule, as it has done before. Yet reaching a political solution is not going to be easy.

The government deserves praise for taking a fresh approach to the ethnic minority question. In contrast with previous leaders, who generally favoured military solutions to ethnic strife, President Thein Sein has made a negotiated peace a top priority of his administration, and the government's lead mediator, minister in the president's office Aung Min, has shown a genuine will to reconsider past entrenched positions (interviews by author, Yangon, December 2012). Like Aung San Suu Kyi, many ethnic leaders in turn have concluded that something truly new is under way. The quick early progress, however, appears to have stalled. Despite unequivocal promises by the government to engage in national political talks, these have yet to proceed. The largely Burman government may not initially have fully understood what it will take in political terms to establish permanent peace with groups who for decades have suffered extreme violence at the hands of Burman soldiers, whose grievances and distrust of the central government run very deep, and for whom insurgency has become "a way of life" (Smith 1999). Moreover, as the brutal conflict in Kachin State has shown, the new government may not be in full control of the armed forces, at least when it comes to the domain of war-fighting which has long been an entirely military affair and is a responsibility that the new *Tatmadaw* leaders are likely to guard jealously.

Although the ceasefires are holding so far and negotiations between the government and the Kachin Independence Organization (KIO) are ongoing, there is an urgent need to move forward with political talks. As with the NLD, final success in this area will require addressing fundamental questions about power-sharing, which necessarily means reopening questions currently settled in the 2008 Constitution. It will also depend on agreeing on a fairer sharing of the country's natural resources, many of which are located in current or former conflict areas and have long been a major source of conflict. This, again, will demand some very difficult compromises to accommodate core interests of the military and established economic elites while also giving ethnic leaders and local communities enough to convince them to lay down arms and genuinely embrace peace, and become part of the Union of Myanmar. For ethnic armed leaders, such compromise is made more difficult by the likelihood that under conditions of peace and democracy they would lose power locally to civilian elites from their own ethnic group. It should not be forgotten that military rule has persisted for decades not only at the centre of the Myanmar polity, but also in many ethnic areas, and that powerful vested interests across the country are tied up in the status quo.

State-Society Relations

The final set of critical negotiations involves negotiation between the state and Myanmar society more broadly. In this case, the negotiations are more abstract; no explicit deal or pact can be envisioned. But in order to sustain political stability and support for the reform process, the government will need to deliver on popular expectations for material progress. Failure to do so will feed the ranks of opposition *radicals* and create opportunities for military *hardliners* to reassert control.

While political activists, journalists, and NGOs in the main cities are revelling in their new-found civil and political freedoms, to many ordinary Myanmar people the overriding issue is poverty, including jobs, health, and education. The government has made poverty alleviation a high priority and, judging from the economic reforms that are under way, there is no need to doubt its intentions. However, economic change can take even longer than political change to filter down. Weak state capacity means that many high-level policy measures are failing to make an impact on the ground. The civil service is proving to be an obstacle to reform in many areas, due to a mix of bureaucratic inertia and vested interests. And all around the country, local authorities, including military battalions, continue to engage in arbitrary taxation, land grabs, and other long-standing repressive practices.

This gap between expectations and reality (however inevitable it may be in a transition period) constitutes a powder keg. Already social unrest is growing in the freer political environment where people are able to vent their pent-up frustrations over appalling living conditions and official corruption. Within limits, this is a healthy process, which helps ensure that ordinary people are not overlooked and that continuing abuses at the local level are brought to the attention of national leaders. However, any major unrest, especially in the main cities, could invite intervention by military *hardliners* and thus threaten the entire reform process.

The decision by Aung San Suu Kyi and the NLD to work with the new government has extended its period of grace, but there are signs of a struggle within the opposition for "the soul of the people". While Aung San Suu Kyi's leadership of the democracy movement was previously largely undisputed, there are today a growing number of *radicals* who are openly critical of her moderate political strategy and who are actively working to mobilize people for street protests. This is cause for serious alarm. If history is any guide, the combination of still-deep popular economic grievances and radical political activism could well feed another uprising; and should that happen, there is a great risk that the quest for political freedom will suffer as a consequence, as it did in both 1988 and 2007.

Looming in the background of all of these issues is the military and the need to keep the most powerful institution in the country on the side of reform (and eventually bring it under civilian control). Failure to successfully negotiate any of these core socio-political relationships could all too easily produce the conditions for another military coup and a return to the repression and governance style of the old regime. Even short of that, failure to sustain the current momentum of "national politics" would seriously weaken the ability of the government to effectively implement the reforms needed to bring peace, prosperity, and human rights. Myanmar thus risks getting stuck in the same quicksand of partial change that so many other democratizing countries have found themselves in.

CONCLUSION

The recent reforms in Myanmar have transformed political life in the country and substantially improved governance, even as deep-seated structural obstacles continue to impede progress on many major issues. Crucially, the new government is undertaking reform because it *wants* to, not because it had to. While previous military governments since 1962 have essentially been security administrations with a strongly defensive outlook, the current government has a much more progressive development agenda. This agenda may be rooted more in nationalism and a quest for economic development and modernization than in a commitment to liberal values. However, it has created, for the first time in fifty years, real prospects for a "national deal" (or perhaps a series of deals, to be negotiated in succession over time) that could bring together long-standing enemies across political and ethnic fault lines.

The challenge now is for moderates on all sides to negotiate and consolidate the institutions and structures needed to build and sustain long-term peace, democracy, and development. This will require difficult compromises that may be at odds with the immediate interests of each party, but could pay a huge dividend for everyone in the longer run. The NLD will have to find a way to share power, at least in the medium term, with the old elite, including the military. The Burman majority, similarly, must accept that the time has come to live up to the promises made at Independence to give ethnic minority groups genuine autonomy and a fair share of the country's resources. And future governments, of whatever stripe, must commit themselves to improving governance, cleaning up corruption, and instituting economic policies that truly benefit the general population. To achieve this, a lot more still needs to change in Myanmar, and the international community must prove that it, too, is now ready to throw its full support behind an incremental and long-term reform process, even if not everything is picture-perfect.

Notes

1   In one of his first interviews with foreign media, President Thein Sein told Gwen Robinson of the *Financial Times*, "I myself am from a very poor background. I experienced first-hand poverty in this country, and that is not unrelated to my desire, from the moment I became president, to make a priority of poverty reduction in this country. Now I have become president. I have been able to bring together thoughts and ideas about the situation our people face, and combine them with new ideas from scholars and experts, and I now have the opportunity to try to do something about the problems I have long seen, and to act on this concern—especially for the poorest people" (Robinson 2012).

2   It is worth noting in this respect that the only serious effort at reform between 1990 and 2010 happened in the early 2000s when both the UN and moderates in Washington showed a willingness to engage with the military government.

3   This point was reinforced by Aung San Suu Kyi in an interview with the *New York Times* after the NLD joined parliament: "I have to say that the speakers of both houses, they're fair-minded and they don't treat the NLD as the enemy ..." (Keller 2012).

4   The main tensions at this point appear to be between the president and the speaker of the lower house, who are members of the same party but who represent two different institutions and may also have competing personal interests.

5   On several occasions, the military block of MPs has split, with some voting in favour of progressive initiatives such as the release of political prisoners.

6   This was evident, for example, in Aung San Suu Kyi's actions as leader of the commission that investigated the police crackdown on protesters at the Letpadaung copper mine in central Myanmar. While the commission's report recommended that villagers be compensated for lost land and that new environmental safeguards be put in place, it failed to place responsibility for

the violence and rejected calls from locals and activists that the mine be closed down (Letpadaung Investigative Commission 2013). In other words, it carefully avoided stepping on government interests or on those of the main investors in the mine, the military-owned Union of Myanmar Economic Holding and Wanbao, a state-owned Chinese company. Aung San Suu Kyi subsequently explained that it was imperative not to alienate an important foreign investor.

7   According to the 2008 Constitution, no one whose spouse or children owe allegiance to a foreign country can become president. Since Aung San Suu Kyi's two children are British citizens, her ambition to become president will require a constitutional amendment (or a change of citizenship), and thus military support.

References

Bunte, Marco. *Burma's Transition to 'Disciplined Democracy': Abdication or Institutionalization of Military Rule?* GIGA Working papers No. 177. Hamburg: German Institute of Global and Area Studies (GIGA), 2011.

Callahan, Mary. "The Generals Loosen Their Grip". *Journal of Democracy* 23, no. 4 (2012): 120–31.

Englehart, Neil A. "Two Cheers for Burma's Rigged Election". *Asian Survey* 52, no. 4 (2012).

Ghosh, Nirmal. "Childhood Poverty Inspired Thein Sein's Success". *Straits Times*, 15 December 2012. <http://www.straitstimes.com/the-big-story/st-asian-year/story/childhood-poverty-inspired-thein-seins-success-20121215>. Accessed 20 October 2013.

Hindstrom, Hanna. "Is It Foolish to Criticise Aung San Suu Kyi?". *Democratic Voice of Burma*, 24 September 2012. <http://www.dvb.no/uncategorized/is-it-foolish-to-criticise-aung-san-suu-kyi/23942>. Accessed 20 October 2013.

Holliday, Ian. "Myanmar in 2012: Toward a Normal State". *Asian Survey* 53, no. 1 (2013): 93–100.

Human Rights Watch. *All You Can Do Is Pray: Crimes Against Humanity and Ethnic Cleansing of Rohingya Muslims in Burma's Arakan State.* New York: Human Rights Watch, 2013. <http://www.hrw.org/news/2013/04/22/burma-end-ethnic-cleansing-rohingya-muslims>. Accessed 20 October 2013.

International Crisis Group (ICG). *Reform in Myanmar: One Year On.* Asia Briefing No. 136, 11 April 2012. <http://www.crisisgroup.org/en/publication-type/media-releases/2012/asia/myanmar-reform-in-myanmar-one-year-on.aspx>. Accessed 20 October 2013.

———. *Myanmar: Major Reform Underway.* Asia Briefing No. 127, 22 September 2011. <http://www.crisisgroup.org/~/media/files/asia/south-east-asia/

burma-myanmar/b127%20myanmar%20-%20major%20reform%20underway>. Accessed 20 October 2013.

Jagan, Larry. "Burma's President Shakes Up the Chessboard". *Foreign Policy*, 6 September 2012. <http://www.foreignpolicy.com/articles/2012/09/06/burmas_president_shakes_up_the_chessboard>. Accessed 20 October 2013.

Keller, Bill. "A Conversation with Aung San Suu Kyi". *New York Times*. 30 September 2012. <http://keller.blogs.nytimes.com/2012/09/30/a-conversation-with-daw-aung-san-suu-kyi/?_r=0>. Accessed 20 October 2013.

Kivimäki, Timo and Morten B. Pedersen. *Burma: Mapping the Challenges and Opportunities for Dialogue and Reconciliation*. Report prepared for the Crisis Management Initiative, Martti Ahtisaari Rapid Reaction Facility, 2012.

Kyaw Yin Hlaing. "Understanding Recent Political Changes in Myanmar". *Contemporary South East Asia* 34, no. 2 (2012): 197–216.

Letpadaung Investigative Commission. *Letpadaung Copper Mine Final Report*. 13 March 2013. <http://www.scribd.com/doc/130334549/Letpadaung-Copper-Mine-Final-Report-by-Investigation-Commission-March-11-2013>. Accessed 16 January 2014. (No English translation available.)

Lintner, Bertil. *Aung San Suu Kyi and Burma's Struggle for Democracy*. Chiang Mai: Silkworm Books, 2011.

Lloyd-George, William. "The Dicey Democrat: How a pillar of the old regime in Burma is working to prove his democratic credentials". *Foreign Policy*, 28 November 2012. <http://www.foreignpolicy.com/articles/2012/11/28/the_dicey_democrat>. Accessed 20 October 2013.

Magnusson, Anna and Morten B. Pedersen. *A Good Office? Twenty Years of UN Mediation in Myanmar*. New York: International Peace Institute, 2012.

Malinowski, Tom. *Testimony before Tom Lantos Human Rights Commission hearing on "Human Rights in Burma"*. Washington DC, 28 February 2013. <http://www.hrw.org/news/2013/02/28/testimony-tom-malinowski>. Accessed 20 October 2013.

Maung Aung Myoe. *A Historical Overview of Political Transition in Myanmar Since 1988*. Asia Research Institute Working Paper Series No. 95. Singapore: Asia Research Institute, National University of Singapore, 2007. <http://www.ari.nus.edu.sg/docs/wps/wps07_095.pdf>. Accessed 16 January 2014.

Maung Maung. *The 1988 Uprising in Burma*. New Haven: Yale University Southeast Asian Studies, 1999.

Nyein Nyein. "Is Shwe Mann Trying to Steal Thein Sein's Reform Mantle?". *Irrawaddy*, 16 March 2012. <http://www2.irrawaddy.org/article.php?art_id=23227>. Accessed 20 October 2013.

Nyein, Susanne Praeger. "Expanding Military, Shrinking Citizenry and the New Constitution in Burma". *Journal of Contemporary Asia* 39, no. 4 (2009): 638–48.

Pedersen, Morten B. "The Politics of Transition in Burma: Opportunities for Change and Options for Democrats". *Critical Asian Studies* 43, no. 1 (2011).

Pedersen, Morten B. *Promoting Human Rights in Burma: A Critique of Western Sanctions Policy*. Lanham: Rowman & Littlefield, 2008.

Robinson, Gwen. "Transcript of Interview with Thein Sein". *Financial Times*, 12 July 2012.

Smith, Martin. *Burma: Insurgency and the Politics of Ethnicity*. 2nd ed. London: Zed Books, 1999.

Thein Sein. Statement at the General Debate of the Sixty-Seventh Session of the United Nations General Assembly, 27 September 2012. <http://gadebate.un.org/sites/default/files/gastatements/67/MM_en.pdf>. Accessed 20 October 2013.

Transnational Institute. *Access Denied: Land Rights and Ethnic Conflict in Burma*. Burma Policy Briefing No. 11, 2013*a*. <http://www.tni.org/node/70443/publications>. Accessed 20 October 2013.

———. *The Kachin Crisis: Peace Must Prevail*. Burma Policy Briefing No. 10, 2013*b*. <http://www.tni.org/node/70443/publications>. Accessed 20 October 2013.

III

Encouraging Signs

4

MYANMAR'S PARLIAMENT
From Scorn to Significance

Thomas Kean

Like much about Myanmar's transition to discipline-flourishing democracy—as the State Peace and Development Council (SPDC, 1997–2011) so regularly called it—the *hluttaw* (parliament) established under the 2008 Constitution was widely written off before it even came into being. The conventional wisdom among commentators, analysts, and politicians was that the constitution was designed to perpetuate decades of military rule, the 2010 general election would be a sham, and the *hluttaw* would be a rubber stamp for the new military-backed national government.[1] The one-sided result of that general election, the rules of which heavily favoured the military-aligned Union Solidarity and Development Party (USDP), only served to reinforce this view.

Despite the strong majority enjoyed by the USDP,[2] and the presence of appointed military representatives, who fill 25 percent of all seats in each national, state, and region parliament, over the past two-and-a-half years the *hluttaw* bodies have been anything but a rubber stamp. On the contrary: one of the defining features of the *Pyidaungsu Hluttaw*, or National Parliament, has been the regular tension, and even conflict, with President U Thein Sein's government and other institutions in Myanmar's political landscape, including the judiciary, political parties, media, and civil society. The parliament has vigorously asserted its independence from these other institutions—to the point of potentially harming the reform process—and its members have taken particularly seriously the task of acting as a check on the Union government, cutting budgets and discussing and investigating reports of corruption and illegal land confiscations. As writer and historian Thant Myint-U has noted, because it is a new institution the parliament does not suffer in the same way as the judiciary and bureaucracy from corruption, red tape, and other legacies of decades of military rule (Kean 2012). For the same reason, however, the *hluttaw* and its members are still feeling their way around a system bequeathed by the SPDC through its tight management of the constitution-drafting process. Inevitably, this has led to some missteps and misunderstandings.

Given Myanmar's fraught political history and the binary nature of post-1988 politics, particularly in areas dominated by ethnic Burmese, a surprising degree of cooperation between its representatives has characterized the parliamentary system at the national level. Even after the addition of representatives from the National League for Democracy (NLD) in May 2012 there has been a consistent and notable lack of adherence to party political lines.[3] While still a controversial presence, some of the appointed military representatives have earned a grudging respect from their elected peers for their contribution to *hluttaw* discussions and they operate with a significant degree of independence on the majority of issues. The dialogue between the military and the opposition in the parliament appears to have been beneficial for both sides. At the same time, however, the USDP/ military control over the parliament has never been under threat on the important questions of Myanmar's future, such as the military's formal role in politics. Because of their small overall numbers, the gains made by the Burmese and ethnic minority opposition, while impressive, have been confined to issues that do not seriously challenge USDP/military interests.

Although the *hluttaw* is still off-limits to the broader public, another feature of the past two years has been the gradual opening-up of the National Parliament to outsiders, both local and foreign. The secretive nature of the first session, from which independent observers were banned, was quickly discarded. International delegations, non-government organizations, and even groups from local schools have watched sessions from the chambers' galleries, much as they would in Western parliamentary democracies. Myanmar journalists regularly attend and report on the *hluttaw* sessions without censorship. The relationships that parliamentarians have developed with these journalists have contributed to the dramatic shift in public perceptions of the *hluttaw* over the past two years.

It is in this context that this chapter seeks to analyze the place of the parliament and its members in Myanmar's new political landscape. While Myanmar-language coverage of the parliament has grown significantly since March 2011, internationally it remains an overlooked piece of the reform jigsaw. The *Myanmar Times* has been one of the few English-language sources of information on its activities and dynamics, and much of my understanding has been informed by the reporting of my Myanmar colleagues, in my capacity as editor of the English-language edition. Largely because of my position at the newspaper I have had the opportunity to conduct extensive interviews with around a dozen members of parliament (MPs) about the parliament's activities and dynamics, as well as many other individuals who regularly interact with the institution.

This chapter begins by outlining the process through which the parliamentary system was created under the controversial 2008 Constitution, how parliamentarians were elected in an even more controversial general election in 2010, and the historic handover from the SPDC to President Thein Sein's quasi-civilian government in March 2011. Second, it details the factors behind parliament's assertion of independence vis-à-vis the government and individual members of the administration, and the importance of a number of individuals to this process, particularly the *Pyithu Hluttaw* (People's Assembly) Speaker Thura U Shwe Mann. It also looks at the interaction between the parliament and other actors in the political process. Third, this chapter considers some of the achievements of the parliament and how MPs have gone about representing their immediate constituents and other people they perceive they represent. Finally, the chapter concludes by considering the possible implications for the parliament and its members of the 2015 general election. The first national vote to pit the USDP against the NLD and its popular leader Daw Aung San Suu Kyi is a potential flashpoint for conflict in what has so far been a relatively smooth transition from military rule to "disciplined democracy". The competition for 2015—and for control of the legislatures and the reins of government—has already begun, with political alliances, constitutional amendments, and changes to voting systems being discussed. All major parties have held, or are preparing to hold, national party conferences. There is also a risk of conflict if fundamental political issues that have so far been off the table, such as the 2008 Constitution, are questioned and challenged.

However, as seen by the smooth integration of NLD representatives following the 2012 by-elections, there has so far been little visible impact on activities inside the parliament. Members of parliament express surprising insouciance about their own prospects for 2015 and argue that working both individually and with members of other parties to deliver results to constituents is the best insurance policy against electoral defeat. Cooperation, rather than confrontation, is likely to remain the dominant feature of the parliament until much closer to the election proper, particularly as a number of the factors that have led to the bipartisan atmosphere, such as the strong USDP majority, will not change before 2015.

LEAD-UP TO THE 2010 ELECTION

The Constitution of the Republic of the Union of Myanmar established a bicameral national parliament, known as the *Pyidaungsu Hluttaw*, which comprises a 440-seat *Pyithu Hluttaw*, or lower house, and 224-seat *Amyotha Hluttaw*, or upper house. Additionally, fourteen State and Region *Hluttaw*s were created.[4] In all parliamentary bodies, the military is guaranteed 25 percent of seats, which are filled by serving military personnel appointed by the Commander-in-Chief of the Defence Services.[5] Unlike elected representatives, who serve for terms of five years, military members of parliament can be, and have been, reshuffled at any point by the Commander-in-Chief. The process of drafting the constitution, initiated in 1993 through the convening of the National Convention, was concluded in late 2007 and early 2008. In February 2008 the SPDC announced that the draft constitution would be put to a referendum on 10 May that year. The government later announced that it had been approved with 92.48 percent support from 98.12 percent voter turnout, figures that look all the more unlikely when compared to voter turnout in the subsequent 2010 general election and the 2012 by-elections (MOFA 2008).

In March 2010, the SPDC released a set of restrictive election laws that would set the tone for the rest of the campaign period until the vote in November of that year. Later the same month, the NLD announced it would not take part in the election because that would mean "safeguarding" the constitution and consequently abandoning its members in detention, including, it appeared at the time, Aung San Suu Kyi (BBC 2010). The extent to which the public supported this decision is unclear, although anecdotal reports suggest the reaction was mixed.

Other politicians, however, sensed that the elections provided an opportunity to challenge the military establishment within the legal framework, and had begun mobilizing in late 2009. In many of Myanmar's ethnic minority regions this process was even more pronounced, with all major ethnic minorities having some form of representation. In Kachin State and northern Shan State, however, the Union Election Commission refused to allow parties linked to the Kachin Independence Organization to register,[6] while in some areas under the control of ceasefire groups such as the United Wa State Party, voting was cancelled.[7] Between April and the end of the August, when the window to register candidates closed, more than 40 parties had initiated the registration process, of which 37 would compete on 7 November, fielding 3069 candidates across 1154 constituencies, including 82 independent candidates (Union Election Commission 2010). The largest opposition groups in terms of candidates fielded were the National Democratic Force (NDF), formed by former NLD members, the Shan Nationalities Democratic Party (SNDP), and the Democratic Party (Myanmar).

The vehicle for the military establishment to contest the elections was the USDP, formed in June and led by Thein Sein, then prime minister. The USDP was built upon the Union Solidarity and Development Association, formed in the early 1990s by Senior General Than Shwe. The USDP inherited its predecessor's leadership, administrative apparatus, offices, and most of its members. Its leaders were mostly former senior military officials, who resigned from the *Tatmadaw* (armed forces) formally in August 2010 to contest the election. The party ran in almost every constituency and its representatives comprised a mixture of former military officials and civilians, including administrative officials, former civil servants, prominent businessmen, and professionals such as doctors and lawyers. In many ethnic minority areas the USDP recruited candidates from the local major ethnic group, including, controversially, in Rohingya-dominated northern Rakhine State.[8]

Election day proper was marred by widespread accusations of fraud and vote rigging, with the USDP winning almost 80 percent of all seats.

While these well-founded accusations garnered significant media coverage outside Myanmar and confirmed the negative perceptions of the election, the extent to which a completely free and fair election on 7 November 2010 would have altered the results is questionable. None of the newly-formed opposition parties were in a position to challenge the USDP as they lacked funds, candidates, and popular support. In hundreds of constituencies the USDP was challenged only by the National Unity Party (NUP), essentially a continuation of Ne Win's Burma Socialist Programme Party that had been formed in 1988 and which lacked credibility as a viable opponent. In the majority of constituencies, particularly in rural areas, the USDP candidates won emphatically. Nevertheless, the large number of parties and candidates, and the use of the first-past-the-post voting system, meant that the USDP victory, like that of the NLD in 1990, was not as comprehensive as it may appear: the USDP received some 57.9 percent of all votes cast (Network Myanmar undated), with turnout varying from 77.26 percent for the *Pyithu Hluttaw* and 76.62 percent for State and Region *Hluttaw*s (Maw Maw San 2010).

UNCERTAINTY FOLLOWING THE ELECTION

The immediate post-election period was one of uncertainty. It was not clear what the next step by the government would be and when it would occur. In mid-January 2011 the SPDC announced that the first session of parliament would convene in Naypyitaw on 31 January. Its first actions were to enact the constitution and, over the course of the next week, select the president—U Thein Sein. A former Secretary-1 of the SPDC, Thiha Thura U Tin Aung Myint Oo, was selected as Vice President-1, while Dr Sai Mauk Kham filled the second vice presidential position. The selection of this little-known Shan doctor from Lashio as a vice president was widely interpreted as a concession to ethnic minority groups.

The first session of parliament took place in an unusual context: although the president had been selected at the beginning of the session, power had not yet been handed over, and it was SPDC ministers who initially fronted the legislature. The ministers mostly took the opportunity to tout the military regime's achievements. For this reason, the NUP, which held the third-largest number of seats, essentially abstained from asking questions or submitting proposals. Representatives have privately conceded they were initially afraid to speak up but many, particularly from opposition parties, submitted questions. While many SPDC ministers stonewalled, there was still "a level of accountability—or at least disclosure—from the military that has probably not been present for several decades" (Kyaw Kyaw 2011). Independent analyst Richard Horsey noted after the first session that a range of "sensitive topics" had been raised, with the speakers "allowing rather open and free-flowing debate" (Horsey 2012, p. 43). He concluded that the first session of the national parliament was not a dramatic break with the past but still represented a substantive change.

Nevertheless, opposition lawmakers made up just 105 of the 493 elected positions, and barely 15 percent of all parliamentarians. During the first session journalists were barred from watching proceedings, and members of parliament were threatened with jail terms for passing on information under a set of seventeen restrictive laws promulgated by the SPDC that constitute parliament's standing orders. Reports of the proceedings in state media were extensive but still showed signs of government censorship: MPs said discussions were not reported in full, and some topics were omitted completely. Opposition activists and observers, mostly those in exile, soon dubbed the national legislature the "15-minute parliament" because of the brevity of the initial sessions that saw U Thein Sein elected president (RC 2011). Some critics went so far as to question whether opposition MPs ran for office for the 300,000 *kyats* a month salary, the equivalent of about US$350, and accused them of "pay[ing] lip service to the new era of democracy that has supposedly arrived in Myanmar" (Aung Din 2011).

Like assessments of the overall political process, these negative perceptions changed rapidly over the course of the next twelve months. When the third session began on 26 January 2012, news agency Reuters published a feature article with the headline "In Myanmar, a 'sham' parliament stirs to life" (Szep 2011), describing how MPs were drafting anti-corruption legislation and preparing to discuss the national budget, which had previously been passed in secret by the military with no public consultation or civilian oversight.

ASSERTING INDEPENDENCE: THE EVOLUTION OF THE *HLUTTAW*

The first session of parliament concluded on 23 March 2011, and a week later Senior General Than Shwe signed the order to dissolve the SPDC and hand power to Thein Sein's new government. The second session, which began on 22 August 2011, was essentially the first under the new political structure with its quasi-civilian government. Up to this point, the government had not yet chalked up any major reform victories to win over its critics, and although there were some positive signs, for many observers the jury was still out on the sincerity of the changes. However, this changed dramatically just three days before the second session opened, when the president met Aung San Suu Kyi at his official residence in Naypyitaw. This historic meeting set the tone for the open and frank debates that took place during the second session, right up until its conclusion in November.

Among some MPs, though, there was already optimism that the second session would mark a turning-point in the life of the fledgling legislature. A chief source of this optimism was the formation during the first session of four 15-member permanent parliamentary committees in each house: a Bill Committee, Public Accounts Committee, *Hluttaw* Rights Committee, and Government's Guarantees, Pledges and Undertakings Vetting Committee (Shwe Yinn Mar Oo and Soe Than Lynn 2011). While senior positions on the committees went uniformly to USDP members, a surprising number of the overall committee members were from other parties—in most cases around one-third. Representatives on the two Bill Committees spent the months before the start of the second session examining existing and new draft legislation in cooperation with the government and gained an insight into the scope of President Thein Sein's reform plans.

The formation of the permanent committees—comprising many of the more capable legislators—initially did not attract much attention, but it was an important development for a number of reasons. A significant amount of parliamentary work was taken out of the USDP-dominated chamber and into an environment where MPs could mix and converse openly on a more intimate basis. The Public Accounts Committee, which vets the budget, and the Bill Committee have proven to be particularly influential bodies. The authority of the three Bill Committees—the upper house, lower house, and joint committees—derives from parliamentary procedure; when legislation is submitted to parliament, the relevant Bill Committee's report is read out and debated. More often than not, the other parliamentarians adopt the committee's recommendations, although dissent is not uncommon.

The strong emphasis on committees—there are more than twenty,[9] mostly comprising fifteen members—has also forced members of the USDP to mix with representatives of other parties, and this has been one of a number of factors behind the rise of a parliament with an unusual lack of party divisions and verbal conflict. Other factors include the weaknesses of Myanmar's fledgling political parties, the lack of strong ideology and the weak party allegiance among USDP representatives, and the relative independence that has been afforded armed forces representatives. The physical layout of the parliament also has a significant impact: MPs face the Speaker rather than each other, which does little to encourage divisions between parties.

Perhaps most credit for the emergence of a credible parliament should go to *Pyithu Hluttaw* Speaker Shwe Mann, who until the dissolution of the SPDC was Joint Chief of Staff of the Army, Navy and Air Force, its third-highest ranking position, and *Amyotha Hluttaw* Speaker U Khin Aung Myint, a former Major General and Minister for Culture. Under the existing standing orders, the two Speakers have wide-ranging powers, including control over the agenda of each chamber and the right to censure MPs, but while both are senior USDP members, neither has attempted to force their representatives to adhere to a party line: Shwe Mann regularly encourages members of parliament to shed their party allegiances; U Khin Aung Myint exercises more control over debates than his counterpart, and will sometimes turn off MPs' microphones if they run over their allotted fifteen minutes during discussions, broach taboo topics such as federalism, or generally speak out of line.

INSTITUTIONAL RIVALRIES: LEGISLATURE, EXECUTIVE, AND JUDICIARY

The separation of powers enshrined in Myanmar's constitution, with the executive being outside the legislature, means that most of the conflict that has occurred to date in the parliament has been between the executive government and the legislature, rather than among parties and individuals within the *hluttaw*. Unused to any scrutiny, some ministers— even so-called reformers—have complained that too much of their time is spent fronting parliament to answer questions of little importance from members. "They especially don't like the role of committees because for a long time [ministers] had the right to exercise the administrative power with no questions, no checks. So now some people check and ask many questions, they don't understand and don't accept the habit", said one representative.[10] In one notable case, the Minister for Agriculture and

Irrigation U Myint Hlaing was forced to apologize in parliament for being quoted in the domestic press as calling MPs uneducated and ill-informed after they significantly cut his ministry's budget for 2012–13.

In early 2012 the Constitutional Tribunal found itself at the centre of an important and troubling dispute between the parliament and the executive. This conflict highlighted the growing strength and independence of the *hluttaw*, but also brought it significant, and warranted, criticism. In February the Auditor-General, on behalf of President Thein Sein, asked the Tribunal to decide on the status of bodies created by parliament, and whether they are "union level", that is, essentially of the same status as the government. On 28 March the Constitutional Tribunal ruled they were not union-level bodies, setting the course for a showdown between the legislature and the executive. The conflict came to a head during the fourth session of parliament, when more than three hundred legislators, arguing that the definition adopted by the Tribunal would impair their ability to act as a check and balance on the government, signed a petition to impeach the Tribunal for "improper discharge of duties" and "failure to comply with the provisions of the constitution". Both the upper and lower houses approved this resolution, but rather than wait to be formally impeached, the Tribunal's members resigned en masse in September 2012.

For such an antagonistic gesture, the public response from the government has been surprising: one member of parliament said that after the impeachment, ministers were more likely to front the parliament than send their deputy or a director-general. "At first they didn't care about us but … now some of the union ministers come. This is one of the changes in the parliament. It is because of the crisis of the Constitutional Tribunal."[11] However, in their eagerness to ensure the strength of the parliament, MPs responded in a way that could undermine judicial independence, and were criticized for it both inside Myanmar and abroad. Some have expressed concerns about the precedent it will set for the Tribunal, given its important role as an arbiter in future disputes (Nardi 2012). Acknowledging this criticism, one MP said that although the *hluttaw* had succeeded in impeaching the Tribunal's members, this represented a "failure" for the parliament. Unable to resolve the dispute through dialogue, it had responded in a way that ultimately hurt the parliament's credibility, he said.[12]

If there was any realization that impeaching the Tribunal represented a failure for the parliament, it did not last long: in early 2013 MPs approved a bill amending the Constitutional Tribunal Law which seemed to introduce ambiguity over whether the Tribunal's decisions are final. This was despite President Thein Sein attending parliament and urging members to vote against the changes because they were, he said, "unconstitutional". The impact of these parliamentary decisions is not yet clear, but they constitute a disturbing use of legislative power to overwhelm perceived political opponents.

However, in other cases, parliamentary representatives appear to have made a conscious attempt to avoid confrontation in their dealings with the government and ministers. Following a discussion about corruption in fifteen ministries that was uncovered by the Auditor-General, one NLD representative said he expected cases of misappropriation would be resolved through a mixture of "some action and … some negotiation so that the funds lost will be reimbursed by the persons concerned. It is important that it is not confrontational. Because we discuss it openly it will help transparency and I think it will improve later and they will manage [budgets] properly."[13]

Similarly, Speaker Shwe Mann made a deliberate decision not to use the term "oversight" to describe the role of parliamentary committees vis-à-vis the government, preferring instead "reciprocal checks and balances" because "he thinks the words are a little softer than 'oversight power'".[14] Where in 2012 debates over national planning and the budget had divided parliament and the government, in 2013 the *hluttaw* invited the officials from each ministry who oversaw the drafting of the legislation to attend sessions when it was being discussed by members. In a meeting with journalists on 31 January 2013, to mark the second anniversary of the convening of parliament, Shwe Mann conceded there had been "misunderstandings" between MPs and members of the government, which he attributed to a lack of knowledge about the parliament's role.

While on the whole eager to act as a check on government, parliament has been less excited about the prospect of the other branches of government acting as a check on it. There remains no formal process to impeach or remove an MP,[15] and parliamentarians rejected a proposal to force all government ministers to declare their assets after the Attorney-General said the proposal should be expanded to include members of parliament (Yan Pai 2012). In another example, the Inter-Parliamentary Union took the final draft report of its assessment mission down from its website because of a complaint about the parliament's weaknesses being made public.

The response to the Constitutional Tribunal dispute has been particularly controversial. As one editor said: "At the start [the parliament] respected what the constitution said, but after it became a problem for MPs they simply ignored it". When an anonymous blogger criticized members of parliament for approving the Constitutional Tribunal Law amendments, MPs—convinced the blogger was a member of the government—responded by forming a committee to investigate the author's true identity so defamation charges could be filed. To most outsiders—and even to some MPs on the investigation committee—the decision appeared petty and counterproductive, and it attracted domestic and international scorn.

UNPREDICTABLE VOTING

On many occasions over the past two years, parties have split when it has come to voting on proposals and bills—even in the tightly-controlled first session (Kyaw Kyaw 2011). On one notable occasion when the president returned the parliament-approved draft of the *Ward and Village-Tract Administration Law* with the recommendation that one stage of the selection process for local administrators be changed from secret vote to "negotiated selection", representatives narrowly voted against the proposal, 278 to 236. Splits have also occurred along more easily discernible lines, such as the vote in September 2012 on the proposal to impeach the Constitutional Tribunal: all *Tatmadaw* representatives voted against the proposal, while all elected MPs voted for it. On a subsequent vote in the *Pyithu Hluttaw* to amend the Constitutional Tribunal Law, two elected MPs from the SNDP sided with the military against the bill. "Now there are so many committees and we are all cooperating. We are basically party-less in terms of how we think and operate," said U Khin Maung Yi of the NDF.[16]

This pattern of unpredictability has continued, despite the arrival of more than forty NLD representatives who won seats in the April 2012 by-elections.[17] As a minority party, holding less than 10 percent of seats, the NLD representatives have seemingly little to gain at this point from casting themselves as the opponents of the USDP, and operate under instructions not to antagonize their counterparts in the USDP or the military.

> Our NLD representatives enter into this parliament with two main objectives. We want reconciliation and we want to cooperate with the other parties for the betterment of our country and for the people. If the proposal is better for the people and our country, we will agree—we will never disagree.... We have to cooperate with the other members, including ethnics and the USDP.[18]

There is no guarantee that this atmosphere of cooperation will persist. The parliament's stakeholders could deem it in their best interests, particularly as the general election in 2015 approaches, to begin defining themselves more clearly as political adversaries rather than partners. However, given that the numerical composition of the parliament—and the NLD's minority status—will not change before 2015, bipartisanship is likely to remain a strong feature of parliament for several more years.

COMPETING PERSONALITIES: POLITICAL AMBITIONS ON SHOW

A significant contributor to the progression of the parliamentary system has been the Speaker of the *Pyithu Hluttaw*, Shwe Mann, who is also leader of the USDP.[19] Despite the fact they are from the same party, he has not shied away from publicly criticizing government ministers who he believes have shirked questions from members of parliament (Soe Than Lynn 2011). Considered a likely presidential prospect before Thein Sein was elected, there is speculation that his attempts to build the institutional strength of the *hluttaw* are based on ambitions to be president after the next general election in 2015. Despite this speculation, he is popular with parliamentarians, including those from the NLD—he has a warm relationship with Aung San Suu Kyi and the two meet regularly—and most find him sincere.

On occasions Shwe Mann has used his position and status to influence the result of voting in the *hluttaw*: instead of putting proposals he wants approved to a vote, he asks three times if there are any objections, a process permitted under the laws governing how the parliament operates. This sends a clear signal to both USDP and military representatives that Shwe Mann, their superior, wants them to vote in the affirmative. One example was in August 2011, when Thein Nyunt of Thingangyun put forward a proposal to release prisoners of conscience. More recently, a motion to form a commission to investigate unrest at the Letpadaung mine project was approved in a similar manner, despite objections from the Ministry of Defence and it seemingly being contrary to the interests of the military (Soe Than Lynn 2012).[20] This style of leadership has undoubtedly helped the Speaker gain the support of opposition parliamentarians.

While reports of Shwe Mann's ambitions are difficult to verify, the *Pyithu Hluttaw* Speaker has appeared on a number of occasions to deliberately put the parliament on a collision course with the government. In February 2012, when parliamentarians were assessing the government's proposed budget for 2012-13, he announced that a pay rise was needed for civil servants in order to combat corruption (Myo Thant 2012). Then Minister for Finance and Revenue U Hla Tun rejected the proposal on the grounds it would be fiscally irresponsible, and parliament refused to pass the budget. Finally, a compromise was reached under which the lowest-paid civil servants received a 30,000 *kyat* a month increase (Reuters 2012).

The divisions were plain to see at the USDP national assembly in Naypyitaw in October, when Thein Sein managed to hold on to the party chairmanship, to the apparent surprise and disappointment of many representatives, who had expected the Speaker to take over. While Thein Sein has furthered the cause of national reconciliation and brought previously opposed groups, such as the NLD and exiled activists, together behind his government, he has not, in the eyes of some members of parliament and observers, been able or willing to do enough to support the USDP party cause. Similarly, they argue he has not shown enough respect to the parliamentarians that selected him as president through the constitution's electoral college system. U Ye Tun commented:

> [Thura U Shwe Mann] is honest and he can see the way forward for the party better than U Thein Sein. He is president but he did not understand politics well, such as the check and balance process ... U Shwe Mann wants to increase the parliament's activities to make it more effective and if U Thein Sein understood and cooperated well the USDP party's situation would be better in 2015.[21]

Given its large majority in the *hluttaw*, the USDP could pursue other means of protecting its interests in the 2015 election. In March 2013, two senior members submitted a proposal to form a committee to review the constitution which both houses approved unanimously. While constitutional change has been an ever-present issue in Myanmar politics since 2008, the Burmese and ethnic minority opposition have almost always advocated it. The submission of the proposal appears to be a strategic decision based on the recognition that the USDP's majority in parliament will likely disappear after the next election and therefore should be utilized now. By taking the initiative on the issue, the USDP can better seek to leverage its majority to make amendments that will support its interests in 2015, such as changes to the voting system in the lower house,[22] possibly by negotiating a deal with the NLD on amendments that the opposition wants passed.

In June 2013, the USDP called the first meeting of the party's executive committee since its national assembly in October 2012. USDP leaders were expected to begin preparing a policy platform for 2015, including the party's stance on constitutional amendments and the voting system.

INCREASINGLY INCLUSIVE BEHAVIOUR

Myanmar's national legislatures may be physically remote from most of the country but different sectors of society, as well as the international community, have been quick to explore avenues for engagement. This engagement has varied from journalists and international delegations seeking interviews and meetings to civil society organizations providing briefing documents on specific issues with the intention of influencing lawmaking. However, the engagement has worked both ways, with committees and commissions established to allow the public to file complaints, an important means of interaction with constituents.

One of the most prominent—and successful—examples of engaging with members of parliament to influence legislation was the 30 June 2012 meeting between hundreds of members of the Myanmar business community, including a number of well-known business cronies, and a parliamentary delegation led by Shwe Mann. The purpose was to gather feedback on amendments to the draft Foreign Investment Law that was before the parliament. Subsequently, dozens of amendments were submitted and passed to make the law more favourable to local interests and less to foreign investors. After the draft was approved—following considerable debate both in the parliament and the media—the government returned the draft with suggested amendments to make it more investor-friendly, most of which were eventually accepted.

Another, less well-known, example of successful lobbying by stakeholders concerned the Farmland Law and Vacant, Fallow and Virgin Lands Management Law. A network of NGOs focusing on land rights issues analyzed the draft laws while they were still before the parliament in the second half of 2011 and disseminated briefing papers to MPs, including one who was on the Bill Committee tasked with recommending changes to the drafts. The draft laws were held up in parliament, and network members said subsequent revisions addressed some, but not all, of their concerns. When one of the key members was asked how they felt about their new ability to influence lawmaking, he said:

[It is] really empowering.... It is a really big change.... This is really encouraging for us to move our agenda forward. If we don't say this is empowerment, what else can we call empowerment? It's really powerful.[23]

While the network was able to have an impact on the land laws, it should be acknowledged that, like the business owners who lobbied parliament about the *Foreign Investment Law*, it was able to do this because of its elite-level status in society, which helped to facilitate its engagement with members of parliament. While the network's members profess to represent the interests of farmers, there was little opportunity for farmers themselves, or for newly-formed farmer associations, to get involved directly in the process of lobbying MPs.

These examples highlight an important shortcoming of the parliamentary system: the lack of a formal consultation process. Bill committees rarely look for outside expertise to inform their decision-making, while under the standing orders drafts of legislation are secret until submitted to parliament—members can be punished for distributing them beforehand—and even then copies remain hard to obtain, limiting the options for other actors to engage. For the outside world, obtaining information about the activities of parliament and its committees remains difficult, as there is no online dissemination service.

In this context, the role of the media has been important. While journalists were barred from entering the parliament during the first session, this ban was rescinded for the second session in August 2011. On any given sitting day there are up to fifteen journalists from private print-media publications present. However, this small press corps struggles to cope with the sheer amount of information coming out of the parliament, and is able to cover only a fraction of the discussions that take place. They also do not have reliable access to information, and have to record the session or ask MPs directly for transcripts of their speeches.

Numerous foreign delegations have visited the parliament and met representatives; amongst the visitors was a team from the Inter-Parliamentary Union carrying out a needs assessment in April–May 2012. The most detailed assessment conducted to date, it made a number of important recommendations on the administration of parliament, its processes and procedures, and parliamentary services. These included the creation of committees to oversee the operations of parliament, an overhaul of the committee system, and capacity-building programs for members of parliament and parliamentary staff. The report also emphasized the importance of international organizations coordinating support to avoid overlap and confusion. "Given the number of organizations proposing their support to the parliament, cooperation and coordination will be paramount in ensuring that the parliament receives relevant, timely and beneficial support", the report concluded.[24] There is no evidence, however, that any of the report's recommendations have yet been acted on.

DELIVERING RESULTS, GAINING RESPECT

Up to time of writing, the parliament has approved 52 bills, including key legislation on foreign investment, labour unions and peaceful protests (ALTSEAN 2013b). As of June 2013, 34 submitted bills had not yet been approved. But arguably the single most important achievement of parliamentarians has been building institutional credibility. Undoubtedly, the presence of the NLD since May 2012 has been a major factor in increasing public interest and trust significantly. But much of the scepticism of early 2011 had evaporated even before the entry of NLD representatives, because the parliament had shown itself to be an institution independent of the government and military, through, for example, its scrutiny of the budget. The speed with which this independence was achieved has been as much a surprise to representatives in parliament as it has been to observers.

Many representatives have worked hard to bring tangible benefits to constituents. Admittedly, the extent to which the debate over proposals and legislation, the questioning of ministers, and the examination of budgets has directly affected the lives of ordinary Myanmar people is limited. However, some actions that do not immediately appear significant have had a material impact. Parliamentarians have, for example, successfully pushed the government to amend policies that force farmers to grow unsuitable crops, to give ethnic minorities greater freedom to teach their languages and hold cultural events, and to significantly increase salaries for hardship postings to encourage more civil servants to accept jobs in remote areas.

In many cases, members of parliament work to address issues not only for their constituents but also for members of their ethnic or religious group. *Amyotha Hluttaw* representative J Yaw Wu said he had regularly raised the issue of how the ethnicity of Lisu people is written variously as Lishaw, Lawlaw and Loiyaw on National Registration Cards. This practice allows immigration officers to extort money from Lisu around the country because only the name "Lisu" is officially recognized by the government, he said. J Yaw Wu said he also ensured action was taken against military or police force personnel responsible for three illegal killings in his constituency.

> Being able to [ensure the officers were punished] was really wonderful, I never imagined it would be possible. Before I thought that this parliament was also just under the USDP and we have to follow whatever they do but there are many things we can raise.[25]

A number of parliamentary committees have also been established to handle complaints from the public, notably the *Pyithu Hluttaw* Judicial and Legal Affairs Committee chaired by Thura U Aung Ko, the *Pyithu Hluttaw* Rule of Law, Peace and Stability Committee chaired by Daw Aung San Suu Kyi, and a joint commission that includes more than sixty MPs which is investigating complaints over land confiscations.[26] As of October 2012, the Judicial and Legal Affairs Committee had received two thousand complaints and said it had resolved about twelve hundred. The committees, however, do not have the right to change or make legally-binding decisions; they can only forward cases to the relevant authorities with recommendations. Nevertheless, as one experienced journal editor noted, "People are coming to believe that they can rely on the parliament to resolve issues by using the committees".[27]

Many observers and representatives agree that MPs have become savvier about how they raise issues in the *hluttaw*. A number of MPs credited the arrival of the NLD as a factor in improving the quality of debate in the parliament and making discussions more vibrant, but each session has shown a gradual improvement as members gain experience and knowledge. Questions have become more pointed and focused, and MPs are beginning to ask follow-up questions when the response from a government official does not properly answer the question. U Thein Nyunt from Thingangyun said he believed he had been able to speed up the release of political prisoners—including specific individuals—by submitting a motion during each of the five sessions.[28] Knowing that U.S. President Barack Obama's visit would likely be accompanied by an amnesty, in the week leading up to it, Thein Nyunt raised the case of one man who had been in prison for more than two decades, after the man's family asked him for help. The prisoner was subsequently released, along with at least forty-three other political detainees.

Inactivity, however, remains an issue. Visitors to the hluttaw will notice that while normally at least three-quarters of MPs attend sessions, many do not participate in discussions.[29] Most observers estimate half to two-thirds of members are almost completely inactive. U Khin Maung Yi of the NDF said most USDP representatives were too "afraid of their party leaders, government, and losing their seats" to speak up on issues of importance. Another reason behind their inactivity is the fact that many USDP representatives ran in the election somewhat reluctantly and lack any political experience. This phenomenon is not confined to the USDP: one 75-year-old NUP representative from Mon State conceded he had no real wish to be a parliamentarian. "The party selected me to run [in the election] and the people voted for me over the USDP candidate: that's why I'm here," he said.[30]

VICTORIES OUTSIDE THE CHAMBER

Representatives have also been able to use their status and authority to assist constituents in other, less formal ways. One of the most common complaints they receive is of corruption and misuse of authority among low-ranked government officials. U Ye Tun of Hsipaw said he had devised a simple but effective method of resolving complaints such as these:

> I have the right to put forward [the complaint] in the *hluttaw* to their minister … but instead I first telephone him [the official], "Officer, our people come to me and complain about your activities. You must take action within 15 days or I will write down what you are doing and put forward some questions about it to the parliament".… After I was elected I could do that and they are very, very afraid now, because they have many faults. Every department. Bribery. Corruption. So they say, "Okay, U Ye Tun, don't put forward this question, I will solve it now".[31]

According to Daw Phyu Phyu Thin, Aung San Suu Kyi has instructed NLD members of parliament to "get out and meet with the people we represent" and listen to their concerns. Instead of raising every issue in parliament, she has told them to "try to solve these issues ourselves, especially complaints about crime and municipal-related issues" (Kyaw Hsu Mon 2012). Similarly, at its party conference in Tachileik in January 2013, the SNDP made grassroots engagement with communities a central element of its plan for the 2015 election. But MPs like U Ye Tun are still in the minority; most lack the confidence or knowledge to tackle local government officials outside the *hluttaw*. In the case of USDP representatives, these township officials were sometimes their superiors before they won a seat in parliament, making any potential confrontation undesirable. Additionally, the national, state, and region governments have taken some steps to limit the involvement of parliamentarians in "administrative" affairs, arguing that it contravenes the separation of powers enshrined in the constitution (Win Ko Ko Latt 2012). As more MPs begin to exercise the formal and informal power that comes with their office, these conflicts are only likely to increase.

It is important to acknowledge the difficulty of assessing and verifying the exact impact of parliamentarians' efforts. On issues of significance, there are nearly always other forces at work. In the case of political prisoners, for example, numerous international and domestic actors have lobbied the government for decades on both the broader plight of prisoners as well as individual cases. Additionally, it is usually hard to confirm what follow-up action, if any, has been taken as a result of interaction between MPs and officials from the government, judiciary, or military. In one case, U Ye Tun submitted a complaint letter to the military over land confiscation in his constituency. After an internal investigation, the military agreed in June 2012 to pay compensation for land that was registered (a significant proportion of the land was classified as vacant). However, by late 2012 it had still not paid the money and had not indicated when it would do so.

Despite the gains made by some MPs since early 2011, at the time of writing there were still some clear limits on what is possible in the *hluttaw*, particularly for the opposition. Military spending is one such matter: During debates on the 2013-14 budget, one member of parliament proposed a modest reduction in the Ministry of Defence budget. This proposal was overwhelmingly defeated and the numbers suggest that even a number of non-USDP and non-military representatives voted against it.

The parliament also has a number of physical, administrative, and capacity issues that place a significant burden on representatives. Both the parliament as a whole and individual parliamentarians lack access to proper law-making resources. While the hluttaw itself is a palatial complex of thirty-one buildings, representatives have no personal offices, as the majority of the buildings are used for parliamentary committees. Most members are on at least one committee, but these offices afford them no privacy from members of other parties. There are few reference materials available to lawmakers and Internet access was installed only in 2012 in the hluttaw complex. Most parliamentarians have no staff, such as research assistants or people to handle media enquiries. Representatives on committees even have to make a small contribution, normally 10,000 *kyat*s per month (around US$12), to cover the costs of stationery and coffee mix. The remoteness of Naypyitaw is another issue, which is particularly a burden for ethnic representatives, some of whom come from areas barely accessible by road. With the parliament in session six or eight months of the year, for long periods members of parliament have no opportunities to return home to meet constituents.

MILITARY AND ETHNIC MINORITY REPRESENTATIVES

One of the more controversial elements of the parliament—and one the NLD has vowed to tackle—is the presence of serving military personnel, who are appointed to fill 25 percent of seats. For the most part, the military has been a benign presence, its representatives introducing no bills and submitting few proposals or questions. Occasionally *Tatmadaw* representatives have participated in discussions. However, when called upon to vote on a bill or proposal that is not contrary to the military's interests, their involvement has been unpredictable and it remains unclear exactly whether their loyalties lie more with the government, the parliament, or with neither. While they voted against impeaching the Constitutional Tribunal, seemingly in line with the government's wishes, they sided with the parliament and against the advice of the Ministry of Defence to establish a commission to investigate the Letpadaung mine project (see Note 20). The majority of *Tatmadaw* representatives also voted against an amendment proposed by President Thein Sein to the *Ward and Village Tract Administration Law*.

However, *Tatmadaw* representatives have personally made it clear to other members of parliament that they will not consider any changes to the constitution, a standpoint that could put them on a collision course with elected representatives. "The *Tatmadaw*'s main objective in parliament is to protect the constitution. And they take 'protect the constitution' to mean not changing the constitution", said one journalist who has covered all *hluttaw* sessions to date. Another journalist who regularly attends parliament said *Tatmadaw* representatives were able to vote freely as long as the topic was not likely to "create instability". Nevertheless, on such an important issue military members of parliament would almost certainly look to Commander-in-Chief Senior General Min Aung Hlaing for direction on how to vote.

In his 2013 Armed Forces Day speech, Min Aung Hlaing said the military would continue to play a formal role in politics. However, he also hinted that if permanent stability could be obtained, the military would leave the political scene. While the NLD continues to call for their removal at some point, one of the NLD representatives said the opportunity to interact with military members of parliament on a regular basis had been beneficial for the party as it enabled regular and informal dialogue, which he believed helped both sides understand each other better.

For many ethnic minority MPs, the opportunity to enter parliament brought a number of hopes: peace, equality, and autonomy. For the most part, these hopes are yet to be fulfilled. Even within the parliament, there appears to be discrimination against ethnic minorities. A number of members said they were frustrated that the USDP had allocated few positions of authority to non-Burmese, with only a handful of committee chair and secretary positions held by ethnic representatives.[32] The composition of the government tells a similar story. J Yaw Wu said he had been nominated several times to be part of delegations to foreign parliaments but had always been rejected. Only after complaining to the Speaker was he finally accepted on an international delegation.

One particularly serious issue has been the parliament's apparent inability to play any effective role in efforts to resolve conflicts with ethnic minority groups, particularly in Kachin State. One member of the parliamentary peace-making team said he believed individuals in the government had undermined the team's efforts to broker a ceasefire shortly after the conflict broke out in June 2011. J Yaw Wu said it was "useless" to submit proposals on the issue because they were just forwarded to the committee, which, he said, was powerless. "It's very difficult to solve [the conflict] between this military and KIA. We also cannot communicate with the KIA, because they will say we are guilty of contacting the rebels", he said. The conflict has highlighted the current limits of parliament's ability to influence the *Tatmadaw*. Similarly, parliament has struggled to make a meaningful contribution to the Rakhine State crisis, with the executive taking the lead.

Much of the ethnic minority representatives' frustrations, however, rest with the constitution. Like the USDP, NLD, and Burmese opposition groups, ethnic minority parties have their own constitutional amendment wish-list. Aside from the perennial issue of federalism, many want more power to be delegated to regional governments. In particular, they make a compelling argument that the power to form regional governments should be taken away from the president. The current set-up effectively gives a Burmese leader the right to choose the chief ministers in all ethnic minority states, and reduces the prestige of the regional parliaments.

TOWARDS THE 2015 GENERAL ELECTION

The past two years have been remarkable for Myanmar—a rare period of optimism and political progress after decades of grinding socialist and military rule. Members of the inaugural post-military-rule parliament have had a front seat on a roller-coaster ride that so far has had more ups than downs. The growth and development of the parliament and its members has exceeded the expectations of even the most optimistic observers, and, indeed, of the representatives themselves. This progress has been forged in the unique atmosphere of cooperation created by the end of direct military rule, an atmosphere that has allowed a number of previously diametrically opposed groups, particularly the military and the NLD, to agree to work within the same framework towards similar goals.

There is no guarantee that this atmosphere, this optimism, and this cooperation, will continue until the next election, expected around the end of 2015. A number of major issues remain unresolved, particularly in relation to the constitution. Much of the progress has been forged through the personal ties between Thein Sein, Shwe Mann, and Aung San Suu Kyi, and relations between the two former generals appear to be fraying. Unless the USDP can improve its popularity in the electorate over the next few years, it is easy to foresee an increase in tension between the two major parties as they jockey for position before the vote.

Shwe Mann will continue to be a dominant figure in the parliamentary set-up. The wide powers of the Speaker's position have enabled him to drive the *hluttaw* forward. However, he could easily use his position as the *Pyidaungsu Hluttaw* Speaker in the second half of the *hluttaw* term[33] to more clearly push his party's—and his own—interests and ambitions. Indeed, he is likely to come under pressure from the more conservative elements of the party—particularly SPDC-era ministers, most of whom hold seats in parliament—to do so. With the current emphasis on allegiance to national or institutional interests above those of political parties, it is easy to overlook the fact that the USDP maintains a massive majority in both houses. This majority has only rarely been invoked to reject proposals, such as that on reducing military spending, but the impeachment of the Constitutional Tribunal shows the extent of the power of USDP members of parliament in the current political set-up (ICG 2012).

While less likely, it is also possible that Shwe Mann and Aung San Suu Kyi could reach an understanding that ensures party conflict and instability are avoided before and immediately after the election in 2015. The NLD leader—with the support of much of the Burmese population—appears to have placed great importance on securing the presidency after Thein Sein. Through negotiation, this could be achieved in a way that also avoids the potentially-destabilising outcome of a massive election win for the NLD, with the result being a government of national unity.

An important indicator of whether this is possible will be the stance parties take if, as expected later in 2013, the Union Election Commission submits a proposal to change from first-past-the-post voting to a more proportional system for the 2015 election. This change would likely disadvantage the NLD, be beneficial for the USDP and other Burmese parties, and have both positive and negative outcomes for ethnic parties. So far the NLD has said it opposes the measure, while the USDP has been non-committal. A change in the voting system would also potentially address another worrying prospect: a large turnover of MPs that would see much of the knowledge and experience gained during the 2011–2016 period lost.

It is also unclear what the election will hold for ethnic parties. Under Myanmar's first-past-the-post system, in some constituencies competition between ethnic parties—such as the SNDP and Shan Nationalities League for Democracy (SNLD)[34]—could split the vote and give the USDP or NLD a much greater chance of victory. In other areas, such as Kachin State, there is still no party that the majority of the population feels represents its interests. The NLD has also given no assurances that it will refrain from competing against ethnic minority parties. In addition, non-state armed groups in the United Nationalities Federal Council (UNFC)[35] have so far rejected the government's vague overtures to resolve their demands for greater autonomy in the parliament by establishing political parties. In June 2013, a number of the larger registered ethnic political parties announced their intention of forming a single party in order to better compete against the NLD and USDP in 2015.

Criticism has emerged in relation to two parliamentary commissions, one that investigated land disputes, and another (in which a number of members of parliament, including Aung San Suu Kyi, participated) that looked at the Letpadaung mine conflict, Undoubtedly, the early and surprising successes of the parliament have created heightened public expectations about its activities. Managing those expectations will be a challenge, particularly when the administrative processes of parliament—the committee meetings and debates—appear from the outside to be unwieldy.

Nevertheless, there are numerous reasons to be optimistic about the future of the national parliament. Public confidence in the *hluttaw* continues to grow, and MPs enjoy a level of respect and public support that is remarkable, given the deep divisions over the 2010 election. International organizations, including the United Nations Development Programme, Inter-Parliamentary Union, International Institute for Democracy and Electoral Assistance, and National Democratic Institute, are in the process of assessing and attempting to address some of the issues related to human capacity, parliamentary administration and resources for members of parliament.

Parliament's occasional conflicts with the president, government, and individual ministers have underscored the evidence that all stakeholders, including the military, appear committed to the principle of an independent legislature. A large number of MPs exhibit an admirable level of commitment to the office despite the low pay and other difficulties. Most seem acutely aware that the parliament is a work in progress, and will continue to be so well into its second and third terms. "I think of the experience of being a member of this first parliament as like trying to lay the foundations to build a house," said Tun Aung Kyaw of the Rakhine Nationalities Development Party. "We can't build a house immediately. First we make the foundations. And that's what we are doing now."[36]

Appendix: Parliamentary Committees as of May 2013

Table 4.1
Pyithu Hluttaw Committees

	Committee	Chairman	Party
1	Bill	T Khun Myat	USDP
2	Public Accounts	Thurein Zaw	USDP
3	Rights	Nanda Kyaw Sar	USDP
4	Government's Guarantees, Pledges & Undertakings Vetting	Win Sein	USDP
5	Representatives Vetting *	Maung Oo	USDP
6	Citizens' Fundamental Rights, Democracy & Human Rights	Htay Oo	USDP
7	National Race Affairs & Internal Peace-Making	Thein Zaw	USDP
8	Banks & Monetary Development	Aung Thaung	USDP
9	Planning & Financial Development	Soe Tha	USDP
10	Farmers, Workers & Youth Affairs	Tin Htut	USDP
11	International Relations	Hla Myint Oo	USDP
12	Economic & Trade Development	Maung Maung Thein	USDP
13	Transport, Communication & Construction	Thein Swe	USDP
14	Sports, Culture & Public Relations Development	Aye Myint	USDP
15	Agriculture, Livestock Breeding & Fishery	Soe Naing	USDP
16	Investment & Industrial Development	Htay Myint	USDP
17	Resources & Environmental Conservation	Lun Thi	USDP
18	Health Promotion	Kyaw Myint	USDP
19	Education Promotion	Chan Nyein	USDP
20	Judicial & Legal Affairs	Aung Ko	USDP
21	Public Affairs Management	Maung Oo	USDP
22	Social Development	Maung Maung Swe	USDP
23	Reform & Modernization Assessment	Aung Thein Linn	USDP
24	Water Transportation Development	Kyi Min	USDP
25	Legal Affairs & Special Affairs Assessment Commission	Nanda Kyaw Sar	USDP
26	Rule of Law, Peace & Stability	Aung San Suu Kyi	NLD

*Dissolved 11 January 2013
Source: ALTSEAN 2013*a*

Table 4.2
Amyotha Hluttaw Committees

	Committee	Chairman	Party
1	Bill	Mya Nyein	USDP
2	Public Accounts	Thein Win	USDP
3	Rights	Mya Nyein	USDP
4	Government's Guarantees, Pledges & Undertakings Vetting	Aung Tun	USDP
5	Representatives Vetting *	Than Swe	USDP
6	National Races Affairs	Paung Nap	WDP
7	Citizens' Fundamental Rights, Democracy & Human Rights	Aye Maung	RNDP
8	Education, Health & Culture	Khin Shwe	USDP
9	Women & Children Affairs	Mya Oo	USDP
10	Public Complaints & Appeal	Aung Nyein	USDP
11	UN, ASEAN, AIPA & International Relations	Col.Maung Maung Htoo	Military
12	Farmers & Local & Overseas Workers Affairs	Myint Kyi	USDP
13	National Planning	Zaw Myint Pe	USDP
14	Monetary & Customs	San Tun	USDP
15	Commerce	Nan Ni Ni Aye	USDP
16	Financial & Legal Affairs Commission	Aung Tun	USDP
17	Non-governmental Organizations	Win Naung	USDP
18	Mines & Natural Resources	Nay Win Tun	PNO

* Dissolved 11 January 2013
Source: ALTSEAN 2013*a*

Table 4.3
Pyidaungsu Hluttaw Committees

	Committee	Chairman	Party
1	Joint Bill	Mya Nyein	USDP
2	Joint Public Accounts	Mya Nyein	USDP
3	Representatives Vetting	Maung Oo	USDP

Source: ALTSEAN 2013*a*

Notes

1 See, for example, Burma Campaign UK 2011, Clegg 2010, *Economist* 2011.
2 The USDP holds 212 of 325 seats for elected representatives in the *Pyithu Hluttaw*, and 124 of 168 seats in the *Amyotha Hluttaw*.
3 Naturally, members of parliament are often divided on specific issues. However, these divisions are on an issue-by-issue basis, rather than along party lines, such as over the Constitutional Tribunal debates.
4 The fourteen state and region legislatures are not examined in this paper. Much less attention has been given to these legislatures and their members than to the national parliament, probably because they meet infrequently and the constitution vests most law-making power in the national parliament.
5 Since the handover from the SPDC, this person has been Min Aung Hlaing, who in early 2013 became Senior General, the position formerly held by Than Shwe.
6 The Kachin State Progress Party and Northern Shan State Progress Party were not given approval to register. A Kachin party closely aligned with the military regime and the USDP, the Unity and Democracy Party of Kachin State, was allowed to register and won a handful of seats.
7 Voting was cancelled in five *Pyithu Hluttaw* constituencies and twelve state or region *hluttaw* constituencies because of security concerns. In the April 2012 by-elections, voting did not take place in three *Pyithu Hluttaw* constituencies in Kachin State because of the conflict with the Kachin Independence Army.
8 Myanmar does not officially recognize the Rohingya as an ethnic group and generally refers to them as Bengalis. They are considered illegal immigrants from Bangladesh and the majority do not have citizenship. However, the USDP issued temporary identity cards to many Rohingya prior to the 2010 election, enabling them to vote for Rohingya candidates from the USDP, generally against Rakhine candidates from the Rakhine Nationalities Democratic Party (RNDP). In mid-2013 Rakhine parties began lobbying the Union Election Commission to deny temporary identity card holders the right to vote in the 2015 election and to ban Rohingya candidates from standing for election.
9 See Appendix to this chapter.
10 U Ye Tun, *Pyithu Hluttaw* representative for Hsipaw, SNDP. Interview with author, 18 November 2012.
11 U Tun Aung Kyaw, *Pyithu Hluttaw* representative for Ponnagyun, RNDP. Interview with author, 19 November 2012.
12 U Khin Maung Yi, *Pyithu Hluttaw* representative for Ahlone, NDF. Interview with author, 8 October 2012.
13 U Win Htein, *Pyithu Hluttaw* representative for Meiktila, NLD. Interview with author, 19 November 2012.

14 According to U Ye Tun, Speaker Shwe Mann generally says "reciprocal checks and balances" when speaking in Myanmar rather than the Myanmar term, *apyan ahlan htein hnyi yay y*. Some Myanmar writers also translate "checks and balances" as *ahtein ahtay* but the term is relatively new and the English version is more common. There is no agreed-upon translation of "oversight" so the English term is generally used.

15 Legislation governing the process of "recalling" an MP, as permitted under Section 38(b) of the constitution, was submitted to the *hluttaw* in October 2012 but had not been approved as of June 2013.

16 U Khin Maung Yi, *Pyithu Hluttaw* representative for Ahlone, NDF. Interview with author, 8 October 2012.

17 The by-elections were mostly for constituencies that had been held by MPs appointed to the government, as under the constitution members of the executive have to resign from the legislature.

18 U Zaw Myint Maung, *Pyithu Hluttaw* representative for Kyaukpadaung, NLD. Interview, 20 November 2012.

19 The formal handover of the USDP chairmanship from President Thein Sein to Shwe Mann took place at the party's youth conference in early May 2013. The issue of the chairmanship has been controversial, as under the 2008 Constitution members of the government are not permitted to engage in party activities. The handover was expected to take place at the party's first national assembly, in October 2012, but Thein Sein retained the position and Shwe Mann was instead confirmed as the most senior of three vice-chairmen and therefore acting chairman.

20 The mine is a joint venture between Union of Myanmar Economic Holdings Limited, which is owned by the *Tatmadaw*, and China's Wanbao Mining.

21 U Ye Tun, *Pyithu Hluttaw* representative for Hsipaw, SNDP. Interview with author, 18 November 2012.

22 Under the constitution, lower house constituencies are tied to township boundaries, effectively ensuring that proportional representation cannot be used unless the constitution is amended.

23 Member, Food Security Working Group. Interview, 15 February 2012.

24 Copy of report on file with author.

25 J Yaw Wu, *Amyotha Hluttaw* representative for Kachin State Constituency 12, National Unity Party. Interview with author, 18 November 2012.

26 Additionally, the Myanmar National Human Rights Commission, which was established by the president without parliamentary approval in late 2011, had received more than three thousand complaints by early December and assessed most of them.

27 Senior editor, Yangon-based news journal. Interview with author, 5 December 2012.

28 U Thein Nyunt, *Pyithu Hluttaw* representative for Thingangyun, New National Democracy Party. Interview with author, 19 November 2012.

29 In early November 2012, attendance hit an all-time low, when 168 MPs were absent from a *Pyidaungsu Hluttaw* session.

30 *Pyithu Hluttaw* representative from Mon State, National Unity Party. Interview with author, 20 November 2012.

31 U Ye Tun, *Pyithu Hluttaw* representative for Hsipaw, SNDP. Interview with author, 18 November 2012.

32 U Khat Htein Nan, *Amyotha Hluttaw* representative for Kachin State Constituency 1, Unity and Democracy Party of Kachin State. Interview with author, 19 November 2012.

33 Under Section 76(a) of the constitution, each Speaker serves half of the parliament's five-year term as *Pyidaungsu Hluttaw* Speaker. *Amyotha Hluttaw* Speaker Khin Aung Myint was *Pyidaungsu Hluttaw* Speaker from 2011, with Shwe Mann due to take over in the middle of 2013.

34 The SNLD contested the 1990 election and won 23 seats, but it was deregistered in 2010 after the party, like the NLD, refused to re-register to contest the election that year. At the time its leader, Khun Htun Oo, was serving a 93-year jail term imposed in 2005. Some former members, however, formed the SNDP to contest the election. Khun Htun Oo was released in an amnesty in January 2012 and the party re-registered later that year.

35 The UNFC comprises 11 non-state armed groups and was formed in February 2011.

36 U Tun Aung Kyaw, *Pyithu Hluttaw* representative for Ponnagyun, RNDP. Interview with author, 19 November 2012.

References

Alternative ASEAN Network on Burma (ALTSEAN). Parliament Watch. Updated 15 November 2013a. <http://www.altsean.org/Research/Parliament%20Watch/Home.php>. Accessed 16 January 2014.

———. Parliament Watch: List of New Laws. Updated 2 July 2013b. <http://www.altsean.org/Research/Parliament%20Watch/Laws.php>. Accessed 22 October 2013.

Aung Din. "15 Minutes of Fame for Myanmar MPs". *Asia Times* Online, 24 March 2011. <http://www.atimes.com/atimes/Southeast_Asia/MC24Ae01.html>. Accessed 22 October 2013.

British Broadcasting Corporation (BBC). "Suu Kyi's NLD Party to Boycott Burma election". BBC, 29 March 2010. <http://news.bbc.co.uk/2/hi/8592365.stm>. Accessed 22 October 2013.

Burma Campaign UK. "Burma's Rubber Stamp Parliament Can't Hold Government To Account". 31 January 2011. <http://www.burmacampaign.org.uk/index.php/news-and-reports/reports/title/burmas-rubber-stamp-parliament-cant-hold-government-to-account>. Accessed 22 October 2013.

Clegg, Nick. "Myanmar's Sham Election". *International Herald Tribune*, 3 October 2010. <http://www.nytimes.com/2010/10/04/opinion/04iht-edclegg.html? <http://www.nytimes.com/2010/10/04/opinion/04iht-edclegg.html?_r=0>. Accessed 22 October 2013.

Economist. "A Parliament, But Not As You Know It". *Economist*, 27 January 2011. <http://www.economist.com/node/18014087>. Accessed 22 October 2013.

Horsey, Richard. "Myanmar's Political Landscape Following the 2010 Elections: Starting with a Glass Nine-Tenths Empty?". In *Myanmar's Transition: Openings, Obstacles and Opportunities*, edited by Nick Cheesman, Monique Skidmore and Trevor Wilson. Singapore: Institute of Southeast Asian Studies, 2012.

International Crisis Group (ICG). *Myanmar: Storm Clouds on the Horizon*. Asia Report No. 238, 12 November 2012. <http://www.crisisgroup.org/en/publication-type/media-releases/2012/asia/myanmar-storm-clouds-on-the-horizon.aspx>. Accessed 22 October 2013.

Kean, Thomas. "Burma's Parliament Emerges From the Shadows". *Inside Story*, 26 March 2012. <http://inside.org.au/burma-parliament-emerges-from-the-shadows/>. Accessed 22 October 2013.

Kyaw Hsu Mon. "Public Is 'Waiting to See' What The NLD Can Do For Them: MP". *Myanmar Times*, 31 December 2012. <http://www.mmtimes.com/index.php/national-news/3679-public-is-waiting-to-see-what-the-nld-can-do-for-them-mp.html>. Accessed 22 October 2013.

Kyaw Kyaw. "Burma's Parliamentary System Explained". *New Mandala*, 1 April 2011. <http://asiapacific.anu.edu.au/newmandala/2011/04/01/burmas-parliamentary-system-explained/>. Accessed 22 October 2013.

Maw Maw San. "Election Turnout Higher than 1990". *Myanmar Times*, 13–19 December 2010. <http://www.mmtimes.com/2010/news/553/news55301.html>. Accessed 22 October 2013.

Ministry of Foreign Affairs (MOFA) (Myanmar). "Union of Myanmar: Commission for Holding the Referendum: Announcement No. 12/2008". 26 May 2008. <http://www.mofa.gov.mm/news/Announcements/26may08.html>. Accessed 22 October 2013.

Myo Thant. "Speaker Shwe Mann again pushes for pay increase". *Mizzima News*, 21 February 2012. <http://www.mizzima.com/news/insideburma/6626-speaker-shwe-mahn-again-pushes-for-pay-increase.html>. Accessed 22 October 2013.

Nardi, Dominic J. "After Impeachment, a Balancing Act". *Myanmar Times*, 1 October 2012. <http://www.mmtimes.com/index.php/opinion/2013-after-im-peachment-a-balancing-act.html>. Accessed 22 October 2013.

Network Myanmar. "A Comparative Analysis of the Number and Percentage of Votes Secured by the Top Eight Political Parties (Who Won 10 Seats or More in the Assemblies)". Network Myanmar, undated. <http://www.network-myanmar.org/images/stories/PDF7/votes%20per%20party.pdf>. Accessed 22 October 2013.

RC. "The 15-minute Parliament". *Economist*, 2 March 2011. <http://www.economist.com/blogs/banyan/2011/03/myanmars_government>. Accessed 22 October 2013.

Reuters. "Myanmar Raises Civil Service Salaries as Prices Soar". 14 March 2012. <http://in.reuters.com/article/2012/03/14/myanmar-wages-idINDEE82D-0AD20120314>. Accessed 22 October 2013.

Shwe Yinn Mar Oo and Soe Than Lynn. "MPs encouraged by committees". *Myanmar Times*, 14–20 March 2011. <http://www.mmtimes.com/2011/news/566/news55605.html>. Accessed 22 October 2013.

Soe Than Lynn. "Myanmar Parliament Approves Letpadaung Mine Probe". *Myanmar Times*, 24 November 2012. <http://www.mmtimes.com/index.php/national-news/3343-myanmar-parliament-approves-letpadaung-mine-probe.html>. Accessed 22 October 2013.

———. "Thura U Shwe Mann Warns Government to Ready for Free Trade". *Myanmar Times*, 12–18 September 2011. <http://www.mmtimes.com/2011/news/592/news59202.html>. Accessed 22 October 2013.

Szep, Jason. "In Myanmar, a Sham Parliament Stirs to Life". Reuters, 26 January 2011. <http://www.reuters.com/article/2012/01/26/us-myanmar-parliament-idUSTRE80P1U720120126>. Accessed 22 October 2013.

Union Election Commission. "Announcement on Figures of Multiparty Democracy General Elections for Respective *Hluttaws*". Notification No 143/2010, 7 December 2010. Available at: <http://www.burmanet.org/news/2010/12/08/new-light-of-myanmar-figures-of-multiparty-democracy-general-elections-for-respective-hluttaws-announced/>. Accessed 16 January 2014.

Win Ko Ko Latt. "NLD Member Warned for 'Intervening' in Govt Affairs". *Myanmar Times*, 27 August–2 September 2012. <http://www.mmtimes.com/2012/news/641/news21.html>. Accessed 22 October 2013.

Yan Pai. "MPs' Assets Declaration Motion Shot Down". *Irrawaddy*, 10 August 2012. <http://www.irrawaddy.org/nld/mps-assets-declaration-motion-shot-down.html>. Accessed 22 October 2013.

5

VILLAGE NETWORKS, LAND LAW, AND MYANMAR'S DEMOCRATIZATION

Tamas Wells and Kyaw Thu Aung

There is broad agreement among observers both inside and outside the country that "something significant has happened in Myanmar" since the 2010 elections (Egreteau 2012, p. 30). However, defining the nature of this change has proved contentious.

In this debate, most attention has been focused on the elite level and the new roles of the "triumvirate" of President U Thein Sein, Lower House Speaker Thura U Shwe Mann and "opposition" leader Daw Aung San Suu Kyi (Tin Maung Maung Than 2012). This has meant that the political changes in Myanmar have been described as "a top-down transition" (Egreteau 2012), with democratization coming from above through an elite-led reform agenda. In this top-down reform process, local level politics in most parts of the country is assumed to be largely unchanged. As Holliday (2013, p. 100) suggests, "much changed in Myanmar in 2012, yet for ordinary people much remained the same as reform impacts were confined largely to elites".

This case study asks whether and how things may have changed for ordinary people in rural areas in Myanmar. Is the process of political change only top-down, or are there ways in which it is also bottom-up? In other words, are rural people waiting for elite-led reforms to reach them, or are they, too, agents of democratization?

In order to answer these questions, this paper examines the situation among networks of village groups in the Ayeyarwady Delta area in southern Myanmar, and particularly their engagement in advocacy related to Myanmar's new land laws. It is based on in-depth interviews conducted in February 2013 with sixteen male and three female members of the networks. It also draws on project records and interviews with five staff from Paung Ku, a civil society-strengthening initiative started in Myanmar in 2007 by a consortium of local and international non-government organizations (NGOs).[1] All five staff members have been engaged with village-based groups in the Delta since 2008.[2]

DEMOCRATIZATION "FROM BELOW"

In considering the changes in Myanmar, we first acknowledge that "democracy" and "democratization" are contested concepts. While authors such as Schumpeter (1947) focus on a narrow procedural definition of democracy (based primarily on free and fair elections), others broaden the concept to include state accountability through other mechanisms, especially through a watchdog role performed by civic organizations and media (Schedler 1999). This paper takes the wider definition, acknowledging that civil society networks can contribute to democratization "from below" by increasing the voice of citizens about key issues that affect their lives.

This wider role in democratization taken by civil society networks in Myanmar during the mid-2000s has been given some attention by authors such as Ashley South (2004). With a perceived deadlock in negotiations between the government and opposition groups, and seemingly bleak prospects for democratic transition, South looked to emerging civil society networks as "an important vehicle for long-term, 'bottom-up' democratization" (p. 234). Civil society networks were seen to be critical in mobilizing the grassroots to organize and "reassume control over aspects of their lives which since the 1960s have been abrogated by the military" (p. 243). In other words, while "top-down" democratization in Myanmar in the short term seemed unlikely, civil society networks offered some hope of gradual democratization from below.

Since the period of political reform began in Myanmar following the 2010 elections, the reverse observation has become the norm. The outlook for continued elite-led democratization is cautiously optimistic, while authors such as Holliday (2013) portray ordinary people as being relatively peripheral to change.

This case study of networks in the Delta presents a different picture. First, it highlights that in some cases there have been important changes in local-level politics related to freedom of association and expression. Second, it provides evidence that while the transition could in some ways be characterized as top-down, there are also significant ways in which civil society networks are contributing to democratization from below through actively increasing the voice of citizens. In other words, it is not only the elite that is sensing change in Myanmar's politics, and it may not only be the political elite that is affecting it.

NETWORKS OF COMMUNITY GROUPS IN THE AYEYARWADY REGION

In August 2010, over forty community-based groups in villages in the Ayeyarwady Delta region decided to form a set of local networks across four different townships. Informal connections between village groups in the area had grown over the previous two years—largely due to the enormous scale of the relief response to Cyclone Nargis—and group leaders thought that these relationships should be formalized. The central idea was that many of the local development problems they experienced in their own village were also present in other villages in their area, and the answers to those problems were often collective in nature. "We realized that the problems weren't just in our village, other villages were struggling with the same things", said one farmer involved with the network.

Until 2011, under the rule of the State Peace and Development Council (SPDC) Myanmar had some of the world's most restrictive laws in relation to freedom of association and expression, so this kind of networking represented a substantially different dynamic of political engagement. What had changed in these grassroots communities to make this possible?

At time of interviews in 2011 it was clear that Delta communities still faced longstanding problems, such as the inability of most people to achieve a viable livelihood and a lack of access to basic health and education services, but network leaders in these areas also described significant local political change that had been brought about by Cyclone Nargis, and indicated their perceptions that a national-level political transition was occurring.

Cyclone Nargis and Freedom of Association

Cyclone Nargis occurred in May 2008. It was a critical event for Delta communities, one of the worst natural disasters worldwide in the last hundred years, with more than one hundred thousand people killed and over a million left homeless. The cyclone's impact was concentrated in the flat, heavily-populated Ayeyarwady River Delta. The subsequent relief and rehabilitation efforts, led by local people across the Delta area, catalyzed the formation of a vast set of new community-based organizations. While there had always been formal groups within Delta villages, such as *thayenaye* funeral groups, parent-teacher committees, and religious organizations, these were strictly limited to social and religious affairs, and in most cases did not consider strategies aimed at wider village development. As one network leader said, "We definitely weren't allowed to form this kind of group before [the cyclone]".

A number of external development organizations, including Paung Ku, were also involved in funding and actively bringing these village-level groups together. With this help, not only were local groups able to take a role in development decision-making following the cyclone, they were also empowered by having access to new external resources and connections. This freedom of association and access to resources in turn allowed the groups to gain new organization and project leadership experience, which ultimately proved to be a crucial factor for the success of the wider networks.

The freedom of association needed to create this vast set of new groups was largely seen to be a result of the scale of the disaster, and the inability of authority structures to maintain pre-cyclone restrictions. Even after the initial relief phase, when authority structures were re-established at the village level, the new freedom of association continued. Despite the fact that the formal legal context had not changed, authorities no longer questioned local gatherings, and sometimes attended meetings themselves. This was in part due to the perception by local authorities of the positive impact of local groups in village rehabilitation and development.

One network member also mentioned Myanmar's 2008 Constitution, which allows citizens "to form associations and organizations" (Article 354). He said that even though the constitution did not come into force until 2011, in the period following Cyclone Nargis this provision gave some confidence to local leaders in continuing to develop new community groups and networks.

As a general proposition, it can be said that following Cyclone Nargis the Delta region of Myanmar in some ways experienced an associational revolution, with the formation of thousands of new village groups disrupting decades-old restrictions on freedom of association. Yet this kind of disruption of norms may not be unique to the Delta. Other recent natural disasters—notably the 2010 Mandalay floods and Cyclone Giri in 2010 in Rakhine State—also sparked growth in civil society connections (Paung Ku 2010). Furthermore, the eruption of concerns over other issues in other places, such as the plans for special economic zones in Dawei and Thilawa, or mining rights in Letpadaung, are forcing a renegotiation of norms of freedom of association.

While the devastation following Cyclone Nargis is perhaps the most extreme example of an exogenous disruption of local norms, the boundaries to freedom of association are clearly also being extended in other areas of the country, impelled by a range of different drivers.

Freedom of Expression and a New *Dimokarazi*

Network members saw local governance in the period leading up to the cyclone as having been particularly restrictive. One member summarized the culture of governance by quoting a Burmese saying, *"pe da yu, kywe da za, kaing da lôk"*, meaning, "take what is given, eat what is served, and do what is ordered". Thus there was little freedom for engagement with local government about development issues.

However, all interviewed network members said that the situation was now different. Along with the growth of freedom of association after Cyclone Nargis, freedom of expression was also increasing. As one network leader said, "We are not scared now to say what we think".

For example, a Paung Ku mentor related the story of a village member who wanted to change the name on his land title and was asked by the official to pay a bribe of 10,000 *kyats* (around US$12). Previously, these kinds of bribes had to be paid in order to progress a request. However, the man said he told the official that he would only pay if he received a formal receipt with the name of the official on it. The official withdrew his demand and changed the name on the land title without receiving any money.

One network leader spoke of local military recruiting meetings. Previously, all families in the village were ordered to attend, and men and boys of eligible age were required to enlist. With increased local freedom of expression and a renegotiated relationship with local authorities, most households in the village now refused to attend, yet did not face any repercussions. "Now hardly any families go and it doesn't matter", he said.

Finally, a member of a women's group within one network told the story of her friend who had wanted to complain to the local authority but said that she was scared. Another person then said, "*Dimokarazi ya pi* (we've got democracy), you can complain. It is no problem".

When asked about what was meant by *dimokarazi*, nearly all network members responded that it was closely related to freedom of expression, that people were allowed to voice their opinions regardless of their background. "It doesn't matter if you are poor, or if you are a woman, you can say what you think if there is *dimokarazi*", said one female leader. Some other respondents pointed to *dimokarazi* meaning not only freedom of expression but also responsiveness of government to community voices. Yet interestingly, when asked to define *dimokarazi*, none of the respondents mentioned elections. Thus at the grassroots level, *dimokarazi* was seen primarily to be a "culture" of freedom of expression rather than a procedural focus on electoral democracy.

Asked why this freedom of expression had developed at the village level, network members pointed to perceived changes in national-level politics. Positive interpretations of elite political change—particularly with a new president replacing Senior General Than Shwe and the presence of Daw Aung San Suu Kyi in parliament—were seen to have propelled new perspectives at the local level. There were still some problems with local authorities, since many of the same people, with the same interests, remained in place, but the overall dynamics of the relationship were perceived to be significantly different, and characterized primarily by a change in freedom of expression.

When asked how local communities became aware of national-level political changes, all persons interviewed said that they received national news through listening to the Burmese language services of the BBC World Service, Voice of America, and Radio Free Asia. Some network leaders also pointed to the role of local and international organizations in conveying political news and analysis to them. Although some analysts see the print media as being a new watchdog (Nwe Nwe Aye 2012), none of the network members who were interviewed reported regularly reading local print media of any kind. However, as we outline in the next section, with support from Paung Ku the networks were able to use the media to support their own land law advocacy.

Overall, local community leaders involved with the Delta networks felt that there had been significant movement toward *dimokarazi*. Political change in Myanmar was seen by many community leaders to be reaching the grassroots in significant ways—yet this *dimokarazi* may represent a different vision from that expressed in elite circles in Yangon or Naypyitaw. While there is much discussion about the importance of the 2015 elections for Myanmar's democratic future, network leaders focused more on their experience of freedom of expression. And while many urban actors may point to the significant relaxing of media censorship as evidence of growing freedom of expression, village-level leaders were more likely to identify examples from local political culture related to their engagement with authorities.

Elite actors and grassroots network leaders may agree that there has been a shift in Myanmar towards *dimokarazi*, yet they may be talking about different things. However, it is important to recognize that democratization may not look the same from above as it does from below.

LAND LAW AND DEMOCRATIZATION "FROM BELOW"

We turn now to the second question of how grassroots communities and networks may also be contributing to political change. Myanmar's recent political shifts have been characterized as top-down, but in what ways may they also be "from below"? In what ways may ordinary people also be agents of democratization in Myanmar?

Land Rights in the Delta

Before outlining the case of networks in Ayeyarwady region and their advocacy related to land law reform, it is important to highlight the context of land rights in Myanmar's Delta region.

The issue of land rights has long caused tension in Burmese society. For example, in the British colonial period, the Saya San rebellion of 1930–32 was in part catalyzed by land issues—with a wealthy group of moneylenders having gained control of substantial amounts of Burma's productive agricultural land (Turnell 2009). During the 1920s and 1930s, Burmese newspapers such as the *Sun* and the *New Light of Burma* (Adas 2011) gave prominence to land issues—and their associated conflicts.

In response to the perceived injustices of the colonial period, the socialist era in Burma (1962–1988) emphasized—at least in official policy—the land needs of smallholder farmers, particularly through the 1963 *Protection of Peasants' Rights Law*. However, after the widespread failure of the Burmese economy in the late 1980s, new land laws were introduced, with the aim of promoting private sector development of "fallow" land or "wastelands", which in many cases was land already occupied by smallholder farmers. With trade sanctions and a restrictive foreign investment law in place, this meant that control of land increasingly went to domestic political, military, and economic elites (Loewen 2012).

Myanmar's 2008 Constitution contains a number of provisions relevant to land. In particular, it strengthened the position for private ownership of user rights (also of other resources), the right of private property, the right of inheritance (Article 37(c)), and for non-discrimination on the basis of wealth or culture (Article 348). Yet the 2008 Constitution also retains the stipulation that the Union "is the ultimate owner of all lands and all natural resources above and below the ground, above and beneath the water" (Article 37(a)). Against this constitutional background, the new Thein Sein government named land law reform as a priority, and during the second half of 2011 parliament began the process of drafting new laws. In March 2012 the revision of the *Farmland Law* and the *Vacant, Fallow and Virgin Lands Management Law* was approved.

In parallel with the development of the new laws came increased national attention to land-grabbing. With the rapid increase of foreign investment and (largely unregulated) private sector activity around the country, especially in the areas of mining, agribusiness, infrastructure, and oil and gas, many local communities reported incidents of land confiscation, and these reports increasingly made their way into the local media. For example, in the first half of 2012 protests by local farmers about land confiscation by the company Zaykabar on the outskirts of Yangon were highlighted in several local journals, including the *Myanmar Times* (Noe Noe Aung 2012) and *Weekly Eleven* (2012).

These pressures were also being felt in the Delta area, with ongoing economic recovery following Cyclone Nargis still an issue. A report on the socio-economic status of one Delta township (Soe Lin Aung 2012) highlighted the fact that cycles of debt, exacerbated by the losses of Cyclone Nargis, had forced many smallholder farmers to sell their land, and that land had now become concentrated in the hands of fewer owners.

From the perspective of the Delta region farmers who were members of the network, the issues associated with land rights were both acute and chronic.

They were acute in the sense that Cyclone Nargis had had a devastating impact on rice yields. At the time of the cyclone almost all rice crops in the most affected townships had been lost, and subsequent harvests in 2009 were lower in yield than normal, because the soil had been heavily damaged by salt water flooding. Finally, due to the losses associated with the cyclone, farmers were keen to maximize their yields in both wet and dry seasons, and to do this they turned to increased use of fertilizer. However, while fertilizer use and its associated costs increased seasonally, yields remained stagnant and well below pre-Nargis levels. "This year I only got about 60 percent of the yield I got before Nargis", said one farmer.

The problems were chronic in the sense that there were long-term issues related to the government's land and agricultural policy that were seen to stifle development and production. Farmers were unable to formally own their land (as the constitution claimed state ownership of all agricultural land) and had only limited freedom in their choice of crops. Furthermore, due to the highly uneven nature of costs and returns in paddy farming— for example, the high inputs required during planting and harvesting seasons—access to credit was essential, but while the Myanma Agricultural Development Bank (MADB) gave low-interest loans to farmers, the amounts given were well below farmers' real credit needs. For example, one farmer said, "For the wet season crop I need 100,000 *kyats* [around US$1200] per acre for fertilizer, hiring of motorized ploughs and labour, but I can only get 20,000 [from the government loan]". If they required more up-front capital, farmers would have to turn to private lenders, whose interest rates would be up to ten times higher (up to 20 percent per month).

These issues of uneven investments and returns existed for rice farmers across the whole country, but in the Ayeyarwady region they were felt more acutely because the Delta is one of the few areas in Myanmar where two rice crops (wet season and dry season) can be planted profitably. With two rice crops per year, a farmer's credit needs are significantly higher than with only one.

The combination of these new and longstanding land-rights issues has meant that many farming families with large accumulated debt have been forced to sell their land. As one farmer said, "Before the cyclone half the families [in our village] had land for paddy, now only a quarter do".

Citizen "Voice" and Land Law Advocacy

While land rights have long caused tension in Myanmar, in the Delta area this tension has reached a critical point. In early 2012, the Delta networks formulated a set of recommendations about the new national-level land laws—addressing the issues of agricultural loans, land ownership, freedom to choose crops, and fairer market practices. These recommendations— along with a petition from farmers that contained over fifteen hundred signatures—were sent to President Thein Sein, the Speakers of the upper and lower houses of parliament, and to local members of parliament.

The petition represented one of the first examples of mass, grass-roots-to-national policy engagement since the 2010 elections. How does it relate to democratization from below? The example of the Delta networks and their land law advocacy presents a mixed picture. On the one hand democratization requires the development of *voice*, whereby citizens are able to express their needs or perspectives to decision-makers, but on the other hand, it also requires an increase in *responsiveness* by the government. From the perspective of the Delta network leaders engaged in land law advocacy, it seemed that networking had significantly increased the voice of citizens—yet while small changes on the government side can be observed, questions remain about whether there has been a real increase in responsiveness.

In terms of increasing the voice of citizens, the Delta region networks operated in three ways—facilitating communication, aggregating citizen voices, and sharpening advocacy messages.

Of importance to network leaders was the new ability to communicate between village groups by using mobile phones. Before Cyclone Nargis there had been virtually no phone use in villages in the area, which made it extremely time-consuming to organize or share information between geographically-separated villages. By early 2013, however, all network leaders had mobile phones and almost all villages involved had at least one person with a phone.[3] In the post-cyclone period this development transformed the flow of information and, consequently, the ability to organize.

The existence of the network also fostered a new aggregation of citizen voices. This was particularly apparent in the land law campaign where—aided by new flows of information—a large number of farmers (almost 1500 across four townships) were able to add their signatures to the recommendations.

Finally, the network was also able to sharpen advocacy messages. In the case of the land law campaign, the network used its new connections (facilitated by local and international agencies) to legal and policy expertise to shape widespread grassroots perspectives into concrete policy recommendations. Network leaders said that the input of legal expertise had raised their capacity to analyze the laws and therefore to engage more informatively with policy-makers. In addition, using external linkages with the Yangon-based print media—facilitated by Paung Ku and other external agencies—the network was able to secure publication of several journal articles about their campaign, thereby amplifying the message both to a wider public audience and to government.

This sharpening of citizen voices into formats that could be presented directly to policy-makers was also perceived to be channelling action in a non-violent way. Myanmar has recently seen clashes between police and protesters over issues of land, for example in Ma-ubin in February 2013 (Nyein Nyein 2013). In contrast, the Delta networks were seen to have created a forum in which citizen voice could be presented in a less adversarial manner.

The actions of the Delta networks in creating this forum were clearly enhanced by the assistance of external agencies such as Paung Ku. Crucially, through linking network members with journalists and land law experts, Paung Ku was able to assist the connection of local policy ideas to discussions within the media and in parliament. In other words, it supported a narrowing of the distance between grassroots mobilization and elite-level policy debate.

Did this increase in citizen voice bring any change in government responsiveness? What impact did the network's land law advocacy have?

Ultimately, the final approved *Farmland Law* received a mixed reaction from the network. It was seen to contain some positive changes for farming families, in that the law allows greater freedom of choice in relation to crops; the right to sell, pawn, and buy user-rights has been formalized; and it includes potentially better rights of appeal against unfair land confiscation. Also, at the policy level, agricultural loan amounts have been increased. Network members thought that these changes—particularly those related to agricultural loans—would impact significantly on their livelihoods in the future.

However, in other respects the final law fell short of the networks' expectations. Formal land ownership remains with the state (as stipulated in the 2008 Constitution) and there was little progress in formalizing fairer market rules (especially to do with measurement of rice). Overall, there was only limited change between the draft stage of the law and the final version as approved by parliament, which meant that civil society advocacy efforts—including from the Delta networks—had had only limited impact.

Although the direct impact of their advocacy on the law was limited, network leaders expressed the feeling that there had been some change in their relationship with the government: fewer restrictions were applied and there was more opportunity to communicate directly with members of parliament. For example, after the land law recommendations had been submitted, U Myat Thein, a member of the Union Solidarity and Development Party and lower house Member of Parliament for Bogale,[4] met with the Delta network's leadership to discuss the recommendations and report back on the parliament's decisions—including both areas of agreement and disagreement. With an increased sense of connection to policy processes, network leaders were confident to continue their land law advocacy as well as branching into other policy processes, especially in relation to the critical issue of a fisheries law.

CHALLENGES FOR THE DELTA NETWORKS

While the networks clearly have an important role, several questions remain about the way they can contribute to democratization.

First, the growing freedom of association and expression that these Delta townships are experiencing means that a new set of voices is being heard. However, this does not mean that *all* voices are now represented. In particular, women's participation is still limited. Village and village tract leaders in network areas were all male, and the Delta network leadership groups themselves were comprised entirely of men. A growing awareness of gender issues within the network has recently led to the formation of women's associations, but this is no guarantee that women's leadership either inside the network or at the village level will increase.

Second, most of the vast set of new community groups and networks in the Delta were formed in response to the need for relief activities following Cyclone Nargis. A key strength during this period was the flexibility of organizations to adapt and form new informal connections both within and outside their villages. Over time, however, the networks have become increasingly institutionalized and hierarchical in their structure—with an overarching leadership committee and four subgroups (women's, youth, farmers', and fisheries' associations). One question is whether the increasing institutionalization and hierarchy of the networks will limit their flexibility to act, and particularly, their ability to contribute to democratization.

Third, while the networks sent their land law recommendations to the national level of government leadership, they remain relatively disconnected from national policy debates. The new freedoms enjoyed by Myanmar's print media have created a forum for policy dialogue in which journals can present information and opinions on many issues, but due to their limited distribution and relatively high prices (around 500 *kyats* or US$0.60 for a journal), the print media is still really only accessible to the urban middle class. The Delta networks were reliant on organizations such as Paung Ku to connect them to journalists and to inform them of relevant articles. If rural networks are to contribute more widely to democratization, they will need to be more closely connected to Myanmar's new print media.

Ultimately, while the development of new grassroots networks in Myanmar may be significant, these networks continue to face challenges and will not automatically become vehicles for the promotion of democratic values. Networks may be inclusive and participatory, yet they can also be exclusive and hierarchical.

CONCLUSION

Since the 2010 elections Myanmar has entered a period of significant political change. These changes should not be seen as affecting only elite-level actors. The example of the Delta networks shows that while longstanding hardships in relation to the pursuit of a livelihood and the lack of services persist in rural areas, in some cases substantial political changes are occurring, particularly in relation to freedom of expression and association.

These changes are also important for other areas of the country. While Cyclone Nargis may be the most profound example of exogenous disruption of local norms of freedom of association, other accepted norms are being disrupted in a variety of ways, particularly through the pressures of rapid socio-economic change. Around the country, from Letpadaung to Dawei, this disruption is encouraging new forms of networking.

This example of land law advocacy by the Delta networks is important because it shows the active engagement of rural networks in increasing citizen voice in a manner which would not have been possible three years ago. Yet it also shows that an increase in citizen voice—and even an increase in dialogue with government—is no guarantee of increased responsiveness about issues.

The case is also important because it shows that in one sense the existence of the networks was only made possible because of local changes in freedom of expression and association. In another sense, though, the networks were also able to actively propel these changes by raising citizen voice. As one farmer said, "Where you push, you get change". The networks can thus be seen as both a result of, and a driver of, local political change.

Finally, the case study also highlights not only that some grassroots civil society networks are experiencing new freedoms, but also that they are actively pushing for further change, even to the national level. It is unclear to what degree this advocacy had an impact on the policy process, but it does demonstrate how networks can increase citizen voice, contributing to democratization from below. External agencies such as Paung Ku can play a crucial role in helping to connect the voices of grassroots issue-based networks to elite-level debates.

Ultimately, this study shows that the impacts of recent political reforms in Myanmar are not confined only to elites, nor is it only elites who are capable of effecting change. Ordinary citizens and civil society networks may also be agents of democratization.

However, the vision of democracy itself may remain contested. While the shift towards establishing the procedures of electoral democracy, along with the development of an uncensored urban-based media, may fulfil some elite definitions of "democracy", without a corresponding change in local freedom of expression this may not suffice to meet grassroots expectations of *dimokarazi*. It is important to recognize that democracy may not look from same from above as it does from below.

Notes

1   The Paung Ku initiative was started in 2007 by a wide consortium of local and international organizations with Save the Children as lead agency. Paung Ku is now a Myanmar organization that provides funding and capacity-building to local civil society organizations across a range of sectors for service delivery (in particular to poor and marginalized people), networking, and advocacy projects.

2   It is important to note that this paper gives only one particular perspective on Myanmar's changing political context—one largely given by network leaders from four Ayeyarwady Region township networks. While we do reflect on the wider implications of this view for Myanmar's politics, we also recognize its limitations and the presence of a broad range of other, and perhaps conflicting, perspectives.

3   According to government figures, in early 2012 there were 2.8 million mobile phone users in Myanmar (MCPT 2012). This represents a dramatic increase from an estimated 600,000 users in 2010, with the main reason for the increase being the gradual reduction in SIM card costs to more accessible—though still expensive—prices of around US$250. While Internet access has increased in urban areas, with growing numbers of cyber cafes, access to mobile phones constitutes the most important development in communications in rural areas and was a critical factor for the networking of the Delta groups.

4   Bogale is one of the larger towns on the coastline where the Ayeyarwady River enters the Andaman Sea. It was one of the towns most severely affected by Cyclone Nargis.

References

Adas, Michael. *The Burma Delta: Economic Development and Social Change on an Asian Rice Frontier, 1852–1941*. Wisconsin: University of Wisconsin Press, 2011.

Constitution of the Republic of the Union of Myanmar (2008). Naypyitaw: Printing and Publishing Enterprise, Ministry of Information, Union of Myanmar. <http://www.burmalibrary.org/docs5/Myanmar_Constitution-2008-en.pdf>. Accessed 31 October 2013.

Egreteau, Renaud. "Burma/Myanmar". *Political Insight* 3, no. 2 (2012): 30–33.

Holliday, Ian. "Myanmar in 2012: Toward a Normal State". *Asian Survey* 53, no. 1 (2013): 93–100.

Loewen, Elizabeth. *Land Grabbing in Dawei (Myanmar/Burma): A (Inter) National Human Rights Concern*. Briefing Paper, Agrarian Justice program, Transnational Institute. Amsterdam: Paung Ku and Transnational Institute, 2012. <http://www.tni.org/report/land-grabbing-dawei>. Accessed 31 October 2013.

Ministry of Communications, Posts and Telegraph (MCPT). "MCPT Newsletter", 29 February 2012. Reproduced in *Smart News Journal* 1, no. 1, 21 March 2012. <http://www.mcpt.gov.mm/sites/default/files/pdf/1-1%20Smart-News-Journal%20.pdf>. Accessed 22 June 2013. (In Burmese.)

Nwe Nwe Aye. "The Role of the Media in Myanmar: Can it be a Watchdog for Corruption?". In *Myanmar's Transition: Openings, Obstacles and Opportunities*, edited by Nick Cheesman, Monique Skidmore and Trevor Wilson. Singapore: Institute of South East Asian Studies, 2012.

Noe Noe Aung. "Zaykabar Defies Order on Farmland". *Myanmar Times*, 14–20 May 2012. <http://www.mmtimes.com/2012/news/626/news62602.html>. Accessed 31 October 2013.

Nyein Nyein. "Land Protest Leaves One Dead, Dozens Injured". *Irrawaddy*, 27 February 2013. <http://www.irrawaddy.org/photo/land-protest-leaves-one-dead-dozens-injured.html>. Accessed 31 October 2013.

Paung Ku. "Reflections on the Giri Response". November 2010. <http://www.scribd.com/doc/67205436/Paung-Ku-Reflections-on-Giri>. Accessed 19 June 2013.

Schedler, Andreas. *The Self-Restraining State: Power and Accountability in New Democracies*. Boulder: Lynne Rienner, 1999.

Schumpeter, Joseph. *Capitalism, Socialism, and Democracy*. 2nd ed. New York: Harper, 1947.

Singh, U.B. "Do the Changes in Myanmar Signify a Real Transition?". *Strategic Analysis* 37, no. 1 (2013): 101–04.

Soe Lin Aung. *Socioeconomic Trends in Bogale: Livelihoods Land Tenure, and Market Activities in a Delta Township of Myanmar*. Paper written for Heinrich Boll Foundation, 2012, but as yet unpublished.

South, Ashley. "Political Transition in Myanmar: A New Model for Democratization". *Contemporary Southeast Asia* 26, no. 2 (2004): 233–55.

Tin Maung Maung Than. "Burma/Myanmar's By-Elections: Will Personalities Trump Institutions?". *Asia Pacific Bulletin*, no. 161, 20 April 2012. <http://www.eastwestcenter.org/sites/default/files/private/apb161.pdf>. Accessed 31 October 2013.

Turnell, Sean. *Fiery Dragons: Banks, Moneylenders and Microfinance in Burma*. Nordic Institute of Asian Studies (NIAS) Monograph Series 114. Copenhagen: NIAS Press, 2009.

Weekly Eleven. "Farmlands Will Not Return to Farmers, Says MP". *Weekly Eleven*, 28 July 2012. <http://elevenmyanmar.com/national/409-farmlands-will-not-return-to-farmers-says-mp>. Accessed 31 October 2013.

6

FROM EXILE TO ELECTIONS

Than Than Nu

A spirit of resistance was impressed upon me from an early age by my parents. I had, of course, grown up with stories of how my father, former Prime Minister U Nu, General Aung San, and countless other Burmese patriots had fought against British and Japanese imperialism, and won independence for the nation. In my father's case, his long career in resistance started at the tender age of fourteen, when he was part of a group of villagers that had assembled to give some visiting British colonial officers a less-than-warm reception at the local docks. He was arrested for his part in this incident, the first of many sojourns in prison over the course of his life (Butwell 1965; U Nu 1975). I was fifteen years old when armed soldiers loyal to General Ne Win stormed into our house in Rangoon in the early hours of 2 March 1962. In order to avoid any violence, my parents did as they were told, and my father was led away to prison that night. As soon as the soldiers and tanks moved away from our house, however, my mother made sure my brothers and I went to school as though nothing had happened. This was her way of showing any who supported the military's actions that we were not cowed by the previous night's events, and that we had nothing to fear either.

As we all know, General Ne Win's actions on that night have had a deep and lasting effect on the course of modern Burmese history. In the years following my father's release from prison, in October 1966, we lived in exile, initially by the Thai-Burma border. It was during the five years spent at various rebel pro-democracy camps in these forests that I met my husband, U Aung Nyein, who was at the time an officer in the rebel army. At the invitation of the Government of India, my parents and I moved to Calcutta, and then to Bhopal. My parents were allowed to return permanently to Burma in 1980, and my husband and I settled down in New Delhi in the same year.

WORKING IN INDIA AND THE 1988 UPRISING

At the time of the 1988 student uprising in Burma, I was working as a translator-announcer in the Burmese Language Unit of All India Radio, the state-owned national radio service of India. My five colleagues—including my husband—and I performed the daily task of translating the latest news, commentaries, and editorials from English to Burmese, and of going on air to broadcast our translated scripts for the morning and evening programs. These were aimed primarily at listeners in Burma. We had always had a broad base of listeners, judging from the letters we received each week through the Indian Embassy in Rangoon, containing song requests, words of appreciation, comments on recent newsworthy occurrences, or general enquiries. I remember our sense of excitement and anticipation when news of the student protests first broke—anticipation that change was perhaps imminent, and that the long decades of the country spiralling ever-deeper into poverty under the heavy weight of military rule were soon to be over. We, and the rest of the world, watched with bated breath, but our euphoria quickly turned into dismay as stories and images of shootings, arbitrary executions, and arrests came out of Burma in quick succession. The government crackdown was in full swing.

At the height of the crisis, we received several hundred letters a week from our listeners in Burma, many of which reflected their unadulterated anger at what the military government was doing to its own people. We went about our business of making our usual professional translations of the news and editorials provided to all language units by All India Radio, and of reading out some of the listeners' letters that we, as a group, deemed suitable for broadcasting. In all, we devoted around half our daily time-slot to covering the pro-democracy movement in Burma. All this was made possible through the backing of the then Prime Minister of India, Mr Rajiv Gandhi, who was one of the first world leaders to express support for the students' cause in international forums. This brief period of support from the Indian government came to an abrupt end after Mr. Gandhi's assassination in 1990. As usual, the appropriateness of our broadcasts was monitored by another All India Radio staff member, who was competent in the Burmese language, but who was not affiliated with our unit. Nevertheless, the military junta lodged a formal complaint with the Indian Embassy in Rangoon, saying that I was personally abusing the junta with vulgar language. Failure to take appropriate action against me could well result in the closure of the Indian Embassy in Rangoon, they threatened.

My colleagues and I were astonished at the speed with which the new Indian government moved to comply with the junta's demands, and at the extent to which they went to placate the generals. I was allowed to continue working at All India Radio, but was barred from all broadcasting. I was informed of this policy decision within a week of Rajiv Gandhi's assassination; there was no paperwork to make the order official, and all it took was a phone call from the Ministry of Information and Broadcasting to the relevant senior official at All India Radio. The timing of this action says much about the unpopularity of Mr. Gandhi's support for the Burmese cause among his coalition allies, and about the latter's eagerness to appease the military rulers of a neighbouring country with which India shared (and still shares) a volatile border. Economic and political aspirations also likely played a large part in driving Indian foreign policy to develop a more positive stance towards the military regime; these are summarized in detail in Egreteau (2008).

Taking me off-air was not enough, however, as the Burmese government also wanted regular, written updates on all the news content that was aired by the radio station. The resulting situation, had it not been so distressing to us at the Burmese Unit, would have otherwise been laughable—the state broadcasting service of the world's biggest democracy began to meekly and regularly hand over original transcripts of its Burmese language program to the world's longest running military dictatorship, so that the latter might satisfy itself that nothing uncomplimentary was being said about it. Ironically, this incident helped to inform our listeners in Burma that I was the daughter of U Nu, a fact that had not previously been made public. Caricatures appeared in the state-owned newspaper naming both me and my father, and claiming that I was abusing the country's leaders by using foul language.

I was barred from broadcasting for the next eleven years. It was only in the year 2000, when the outgoing Secretary of the Burma desk of the Ministry of External Affairs wished to present me with a "special gift", as he called it, that I was told I would be allowed to go on-air exclusively for the "Listeners' Requests" music program. The regular news and editorial programs were still off-limits to me, and I politely refused the offer, shortly before resigning from All India Radio.

POST 1990: LIFE WITH OTHER EXILES

As the 1988 uprising slid further back in time, and the junta showed little willingness either to engage constructively with pro-democracy activists or to honour the results of the 1990 election, more and more political refugees crossed over into neighbouring India and Thailand (see Zaw Oo (2006) for an account of student activism in exile in countries other than India). Among them were student activists who had taken part in political rallies and, later, elected members of parliament who had not been allowed to take office when the election results were annulled. Most of those arriving in India eventually made their way to New Delhi, and for many of the early refugees, our home was their first port of call. Some would show up unannounced in the middle of the night, and we would provide them with whatever hospitality we could. Once these early arrivals were settled in their own homes in New Delhi, they were able to help others who arrived later.

In late 1990, two courageous and determined young men, Ko Soe Myint and Ko Htin Kyaw, hijacked a Thai Airways flight from Rangoon to Bangkok and forced the plane to land in Calcutta. They were completely unarmed, and their sole intention was to raise awareness of the pro-democracy movement in Burma. The two men gave themselves up to authorities upon arrival in Calcutta, and were immediately arrested by the Indian police. My husband travelled to Calcutta to meet them and offer any assistance as seemed appropriate. I did my part in New Delhi, and called upon Mr Rajiv Gandhi to help the two young men, who were, not surprisingly, facing serious criminal charges. Once again thanks to the direct involvement of Mr Gandhi, we were able first to secure the release of Ko Soe Myint and Ko Htin Kyaw on bail, then to have the criminal charges against them dropped (readers are directed towards Sen and Thein Oo (2003) for an account of later legal issues arising from this case). Both went on to become prominent figures in the pro-democracy movement; Ko Soe Myint is the founder, and currently managing director and editor-in-chief of the well-known magazines *Mizzima* and *M-Zine*, which cover current social, political, and economic affairs in Myanmar.

The first long-term priority for pro-democracy activists arriving in New Delhi in the early 1990s was to be formally recognized as political refugees by the United Nations High Commission for Refugees (UNHCR). In the early days of the pro-democracy movement, this was a relatively straightforward matter, especially with Rajiv Gandhi as a sympathetic and willing ally. I helped arrange for a Burmese-English interpreter for their assessment interviews, and accompanied potential refugees to the UNHCR office, where I would sign the necessary paperwork, naming my husband and myself as guarantors. Sometimes there were minor bureaucratic hurdles to be overcome, and I would have to meet officials from the Indian government or UNHCR to assist students who, for some administrative reason or another, had trouble completing the required formalities. Significantly, a senior staff member from the Burmese Embassy defected in mid-1989 in protest against the military government's violent crackdown, and was also forced to seek refugee status in India. By then I had a good rapport with UNHCR staff, and was able to help expedite formalities to not only get the embassy officer and his family recognized as refugees, but also for them to receive a substantial allowance for subsistence.

Before long I lost count of the number of times I was required to appear at the UNHCR office in New Delhi. In the majority of cases, I was signing papers of guarantee for people whose backgrounds I knew absolutely nothing about. In retrospect, I am happy to note that in most cases, the people I helped to be recognized by the UNHCR were, indeed, genuine political refugees.

My family kept in constant contact with a great many of the students as long as we remained in India, and some even stayed in our home for periods of time. Eventually, I returned to Myanmar with my husband in July 2003, and many of the students, now independent professionals, moved to countries such as Thailand, the United States, and Australia. A number of these former students remain close family friends to this day.

Because of our role in helping students and other refugees while in India, between 1988 and 1993 the Burmese Embassy in New Delhi refused to renew our passports. My mother, still living in Rangoon at the time, passed away in early 1993, and it was only through the goodwill of the governments of India and Thailand that I was able to travel to Burma for her funeral, using alternative identity papers. Towards the mid-to-late 1990s, travel restrictions for those wishing to leave Burma had eased somewhat, and several Buddhist monks took this opportunity to travel to India for post-graduate education in Indian institutions. All wished to enroll in Masters or PhD programs in Buddhist studies, and approached me to help them gain admission at various universities. The Congress-I was back in power by then, and I felt confident enough to ask senior bureaucrats at the Ministry of Human Resource Development (HRD) for assistance. Following an agreement between my father and former Prime Minister Pandit Jawaharlal Nehru, two places had been reserved for Burmese students each year at state-run Indian universities. The HRD Ministry was able to make good use of this provision, and by the time we left India in 2003, close to twenty-five monks had taken up places in Indian universities, and many had even completed their degrees. During the same period, three or four student refugees were also able to enrol to study in the same way, in subjects ranging from politics to business administration.

U Aggasara was one of the monks who received a full scholarship for a Masters and PhD at Delhi University, and he wrote his doctoral thesis on "The Role of the Burmese Clergy in Political Activism", but only after he had taught himself English from audio cassettes obtained from the British Council office in New Delhi. It was a sad reminder of how things were in Burma that when he returned home after completing his studies, he did not dare take a copy of his PhD thesis back with him. Nevertheless, he was determined to give something back to his community, and he approached me with a proposal to set up a free school for underprivileged children from his home village of Shwejin in Bago Division. I was still living in India at the time, and was only able to provide financial support, while U Aggasara had to do all the groundwork required for such an undertaking. The school has since flourished and, due to continued financial support from my family and other donors, now offers free education and a midday meal to over five hundred students. It even has an orphanage that houses, feeds, and educates children from around the region, including many whose parents were killed by Cyclone Nargis.

RETURNING TO MYANMAR

I took voluntary retirement from All India Radio in the year 2000, after two decades of continuous service. After that, I volunteered with the non-government organization (NGO) Wings, teaching children in a Delhi slum, as well as teaching Burmese to Indian civil service and military personnel at the School of Foreign Languages, a Government of India-administered institution. In 2003, my husband and I decided it was time to return to Myanmar. Two decades earlier, my parents had returned, and for them, the primary motivation had been not politics or political activism, but a desire to continue their translation of key Buddhist texts from Pali into Burmese and English. There was nothing dramatic about our reasons for returning either: they were partly sentimental, and partly pragmatic. The sentimental reasons were that we yearned to live once again in the country in which we had grown up. I also had in the back of my mind the promise I had made to my father that I would return and work for my country's welfare. At that time, I only had a faint notion that I might one day be involved in politics. The pragmatic reasons included the fact that as we were foreign nationals resident in India, we were not eligible for government pensions, in spite of our many years of employment.

My participation in modern politics in Myanmar came about in a gradual and informal way. Once a week, my husband and I would be invited to lunch at the home of a family friend—the gentleman, now passed away, was U Ba Swe Lay, who had been Secretary in the Ministry of Religious Affairs while my father had been Prime Minister. Several experienced politicians from my father's time were also invited; they would use these gatherings to discuss their political views and experiences and the current state of affairs, as well as the way forward for the country. Since public political assemblies were not allowed at this time, informal gatherings—organized with the pretext of having lunch—were one way politically-minded people could meet to openly discuss topics that were taboo as far as the government was concerned. It was at one of these meetings that I met an old acquaintance, U Thu Wai, who is the current President of the Democratic Party (Myanmar) (DP(M)), and was formerly Personal Secretary to U Kyaw Nyein, who had served as Deputy Prime Minister in the 1950s. The idea of forming a political party, should the opportunity arrive, slowly took shape over several such meetings, but it was not until 2010 that we were able to put our plans into action.

THE 2010 ELECTIONS

Establishing a Party: Challenges and Successes

Once we became convinced that elections would really be held, we scrambled to complete the myriad administrative and logistic tasks required to form a political party. We were at first euphoric—we were able to field close to two hundred candidates from around the country, people willing to contest the upcoming election under our party banner. These were mostly professionals and intellectuals from urban centres, who either approached us directly after having heard of the DP(M) and its "clean" image, or were already known to the party leadership. At this stage, we did not think it would be too challenging a task to obtain the requisite number of signatures from potential party members. This was, of course, before any of the electoral regulations had been officially released. The release of each new regulation was a cause for anxiety and frustration, and we gradually realized not only that we faced nearly insurmountable challenges in the months before the election, but also that the elections themselves were not going to be free or fair in the slightest.

Our first source of anxiety was the extremely short timeline for the electoral process—as is well known, the first election under the new constitution was held in November 2010, but it was not until March of that year that the call for the official registration of political parties was announced. We acted as soon as possible, but in spite of our best efforts, it was not until May 2010 that the Democratic Party (Myanmar) formally came into being. The first significant task that we faced was the collection of one thousand signatures from potential party members. This would have been a simple enough process under ordinary circumstances, but in March 2010 the political climate in Myanmar was far from ordinary. People were reluctant to make a formal commitment to an unknown political organization, and even those who seemed genuinely eager to be involved in party affairs sometimes could not bring themselves to sign up as members. Matters were exacerbated by the official requirement for signatories to provide a great deal of personal information, including residential and work addresses, occupation and national ID number. Each political party was, in turn, required to hand over all this information to the Election Commission for approval. Eventually, following a great deal of legwork by the party faithful, we were able to obtain a grand total of 1,500 signatures. Of these, the Election Commission rejected around three hundred for various reasons, but we were still left with enough signatures for a formal application. Throughout this process, we frequently heard reports of Military Intelligence personnel visiting our party members at their residences, bullying them, and aggressively demanding to know their motivation for signing up to a political party. Our membership remained stable during those early months, in spite of the intimidation, and we senior party members drew strength and inspiration from the loyalty of these ordinary men and women. Having no eminent family connections or wealth to fall back on, they were risking much (far more than people like myself, who at least had family connections) and putting their commitment to political change before their personal security, in a highly uncertain social and political climate.

One of the earlier announcements of the Election Commission informed political parties that each and every candidate would need to pay a fee of 500,000 *kyats* (approximately US$500 at the time), in order to register for the upcoming election. For the average citizen of Myanmar, this is an enormous amount of money, even today, and the majority of the candidates who had been willing to contest the elections under our party banner were simply not able to afford the fee. We were left with a total of forty-seven candidates. Even some of these could not afford to pay the registration fee in full, and had to borrow money.

Today, the DP(M) operates on a modest budget, although we continue to broaden our operational base in small increments. We have opened numerous divisional and sub-divisional offices in various townships and hamlets in Ayeyarwady and Yangon Divisions, and we also have a small but significant support base in Mandalay and Tanintharyi. Official party membership continues to grow by small numbers each week, and currently stands at over twenty thousand.

Campaigning and the Official Result

In spite of these challenges, we as a party were committed to channelling all our efforts into the 2010 election campaign. Here too, we had to overcome, more or less on a daily basis, the highly restrictive and arbitrary regulations that governed the actions of political parties, their members, and candidates during campaigning. Every aspect of the campaign process, from the number of people who could attend political rallies, to the text of political speeches, and even the size and positioning of election posters, banners, and the party flag, was strictly regulated by the Election Commission, and prior approval had to be sought for each activity. This had the effect of discouraging most campaign activities among the smaller parties: given the harsh penalties (heavy fines or dissolution of the party), most were reluctant to organize public gatherings for fear of inadvertently contravening a regulation. It was common knowledge that Military Intelligence personnel attended such events to monitor proceedings, and to take note of any breaches of Election Commission regulations.

Once campaigning began in earnest, we found that the process of meeting potential voters on the streets of our respective constituencies was an enormous pleasure that more than made up for the troubles of the previous months. Despite the subdued nature of the election as a whole, most of the people with whom I interacted spoke warm words of encouragement and support, often inviting me into their homes for tea, and thanking me for doing what they said was important and necessary work. Practically every person I encountered at least showed an interest in the election, and many approached me to ask questions, or to obtain more DP(M) campaign leaflets for friends or neighbours. There was only a small handful of instances when I got a negative response, but these were invariably from die-hard supporters of other parties. Readers may remember that this was a time when the National League for Democracy (NLD) had been officially dissolved by the military junta, and Daw Aung San Suu Kyi had not only refused to re-register her party and contest the election, but had actually called for a nation-wide boycott of the polls. We felt at the time that the latter decision was unnecessary and counter-productive. We and the other democratic forces contesting the 2010 elections were trying our hardest to do good, useful work under very difficult circumstances, and we did not need the added worry of having to defend our actions to a confused and worried electorate.

Nevertheless, my colleagues campaigning in other parts of the country were as encouraged as I was by the reactions of potential voters in their constituencies, and this gave us reason to believe that the DP(M) had a reasonable chance of winning some seats in the 2010 elections. Needless to say, we would only have a reasonable chance of winning if the elections were free and fair. When election day finally came, we tried to organize as many volunteers as we could to be posted as observers at polling stations. I was contesting from Mandalay, while the DP(M) President U Thu Wai and my husband, U Aung Nyein, were stationed in Yangon. Regardless of location, we were horrified not only by the scale on which Election Commission staff broke their own regulations in concert with members of the military-backed Union Solidarity and Development Party (USDP), but also by the brazenness with which these offences were carried out. In Mandalay, I was barred from entering any of the polling booths or Election Commission offices, while I could clearly see USDP members freely entering these premises.

In Yangon, strangely enough, U Thu Wai was allowed to observe both polling and counting, but while he held a comfortable lead on the first day of counting, the official result reported a defeat for him. Also in Yangon, my husband received a phone call from an Election Commission officer at noon on election day, asking him to appear at the Commission's office to observe vote counting. This in itself was strange, because polling booths were supposed to stay open until 4pm that day, but staff at the Election Commission office explained they had closed the polling booths early because there were no more voters. Upon arrival at the counting station, my husband was told that counting was over—he was shown an empty ballot box, and told that there had not been any votes for him. Normally, we would have accepted this result without protest, were it not for the fact that the other two DP(M) candidates from the same constituency—for the Regional Assembly—won with comfortable margins. That a third DP(M) candidate, for the People's Assembly, from the same constituency should suffer such a crushing defeat, was a highly improbable outcome.

While none of the senior members of the DP(M) won a seat in the 2010 election (all relevant ballots involving mysterious circumstances), a handful of younger, politically-unknown candidates were able to secure seats in the Yangon and Mandalay Regional Assemblies. Satisfied with this result, we tried to forge links with whichever democratic forces might be interested in working with us in future. Even at the time the Election Commission first called for parties to register, we had considered informal alliances with some of the numerous small parties formed by ethnic minority groups. After some deliberation, it was decided that the DP(M) would postpone such actions until after the 2010 elections, as we were already burdened with a large amount of work to be carried out in a short time.

AFTER THE ELECTIONS

The Ten Fraternal Parties

After the results were announced, we opened dialogues with a number of other parties, and were able to obtain the agreement of nine other parties, both Burman and ethnic minority. These parties were the Chin National Party, the Shan Nationalities Democratic Party, the Rakhine Nationalities Development Party, the All Mon Regional Democracy Party, the Phaloun Sawaw Democratic Party of the Karen, the National Democratic Force, the Party for Democracy and Peace, the Union Democracy Party, and the Party for Unity and Peace. We decided to pool some funds, and on 12 February 2011, Union Day, we officially inaugurated the group of Ten Fraternal Parties. Our reasons for forming this group were threefold. First, we wished to make a very public and unambiguous statement that the only way forward for the Union of Myanmar was through genuine co-operation, goodwill, and mutual understanding between her various ethnic groups. Second, we believed that we would be far more effective drivers of policy change if we were to petition the government not individually but collectively. Third, we wished that as a group we would be able to act as a counterbalance against the absolute domination of the military-backed USDP in all assemblies.

The 2011 inauguration ceremony was successful and well attended, and in 2012 we organized a similar event that saw an even higher turnout, partly due to the attendance of former students from the 1988 uprising, who had recently been released from prison. Since the formation of the Ten Fraternal Parties group, we have collectively taken several initiatives to bring about policy change, relating to both international and domestic policy. These initiatives included the following:

- On 12 February and 11 March 2011, we wrote open letters to the government of the United States of America and to the European Union (EU) calling for the lifting of economic and political sanctions against Myanmar, which we deemed to be counter-productive and detrimental to the welfare of Myanmar's citizens;
- On 26 February 2011, we issued a press release calling for a general amnesty for all political prisoners, as well as for Myanmar citizens living as exiles or as refugees overseas;

- On 30 March 2011, the day President U Thein Sein's civilian government was installed, we issued a press release voicing support for the president's call for clean government and good governance;
- On 28 April 2011, after the European Union had for the first time hinted that it might consider loosening some sanctions if genuine reform were to occur, we wrote another open letter encouraging the EU to follow up its words with firm actions;
- On 20 May 2011, after a general amnesty for many political prisoners was announced by President U Thein Sein as per Presidential Order 28/2011, we called upon the president to immediately extend the amnesty to all remaining political prisoners;
- In April and June 2011, following the outbreak of hostilities in Kachin State, we called upon the president to organize a National Peace Convention with Myanmar ethnic minorities and other stakeholders;
- On 25 July 2011, we wrote a formal letter of complaint to the Election Commission regarding the serious irregularities observed in the 2010 general election;
- On 20 September 2011, we wrote a letter urging the president to take into account the very negative public opinion towards the Chinese-backed Irrawaddy Dam Project, especially keeping in mind the environmental impact and the impact on local populations;
- On 9 November 2011, we called upon the president to address the extreme difficulties being faced by legume farmers by providing financial assistance in the form of subsidies;
- On 22 November 2011, we issued a press release warmly welcoming news of the re-registration of the National League for Democracy as a political party in time for participation in the April 2012 by-election. The press release also included an invitation to the NLD to work together for the benefit of the country;
- On 7 June 2012, we issued a press release stating that the Rakhine crisis is a regional issue that needs to be handled by Myanmar alone. We also stressed that the crisis was the result of various social and economic factors, and should not simply be regarded as a conflict between Buddhists and Muslims.

We cannot be certain that any of the above initiatives have had a concrete impact, but many of our communications to the president have been followed by policy directives that appear to be largely in line with the goals expressed by the Ten Fraternal Parties. On the other hand, we feel confident in claiming that we played a significant role in the shifting of international attitudes towards sanctions, a shift that ultimately led to sanctions being lifted several months later. This was achieved not only through the open letters mentioned above, but also through meetings with politicians and senior bureaucrats from the European Union and the United States.

I can think of at least one instance that made it very clear to me that our efforts in trying to bring about incremental policy change were being rewarded. On 18 July 2012, representatives of each of the Ten Fraternal Parties were invited to meet President U Thein Sein at his Ledaw Retreat near Naypyitaw. Each party was asked to put forward one proposal for the president's consideration, and U Thu Wai and I, representing the DP(M), called for an abolition of the system of blacklists, which contained the names of thousands of Myanmar and foreign nationals. These people had been blacklisted for various reasons, but foremost among them was some kind of involvement in pro-democracy activities during the time of the previous military regime. U Thu Wai and I related to the president instances of blacklisted former Myanmar citizens living in exile in countries such as Australia and the United States who had been granted valid visas from their respective Myanmar embassies, only to be detained at Yangon International Airport and threatened with deportation or worse. The president took copious notes during our presentation, and as we were about to leave, gave us his personal assurance that this matter would be dealt with expeditiously. True to his word, the Presidential Order abolishing the blacklist system was announced within a few weeks of our meeting.

Incidents such as this, along with numerous other policy decisions and concrete actions on the part of the current civilian government lead me to believe that the president is sincere in his desire to bring about as much positive change as is possible during his tenure. I am confident that most of my party colleagues, as well as colleagues in the other Fraternal Parties share this view. The changes that have come about in the past two years range from the superficial to the substantial. At the "superficial" end of the scale, life in big cities such as Yangon appears far more relaxed than it ever was during the more than fifty years of military rule, and people no longer have any need to look over their shoulder when discussing politics or criticizing the government. Yet most reasonable people are nervous about the prospect of a policy U-turn, and all are aware of the strong military presence that still exists in the government. At the "substantial" end of the scale of policy change, the abolition of the decades-old Department of State Censorship has been hailed by the local and international press alike, and has brought about a renaissance of the print media in Myanmar. Once-taboo political subjects are now being openly written about in books and so-called "journals", privately-owned newspapers, are to be allowed later this year. Even my father's autobiography, which had previously been rejected three times by the Department of State Censorship, with no hope of further review, was published and launched legally for the first time in Myanmar in November 2012.

CONCLUSION

While my colleagues and I have much faith in the president's sincerity, we also recognize that he faces some monumental challenges—of having to undo five decades of governmental mismanagement and bad decision-making; of ridding all levels of the government, the bureaucracy, law enforcement bodies, and the judiciary of widespread corruption and nepotism; of reconciling Myanmar's many ethnic groups and forging a sense of unity and nationhood, while overcoming over a century of cultural chauvinism, distrust, and ill-will; and of lifting the majority of Myanmar's fifty million people out of grinding poverty. Perhaps most people will agree with me when I say that no single person or political party can accomplish these goals in a single term, or two, or five. Democracy, on its own, is no panacea capable of making the ills of a past age vanish overnight. It will take perhaps a generation to raise Myanmar's standard of living to a level on a par with that of her affluent Southeast Asian neighbours, and this, in turn, will require countless incremental improvements in governance, as well as the co-operation of Myanmar's diverse peoples, and the support and goodwill of the international community. What Myanmar does not need at the moment is the aggressive, adversarial politics of the past, or threats of sanctions and boycotts from otherwise well-meaning countries, or politicians putting personal ambition before the good of the nation. To put matters bluntly, we need to be patient, open-minded, far-sighted, and realistic about our goals.

References

Butwell, Richard. *U Nu of Burma.* Stanford: Stanford University Press, 1969.

Egreteau, Renaud. "India's ambitions in Burma: More frustration than success?". *Asian Survey* 48, no. 6 (2008): 936–57.

Sen, B.K. and Thein Oo. "Criminal Case For A Cause—India's Democracy on Trial: The Government of India versus Ko Soe Myint & One". *Legal Issues on Burma Journal* 14 (April 2003): 17–22. <http://www.burmalibrary.org/docs08/LIOB_14.pdf>. Accessed 31 October 2013.

U Nu. *U Nu, Saturday's Son.* New Haven: Yale University Press, 1975.

Zaw Oo. "Exit, Voice and Loyalty in Burma: The Role of Overseas Burmese in Democratising Their Homeland". In *Myanmar's Long Road to National Reconciliation*, edited by Trevor Wilson. Singapore: Institute of Southeast Asian Studies, 2006.

7

SIDELINED OR REINVENTING THEMSELVES?

Exiled Activists in Myanmar's Political Reforms

Kerstin Duell

Myanmar's tumultuous post-colonial history has been characterized by decades of direct and indirect military rule and corresponding political mobilizations that have ranged from armed ethnic and ideological insurgencies to mass protests, student movements, and non-violent pro-democracy uprisings. The nationalization and mismanagement of the economy, the militarization of the state, political surveillance and oppression, and the closure of universities are all factors that have triggered the flight from Burma of millions of Burmese. Several main waves of exit can be distinguished, following major political events—(1) the 1962 military coup; (2) the installation of direct rule by the Burma Socialist Programme Party in 1974 and the U Thant funeral crisis; (3) the 1988 mass uprisings; and (4) the 2007 "Saffron Revolution" protests, respectively. The largest exodus occurred in the period from late 1988 until after the 1990 elections (held on 27 May 1990), when the military government indefinitely delayed the transfer of power to the elected opposition. The Burmese diaspora that formed as the result of these movements was comprised mostly of people who had fled repression and conflict, but it also included individuals who had left Burma for educational and professional purposes.

As a prerequisite to studying the nature of Burmese political activism and underlying domestic, transnational and international linkages, the concepts of "diaspora" and "political exiles" need to be revisited. The central defining feature of a diaspora consists in a shared identity that unites people living dispersed in transnational spaces (Soekefield 2006, p. 280) and in transnational "imagined communities" (Anderson 2001).

Political exiles "engage in political activity, directed against the policies of a home regime, the home regime itself or the political system as a whole, and aimed at creating circumstances favourable to their return" (Shain 1989, p. 15). Silenced at home, exiles exit in order to voice their discontent, but also struggle to return home, at least initially (Ma 1993). The central position of threat in the literature on exile and diaspora is paralleled in social movement theory by threat, opportunity, and the cost of contention (Goldstone and Tilly 2004, p. 179f).

Compared to classical diasporas, the Burmese diaspora of up to four millions in Thailand and smaller communities across the rest of the world is relatively large. It can be divided into two groups: one group consists of people who have become well established (perhaps over a long period) in a host country; the other includes the many unskilled and semi-skilled Burmese migrants who work (often illegally) in countries such as Thailand, Malaysia, India, and Singapore, as well as the refugees who live in official refugee camps or in other, unofficial, dwellings in those same countries and Bangladesh. These migrants and refugees form by far the largest segment of the diverse Burmese diaspora and are thus most noticeable to their respective host countries. Despite the size of the Burmese diaspora, it has possessed neither economic power vis-à-vis the home government nor has it generated real political cleavages in host countries (Zaw Oo 2006).

The first group mentioned above can be described as "rooted cosmopolitans"—that is, people who are nationally based both in their host and home countries while simultaneously engaging in transnational activities (Tarrow 2004; Della Porta and Tarrow 2005). Rooted cosmopolitans share "long-distance nationalism", a nationalism that no longer depends on territorial location in a home country (Anderson 2001, p. 43.). Typically, they are well-established professionals, academics, or journalists in host countries; they are not necessarily politically active, but may be easily mobilized. Owing to their education and familiarity with the respective host countries, such rooted cosmopolitans may function as excellent intermediaries between their home country's political opposition or marginalized groups and the international system.

Although, broadly speaking, the Burmese diaspora comprises all Burmese abroad, be they professionals, migrant workers, refugees, asylum seekers, or political exiles, this chapter focuses primarily on the small politically-active subset of the diaspora—the political exiles who led a transnational pro-democracy movement that sustained challenges against the powerful military regime for over twenty years.

The political exiles identified for this study met at least one of three criteria: first, the reason for their flight from Burma was fear of reprisal or experience of realized reprisal for expressing political opinions or participating in political activities; second, anticipation of acute threats to their safety should they go back to Burma prevented a return from exile; and third, they had participated in political activity against military rule in Burma while abroad.

BURMESE OPPOSITION EXILES IN NEIGHBOURING COUNTRIES, 1988–2008

The 1988 uprisings against military dictatorship and economic mismanagement marked a watershed in Burmese political history and the beginning of the opposition movement exiled in Thailand, India, and Western countries. Military suppression of the nation-wide uprisings triggered an exodus of thousands of protestors to border areas controlled by armed ethnic nationality movements, or to neighbouring countries. Thus, the political opposition was effectively divided into those who remained in Burma, either in prison or underground, and those living outside the country, who were beyond Burmese government control and could engage in political action more openly but who were limited by constraints imposed by their respective hosts.

Prominent members of the diaspora, such as U Nu's daughter Daw Than Than Nu in New Delhi, offered support to activists when they fled to neighbouring countries. Later, informal contacts and ties between the members of the diaspora and fleeing activists laid the foundation for an emerging transnational movement network, in which members of the diaspora soon became vital nodes. For instance, individuals like Maureen Aung-Thwin, director of the Open Society Institute's Burma Project, or Dr Zarni, founder of the Free Burma Coalition in the United States, became active after 1988 and helped to publicize and establish the nascent Burmese movement abroad.

Student leaders and prominent individuals founded numerous social movement organizations (SMOs) that, in combination, made up the multi-faceted collective of the Burmese pro-democracy movement. Thailand and India became the countries where most activist organizations (and refugees) were based.[1]

The exiled movement is here conceptualized as a network encompassing the 1988 activists,[2] veteran politicians and 1990 members of parliament elect, the armed ethnic nationality movements (which had mostly been founded in the 1940s and 1950s), some of the politically-active Burmese diaspora or "rooted cosmopolitans" in Western countries, and some of the refugees who had become politicized abroad. Another "generation" of political activists went into exile after the 2007 protests, but these simply shifted their location and continued their activities from abroad, without founding new organizations or attracting new members; Generation Wave is one example.[3]

Despite the movement's heterogeneity, overarching political objectives were expressed publicly as:
- the establishment of a genuine federal union;
- the abolition of all types of dictatorship;
- the promotion of democratic governance; and
- the guarantee of human rights, political equality, and ethnic self-determination.[4]

Privately though, political agendas diverged substantially, especially between armed ethnic leaders and Burman student activists, who had experienced vastly different realities.

Urban, educated, and predominantly ethnic Burmans came to dominate the movement in exile. The noticeable social stratification among its leaders derived from the fact that the movement emerged from the traditionally strongly-politicized student unions. The few ethnic-nationality members of the student and member of parliament organizations hence adhered to the mainstream democratic agenda, rather than explicitly propagating ethnic-nationality causes.

In contrast with exiles abroad, many of the influential ethnic-nationality leaders of opposition groups inside Burma had spent only their university years in cities, either Rangoon or Mandalay, and otherwise lived in their respective communities in remote areas.[5] These differences in experience also conditioned the strategic orientation of different groups within the opposition movement on the question of using armed resistance versus non-violence. The ethnic nationality movements continued armed resistance against the Myanmar military while their political wings actively participated in mainstream SMOs. The Burman organizations, on the other hand, adhered mainly to non-violence, with the notable exception of the All Burma Students' Democratic Front (ABSDF) student army (formed in 1988) and the small group Vigorous Burmese Student Warriors. The ABSDF split into two groups precisely due to conflicts over the non-violence paradigm. The student-based Democratic Party for a New Society (DPNS) did not join but supported armed resistance.

In exile, activists pursued various strategies to effect systemic change in Myanmar by creating pressure on the military regime both from within the country and from the international community. Key strategies included the lobbying of foreign governments and multilateral agencies to exert pressure on the military government, campaigns against human rights violations, boycotts of companies investing in Myanmar, and channelling training and other resources to activists inside the country.

Some SMOs also focused on giving political education to refugees and migrants, while publicizing their plight, both in their home and host countries. The majority of internationally displaced persons (IDPs), refugees, and migrants belonged to the uneducated, rural population and were unlikely to join SMOs, but their mere existence and experiences were living proof of the regime's crimes, and gave activists further useful evidence for advocacy.

Opportunities and the Shift in Norms at Cold War End

Following the 1988 uprisings, the historic changes brought by the end of the Cold War—in terms of norms, resources, and the re-balancing of powers—had a significant influence on the overall trajectory of the exiled opposition movement. In particular, an ideological shift towards normative-idealist discourses of democracy, non-violence, human rights, and the rights of ethnic minorities and of women, played a pivotal role in framing the opposition as a "pro-democracy movement". Western policy instruments that promoted democratization, acting in tandem with new resources available to non-state actors pursuing these agendas, sustained the Burmese movement's exceptionally long tenure of over twenty years (Tabori 1972, p. 38).

Transnational advocacy networks (TANs) were instrumental in internationalizing the Burmese cause and gathering worldwide support. TANs offer a major advantage: they can bypass a home government and amplify demands internationally until these demands echo back into the domestic arena. This triangular "boomerang effect" occurs when domestic actors convince third-party states and other international allies to pressure the activists' home government (Keck and Sikkink 1997, p. 12; Klotz 1995). The use of transnational advocacy networks implies that activists perceive domestic political opportunity structures as closed, but international opportunities as open.

Burmese activists swiftly employed the political opportunities created by the increased attention being given to human rights and democracy, especially since the Myanmar government's failure to respect human and civil rights provided ammunition for the movement, enabling it to generate international criticism and put pressure on the regime. The documentation of actual and structural violence, as well as, to a lesser extent, of psychological consequences, served for constructing images of injustice in order to mobilize support from international audiences. Activists framed grievances suffered in the home or neighbouring host countries in ways that resonated with their distant (mainly Western) target audiences, stressing the injustice, arbitrariness, and brutality of repression. Indeed, human rights became "the mother of all successful transnational framing efforts" (McCarthy 1997, p. 246). Consequently, SMOs that strongly embedded their agendas in this frame (for instance, the Assistance Association for Political Prisoners (rights of political prisoners); the Ethnic Nationalities Council (ENC) and the Euro-Burma Office (ethnic minority rights); and the Women's League of Burma (women's rights)) attracted vital resources, including international endorsements, access to new political platforms, and training programmes.

Similarly, the Gandhi-inspired non-violent, Buddhist stance of Daw

Aung San Suu Kyi matched the new *zeitgeist* at a time of peaceful revolutions and the lifting of the Iron Curtain, earning her the 1991 Nobel Prize for Peace. Charismatic leaders who appeal to both domestic and external audiences tend to play a pivotal role in "marketing" social movements (Bob 2005, p. 46; Brooten 2005). Aung San Suu Kyi rose to international prominence and came to embody the democratic arm of the Burmese opposition, while, in the absence of an overarching leader of their own, most of the diverse ethnic nationalities rallied behind her (at least for a time). The emergence of such an iconic opposition leader, however, further polarized—until now—the portrayal of conflict as being a simple struggle between Aung San Suu Kyi and the military, and between democracy and authoritarianism, while armed ethnic movements took a back seat.

In countries where the emphasis on human rights and democracy alienated ruling elites, activists stressed Myanmar's instability and its deleterious effects on human, non-traditional, conventional security and, not least, on economic stability in the region.

The movement's need for new resources was not the only reason behind its search for external assistance; historical and identity-related factors were also involved, but these are beyond the scope of this chapter.[6]

Resources and Donors

The new resources that the movement obtained included access to networks and to important policy-makers as well as funding. Transnational advocacy networks played a pivotal role in enabling Burmese activists to convince most Western countries to impose sanctions on the Myanmar government, while extending financial, moral, and diplomatic support to activists. Some SMOs appropriated existing solidarity networks, for example, the All Burma Federation of Student Unions (ABFSU) linked up with international student movements, the Federation of Trade Unions-Burma (FTUB) with the International Trade Union Confederation (ITUC), while the National Coalition Government of the Union of Burma (NCGUB) and the Members of Parliament Union (MPU) linked up with regional and global parliamentarians' networks, such as the International Parliamentary Union. The 1990 members of parliament elect, for instance, lobbied the Inter-Parliamentary Union, the European Parliament, and the Inter-Parliamentary Myanmar Caucus of the Association of Southeast Asian

Nations for parliamentary action. Over time, a sophisticated transnational pro-democracy movement emerged in both neighbouring and Western countries. As the mobilization of tangible and intangible resources provided the movement's lifeline, funding became a core concern. Donor constraints and funding flows therefore began to bear heavily on the movement's leadership, cohesion, strategies, and overall trajectory.

The movement's principal donors of funds, training, and travel grants were the American National Endowment for Democracy (NED), the Soros Foundation's Open Society Institute (OSI), and the International Republican Institute (IRI), but there were also many other significant donors.[7]

Major governmental donors (principally the development agencies but also the foreign ministries) included the U.S. Agency for International Development (USAID), Canadian International Development Agency (CIDA), Norwegian Agency for Development Cooperation (NORAD), Danish International Development Agency (DANIDA), Sweden (SIDA), and the Netherlands' National Committee for International Cooperation and Sustainable Development (NCDO). In contrast, and despite the presence of vocal advocacy groups, the British and Australian governments gave humanitarian assistance to Myanmar but no resources to the opposition-in-exile. Likewise, no resources came from Southern Europe or France.

Two principal donors, NED and OSI, took a lead in the Burma Donors Forum (BDF), a coordinating body for the movement's core donors that met periodically. The BDF membership did not include countries outside North America and Europe. The organization lacked definitions to assess whether a potential grantee organization was "committed to democratic development" or "working towards democracy".[8] In other words, in the absence of clear criteria, the process of selecting recipient organizations was left to the discretion of the respective donor organizations and the few decision-making individuals therein.

However, the multiple agendas of the diverse supporters strongly impacted the movement's priorities, strategies, and overall direction (Duell 2011). In particular, discourse about democracy, ideological rifts over non-violence versus armed struggle, and discussion over whether to support sanctions or favour engagement with the Myanmar government were all issues that provoked disagreement. Competition for funding and the broader politics of resource distribution within transnational advocacy networks fuelled the existing tendency for factionalism and splintering. Finally, disunity and conflict among the various pro-democracy groups became an overarching characteristic of the entire movement (Kyaw Yin Hlaing 2007).

THE ONSET OF POLITICAL CHANGE

By the mid-2000s, a process of self-reflection was well under way among prominent exiled activists. They criticized the movement's policies of exclusion and overprotection, its lack of freedom of expression, transparency, accountability and gender equality; they also pointed at burnt-out elders who clung to their positions for reasons of livelihood or identity, but who blocked younger leaders (Aung Naing Oo 2002; Dictatorwatch 2006). Allegedly, exiled dissidents, in-country opposition, and even some Western and Asian governments, practised political orthodoxy in much the same way as the Myanmar regime (Steinberg 2010, p. 9). Repeated calls were made for an open debate, honest assessment of failures, constructive criticism, and general discipline in place of the usual "highly polarized emotions and often slanderous attacks".[9] Other exiles, however, cautioned that self-criticism would undermine the unity of the movement and embolden the regime (Htet Aung Kyaw 2008). In short, activists grappled with implementing within their own ranks the very ideals they were striving for—democratic rights and practices. They were compelled to do so because movements striving for democracy in their home country are particularly likely to be scrutinized for (any lack of) democracy within their own organizations (Ma 1993, p. 379). Frustration with Myanmar's political stalemate increased in January 2007 when China and Russia blocked—with a historic double veto—a discussion in the UN Security Council of Myanmar's political repression and human rights violations. Exiles felt that another mass movement was necessary.

Inside the country, prominent dissident "students" of 1988, including Paw Oo Htun (alias Min Ko Naing), Ko Ko Gyi, Htay Kywe, Pone Cho, and Min Zeya, as well as students arrested in the 1996 and 1999 protests, were released in the mid-2000s.[10] They formed the "88 Generation Students" group, a movement deliberately without formal leadership or organizational structure in order to minimize repression from the authorities. In 2006, the group reaffirmed Aung San Suu Kyi's leadership qualities as "the one person that can bring about reconciliation and lead us into a new, democratic future" (Lintner 2007, p. 78). Despite re-arrest on several occasions, 88 Generation Students group leaders succeeded in broadening and strengthening the in-country opposition's informal connection with local civil society organizations, lawyers, journalists, and the intelligentsia (Min Zin 2010).

From late 2006 on, the 88 Generation Students group initiated some of the most significant acts of political defiance since 1988, such as the "White Expression Campaign", during which supporters dressed in white, the symbol of Burma's many martyrs, to demand the release of political prisoners. The "Multiple Religious Prayer Campaign" sent worshippers dressed in white to Buddhist, Christian, Hindu, and Muslim holy sites. During the "Signature Campaign", 535,580 signatures demanding the immediate release of political prisoners and the initiation of genuine national reconciliation were collected and sent to the Burmese government and the UN headquarters in New York. This was followed by the "Open Heart Campaign", when over 25,000 letters expressing hardship and grievances were collected and sent to Senior General Than Shwe in January 2007, and the "Sunday White Campaign", when supporters dressed in white visited families of political prisoners on Sundays during April 2007 (88 Generation Students 2008). In addition, remnants of the communist underground provided a key network for mobilizing participants for political action.[11] Activists inside the country also downloaded information from the Internet and received illegal publications from the exiles (for example, material published by the ABSDF); nonetheless, the flow of information was much stronger towards the exiles outside Myanmar than into the country.[12]

Some individuals from the younger "2007 Generation" received training in community organization, political defiance, the use of Internet communications technology, and capacity-building from exile groups.[13] Others were trained not by exiles but in the American Centre and the British Council in Yangon.[14] However, it seems that only individuals who were already putative leaders succeeded in receiving additional training.

The "Saffron Revolution" demonstrations between 19 August and early November 2007 became the next watershed in terms of mass mobilization against the regime.[15] Burmese activists inside and outside the country have since claimed responsibility for preparing the ground for the uprising. People interviewed inside the country tended to downplay the role of the exiles. Some observers consider the 2007 protests as unplanned, as a cycle of contention generated at home, with very limited involvement of exiled activists and other external players (Kyaw Yin Hlaing 2008, p. 141; Selth 2008, p. 284). Exiles, on the contrary, argue that the clandestine nature of training and other activities prevented people on the inside from realising the scale of assistance given by exiles.[16]

Such ambiguity regarding the role of exiles in domestic political contention is symptomatic of the difficulty of assessing the diaspora's contribution to ending the military dictatorship. It seems that neither activists in exile nor activists at home are ready to objectively assess the results and achievements of over twenty years of Burmese transnational activism.

Mobilization of Civil Society During the Saffron Revolution and Cyclone Nargis

Although the Saffron Revolution failed to bring about political change, it nonetheless saw a new generation of activists come to the fore. The year 2007 was an eye-opener for the younger generation, who had not experienced the events of 1988. Discouraged from engaging in politics by their parents, this generation was considered by some to be neither interested in, nor informed about, politics (Kyaw Yin Hlaing 2004). Nonetheless, "Generation Wave" and other groups emerged during that year. They did not join established political parties but engaged in political action, and continued to do so even after the military crackdown on the protests. As in 1988, there was not one protest leadership but many small groups led by various activists according to participants interviewed.

A number of networks linking civil society and political groups emerged or were revived during the events of 2007, and these were further strengthened during the response to Cyclone Nargis in May 2008. The unparalleled damage caused by the natural disaster was severely aggravated by weeks of delay on the part of the regime followed by arbitrary distribution of international aid. The absence of immediate help from the government catalyzed a strong response from youth, civil society, and opposition groups to mobilize charity drives for the affected areas. This response opened up space for humanitarian assistance, which led to an increasing number of local and international organizations becoming active.[17]

The killing of at least dozens (but possibly hundreds) of Buddhist monks

and unarmed protestors in 2007,[18] and the refusal of humanitarian aid that
could have saved thousands of lives in 2008, demonstrated dramatically
the regime's intransigence and disregard for the population. International
condemnation, including from Asian states usually reluctant to "interfere
in internal affairs", further reduced the military's diminished legitimacy.

2008 Election Announcement Divides Regime Opponents

In February 2008, the regime announced that there would be a referendum
on a new constitution and that general elections would be held. The
referendum on the constitution was held according to plan on 10 May
2008, the government showing total disregard of the destruction wreaked
by Cyclone Nargis only eight days before (Jagan 2008), not to mention of
demonstrations that had been held in several cities in April 2008.

The prospect that the government planned to hold elections effectively
split the opposition movement both inside Myanmar and in exile into
pro- and anti-elections camps. Various exile groups began anti-election
campaigns in early 2009.[19] Groups such as the NCGUB, which had primarily
engaged in lobbying foreign countries while rarely experiencing the realities
in the country, opposed the elections. Conversely, groups such as the Ethnic
Nationalities Council that were in touch with people at the grassroots level
inside the country or at the borders saw the elections—however flawed—as
the first prospect for change in decades. Keenly aware of the people's daily
struggle, these groups worked towards seizing this opportunity.

Within Myanmar, the National League for Democracy (NLD) announced
it would boycott the 2010 elections, and eventually those NLD members
willing to stand for election formed a new party, the National Democratic
Force (NDF).

The multi-party elections in November 2010 fell short of international
standards in terms of free and fair process and were highly criticized by
exiles. However, the release of Daw Aung San Suu Kyi a week later and the
inauguration of the new administration in March 2011 triggered a flurry of
visits by high-profile foreigners. The influx of international journalists as
well as other new international players, and, later, the relaxing of media
censorship, all offered opportunities for activists to regroup. President
Thein Sein announced a programme of reform in his inaugural address
on 30 March 2011, but for many exiles the reforms only gained credibility
with the by-elections that were held in April the following year.

Could Exiles Return Without Legal Guarantees or Binding Policies?

In August 2011 at an economic forum, and again in May 2012, President Thein Sein publicly invited exiles who had not committed "serious crimes" to return to the country. Inviting regime critics back could have been motivated by the desire to mitigate further criticism while also using the well-educated members of the Burmese diaspora as an asset in dealing with the challenges that would come with moves to transform Myanmar. In any case, no further explanations, formal procedures, or laws were issued and it was left to individual exiles and Myanmar embassies in the respective countries to proceed. Moreover, instead of introducing a nation-wide policy applicable to all exiles wishing to return, the central government delegated responsibility for returnees to the new regional governments, which were to decide on a case-by-case basis (Mizzima 2011).

A few prominent exiles visited during 2011—for instance, members of the Chiangmai-based Vahu Development Institute group and Shan exile Harn Yawnghwe—but without making permanent arrangements or bringing their families along (Sai Zom Hseng 2011; Murayama 2011). The arrest in August 2012 of a returning lawyer who had defended NLD members in 2007 was taken by the diaspora as an indication that security for returnee exiles was not guaranteed (Zarni Mann 2012).

In September 2012 the president's office published online a list of some two thousand Burmese and foreign activists, journalists, scholars, diplomats, UN staff, and others whose names were to be removed from the immigration blacklist.[20] However, over four thousand names remained on the blacklist, which also included Burmese who are prevented from leaving the country. The government imposed a one-year travel ban on former political prisoners before it would issue them with passports (Weng 2012). In addition, some returning exiles had to sign a five-point statement to give assurance that they would refrain from political activities (Sai Zom Hseng 2011).

In general, the lack of systematic, transparent policies applied to exiles and in-country activists alike.[21] The 88 Generation Students group, for instance, was not registered as a group at all, and therefore needed the assistance of registered local NGOs to hold training programs funded by third parties.[22] The best-known student organization, the ABFSU, did not even maintain membership lists or cards, since university rules stipulate that students must not be part of any organization. The ABFSU complained about being watched by the authorities, and campaigned to be given legal status and for the passing of a new university law to replace the law of 1917.[23] In 2012, NGOs were still required to register under the 1988 *Law relating to Forming of Organizations*, which meant fees and lengthy registration processes at several administrative levels for all local and international organizations.

In the meantime, President Thein Sein's verbal invitations did not translate into legal assurances, and the absence of an official amnesty discouraged the majority of exiles from returning home permanently. In the enduring legal limbo, members of the Asia-based diaspora found it unproblematic to commute to Myanmar, whereas many members of the diaspora in Western countries resolved to undertake fewer visits and otherwise engage in long-distance politics towards their homeland. However, all encountered similar obstacles in considering whether or not to settle back home after decades abroad, including the risk of giving up secure careers, incomes, and homes that could not be matched by opportunities, least of all salaries, in Myanmar. Families also considered the dearth of international schools for their children, who had never attended classes given in the Burmese language.[24]

THE ROLE OF EXILED ACTIVISTS IN THE POLITICAL TRANSFORMATION

Exiles acted as crucial intermediaries for relaying political messages from imprisoned leaders to the exiled movement and the outside world, and vice versa, and acted as brokers between foreign donors and in-country activists. Interlocutors became important channels through which transnational and international players learned about the opposition movement inside the country. In the process, power inequalities between Burmese exiles on the one hand and their donors, coalition and network partners within transnational advocacy networks in the global North on the other, were reproduced in interactions between Burmese exiled and domestic activists. With the opening of political space in Myanmar, including increased freedom for the media and improved access to the government, exiles may only play this role a little longer, until local activists have acquired similar skills and connections and have no further need of their help.

Exiles watched closely the events that unfolded after the 2010 elections, and especially the authorities' treatment of different social movement organizations, political parties, and protesters. They approached the government through local intermediaries, such as the civil society organization Myanmar Egress. U Aung Min and other government representatives went to Chiangmai to meet with exiles. U Tin Maung Than from the exile Vahu Development Institute based in Chiangmai was among the first to return. He faced strong criticism in 2011 from exile groups that opposed engagement with the government's reform agenda, but others such as U Zaw Oo, also from Vahu, soon followed his example.[25] One of the president's advisors, economist Dr U Myint, proposed the establishment of an "independent, non-political, and legal institute of excellence … the Myanmar Development Resource Institute (MDRI)" (U Myint 2011). Several Vahu members and prominent exile leaders soon joined MDRI.

Following the NLD's strong showing in the April 2012 by-elections and Aung San Suu Kyi's entry into parliament, the number of visiting exiles increased. The leading exile media—*The Irrawaddy, Mizzima News*, and *Democratic Voice of Burma*—started to openly report from the country again. Some activists began to shift some or most activities of their organizations to Myanmar.

Exiles have so far focused on building the capacities of the main political actors in the country—the government and parliament, leaders of political parties, and groups associated with the opposition movement. As a result, well-known dissidents are represented on the MDRI and presidential advisory boards, as well as in special commissions—for instance, to investigate the Buddhist-Muslim communal violence or the security forces' treatment of the protestors at the Letpadaung copper mine. The executive committee members of the government-founded Myanmar Peace Centre, which oversees peace negotiations with the ethnic armies, includes a returned political exile and a scholar from the diaspora. Another scholar from the diaspora and contributor to this book, U Winston Set Aung, became Deputy Minister for National Planning and Economic Development.

Exiles from ethnic minorities, by contrast, focus on building the capacities of their respective communities but are less involved with government initiatives at the centre.

The area of human rights offers another focus for exile expertise. Due to the extreme sensitivity surrounding this subject, in the past very few organizations inside Myanmar were able to operate openly on human rights issues. Exile organizations based in Thailand and India are widening the scope of their existing capacity-building initiatives for the documentation of local human rights issues and improving the knowledge and skills of those who defend human rights, while also expanding their (underground and above-ground) networks across the country.

For political exiles who needed to continue voicing dissent in order to maintain their identity over a period of twenty years, recent pragmatic cooperation with what is a new but also a partially-old leadership in Myanmar must feel like a major compromise (Ma 1993, p. 383).

Differing Attitudes of In-Country and Exile Activists

Many activists in Myanmar are acutely aware of their lack of formal education, theoretical knowledge, international exposure, and organizational capacity that has been the result of decades of censorship, the undermining of the education system, and in recent times a lack of Internet access. They also lament the fact that no one in the country has ever experienced the democratic freedoms and practices that are envisioned for Myanmar's future (Hkun Htun Oo 2012). Representatives of youth organizations have, therefore, stressed that the primary contribution of returning exiles should consist of bringing know-how, international experience, and organizational skills for the development of the country.

Another important area of exile experience has been interaction with people from minority ethnic groups, and hence they have an understanding of ethnic relations that differs from that of people within Myanmar. In exile, Burmans were in regular contact with ethnic movement organizations as well as with the armed groups. Not least, key organizations such as the NCGUB, Democratic Alliance of Burma, and the National Coalition of the Union of Burma (NCUB) were founded in Manerplaw, the former Karen National Union headquarters, at the inception of the pro-democracy movement between 1988 and 1990. During the exodus into territories controlled by the respective rebel armies, minority groups provided vital help for the activists' survival in the jungle and eventual crossing to neighbouring countries. Although Burman-ethnic relations were far from smooth, identifying common goals, as well as exposure to international perspectives on ethnic rights, increased mutual acceptance.

Beyond politics, many activists living in Myanmar believe diverse fields could benefit from the valuable expertise and skills of foreign-educated Burmese returnees, whereas a minority seems to think that returnees would be too out of touch to make valuable contributions to the country's development. To the external observer, it seems obvious that exile media organizations could become catalysts for media development, through training young journalists, setting standards for journalistic ethics, connecting local and international media, and otherwise contributing to putting Myanmar indigenous media outlets on the global news network map. While the government appears to encourage returning exile media organizations, these organizations still need to struggle with cronies who own some of the private media, as well as with local journalists who oppose this new competition.[26]

In-country activist leaders are proud of the sacrifices they made over many years to maintain, at great personal risk, underground networks across the country and contacts with the people at the grassroots level. A common criticism voiced by youth activists among the 1988 exiles is that they remain close to their peers from the 88 Generation Students group and to political prisoners but are not close to ordinary people in the Myanmar population; accordingly, exiles work mostly with the political leaders and stakeholders but hardly at all with the broader civil society that does not focus on strictly political issues.[27] There is a perception that exiles fail to approach and to understand the general population's needs and aspirations.[28] Yet, considering the circumstances of their previous transnational or in-country clandestine work, it is no surprise that exiles have had limited exposure at best to people at the grassroots level. However, such criticism contradicts the claims of exile organizations such as the ABSDF, DPNS, and FTUB to have worked extensively at the grassroots during the years of dictatorship (Duell 2011). Whatever the case, as 88 Generation Students group leader Ko Ko Gyi has pointed out, returning exiles need to intensify their approach to the grassroots in order to work efficiently with the population and use funds wisely.[29]

Incongruent expectations pose another point of contention between activists living in Myanmar and exiles. Local activists are well aware that decades of pent-up frustration and grievances fuel the extremely high expectations of ordinary people to see immediate improvements in matters of daily survival such as food, housing, electricity, transport, land issues, and other matters. Exiles seem to hold equally unrealistic expectations, but in terms of fundamental institutional changes rather than in relation to daily hardships. With education and experience often acquired in established democracies and industrialized countries, exiles tend to measure Myanmar against the political freedoms of their host countries.[30] On the one hand, such comparisons imply how removed from current local conditions some exiles may have become. On the other hand, the vision of a fully-fledged federal democracy will drive the country's reform ahead and prevent it from stagnating at an early stage.

Resentments that have built up over a twenty-year history of activism continue to affect relations between the in-country and exile opposition movements. Activists in Myanmar have tended to perceive themselves to be the real martyrs and crucial players, while to varying degrees portraying exiles as hypocrites who lead their lives in security and material comfort. Beyond the issue of who shows real dedication to the country's political progress, what lies at the core of the matter is the question of power. In 2007, for instance, some former political prisoners of the 88 Generation Students group stressed their unwillingness to grant political positions to returning exiles in the event of transition.[31] In 2012, in-country activists were still questioning whether returnees are driven by concern for their country or by personal gain. As a member of the Myanmar Youth Union explained, "We need to call the exiles back to see their attitudes—whether they return for their own interests or to really help the country."[32] Others, in contrast, believe the returnees to be very committed to broad-based reform and therefore actively working with many different groups and parties.[33]

There is also conflict over past exile activities—focussing on the exact nature and effectiveness of programmes and the use of funds.[34] Exiles account for any lack of transparency in the use of aid money as being due to the clandestine nature of their previous work. Despite this, it appears that some activists inside Myanmar continue to doubt the exiles' honesty. It is ironic that the competition for funding that exacerbated some of the internal problems of the exiled opposition movement now causes friction between exiles and activists inside Myanmar.

Changes in Donor Agendas since 2011

The reform process has had substantial ramifications for donors. In the last two years the flow of people, capital, and information into Myanmar has greatly increased. The suspension of most international sanctions has paved the way for formal bilateral and multilateral engagement by foreign governments and other international bodies with the new administration. International non-governmental organizations (some of which have a long history of supporting Burmese refugees, IDPs, and migrant workers in the region as well as a number of political exiles) are increasingly entering Myanmar to carry out their humanitarian programmes. Several trends can be observed.

First, some organizations that traditionally donated to the exile movement have shifted their focus to supporting projects inside Myanmar, projects that are run by newly-established organizations or returning exiles. Even regime critic George Soros visited Myanmar in January 2012, underscoring how circumstances and priorities have changed.

Second, a different set of donors—international and multilateral agencies that support political parties, parliaments, and multi-party platforms—are setting up or expanding Myanmar-specific programmes and staff.[35]

Third, funds for exile and cross-border projects are drying up. The major donors to the opposition movement—the Soros Foundation, the National Endowment for Democracy, the International Republican Institute (IRI)— continue to support some initiatives, but grants will be phased out before 2015. Donors may also feel compelled by their respective governments to officially enter Myanmar. Yet this quick shift combined with "donor fatigue" has had detrimental effects on humanitarian assistance to IDPs and refugee communities in border areas and neighbouring countries.

As a result of these changes, exile organizations will need to re-invent themselves in order to stay relevant. The political opening-up of Myanmar undermines arguments to "stay behind" in exile. The government in exile, the NCGUB, was dissolved in September 2012 after twenty-one years. With Aung San Suu Kyi in parliament and progress being made in other areas, the NCGUB had lost its *raison d'être*, in addition to which the group's budget was reduced to a quarter of what it was five years ago (interview with Dr Sein Win, 2012).

At the same time, human rights groups working in exile continue to publicize repression by the government, restriction of freedoms, and Myanmar's many unchanged problems. Perhaps the last role for exile organizations would be, over the next few years, to keep a check on whether progress is being made towards true democratization, rule of law, and respect for human rights.

Myanmar's lack of development, its desperate need for humanitarian aid, and the changes in its political system have together engendered a "gold rush" of investors as well as donors of political, humanitarian, and technical assistance. International firms have been seeking skilled members of the Burmese diaspora in Asia to staff their new offices in Yangon. As a result, non-political members of the diaspora have met with a comparatively better situation for return than members who had been politically active.

For their part, what activists have mainly requested from international organizations and donors has been training and capacity-building. These requests have brought a flood of training programmes, offered by a multitude of international and exile organizations, which has resulted in some duplication of effort and lack of transparency. Attempts to increase transparency and minimize such duplication have led to the establishment of various informal donor working groups, none of which seems to be particularly influential. While several donor forums that focus on political education alone have emerged, plans to share information on programmes, strategies, and recipients of funds have not been realized, and links to local NGO forums such as the Local Resource Centre or Paung Ku remain limited at best.

Furthermore, power asymmetries between donors and recipients, between exiles and insiders, and between local well-established and newcomer organizations, have created a difficult web of relationships and dependencies. In addition, the sudden availability of resources as well as more political space has also motivated Burmese groups to do more projects and work more openly, especially since everyone is preparing for the next general election in 2015. Genuine efforts notwithstanding, some organizations also appear to have been set up hastily in order to siphon off some funds without actually offering useful programmes.

CONCLUSION

While the tangible results of exile transnational activism are not highly visible, a path for exiles to contribute to the current reforms can be discerned. The politically-active members of the diaspora can be credited with having influenced international attitudes and responses to their homeland, as well as its domestic politics. Transnational activism influenced world opinion towards according the status of international pariah to Myanmar's military regime, with resulting limitation on international investment, economic assistance, and diplomatic standing. The latter certainly counted among the multiple factors that induced top-down political reform.

As for the present situation, local activists express clear expectations about the roles that returning exile activists will be able to play in the transition to democracy, and about the potential role of the broader diaspora in Myanmar's overall development. Exiles in turn demonstrate commitment to positive change and are making their skills and experience available to their respective peers as well as to the president and other state actors. The extent to which returning exiles have political ambitions remains unclear, but more than one former exile has openly declared an intention to run for election in 2015.[36] It is likely that such ambitions will fuel competition over power among a greatly increased spectrum of stakeholders in Myanmar politics that now includes the government, the national and regional parliaments, opposition parties, ethnic leaders, returned exiles and other members of the diaspora, and international players. Many of these have already started to position themselves strategically for the 2015 general elections and various post-election scenarios.

How things will balance out for former exiles will hinge in part on the will of local activists to integrate them into existing organizations, and in part on the government's willingness to embrace its former critics with a full amnesty.

A pivotal external factor affecting local politics will be the agendas of international donors, changes in which may cause shifts in programme priorities; and funding flows from donors may engender competition instead of cooperation, increasing the proverbial tendency among Burmese activists to establish ever more organizations.[37]

So far it seems that the transfer of know-how is perceived as a one-sided process from "outside" to "inside", but missing in this perception are the issues about which the returning members of the diaspora could learn from peers in the country. Returning exiles will only be able to engage in a sustained and effective way with Myanmar's political process if they are able to cooperate closely with local activists and people at the grassroots level. It is not surprising that conflicts exist among dissident groups in a movement that was split between home and exile over twenty years ago. Now, however, these different realities and experiences need to be forged into one combined effort directed towards a transformation in Myanmar that will prevent a return of dictatorship.

Notes

1   Although some flagship SMOs such as the Burma Campaign UK, Free Burma
    Coalition US, and its splinter group US Campaign for Burma, operated
    from Europe, the United States, Canada, and Australia, core SMOs had their
    headquarters in Thailand, with branches in India. Information exchange,
    cross-border and grassroots work was carried out there and information about
    activities was distributed within the transnational network (Duell 2011).

2   The 88 Generation Students group continues to be referred to as "students",
    since shared experiences of the 1988 uprisings and opposition to military
    dictatorship defined activist identity in exile even more than in Myanmar. Yet
    decades in exile have altered the notions of "exile" and "home", especially for
    younger generations born in exile.

3   Young activists formed "Generation Wave" after the "Saffron Revolution"
    because they felt that nothing had been achieved. Between 2008 and 2010,
    Generation Wave activists provided training for Burmese youth aged 17-35
    from a safe house in Mae Sot at the Thai border (Interview with Generation
    Wave, Yangon 2012).

4   These objectives were stated prior to 2010 in various wordings by the National
    Coalition Government of the Union of Burma (NCGUB), National Coalition of
    the Union of Burma (NCUB), Ethnic Nationalities Council (ENC), Federation
    of Trade Unions-Burma (FTUB), All Burma Federation of Student Unions
    (ABSDF), and others.

5   Interviews with the Chin National Front (CNF) 2007, at Mizoram; with Mahn
    Sha of KNU, 2007, at Mae Sot; and with Sao Seng Suk of the Shan State Army
    (SSA) 2007, Chiangmai.

6   According to an interview with Burmese journalists and activists, Aung
    San, the leader of the anti-colonial student movement and the independence
    movement—and the founding father of both the nation and the military—
    continues to serve as a role model for young activists today, as he did in 1988
    for the All Burma Students' Democratic Front. Aung San was never imprisoned,
    but went underground and ultimately travelled to Japan to receive support
    and military training. In 1988 when fleeing students arrived at the borders of
    Burma, they expected to get military training from the ethnic armies in border
    areas, as well as from neighbouring India and Thailand. Of similar significance
    for historical reasons is the fact that, since the time of the anti-colonial *Dobama
    Asiayone* movement (founded in 1930), Burmese activists have employed a
    two-pronged strategy of underground activism and above-ground political
    party work, and this was also the strategy adopted in 1988 by the All Burma
    Federation of Student Unions and the Democratic Party for a New Society
    respectively. Exile activism and in-country underground activism cannot be

treated as completely separate matters, since exiles frequently entered the country using the underground networks of the student movement.

7   Key donors included the International Republican Institute, National Democratic Institute, Albert Einstein Institution, Rockefeller Foundation, American Jewish World Service, Danish Burma Committee, Danish Church Aid, Norwegian Burma Committee, Norwegian Church Aid, Norwegian Peoples Aid, Oxfam-Novib, Swedish Burma Committee, Olaf Palme International Centre, International Institute for Democracy and Electoral Assistance (IDEA) (Sweden), Trocaire (the Catholic Church of Ireland's official overseas development agency), Prospect Burma (UK), Canadian Friends of Burma, Canadian Lutheran World Relief, Rights and Democracy (Canada), Inter Pares (Canada), and some of the German political foundations. In addition, a number of medium-sized Christian donor organizations focussed on the Christian minorities.

8   Conversations during the BDF, 2007.

9   Email correspondence with exiled Burman leaders, August 2007.

10 Min Ko Naing, for instance, was imprisoned from March 1989 to November 2004, September 2006 to January 2007, and August 2007 to January 2012 (88 Generation Students 2008).

11 Interview with former 1988 student activist, Yangon, February 2013.

12 Interviews with various youth activists, Yangon, October 2013.

13 Interview with ABFSU, Yangon, October 2012.

14 Interview with ABFSU, Yangon, October 2012.

15 Hundreds of thousands of monks, nuns, and citizens staged at least 227 distinct protests in 66 towns across all states and divisions (Human Rights Documentation Unit, NCGUB 2008, p. 9).

16 Interviews with several activists, Yangon, April 2012–April 2013.

17 Most interviewees stressed this point. See also, South and others 2011, pp. 31–33.

18 None of the interviewed Burmese seems to believe the official figures, which were far below 100.

19 See list of activities at: Mizzima Election 2010: Exile Anti-Election Campaigns. <http://archive-2.mizzima.com/towards-elections/opposition-a-ethnic-election-stance/exile-anti-election-campaigns.html>. Accessed 16 January 2014.

20 The blacklist included prominent dissidents such as Dr Sein Win, president of the government in exile; Aung Din, US Campaign for Burma; Zipporah Sein, secretary of the Karen National Union; Moe Thee Zun and Dr Naing Aung, former leaders of the ABSDF; Aung Moe Zaw of the Democratic Party for a New Society; Maung Maung, of the FTUB; Khin Ohmar, from the Network for Democracy and Development; Naw Lay Dee, of the Burmese Women's Union; Dr Cynthia Maung, director of the Mae Tao Clinic in Thailand; Bo Kyi, Tate Naing, and other members of the Assistance Association for Political Prisoners;

Aung Htoo, from the Burma Lawyers Council; as well as the two sons of Aung San Suu Kyi, well-known authors Bertil Lintner, and John Pilger, and some diplomats (Nyein Nyein 2012).

21 Numerous laws needed to be passed or amended at this point to transform state and society. Nonetheless, the Thein Sein administration gave priority to, for example, passing the *Foreign Investment Law*, while leaving seemingly more pressing political issues unlegislated.

22 Interview with Ko Ko Gyi, Yangon, October 2012.

23 Interview with ABFSU, Yangon, December 2012.

24 Interview with returned exile, Yangon, October 2012.

25 Interview with activist, Yangon, October 2012.

26 Interview with former 1988 activists, Yangon, February 2013.

27 Interview with youth activists, Yangon, October 2013.

28 Interview with youth activists, Yangon, October 2012.

29 Interview with Ko Ko Gyi, Yangon, January 2013.

30 Interview with peace movement organizer, Yangon, December 2012.

31 Interviews with former political prisoners, Yangon, March 2007.

32 Interview with Myanmar Youth Union, Yangon, December 2012.

33 Interview with Generation Wave, Yangon, December 2012.

34 Interview with NLD Youth, Yangon, December 2012.

35 The organizations include IDEA, International Foundation for Electoral Systems, Inter-Parliamentary Union, Danish Institute for Parties and Democracy, Netherlands Institute for Multiparty Democracy, Commonwealth Local Government Forum, Canadian Parliamentary Centre, National Democratic Institute, Konrad Adenauer Foundation, Friederich Ebert Foundation, Friedrich Naumann Foundation, Asia Foundation, and the Burma Centre Netherland/Transnational Institute.

36 Interview with activist, Yangon, January 2013.

37 Many exiles have said in interviews over the years that where there are two Burmese, there will be three organizations.

References

88 Generation Students. *The Findings in the Open Heart Letter Campaign in January 2007*. Washington: The Burma Fund, 2008. <http://www.burmalibrary.org/docs6/OpenHeart-Publication.pdf>. Accessed 19 January 2014.

Anderson, Benedict. *Imagined Communities*. London, New York: Verso, 2001.

Aung Naing Oo. "Spitting Images". *Irrawaddy* 10, no. 5, June 2002. <http://www2.irrawaddy.org/article.php?art_id=2670>. Accessed 19 January 2014.

Bob, Clifford. *The Marketing of Rebellion: Insurgents, Media, and International Activism*. New York: Cambridge University Press, 2005.

Brooten, Lisa. "The Feminization of Democracy Under Siege: The Media, 'the Lady' of Burma, and U.S. Foreign Policy". *National Women's Studies Association Journal* 17, no. 3 (2005): 134–56.

Buncombe, Andrew. "Burma's exiles can return—if they promise to be good". *Independent* (UK), 19 October 2012. <http://www.independent.co.uk/news/world/asia/burmas-exiles-can-return--if-they-promise-to-be-good-8217108.html>. Accessed 6 November 2013.

Della Porta, Donatella and Sidney Tarrow. "Transnational Processes and Social Activism: An Introduction". In *Transnational Protest and Global Activism*, edited by Della Porta and Tarrow. Lanham, MD: Rowman and Littlefield, 2005.

Dictatorwatch. "A Fractured Movement?". Dictatorwatch, 8 August 2006. <http://www.dictatorwatch.org/prbdmfracture.html>. Accessed 6 November 2013.

Dudley, Sandra. *'External' Aspects of Self-Determination Movements in Burma.* QEH Working Paper Series 94. Oxford: Oxford Department of International Development, 2003. <http://www3.qeh.ox.ac.uk/pdf/qehwp/qehwps94.pdf>. Accessed 6 November 2013.

Duell, Kerstin. "Transnational Activism and the Burmese Pro-Democracy Movement in India and Thailand". PhD Dissertation, Department of Political Science, National University of Singapore, 2011.

Egreteau, Renaud. "Burma in Diaspora: A Preliminary Research Note on the Politics of Burmese Diasporic Communities in Asia". *Journal of Current Southeast Asian Affairs* 31, no. 2 (2012): 115–47.

Goldstone, Jack A. and Charles Tilly. "Threat (and Opportunity): Popular Action and State Response in the Dynamics of Contentious Action". In *Silence and Voice in the Study of Contentious Politics*, edited by Ronald R. Aminzade and others. Cambridge: Cambridge University Press, 2001.

Hkun Htun Oo. "A Union For All of Us". *Journal of Democracy* 23, no. 4 (2012): 132–34.

Htet Aung Kyaw. "What's Changed in Burma in the Past 20 Years?". *Democratic Voice of Burma*, 17 September 2008. <http://www.dvb.no/uncategorized/whats-changed-in-burma-in-the-past-20-years/1884>. Accessed 19 January 2014.

Human Rights Documentation Unit (HRDU), National Coalition Government of the Union of Burma (NCGUB). *Bullets in the Alms Bowl: An Analysis of the Brutal SPDC Suppression of the September 2007 Saffron Revolution.* Bangkok: Human Rights Documentation Unit, NCGUB, March 2008. <http://www.burmacampaign.org.uk/images/uploads/BulletsInTheAlmsBowl.pdf>. Accessed 6 November 2013.

Jagan, Larry. "Saffron Revolution Renewed". *Bangkok Post*, 29 April 2008.

Keck, Margaret and Kathryn Sikkink. *Activists Beyond Borders: Advocacy Networks in International Politics.* Ithaca: Cornell University Press, 1997.

Klotz, Audie. *Norms in International Relations: The Struggle Against Apartheid.* Ithaca and London: Cornell University Press, 1995.

Kyaw Yin Hlaing. "Understanding Recent Political Changes in Myanmar". *Contemporary Southeast Asia* 34, no. 2 (2012): 197–216.

———. "Challenging the Authoritarian State: Buddhist Monks and Peaceful Protests in Burma". *Fletcher Forum of World Affairs* 32, no. 1 (2008): 125–44.

———. *The State of the Pro-Democracy Movement in Authoritarian Burma*. Washington: East West Center, 2007.

Lintner, Bertil. "Burma's Warrior Kings and the Generation of 8.8.88". *Global Asia* 2, no. 2 (2007): 70–79.

Ma, Shu-Yun. "The Exit, Voice, and Struggle To Return of Chinese Political Exiles". *Pacific Affairs* 66, no. 3 (1993): 368–85.

McCarthy, John. "The Globalization of Social Movement Theory". In *Transnational Social Movements and Global Politics: Solidarity Beyond the State*, edited by J. Smith, C. Chatfield and R. Pagnucco. Syracuse, NY: Syracuse University Press, 1997.

Min Zin. "Can the Opposition Remain Relevant?". *Irrawaddy*, August 2010. <http://www2.irrawaddy.org/article.php?art_id=19195>. Accessed 10 November 2013.

Mizzima News. "Views on Burmese president's call for citizens abroad to come home". *Mizzima News*, 17 August 2011. <http://burmanationalnews.org/burma/index.php?option=com_content&view=article&id=575&Itemid=1>. Accessed 10 November 2013.

Murayama, Yusuke. "As restrictions ease, activists return to Myanmar". *Asahi Shimbun*, 8 December 2011.

Nyein Nyein. "Burma Releases Names of Those Removed from Blacklist". *Irrawaddy*, 30 August 2012. <http://www.irrawaddy.org/burma/burma-releases-names-of-those-removed-from-blacklist.html>. Accessed 10 November 2013.

Sai Zom Hseng. "Invitation to Return Falls Flat Among Exiles". *Irrawaddy*, 28 October 2011. <http://www2.irrawaddy.org/article.php?art_id=22346>. Accessed 16 January 2014.

Selth, Andrew. "Burma's 'Saffron Revolution' and the Limits of International Influence". *Australian Journal of International Affairs* 62, no. 3 (2008): 281–97.

Shain, Yossi. *The Frontier of Loyalty: Political Exiles in the Age of the Nation-State*. Middletown, Conn.: Wesleyan University Press, 1989.

Soekefield, Martin. "Mobilizing in Transnational Space: A Social Movement Approach to the Formation of Diaspora". *Global Networks* 6, no. 3 (2006): 265–84.

South, Ashley, Susanne Kempel, Malin Perhult and Nils Carstensen. *Myanmar — Surviving the Storm: Self-protection and survival in the Delta*. Local to Global Protection. Denmark: October 2011. <http://www.local2global.info/area-studies/burmamyanmar-delta-nargis-area-study>. Accessed 10 November 2013.

Steinberg, David. I. *Burma/Myanmar: What Everyone Needs to Know*. New York: Oxford University Press, 2009.

Tabori, Paul. *The Anatomy of Exile*. London: Harrap, 1972.

Tarrow, Sidney. "Rooted Cosmopolitans and Transnational Activists". Prepared for a special issue of *Rassegna Italiana di Sociologia*, 2004. <http://government. arts.cornell.edu/assets/faculty/docs/tarrow/rooted_cosmopolitans.pdf>. Accessed 6 November 2013.

———. *Power in Movement*. 2nd ed. New York: Cambridge University Press, 1998.

U Myint. *Reducing Poverty in Myanmar: The Way Forward.* Theme Paper presented to the National Workshop on Rural Development and Poverty Alleviation in Myanmar, Myanmar International Convention Center, Naypyitaw, 20–22 May 2011. <http://www.encburma.net/index.php/archives/burma-government/566-dr-u-myint-reducing-poverty-in-myanmar-the-way-forward. html>. Accessed 6 November 2013.

Weng, Lawi. "Govt Removes Names from Blacklist, But Thousands Remain". *Irrawaddy*, 28 August 2012. <http://www.irrawaddy.org/z_political-prisoners/ govt-removes-names-from-blacklist-but-thousands-remain.html>. Accessed 6 November 2013.

Zarni Mann. "Homecoming NLD Lawyer Jailed for Six Months". *Irrawaddy*, 30 August 2012. <http://www.irrawaddy.org/nld/homecoming-nld-lawyer-jailed-for-six-months.html>. Accessed 6 November 2013.

Zaw Oo. "Exit, Voice and Loyalty in Burma: The Role of Overseas Burmese in Democratising Their Homeland". In *Myanmar: State, Society, and Ethnicity*, edited by N. Ganesan and Kyaw Yin Hlaing. Singapore: Institute of Southeast Asian Studies; Hiroshima, Japan: Hiroshima Peace Institute, 2007, pp. 231–59.

8

UNDERSTANDING RECENT LABOUR PROTESTS IN MYANMAR

Kyaw Soe Lwin

When the subject of workers and the labour movement in Myanmar is discussed, it has been widely assumed that the labour movement became (and remained) very weak after the 1962 military putsch. Before that, under the leadership of political parties during the parliamentary period from January 1948 to March 1962, the labour movement had been very active and quite militant, and workers were incorporated into party politics by politicians. When the military took political power in 1962, all independent workers' movements were curtailed. Instead, the state incorporated workers into the party-state structure, under an institution called the People's Workers' Council (later known as the Workers' Association), and limited their political freedom.

After the military putsch in 1988, in contrast, the State Law and Order Restoration Council (SLORC) and the State Peace and Development Council (SPDC) governments excluded the labour movement from political participation and collective bargaining, and subjected it to repressive measures. Workers held very few strikes in industrial factories but were unprotected and suffered retaliation by the SLORC/SPDC government.

This scenario changed suddenly when, in March 2011, the SLORC/SPDC government handed over political power to a new military-dominated civilian government under President Thein Sein. Upon taking office in March 2011, the president initiated a series of reforms that widened the current political space and allowed many people to enjoy a degree of political freedom that the country had not seen since 1962. In doing so, the Thein Sein government surprised many people both inside and outside the country.

The reform process seemed slow at first, but the pace of reform quickened in 2012. Hundreds of political prisoners were released, in three groups (BBC 2011; Nelson and MacKinnon 2012). Controls on trade unions were relaxed, and censorship of the press was formally abolished in August 2012 (Nelson 2012). Moreover, the parliaments passed a number of new laws, including a law under which peaceful public protests and demonstrations were to be allowed (Win Ko Ko Latt and Ei Ei Toe Lwin 2012).

(Some commentators interpret these reforms as an attempt on the part of the former military generals to avoid huge public protests, like the "Arab spring", in Myanmar. Whatever the reasons behind the changes, it has to be agreed that since 2011 the Myanmar government has undertaken many positive reforms.)

With these reforms, Myanmar's political space was widened and people started taking advantage of the liberalized political environment. Political and labour activists who had been released from prison, including some prominent activists from the time of the 1988 uprising, made the most of the political opportunities arising from the reforms and began immediately to engage again in their former activities. Several prominent labour activists, such as Ko Phoe Phyu and Su Su Nway, started organizing workers from labour-intensive factories in industrial zones in Yangon.[1]

In the period from May to July 2012 a number of spontaneous strikes were held at several factories in industrial zones, more or less simultaneously. It was reported that between 1 May to 30 June more than fifty thousand workers participated in labour protests (MLESS 2012a). A few strikes became violent. Many of striking workers were females working in labour-intensive industries such as garment factories, seafood-processing factories, and shoe manufacturing factories.

Grievances over low pay and poor working conditions played a significant role in the emergence of these labour protests in 2012, yet grievances alone cannot explain the sudden appearance of these strikes or explain why some of them became violent. Why did so many industrial workers from just a few industrial zones in Myanmar suddenly go on strike to demand better wages and better working conditions, whereas the larger part of Myanmar's workforce remained less demanding and more acquiescent in relation to their fundamental rights?

This is the question the author tries to answer in this chapter. The chapter will examine how Myanmar workers attempted to challenge their employers and the state, and how other actors on the scene—politicians, as well as labour and political activists—engaged with these events. Two labour protests that turned violent will be examined as case studies. This chapter argues that a number of factors contributed—the relatively tolerant political climate, the concentration of workers in factories, mobilizing by political and labour activists, and grievances about low pay and appalling working conditions.

LABOUR CONDITIONS IN THE POST-1988 PERIOD

During the period of the SLORC/SPDC government, which followed the military coup of 1988, conditions for workers deteriorated dramatically. Workers were excluded from political participation and collective bargaining, and any attempt by labour activists to organize or mobilize workers was severely suppressed by the Myanmar army. Many labour activists served long prison sentences (ILO 2008, pp. 255–57). Although the use of forced labour had existed in Myanmar since the colonial period, it became more widespread and more serious under the SLORC/SPDC government. As far back as 1996 the International Labour Organization (ILO) began negotiating with senior army leaders in order to end the practice of forced labour (ILO 1998, p. 1).

In overall terms, the situation of many workers declined significantly. For dealing with labour administration and labour policy, the SLORC/SPDC government still used the socialist-era labour laws, but many workers were denied the protection of the basic rights provided by the socialist labour legislation.

This was primarily because mutually beneficial relationships between businessmen and senior army leaders were developed, and businessmen received patronage and protection from the state in exchange for bribes.

Corruption became an incurable problem under the SLORC/SPDC government (Kyaw Yin Hlaing 2001, pp. 279–307, 267–70). In the early 1990s, Myanmar's leaders attempted to promote the national economy by adopting market economic policies. Features of the hoped-for market economy did not develop fully, but, due to mismanagement by senior army leaders, turned into what has been called "crony capitalism" (Taylor 2009, p.455).

Like other government officials, many labour officials had good relations with numerous business people. In one interview with the author, a former businessman who manufactured industrial materials for construction spoke about the corrupt labour officials he had met. He said that handling labour inspectors under the military regime was much easier than he had experienced in the socialist period.[2] With the protection of the state, many employers broke the rules. For instance, it was discovered that employers in factories had recruited young workers whose ages were between 13 years and 15 years, which was not in accordance with the existing rules (Soe Yarzar Htun 2012, p. 13).

In many labour-intensive factories, many workers were paid low wages. For example, in the New Way shoe manufacturing factory the basic pay was 14,500 *kyats*, and allowances for various purposes were added to this basic pay. In addition to basic pay, a worker in the factory would receive additional allowances under the following headings: 1,800 *kyats* for *skill*, 1,700 *kyats* for *position*, 8,500 *kyats* for *non-absence*, 1,500 *kyats* for *service*, 4,000 *kyats* for *meal allowance*, 7,000 *kyats* for *extras*, 7,000 *kyats* for *cost of living allowance*, 4,000 *kyats* for *Sunday attendance*. Deductions were made from a worker's monthly wage when the worker did not fulfil the requirements for some allowances. For instance, if the worker was absent for one or more days from work, he or she would not get the *attendance allowance*; if the worker did not work on Sunday, he or she would not receive Sunday allowance. Therefore, in order to avoid deductions, a worker was required to work every day in the whole month.[3] Several garment workers told of similar situations.

The salary slip of one female garment worker showed that she received 9,800 *kyats* as basic pay, which was calculated for 28 days at the rate of 350 *kyats* per day. In addition, she received additional allowances under different headings: 10,800 *kyats* for *overtime*, 4,000 *kyats* for *non-absence*, 22,000 *kyats* for *dutiful bonus*, 2,700 *kyats* for *travel allowance and pocket money*, and 5,000 *kyats* for *cost of living allowance*. She received a total of

53, 835 *kyats* after a deduction of 465 *kyats* for her social security scheme. There is no doubt that larger deductions could be made from her salary if she chose not to do overtime work.

In some factories, employers raised basic wages while reducing allowances for other purposes.[4] From the figures seen above, it is quite apparent that many workers in labour-intensive factories did overtime work in order to survive. Ko Ko Gyi, a member of the 88 Generation Students group, spoke to the audience at the labour conference held on 3 June 2012, and said that even he could not understand how much a worker received when he saw payment slips like these (Ko Ko Gyi 2012).

At the same conference, one workers' delegate stated:

> A condition has existed between employers and workers: that is to say "workers have been unfairly squeezed". Why I call this condition as "unfairly squeezed" is that I have enough proof. They paid workers at the rate of 50 to 65 *kyats* per hour. If a worker gets 65 *kyats* per hour, how can he eat? If we make a [phone] call, we have to pay 50 *kyats* per minute. If a worker makes a call to his family, it will cost him an hour of his wage. Another thing is that factories pay overtime fees and attendance fees. In addition, they pay production fees, special fees and *Mout-Phoe* (pocket money). These incentives are provided in order to control workers; we have a saying in Burmese, which is "workers are tied with a long rope". This Burmese adage is quite fit for this condition. Why does this condition fit with this adage? A worker cannot skip a day. If he skips any time, the amount equivalent to 10,000 to 20,000 *kyats* will be deducted from his monthly wage. To prevent the deduction, a worker has to attend his work even if he is sick. Therefore, their fundamental rights are infringed. That is why I call this condition "unfairly squeezed" (Kyaw Zin Lin 2012).

Many Myanmar workers do not properly know their statutory rights. When the author interviewed more than one hundred workers from different industries, he discovered that they hardly knew what their rights were. Ko Ko Gyi narrated his experience on this issue:

> Here is a sad situation: in one factory, a group of workers have demanded that their working time be from 7am to 7pm. I felt very sad. They do not understand that the working time should be eight hours only. They made a demand without any knowledge about their fundamental rights (Ko Ko Gyi 2012).

The labour leader from the Tai Yi shoe factory stated that the conditions of workers before 2012 were much worse. She said that the factory did not provide sanitary drinking water; that workers had to work for almost one thousand hours per month free of charge; that when any damage occurred to the final products, deductions were made from their salaries unfairly; and that in spite of the *Social Security Act* (1954), only four hundred workers out of a workforce of two thousand in the factory had been registered for the social security scheme. The labour leader said that the conditions in the factory improved a little after the workers had protested several times.[5]

In many factories, workers' fundamental rights were severely violated. In an interview with a group of workers from Khun Maing block-making factory, they stated that they had not been able to enjoy their existing leave entitlement until after the protest in 2012.[6] An interview with a group of female workers from a seafood-processing factory disclosed the fact that their employer had violated workers' rights through collusion with government officials. For instance, when one female worker from the factory became very sick, she went to see a doctor in a social security office in their township and requested the doctor to endorse a period of sick-leave for her. But the doctor replied to her that even though he wanted to fulfil her request, he could not do it because he had already been phoned by the management of the factory and asked to give her only one day's leave.[7] U Htay, a labour activist and lawyer, explained to the author that even under the new civilian government, many factories in industrial zones in Myanmar did not follow the labour laws and regulations, and many labour officials turned their backs by taking bribes. He further commented, "the conditions of workers in Myanmar are terrible; they are quite similar to the situations of the Industrial Revolution in England".[8]

LABOUR PROTESTS UNDER THE THEIN SEIN GOVERNMENT

On 21 November 2011, the Thein Sein government abolished the 1964 *Law Defining the Fundamental Rights and Responsibilities of the People's Workers* (*NLM* 2011, p. 1). The government had previously, on 11 October 2011, enacted the *Labour Organizing Law* (2011) which repealed the *Trade Union Act (1926)* (MLESS 2012*b*). On 28 March 2012, Parliament passed the *Settlement of Labour Disputes Law (2012)* abolishing the *Trade Disputes Act* of 1929 (MLESS 2012*c*).

Although there had been very few mass strikes in Myanmar since 1974, in May, June, and July 2012 a huge wave of labour strikes erupted in Yangon and several other major cities. Many observers explained the outbreak as a response by workers to the increase of 30,000 *kyats* in monthly salary for all members of the civil services and armed forces that had been ordered by the government on 15 March 2012 (Feng Yingqiu 2012).

It seemed that this news might have enraged many industrial workers who had been getting around 15,000 *kyats* or less per month (excluding overtime fees and other allowances). It is the author's opinion that while the news may have encouraged workers to protest, it was not, in fact, the main reason. Before this announcement there had already been one strike: on 6 February 2012 workers at the Tai Yi shoe factory in Hlaing Tharyar industrial zone outside Yangon staged a strike.[9] Strikes at other factories in several industrial zones, mainly garment factories and shoe factories, followed. Recent government data indicates that a total of 56,551 workers from 90 factories participated in labour protests during the period from 1 May to 30 June (MLESS 2012*a*).

Initially, local authorities mishandled some of the strikes, which pushed the workers to become more violent and passionate. Political activists from the 88 Generation Students group (some of whom had been in prison for many years under the military regime) and other opposition representatives came to assist striking workers in the negotiations with their employers and local officials. Local authorities sided with employers and led many of the negotiations and the conciliation efforts on behalf of employers, a factor that prolonged a number of industrial disputes more than a week, and in some cases, a few months.

In the following sections, two strikes that became violent will be discussed in detail.

The Strike at Tai Yi Shoe factory

On 6 February 2012 workers at Tai Yi shoe factory went on strike for better wages and working conditions.[10] After several attempts, an agreement was reached on 15 February 2012. Although most workers accepted the agreement, a small number, including some leaders of the strike, did not. On 23 February 2012, a total of 687 workers and 78 workers' delegates reached a settlement with the owner, and a contract of agreement was signed. According to the contract of agreement, the employer agreed to pay 48,900 *kyats* per month to each worker, not including overtime pay.

Previously, however, on 17 February 2012, some of the Tai Yi workers had filed a case at the township trade dispute committee. On 1 March 2012, after hearing from both sides, the township trade dispute committee gave its verdict on the disputed terms. As the first issue, the workers demanded that their basic salaries should be 80,000 *kyats* (or 150 *kyats* per hour) plus 8,000 *kyats* per month for non-absence, and that the overtime rate should be the double the basic hourly rate. Second, the workers demanded that the yearly bonus should be one month's salary. Third, the workers claimed that they must be consulted in making decisions on matters such as yearly increment, penalties, and other workplace-related issues. Fourth, the workers claimed wages for strike days. The fifth demand was that an adequate number of toilets be built for female workers.

Regarding the first claim, the court ruled that each worker would receive at least 50,000 *kyats* per month, excluding overtime pay, and that overtime pay would be calculated by the employer in accordance with the rates constituted by the Factories and General Labour Laws Inspection Department. The court overruled the workers' second claim, arguing that the employer had already been paying allowances in different forms. On the third matter, the court decided that the disputing parties must sign a contract of agreement in front of township officials after negotiations were concluded. On the fourth claim, the court directed the employer to make the payments in accordance with the contract of agreement made on 23 February. On the matter of the fifth claim, the court found that the current number of toilets for female workers was not sufficient, and therefore it directed the employer to construct not less than forty-one toilets for the female workers.

The Tai Yi workers were not completely satisfied with the court's decisions, and consequently they filed an appeal with the district trade dispute appeal committee on 14 March 2012.[11] Since the appellate court had not yet issued any judgements, the workers'delegates went to see the president of the court. When the workers' delegates inquired about the delay in the court's decision, the president of the appellate court replied that since a new law for trade dispute settlement was to be passed soon by the parliament, he could not make any decisions right then and would transfer the case to a new arbitration body that would soon be established in accordance with the coming trade disputes settlement law.

Dissatisfied with the president's response, on 30 March 2012 the Tai Yi workers decided to protest against the appellate court's decision and prepared to march to the district trade dispute court. When the workers, who were mostly female, were about to rally, they were blocked violently by riot police, in front of several officials from the township labour department and other departments. During the confrontations between the riot police and the workers, twelve female workers were wounded. Following the violent suppression, on the same day an agreement was finally reached between the workers and the employer. The employer agreed to pay 120 *kyats* per hour as basic wage, with 7,000 *kyats* per month for non-absence, and to provide for four hours of overtime on eighteen days in a month.

After their issues had been addressed, the Tai Yi workers established a labour association. Within a few months, their registration was approved, and the Tai Yi Shoe Workers' Association has become the first lawfully and independently organized labour association in fifty years.

The Strike at Hi-Mo and Hi-Art Wig Manufacturing Factory

There were similar violent incidents at the Hi-Mo and Hi-Art wig manufacturing factory (referred to hereafter as the "Hi-Mo factory"). This case was much tougher for officials to resolve, and it took nearly a month to settle the dispute between the workers from the factory and their employer.

On 9 May 2012,[12] a group of 104 workers from the factory went to the general administration office in Hlaing Tharyar township and submitted a total of seventy-six demands to officials.[13] After lunch, another 204 workers from the same factory went to the Hlaing Tharyar Labour Directorate office and the Mayangone Labour Directorate office and made several demands. At 8:10pm the workers left, after they had been told by officials that their case would be negotiated at 10am on the following day (10 May). On that day, about 1,600 workers gathered outside the Hlaing Tharyar Labour Directorate office, to wait while their leaders negotiated with the employer in the presence of Labour Directorate officers. After intensive discussion, agreement was reached on a total of forty non-monetary demands, and a new level of 30,000 *kyats* as the basic salary, not including overtime pay, was set. Finally, a contract of agreement was signed by both parties.

It was discovered that the factory was owned by a Korean man, and that a Myanmar woman called Daw Nan Thaung Yin had been acting as his representative in regard to the factory ever since the factory was built. When the contract of agreement was made, it was Daw Nan Thaung Yin who agreed on the terms specified in the contract and who signed it on behalf of the Korean owner. However, it turned out that the Korean owner would not accept the agreement that Daw Nan Thaung Yin had signed and would not honour it.

When the workers learnt that the employer would not honour the agreement, they protested again, on 16 May. They were told that since Daw Nan Thaung Yin had been hospitalized, the employer himself would come and negotiate with them. Later, the workers left the factory peacefully, after officials promised that the real employer would come and negotiate with them.

Then it was discovered that Daw Nan Thaung Yin had not been hospitalized but had left town. Since the Korean owner was not officially registered for investing in Myanmar, he could not be held accountable for the contract of agreement signed by Daw Nan Thaung Yin on 10 May.

This discovery infuriated workers, and some began to destroy light bulbs and windows in the factory. On 18 May the mediators, Director-General of the Factories and General Labour Laws Inspection Department U Win Shein and U Aung Thein Lin from the Union Solidarity and Development Party, came to try and settle the bargaining impasse. They failed.

On 21 May, Min Ko Naing of the 88 Generation Students group came with some colleagues and urged the workers not to vandalize the factory. They managed to calm the workers down, and provided them with food and water.

On 22 May, several officers from the Korean embassy came to negotiate with workers, but they also failed.

Another negotiation was attempted on 23 May. It was proposed that each worker would get 10,000 *kyats* per month as basic pay plus 6,000 *kyats* for non-absence, but many workers refused to accept that offer because they wanted a basic pay rate of 30,000 *kyats* per month. When the negotiation failed, the six Korean technicians who had been working in the factory tried to leave, taking some machinery parts. When workers realized the Korean technicians were leaving the factory, they became alarmed and about seven hundred workers blocked the exit, preventing the departure of the Korean engineers.

On 24 May, the workers were persuaded by some activists from the All Burma Federation of Student Unions (ABFSU) to stage a strike in front of the house of Daw Aung San Suu Kyi. When the representatives from the 88 Generation Students group heard about this, they warned the workers not to do any such thing. However, at around nine o'clock that same day, since they were being ignored and their claims were not being heard or addressed by either their employer or the local authorities, the workers' frustration boiled over and a few things inside the factory were destroyed. On 30 May, the factory management decided not to provide any meals or water to the workers, whereupon some activists from the 88 Generation Students group and the ABFSU stepped in and donated food and water to the workers.

The protest dragged on. Since strikes were occurring concurrently in a number of factories, the government could no longer neglect these matters.

On 3 June, officials organized a conference in Yangon of all parties concerned, in an attempt to find solutions for the labour protests. U Hla Maung Shwe, a member of the National Economic and Social Advisory Council and the vice president of Myanmar Egress, told the author that he helped to organize the labour conference on 3 June in order to provide authorities, political and labour activists, employers, and workers with an opportunity to listen to each other's views and to come up with solutions to address the workers' grievances. Many people from government circles, including the Minister of Labour, as well as political and labour activists, workers and journalists, attended the conference, which was held at the Chatrium Hotel.[14]

Following the conference, the impasse in the Hi-Mo factory was finally brought to an end on 5 June 2012; an agreement was reached between the workers and the employer in the presence of Ko Ko Gyi from the 88 Generation Students group, the Deputy Minister of Labour, and other township officials.[15]

Despite the agreement, another fight broke out between workers and the employer in the same factory on 8 June 2012. Normally, the workers in Hi-Mo factory worked overtime up to 9pm, but on the day in question, the employer asked all workers to go home around 7pm, but without arranging any transportation for them. The workers were furious, and locked themselves inside the factory, preventing their employer from leaving. When the employer tried to get the keys from the workers, struggles and fights ensued, and sixteen female workers were hurt. Both sides reported the incident to the Hlaing Tharyar police station.

After this incident, the situation returned to normal, without any further problems.[16]

The Responses of the Thein Sein Government

Before the 3 June conference, the government had taken for granted that the strikes had been largely instigated by opposition activists and representatives of some political parties. In a report submitted to the president by the Ministry of Labour, four groups of people were accused of having encouraged workers to keep the strikes going (MLESS 2012d, p. 2). The groups named were:

- members of the National League for Democracy;
- political activists from the 88 Generation Students group;
- U Htay, a lawyer-cum-activist, and his son from the All Burma Federation of Student Unions;
- Thurain Aung, Kyaw Kyaw, and Saw Kyaw Min from the Federation of Trade Unions-Burma (FTUB).

The report argued that the NLD and the 88 Generation Students group encouraged workers to keep their protests going until their employers agreed to recognize 30,000 *kyats* as the monthly basic wage. Later, the report continued, the NLD ceased its involvement in the strikes after a few attempts to help with negotiations. In addition, the report claimed that the actions of U Htay and his son were leading workers along a destructive path. The report alleged that the FTUB had been attempting to prolong strikes, thereby derailing the government's management. In addition to these allegations, the report revealed that employers, for their part, did not want to honour their agreements and suggested that strikes could be avoided if a daily wage rate was fixed at 2,100 *kyats* per day.

The report's allegations were refuted by Ma Thet Thet Aung of the 88 Generation Students group. Ma Thet Thet Aung argued that she and her colleagues had never instigated protests by workers.[17]

When workers demanded pay rises, the officials from the Ministry of Labour found their claims very difficult to address. However, after discussing the demands with the garment factories owners' association of the Union of Myanmar Federation of Chambers of Commerce and Industry (UMFCCI), they managed to come up with a standard for wages in the garment industry. Including overtime pay and other allowances, the new wages for garment employees were set as follow: 56,700 *kyats* per month for a helper; 70,200 *kyats* per month for a C-level operator; and 82,094 *kyats* per month for a B-level operator.[18]

For many garment workers, the new salary scales seemed reasonable. However, despite salary levels having been determined, many owners of garment factories refused to modify the pay scales for their workers. When protests emerged, politicians from several political parties supported the actions of the striking workers. Officials from the Ministry of Labour, as well as some employers, complained that they could not carry out negotiations with workers due to the intervention of politicians. When it heard of these complaints, the Union Election Commission warned five major political organizations—those believed to be encouraging workers— not to provide any assistance to striking workers (Win Ko Ko Latt 2012). The five parties were:

- the National League for Democracy;
- the Union Solidarity and Development Party;
- the National Democratic Force;
- the Union of Myanmar Federation of National Politics;
- the 88 Generation Student Youths (Union of Myanmar).

Yet in spite of the warning, some independent activists such as Ko Phoe Phyu and U Htay, as well as some members of the 88 Generation Students group, continued to assist the striking workers.[19] When the strikes gained momentum in May 2012, the government refrained from using force against strikers as it had done during the Tai Yi incident. Nevertheless, since many employers were well connected with local officials, a number of industrial negotiations became deadlocked. On 23 May, Min Ko Naing, a prominent political activist who represented the whole 88 Generation Students group, wrote to the Minister of Labour requesting the authorities to resolve these labour strikes as soon as possible.

> Regarding the current labour strikes happening in Hlaing Tharyar industrial zone, Hmawbi Township and other regions, it is believed that the government should step in and settle them. Resolving this issue in the forms of fixing minimum wages and establishing conciliation bodies by the District (or) State government in accordance with the section 10, chapter 3 of the Settlement of the Labour Dispute Law (2011) is desired. It is worrying that if it seems that current labour strikes are disregarded these strikes will take longer and negatively affect current transitional activities. Therefore, it is respectfully requested to settle these issues in order to peacefully end these problems (Min Ko Naing 2012, p. 1).

In addition, the 88 Generation Students group issued an announcement requesting employers to negotiate with their workers.[20]

After the labour conference of 3 June 2012, senior labour officials changed their strategy for managing these strikes and negotiations. The labour authorities invited representatives from the 88 Generation Students group to assist their negotiation and conciliation efforts in factories and workplaces. A labour officer in Mayangone Township commented, "Whenever we have a deadlock situation with workers or when workers became rebellious, we immediately summoned some people from the 88 Generation Students group to assist our negotiation process; normally, workers do not listen to us, but they listen intently to those people from the 88 Generation Students group".[21]

During the labour strikes of May and June 2012, workers began to organize labour associations. As of 17 December 2012, a total of 356 basic labour associations had been registered (MLESS 2013).

PROSPECTS FOR LABOUR CONDITIONS IN MYANMAR

Despite workers in several garment factories having tried to change their appalling working conditions by engaging in labour protests, many garment workers are still being abused. For example, many workers are still forced to work on Sunday. A worker from Kyar Min garment factory said, "If we did not work on Sunday, we were criticized the next day, on Monday. Although officials concerned stepped in and conciliated this dispute, workers were retrenched with compensation. By now, a total of nineteen workers have been dismissed" (May Zin Win and April Oo 2012, p. 27).

When an employer breaks an employment contract with workers, usually no serious action is taken against that employer. U That Naing Oo, the Deputy Director-General of the Department of Labour commented, "If work needs to be done on public holidays, workers may either attend work or take the day off, according to their own wishes. They must not be forced to attend work. Their salaries must not be reduced. Employers are doing what they like, acting as if they have not noticed this." (May Zin Win and April Oo 2012, p. 27).

In regard to the protection of workers, U Htay, a lawyer-cum-activist, explained that the current labour laws dictate to workers how they must work, but these laws do not have any provision for action against employers who break the laws (May Zin Win and April Oo 2012, p. 27).

Under the Thein Sein government, workers are now allowed to organize freely. However, in some factories and workplaces, workers who have been involved in organizing workers' associations have been immediately sacked (April Oo 2012*a*, p. 27). If a worker has been sacked, that worker will not be able to seek employment in other factories since sacked workers are regarded as "trouble-makers" (April Oo 2012*b*, p. 27).

After the strikes in May, June, and July 2012, many employers failed to keep the agreed terms of contracts with workers. As a result, a few strikes took place in September 2012. In one case, about two hundred workers in one industrial zone staged a legal strike on 2 September 2012 (Pyae Phyo 2012*a*, p. 35).

In September 2012, a number of workers from several industrial zones demanded that their employers recognize a standard of 3,000 *kyats* per day as a basic wage. Still many employers refused to meet their demand, arguing that they were not able to pay and that if they were forced to pay, they would shut down their businesses (Aye Myat Thu 2012).

Although a more tolerant political climate has appeared, workers as a group have been largely unorganized and weak. Outside the industrial zones, workers are predominantly disunited and very compliant. Some news agencies have reported that working conditions in other sectors are better, relatively, than they are in factories in industrial zones. For instance, it was reported that the main reason for a lack of strikes in many factories in South Dagon was that the basic salaries of many workers there were higher than those of workers in other industrial zones (Pyae Phyo 2012*b*, p. 27). This is not to ignore the fact that, aside from having better incomes, many workers employed in other industries are not fully protected and their labour rights have also been violated.

U Maung Maung from the Federation of Trade Unions-Burma argued that while some people in the government are assisting the development of healthy trade unions, at the same time there are others who are working to hinder this process. He told the author that his organization had assisted the establishment of labour associations in some ministerial departments with the support of senior officials. He further added that there would always be challenges and it would take time to overcome them.[22]

The International Labour Organization (ILO) has indicated that it already has plans to address labour issues in Myanmar. Under its Decent Work Country Programme (DWCP), the ILO has established three priorities for Myanmar (ILO 2012). The three priorities are:

- the eradication of forced labour by the end of 2015;
- the healthy development of labour associations; and
- putting a Decent Work Country Programme into operation (ILO 2012, pp. 4–5).

Aside from this long-term programme, the International Labour Organization office in Yangon has been working to provide advice on many labour rights violations in Myanmar (Nan Tin Htwe 2012a; 2012b).

CONCLUSION

Grievances about low pay and worsening working conditions were the primary cause of the significant increase in labour protests that was evident in Myanmar in 2012, but other major factors made it easier than before for workers to challenge their employers and the state boldly and to participate courageously in collective bargaining.

The first major factor was the broadening political space that has emerged following the reforms undertaken by the Thein Sein government. Without a doubt, Myanmar is experiencing an unprecedented level of political freedom. Dramatic political and economic reforms have opened up political opportunities, allowing many people to participate in independent associations, public demonstrations, and other events in the political arena—including strikes. It was these political opportunities that allowed sweatshop workers to make claims for better wages and better working conditions. Only a very few people, however, have dared to test the waters.

The number of workers in a factory was a second important factor that encouraged workers to pursue collective demands. On average, labour-intensive factories in industrial zones employ over one hundred workers. Of ninety factories whose workers participated in the labour protests, only nine have a production workforce of fewer than one hundred workers. Eighteen factories have more than one thousand workers, while the remainder have workforces of between one hundred and one thousand workers (MLESS 2012a). The large concentration of workers produced a feeling of solidarity among workers and they were emboldened to go on strike.

The third factor that contributed to the upsurge in strike action in 2012 was the support given to workers by political and labour activists. Ever since the 1990s, labour activists have regarded the labour-intensive factories as fertile soil for campaigns opposing the military regime. Their ample political support gave confidence to striking workers, and may have contributed to strikes being prolonged and becoming violent.

Although the government's reform programme has brought a number of improvements, no one knows how the democratization process in Myanmar will proceed in the future. Since the reforms began, the Thein Sein government has faced several political challenges. It is too early to predict what will happen in regard to labour politics in Myanmar, given that the government has shown itself to be reactive rather than proactive in managing labour issues. How far will the government subjugate Myanmar workers in order to promote the development of a market economy? This is a question that can only be answered in a few decades from now.

Notes

1   Interview with Ko Phoe Phyu on 22 July 2012.
2   Interview with a former businessman, 15 July 2011.
3   Interview with six workers from the New Way shoe factory, 16 July 2011.
4   The author received information about payments from interviews with ten garment workers and U Htay on 21 July 2012.
5   Interview with the labour leader of the Tai Yi shoe factory on 22 July 2012.
6   Interview with five workers from the Khun Main block-making factory on 22 July 2012.
7   Interview with six female workers from Gallant Seafood processing factory on 22 July 2012.
8   Interview with U Htay on 21 July 2012.
9   Interview with the Tai Yi labour leader and Ko Phoe Phyu on 22 July 2012.
10 Information about the events described in this section has mainly been taken from Mayangone Trade Dispute Committee 2012. (The case file was received from Ko Phoe Phyu on 22 July 2012).
11 Interview with Ko Phoe Phyu and the labour leader of the Tai Yi shoe factory on 22 July 2012.
12 Ma Thet Thet Aung from the 88 Generation Students group said that it was on 8 May that the strike broke out, but the government record shows that the protest began on 9 May.
13 Interview with a township labour official on 29 July 2012, and with Ma Thet Thet Aung from the 88 Generation Students group on 20 July 2012.
14 Interview with U Hla Maung Shwe, a member of the National Economic and Social Advisory Council and vice president of Myanmar Egress, on 6 June 2012.
15 Interview with a township labour official on 29 July 2012.
16 Interview with Ma Thet Thet Aung on 20 July 2012.

17 ibid.
18 The author received this information from a township labour official on 30 July 2012.
19 Personal observation and interviews with Ko Phoe Phyu and U Htay on 22 July 2012.
20 Interview with Ma Thet Thet Aung on 20 July 2012.
21 Interview with a township labour official on 29 July 2012.
22 Interview with U Maung Maung, head of the Federation of Trade Unions-Burma, on 29 December 2012.

References

April Oo. "*Akyaungbya Alôk-tôk-chin hma Kinweye Set-yôn 10 yôn-hma Alôkthama-mya UbadeHnin-anyi Sanda-pawtôk-mi*" [Workers from ten factories will go on strike to avoid justified retrenchment]. *Popular News* 32 (2012*a*): 27.

————. "*Alôk-tôkkanya-thaw Alôkthama-mya-a Pyathana Shi-thi-hu-thaw Amyingyaung Alôkthit Yayan Ketkè*" [Getting new employment is difficult due to the view that retrenched workers have problems]. *Popular News* 31 (2012b): 27.

Aye Myat Thu. "*Lôktha Tit-u Tit-ne Achegan Laza 3000 Kyat That-hmatye Alôkshin-myaka Thabaw Matu-naing*" [Employers do not agree to a designated daily wage of 3000 *kyats*]. *7 Day News* 27 (2012): Supplement C.

British Broadcasting Corporation (BBC). 2011."Burma frees dozens of political prisoners". BBC, 12 October 2011. <http://www.bbc.co.uk/news/world-asia-pacific-15269259>. Accessed 26 September 2012.

Feng Yingqiu. "Myanmar grants state employees allowances rather than pay increase". *Xinhua News*, 15 March 2012. <http://news.xinhuanet.com/english/business/2012-03/15/c_131468591.htm>. Accessed 2 June 2013.

International Labour Organization (ILO). "Decent Work in Myanmar: ILO Programme Framework: November 2012–April 2014". November 2012. <http://www.ilo.org/wcmsp5/groups/public/---dgreports/---exrel/documents/publication/wcms_193195.pdf>. Accessed 12 May 2013.

————. "International Labour Office, Governing Body, 301st session, Geneva, March 2008: Eighth Item on the Agenda: 349th Report of the Committee on Freedom of Association". March 2008. <http://www.ilo.org/wcmsp5/groups/public/@ed_norm/@relconf/documents/meetingdocument/wcms_091464.pdf>. Accessed 26 January 2013.

————. "Forced labour in Myanmar (Burma): Report of the Commission of Inquiry appointed under article 26 of the Constitution of the International Labour Organization to examine the observance by Myanmar of the Forced Labour Convention, 1930 (No. 29)". 2 July 1998. <http://www.ilo.org/public/libdoc/ilo/P/09604/09604(1998-81-serie-B-special-suppl).pdf>. Accessed 26 January 2013.

Ko Ko Gyi. Speech at the labour conference held in the Chatrium Hotel on 3 June 2012. Yangon, 2012. (Ko Ko Gyi is a member of the 88 Generation Students group and his recorded speech was received from U Hla Maung Shwe on 6 June 2012.)

Kyaw Yin Hlaing. "The politics of state-business relations in post-colonial Burma". PhD Dissertation, Cornell University, 2001.

Kyaw Zin Lin. Speech at the labour conference held in the Chatrium Hotel on 3 June 2012. Yangon, 2012. (Kyaw Zin Lin is a worker delegate and his recorded speech was received from U Hla Maung Shwe on 6 June 2012.)

Mayangone Trade Dispute Committee. *Pyitaungzu Myanma-nainggandaw Asoya, Myonè*-Wanizza *Padipetka-hmu Kawmati, Mayangôn Myonè, AhmuAhmat (2/2012)* [Union of Myanmar, the Township Trade Dispute Committee, Mayangone Township: Case No. 2/2012]. Yangon, 2012: 1–9.

May Zin Win and April Oo. *"Taninganwe-lè Mana-ya Adamma Acheinpo Sinkaing-chin-dansetyôn Lôktha-acho Kan-ne-ya"* [No rest on Sunday: Some factory workers suffered from forced overtime work]. *Popular News* 33 (2012): 27.

Min Ko Naing. *"Alôkthama-mya-e Lo-at-chethnin Patthetywe Tinbya-taungso-hmu-mya-a Azinbyay-hmu Shi-se-ye-atwet Kunyi-saung-ywet-pebayan Tinbya-chin"* [Requesting assistance for the resolution of claims relating to workers' needs]. Yangon, 2012. (The letter was addressed to the Ministry of Labour and sent on 23 May 2012; the author received a copy of the letter from the 88 Generation Students group office).

Ministry of Labour, Employment and Social Security (MLESS). 2013. *"Alôk-thama Abwè-azi Ubade-aya Pwèzi-ta-thaw Alôk-thama Abwè-chôk, Alôk-shin Abwè-chôk, Achegan Alôk-thama Abwè-azi, Achegan Alôk-shin Abwè-azi 2012"* [The basic workers' associations, basic employers' associations, workers' federated associations, employers' federated associations, and organizations which are organized in accordance with the Labour Organizing Law, 2012]. Yangon: Ministry of Labour, Employment and Social Security, 2013. <http://www.mol. gov.mm/mm/wp-content/uploads/downloads/2013/01/Org-List24-1-2013. pdf>. Accessed 13 February 2013.

———. *"2012 Me-la 1 yet-ne-hma Zun-la 30 yet-ne-ati Laza-todaung-hmu Pyitpwa-thaw Setyôn-alôkyôn-mya"* [The factories and establishments where demands for a pay rise occurred from 1 May to 30 June 2012]. July 2012*a*. <http://www.mol. gov.mm/mm/wp-content/uploads/downloads/2012/07/For-Web-30-6-121. pdf>. Accessed 11 February 2013.

———. *Alôk-thama-abwè-azi Ubade 2011 hnin Alôk-thamaAbwè-azi Ni-ubade-mya* [The Labour Organizing Law 2011 and the Labour Organizing Rules]. Yangon: Ministry of Labour, Employment and Social Security, 2012*b*.

———. *Alôk-thama-yeya Anyinbwa-hmu Pyeshin-ye Ubade 2012 hnin Alôk-thama-yeya Anyinbwa-hmu Pyeshin-yeni-ubade-mya* [The Settlement of Labour Dispute Law

(2012) and the Settlement of Labour Dispute Rules]. Yangon: Ministry of Labour, Employment and Social Security, 2012c.

———. *Alôk-thama-yeya Shinlin-tinbya-chin* [Explanation of labour issues].Yangon, 2012d. (This is an official report that was submitted to the president. The author received a copy of the report from an authorized person on 6 June 2012).

Nan Tin Htwe. "Workers fired for labour roles, says ILO". *Myanmar Times*, 23–29 July 2012a. <http://www.mmtimes.com/2012/news/636/news63614.html>. Accessed 11 February 2013.

———. "ILO meets factory owner over firing". *Myanmar Times*, 6–12 August 2012b. <http://www.mmtimes.com/2012/news/638/news63825.html>. Accessed 11 February 2013.

Nelson, Dean. "Burmese authorities abolish press censorship". *Telegraph*, 20 August 2012. <http://www.telegraph.co.uk/news/worldnews/asia/burmamyanmar/9487465/Burmese-authorities-abolish-press-censorship.html>. Accessed 11 February 2013.

Nelson, Dean and Ian MacKinnon. "Burma releases 650 political prisoners in move to end isolation". *Telegraph*, 13 January 2012. <http://www.telegraph.co.uk/news/worldnews/asia/burmamyanmar/9013254/Myanmar-Burma-releases-650-political-prisoners-in-move-to-end-isolation.html>. Accessed 11 February 2013.

New Light of Myanmar (*NLM*). "The Law Revoking the 1964 Law Defining the Fundamental Rights and Responsibilities of the People's Workers". *New Light of Myanmar*, 22 November 2011, p. 1.

Pyae Phyo. "*Achegan Ubadeba Akwin-aye Chobaukkanya-ywe Hlaingthaya Lôktha-do Sandabya*" [Hlaing Thayar workers staged strikes over violations of their constitutional rights]. *Popular News* 35 (2012a): 35.

———. "*Dagon-taung Set-yôn-mya Achegan Laza-gaung-ywe Sandabya-mu nè-pa-huso*" [A fewer labour protests in South Dagon as the basic pay is better]. *Popular News* 31 (2012b): 27.

Soe Yarzar Htun. "*Alôk-thama Abwè-azi-myapwunbyo-yan Alôk-thama-athaing-waing Lola*" [The labour community desires the development of labour associations]. *Peoples' Age Journal* 98 (2012): 13.

Taylor, Robert H. *The State in Myanmar*. London: Hurst & Company, 2009.

Win Ko Ko Latt. "UEC meets with parties over strikes, protests". *Myanmar Times*, 4–10 June 2012. <http://www.mmtimes.com/2012/news/629/news62924.html>. Accessed 26 September 2012.

Win Ko Ko Latt and Ei Ei Toe Lwin. "Ministry enacts protest by-laws". *Myanmar Times*, 16 July 2012. <http://www.mmtimes.com/index.php/national-news/yangon/396-ministry-enacts-protest-by-laws.html>. Accessed 5 May 2013.

IV

Anticipating Reforms

9

MYANMAR ECONOMIC UPDATE
Macro-economy, Fiscal Reform, and Development Options

Anders Engvall and Soe Nandar Linn

Five decades ago Ne Win set Burma on the *way to socialism*, with a development plan that sought to reduce foreign influence and put the military-controlled government at the centre of the economy. Under President U Thein Sein, an ambitious reform agenda is seeking to undo the legacy of isolation and set Myanmar on the *way to capitalism* by opening up the country to foreign trade and investment.

After decades of military rule and ethnic conflict, a civilian administration was sworn in on 30 March 2011, following elections held in November 2010. The new government immediately embarked on a range of political and economic reforms aimed at attaining national reconciliation, improved governance, and economic development. With a quarter of its citizens living below the poverty line,[1] considerable weaknesses in transport infrastructure, and one of the lowest rates of access to modern telecommunications in the world, Myanmar faces a tremendous development challenge.

Reform achievements to date have been significant, but have largely addressed macro-economic issues and have not required additional budgetary spending. Expectations for real welfare improvements have built up, but little effort has been made to address poverty, fulfil the population's unmet needs for healthcare and education, or upgrade Myanmar's infrastructure to improve domestic competitiveness. Addressing these problems will require massive funds that can only be found through donor support, improved mobilization of internal revenue from those with a taxable surplus, reform of the loss-making state-owned economic enterprise sector, and mobilizing sub-national governments to implement reforms.

The purpose of this economic update is to provide an overview of major economic developments since the government of President U Thein Sein assumed office on 30 March 2011, and to survey trends and outline expectations for future economic development. In this chapter the authors analyze the reforms, their impact, and the needs and prospects for further economic change during the run-up to the 2015 election. Particular attention is paid to the obstacles that will be faced by reformers when they seek simultaneously to develop the economy, reduce the role of state-owned economic enterprises and improve the business climate; to transform the national budget from an instrument for mobilizing funds for the armed forces to a driver of economic development; and to activate sub-national governments. The Thein Sein government is under pressure to deliver on the high expectations for economic improvement. The reformers will continue to struggle against the fundamental challenges created by Myanmar's legacy of under-development.

ECONOMIC REFORMS UNDER U THEIN SEIN

Outside attention has largely focused on Myanmar's political changes, as Daw Aung San Suu Kyi's National League for Democracy (NLD) party has been re-admitted into the country's mainstream politics, ceasefire agreements have been entered into with most of the ethnic armed groups (some of which have waged war with the government for the past six decades), large-scale releases of political prisoners have been carried out, and increased freedom of expression has been allowed. Yet the economic changes that brought about a break with decades of isolationism and an end to the many reckless policies that made Myanmar one of the poorest countries in the world have to some extent been overlooked. Key economic reforms include unification of the exchange rate (a change from a system of up to six parallel rates), trade and investment liberalization, a new land law, rationalization of tax rates, and increased fiscal transparency.

Some aspects of governance at the central level have improved. The government has made efforts to improve transparency—in 2012, for the first time, the national budget was presented to parliament and debated by members, leading to significant cuts in the executive's proposals, and it was subsequently published in national newspapers. As a result of the exchange rate unification, revenue figures have increased. With these changes, the budgetary pattern is expected to change substantially.

With the emergence of parliamentary oversight, figures in the most recent 2013-14 budget show that government spending on health and education is set to increase in comparison with the 2010-11 fiscal year (FY). At the same time, the defence budget has also increased in monetary terms, although the percentage share of the total budget going to the armed forces has decreased.

The government has established a Financial Commission[2] and has undertaken a significant de-concentration of budgeting and planning functions. Myanmar also has a semi-independent Auditor-General, whose purview spans the entire public sector. Transparency has benefited from the lifting of restrictions on the media, which has resulted in greater scrutiny of economic policies.

One important step for improving the government's financial outlook was the conclusion of an agreement, on 25 January 2013, between the Myanmar government and the Paris Club to cancel 50 percent of total outstanding debt owed to large developed country creditors (Paris Club 2013). The agreement lowers Myanmar's external debt burden by US$5,925 million, freeing up significant resources.

The isolationist policies of Ne Win's *Burmese way to socialism* turned Myanmar into a regional economic basket-case. Many of its East Asian neighbours pursued export-oriented development producing rapid growth, while Myanmar's economy was in decline. That lesson has not been lost on President Thein Sein's government, and it has promoted opening up the economy to export-oriented investors. Recognizing the importance of providing a stable legal and economic environment, to compete for investments in the world market, government reformers moved quickly to enact a more attractive foreign investment law.

There is clearly potential for foreign investors to contribute to unleashing productive resources in the country. The economic reform process, including the new Foreign Direct Investment (FDI) law, and the abolition of sanctions imposed by foreign governments, have spurred investment into Myanmar. According to the Myanmar Investment Commission, new realized foreign investments in the country increased rapidly to US$1,400 million in fiscal year 2012-13, compared to US$300 million in the preceding year (Reuters 2013). Most of the investment in fiscal year 2012-13 came from East Asian countries. Significantly, 78 out of 94 new foreign investment projects have been in the labour-intensive manufacturing sector, mostly in garment production, providing important employment opportunities and indicating a shift away from investment in natural resources.

In addition to the economic benefits of foreign direct investment, reformers also hope such investment will bring about a shift in the priorities of future policy-makers. The discipline imposed by world market competition may become an important force for ensuring that future economic policies will be more in accord with international norms and rules, in order for Myanmar to be successful. With a growing share of the electorate employed by multi-national enterprises, it will be political disaster for future governments to impose policies that undermine competitiveness. Through this mechanism, foreign investment may work to keep the government committed to a stable business environment.

Additional benefits of FDI—besides employment creation and the upgrading of skills—will be the impact FDI has on government revenue and fiscal reform. Investors need, and demand, improved public services for creating institutional competition between countries. As the Myanmar government focuses on attracting FDI, it is likely resources will increasingly be used to finance public services as well as the infrastructure investments needed for future investment and growth.

One indication of the attention being given to revenue mobilization is the effort that the Internal Revenue Department of the Ministry of Finance is putting into reform of tax administration and policy. The need for reform is huge, and includes the need to consolidate revenue streams; at present, several line ministries are involved in tax collection and the revenues are retained at these ministries, outside the control of the Ministry of Finance.

The main feature of the economic reforms implemented thus far is that they have focused on macro-economic issues and on opening up the economy to trade and investment. Key economic reforms include the unification of the exchange rate, liberalization of trade and investment, a new law allowing for farmland to be used as collateral, and some improvements in fiscal transparency. The reforms have broken the country's economic isolation and put it firmly on track to becoming a partner in the ASEAN Economic Community (AEC) by 2015.

This initial focus on macro-economic reforms is based on a strategy of starting with areas where improvements can be made quickly and with relative ease. These changes have required little costly investment by the government. There are clearly non-budgetary costs—committing to a unified exchange rate means that state economic enterprises and other favoured firms cannot be granted foreign currency at favourable rates—yet the overall reform strategy has not had any dramatic consequences for the national budget. This has allowed reformers to avoid confronting the issue of privileged budgetary allocations to the armed forces and other sensitive aspects of necessary economic reforms.

DEVELOPMENT CHALLENGES

The Myanmar government has a long way to go before it will be able to provide all the basic services its people need. One-fifth of children in poor families are not enrolled in primary school education, while skilled health personnel do not attend a quarter of births and child mortality is higher than in comparable neighbouring countries (UNCT 2011). To fulfil its commitment to achieving the Millennium Development Goals (MDGs) by 2015, the government must make sizeable investments for expanding and improving the quality of education and health care. The reach of government and its ability to provide services, particularly in rural areas, remains limited. Although the budget share for the health and education sectors has been increased since 2011—both in terms of amount and as a percentage of the total—the sector is still underfunded. In addition, the salaries of civil servants, especially of those who work in rural areas, are often insufficient to cover living costs, even though the monthly salary of civil servants was increased by about US$35 in 2012 plus an additional US$25 in 2013.

A number of critical challenges will need to be overcome if domestic competitiveness is to be improved. These include a weak regulatory environment, a huge infrastructure deficit, and an under-developed financial sector. Infrastructure development is the major challenge, especially for small and medium enterprises, as poor transport and communications systems, and electricity shortages, raise transaction costs to levels that hamper competitiveness.

Decades of under-investment have taken a toll. A substantial portion of economic activity within the private sector in Myanmar is informal, with small and medium-sized enterprises accounting for over 90 percent of firms. Corporate governance within the larger firms has yet to benefit from the same degree of transparency that is maintained in most middle and high-income countries. Finally, the regulations that govern the extractive industries have not been sufficient to protect Myanmar's environment and rich bio-diversity.

Meeting Myanmar's development challenges requires mobilization of development funds both by securing donor funding and by improving revenue collection from segments of the population that have a taxable surplus. Yet Myanmar has one of the lowest ratios of tax collection to gross domestic product (GDP) in the world (ADB 2012). The latest estimate puts the tax-to-GDP ratio at less than 5 percent for fiscal year 2012-13, according to the Internal Revenue Department. With government expenditure at 14 percent, revenues from extractive industries and government lending cover a funding gap of more than one-tenth of GDP.

Decades of centralized, authoritarian rule have starved States and Regions of both the resources and the capacity to implement development programs. To meet the challenge of improving service delivery will require activating sub-national governments to implement reforms in health care, education, and local infrastructure. This may only require a limited transfer of authority from the centre, but, more importantly, it will call for a massive transfer of resources to the sub-national governments. The central government is clearly still reluctant to put the necessary resources at the disposal of States and Regions, as evident from the desperate calls for donor funding from chief ministers at the First Myanmar Development Cooperation Forum, a national-level roundtable held in Naypyitaw on 19–20 January 2013, where planning ministers from States and Regions presented their budget plans and requests for development assistance. The States and Regions were primarily seeking assistance for agriculture, infrastructure, health, and education.

SLOW-MOVING BUDGETARY REFORMS

Under the military government the budgetary system was strictly top-down, and authority was concentrated in the hands of the head of state, who retained full discretionary power. Information about sources of revenue and about how funds were used was kept secret, and a substantial share of the budget went to the armed forces.

In one of its most significant initiatives, President Thein Sein's government has committed to initiating budgetary reforms[3] and to stop financing state economic enterprises from the government budget, starting from fiscal year 2012-13 (*Union Budget Law* 2012; World Bank 2013, Paragraph 358). President Thein Sein addressed this issue on 19 June 2012 at a meeting with national-level organization members, State and Region Chief Ministers, Chairmen of Self-Administrated Divisions and Zones, Deputy Ministers and Departmental Heads. He said:

> We will see increase in job opportunities and income and a triple growth as projected only if we double our current volume of financial investments....
> In addition we must trim down uneconomical and redundant enterprises and cut expenses, while shrinking the State-own business sector and encouraging privatization (Thein Sein 2012).

The details of the Union budget for fiscal year 2012-13 were published in the official newspapers after the 2012-13 budget was passed, but the amount of information given was limited, as it only included consolidated figures for spending and few details about revenue. According to the government's data, the budget deficit in the 2012-13 fiscal year was reduced by 10 percent in comparison with the previous fiscal year.

Political developments have already resulted in increased scrutiny of the budget, primarily through the establishment in 2011 of the parliament's Public Accounts Committee and the Planning and Finance Committee (World Bank 2013, Paragraph 357). Nevertheless, as long as the collection of national statistical data in Myanmar remains weak and figures are unreliable, it will be difficult, if not impossible, to achieve proper policy-based budgeting and planning before the 2015 elections.

Critical lack of transparency relates to the armed forces' revenue and expenditure. Privileged allocations to the military total 18.44 percent of fiscal year budget 2011-12. Despite this funding, the government has had to increase its military expenditures above the budgeted level, due to the outbreak of civil war in Kachin State and violent conflict in Rakhine State.

According to the Union Budget Law for fiscal year 2011-12, the defence budget cannot be questioned, because it is necessary for national security. Moreover, it has never been scrutinized nor adjusted according to the Budget Law of 2011-12 and 2012-13. However, for the first time, members of parliament have raised an issue about the defence budget for 2013-14. During parliament's debate of the budget for fiscal year 2013-14, the defence minister stated that the amount of the defence budget as a proportion of the total national budget was 28.9 percent in 2011-12,[4] 22.8 percent in 2012-13, and 20.9 percent (over 1,000 billion *kyats*) in 2013-14 respectively. However, according to the budget figures for fiscal year 2013-14, the defence budget is 2,245 billion *kyats* (US$ 2.6 billion).

Despite expenditure on defence having declined as a percentage of overall budget expenditure, the Ministry of Defence still receives the largest ministerial allocation, both in terms of capital and of recurrent spending. In fiscal year 2011-12, the major non-defence budget allocations went to the Ministries of Energy, Finance and Revenue, and Construction; in contrast, the government spent least on education and health (expenditure on these were only 4.33 and 1.27 percent respectively). In fiscal year 2012-13, the allocation for health and education was dramatically increased, while there was a huge cut in the amount allocated to the Ministry of Energy, especially for its recurrent spending. The shift in priorities for recurrent government spending is manifested in the fiscal year 2013-14 budget, where the largest allocations are to the Ministries of Finance, Health, and Education. However, the Ministries of Construction, Agriculture and Irrigation, and Border Affairs received the largest shares of the capital budget.

Fiscal transparency is blurred by the "special funds" that have been acknowledged to exist, to cover defence expenditure and the costs of construction projects in Naypyitaw. "Special funds" is a separate item under the Ministry of Defence allocation, with little available information about how this money is used (Wai Moe 2011, Associated Press 2011).

Another step towards improved fiscal governance came when President Then Sein abolished the Ministry of Myanmar Industrial Development, in September 2011. The Ministry had been created only shortly before the transition to a civilian government; its budget was utilized for pet military projects for large-scale industrial development, especially in the new capital, Naypyitaw.

However, in fiscal year 2013-14, there is a new allocation in the Union Budget for the Naypyitaw Council,[5] with a capital budget of 125 billon *kyats* or about US$147 million, under the direct control of the president. The government has not released detailed information to the public about the use of these funds, but it is possible the allocation will fund construction projects in Naypyitaw to prepare for Myanmar's hosting of the Southeast Asian Games in 2013 and taking on the ASEAN chairmanship the following year. These events will put a significant burden on the state coffers, as there as also been a dramatic increase in the 2013-14 capital budget for sports and construction, in addition to the funding of the Naypyitaw Council.

The ratio of tax revenue to GDP in Myanmar in fiscal year 2011-12 was 6.7 percent, a figure that is low in comparison with other Association of South East Asian Nations (ASEAN) countries. To increase tax revenue, in 2012 the Ministry of Finance and Revenue embarked on reform of tax policy and administration, with the support of development partners such as the World Bank, the International Monetary Fund (IMF), the U.S. Treasury and bilateral donors. Collection of tax revenue is likely to be made more transparent during the transition to a reformed system, and will be assisted by the establishment of the Large Taxpayers Unit in Yangon in 2013,[6] as recommended by the IMF. The most important measure required for tax policy reform will be to restructure institutions at both national and sub-national levels.

Since the government signed up to the Extractive Industries Transparency Initiative (EITI) in June 2012, it can be expected that information about the government's revenue from natural resources will become more transparent. Under EITI, independent auditors will identify any gaps between the payments made by companies to the government or its agencies and the income declared by the government.[7]

In 2013, the Revenue Watch Institute ranked Myanmar as the lowest out of fifty-eight countries according to its Resource Governance Index (RWI 2013).

Despite the reforms being in their initial stages, and despite the fact that there is no reform strategy for the budgetary system yet in place, nor have rules and regulations been updated, the World Bank has agreed to partner with the Myanmar government to provide support for public financial management reform (World Bank 2012). By collaborating with the government on a Public Expenditure and Financial Accountability (PEFA) assessment, the World Bank will contribute to improving fiscal processes. This international support will be crucial for realizing the ambitions for transparency and accountability. Since mid-2013, the Government of

Myanmar has developed a Public Financial Management reform strategy and launched a Public Expenditure Review that will address the efficiency of public spending and fiscal decentralization (IMF 2013). Budgetary systems, such as budget classification and reporting, can be improved with technical assistance from international institutions, but accountability and transparency for revenue from natural resource-based sectors will still be a major challenge, due to a lack of strong commitment on the part of the reformist government and a weak Auditor-General, who was formerly the Minster of Mines.

STATE-OWNED ECONOMIC ENTERPRISES

The president has encouraged ministries to reform and to cut the size of state-owned economic enterprises in order to make them more efficient and profitable, since the majority of SEEs have been losing money and the losses have put considerable strain on the national budget in the past. Privatization of some or all SEEs might be a possible solution; however, if that path is pursued, the type of privatization needs to be considered carefully and implemented with caution.

Myanmar started a privatization scheme in 1995,[8] but it was, in effect, a program for selling off state assets and resources, with little transparency. The program continues but, according to the Privatization Commission, in the future the process will be based on sale by auction rather than by the less-transparent method of closed tenders previously used.[9] It will cover SEEs owned by fifteen ministries and government departments, including factories that manufacture textiles, consumer goods, electronic and electrical goods; some mills, land and buildings; as well as cinemas and warehouses. This privatization process is not expected to be completed during the period of President Thein Sein's government. According to government statistics, in 2010 the military government sold 110 state economic enterprises, 32 buildings, and 246 fuel stations, as well as eight wharves along Yangon Port and port areas, through the former tender system.

Aung San Suu Kyi raised the issue of transparency in relation to SEEs—specifically the case of Myanmar Oil and Gas Enterprise (MOGE)[10]—at the International Labour Organization conference in Geneva in June 2011. She urged foreign investors not to engage in joint ventures or partnership with MOGE due to the lack of transparency and accountability. Likewise, she encouraged closer monitoring of the fiscal risk of Build–Operate–Transfer (BOT) arrangements for construction of some highways, and of public-private partnership by the Ministry of Transport and the Ministry of Communications and Information Technology.

Formerly, state-owned economic enterprises used to focus on productivity rather than on maximizing their profits, but SEEs are now finding themselves forced to be stricter in both their financial transactions and their management, in order to become profitable, since their budgets have already been cut. Starting from fiscal year 2012-13, SEEs will have to operate solely with their own funds, because the Union Budget will no longer allocate funds to them. In the case of financial shortages, SEEs will be able to apply for loans from the Myanma Economic Bank (MEB)[11] at an interest rate of 4 percent. SEEs that make a profit will be required to pay 25 percent of that profit as tax, with a further 20 percent of any remaining after-tax profit to be transferred to the government budget. Although SEE budgets have been separated from their line ministries since fiscal year 2012-13, administratively decisions are still made by ministers. With the emergence of sub-national-level administrations, it will be crucial during the transition period to clarify the role of state and region governments with regard to SEEs, and identify how profitable SEEs in their areas can be managed in accordance with state or region plans.

If the new government is to privatize and commercialize SEEs in the future, it will have to develop a proper legal framework for SEE privatization. It will be especially important to ensure that this framework is adequate for dealing with the privatization of large-scale businesses. It will also be crucial for the government to ensure that any sale of an SEE through the tender system is fully transparent to the public, and that details of the assets that have been sold, and of the price received, are declared openly. SEEs may also attract public-private partnership in a proper way through the competitive market.

In this scenario, the status of Union of Myanmar Economic Holdings (UMEH) and Myanmar Economic Corporation (MEC), two military-led companies that still monopolize natural resource-based extractive industries and heavy industries and parts of the service sector, remains unclear.

THE EMERGING ROLE OF STATES AND REGIONS IN ECONOMIC DEVELOPMENT

One of the major changes under the new government has been the formation of sub-national parliaments. Under the provisions of the 2008 Constitution, for administrative purposes Myanmar is divided seven States and an equal number of Regions, one Union territory, five Self-Administered Zones and one Self-Administered Division.[12] After the 2010 general elections, the Myanmar government initiated reforms aimed at decentralization and appointed Chief Ministers in every state and region. While there is a clear ambition to mobilize sub-national governments as key drivers of development, the states and regions are hampered by the ambiguity that surrounds their responsibilities and revenue sources. There are no mechanisms in place for managing the budget allocation between the Union government and the sub-national entities, despite separation of state and region finances from the national budget since October 2011 and the creation of a state and region budget law in fiscal year 2012-13.[13]

Although the capacity of the sub-national parliaments, as well as the rules and regulations under which they will operate, are still unclear, an optimistic observer might expect that parliamentarians will be able to raise issues that could put pressure on governments to be more accountable and transparent. The sub-national governments have the potential to function better and become more powerful in the future, since they are closer to local communities. One indication of this possibility is that there has already been a parliamentary discussion on the role of sub-national governments, in August 2012 (*NLM* 2012*a*).

The sub-national cabinets consist of a Chief Minister and nine cabinet ministers. All states and regions except Chin State have a National Races Affairs Minister. The sub-national budget is divided into three parts; that is, budget for SEEs; for City Development Committees[14] and municipalities; and for state or region-administered organizations, including the offices of the court, the attorney-general, and the auditor-general.

Although there are twenty-four departments at the sub-national level and their budgets are recorded in the respective state and region accounts, from an administrative perspective officers in these departments are attached to their line ministries at the central level. Although there is collaboration between the sub-national governments and the sub-national departments, Chief Ministers and ministers have very limited authority to make decisions, with the exception of Border Affairs Ministers (who are military appointees). For example, the Transportation Minister at sub-national government level has no involvement in large infrastructure investments in his area. Likewise, the Minister of Electric Power and Industry does not have a role in industrial zone development, nor does the Agricultural Minister have authority over farmland management in his state or region. In addition, the key health and education sectors are still controlled by the Union ministries.

It is clear that the ministers of the sub-national governments do not yet have administrative power. Social Affairs ministers have a very small role in the respective sub-national governments. This means that the roles of the state and region Chief Ministers and of the other portfolio ministers will have to be clarified if local economic development is to be realized.

Similarly, the fiscal authority of sub-national level governments is still limited. The budget allocation to them overall is relatively low, at only 7.2 percent of the total national budget in fiscal year 2011-2012. State and region governments are given the authority to prepare a budget, but the ceiling of their budget is limited to an amount determined by national-level ministers. On the other hand, any revenue collected at the sub-national level has to be contributed to the national revenue account.

In regard to tax collection, the constitution gives the sub-national governments the right to collect nineteen types of taxes and fees (Constitution, Paragraphs 193, 194, 254, and Schedule Five). Among the de-centralized departments at the sub-national level, the General Administration Department of the Ministry of Home Affairs, and the Public Works Department under the Ministry of Construction, collect the majority of taxes and fees. Starting from fiscal year 2012-13, 25 percent of tax on non-license motorcycles, of revenue from river-water pumping projects, 2 percent of tax on sales of mobile phone sim-cards, and 5 percent of income tax can be retained at the sub-national level. Nonetheless, the national-level ministries continue to manage the work of tax collection: the Ministry of Border Affairs for example, collects taxes on border trade. Yet there are encouraging signs of efforts to delegate authority and resources. Starting from fiscal year 2011-2012, a fund for poverty-reduction and rural development has been granted to all states and regions.[15] Drawing on these funds may give the sub-national governments an opportunity to initiate their own development programs for poverty reduction. As a first step towards reform of governance at sub-national level, one possible way to strengthen local governments would be to give them a leading role in monitoring community-based projects through collaboration with local communities and civil society organizations. Moreover, developing needs-based plans and policy-based budgeting will be essential for achieving President Thein Sein's goal of *people-centred development* (Thein 2012).

In regard to budget reform, first, more systematic rules and regulations for the transfer of funds from the central government to states and regions are needed. Second, the amount given to states and regions will have to be increased.

Since the deficits of sub-national governments are financed by the Union government, it will be important to develop a clear mechanism for allocating resources efficiently so as to keep the development in all states and regions in balance. In fiscal year 2012-13, Magwe Region registered the largest deficit and Kayah State the smallest. However, not all states and regions received grants in equal proportion: some states and regions received full coverage of their deficits from the Union budget, while only 37 percent of the deficit in Yangon Region was financed by the central government, although Yangon Region contributes the largest share of revenue to the Union. In fiscal year 2013-14, all state and region governments except Tanintharyi Region, Ayeyarwady Region, Mon State, and Rakhine State have received loans for SEEs from the Union Fund.

FUTURE ECONOMIC REFORMS

While there have been significant improvements in the Myanmar economy, great challenges remain. Political will is the key to further economic reforms. Many of the most important policy changes have been driven by clear declarations of the political will to improve welfare and avoid the disastrous impact of the large-scale development policies pursued earlier.

The decision to suspend construction of Myitsone Dam is one case where the government displayed considerable political will, and an unexpected openness to public opinion, in responding as it did. Prior to the decision to suspend the controversial dam project, domestic and international civil society, as well as international development partners, had been alarmed by the government's inattention to the negative impact and lack of transparency surrounding the Myitsone Dam project. In a speech to the first Amyotha Hluttaw on 30 September 2011, President Thein Sein gave an indication of the government's commitment to improving governance when he said:

> As our government is elected by the people, it is to respect the people's will. We have the responsibility to address public concerns in all seriousness. So construction of Myitsone Dam will be suspended in the time of our government (*NLM* 2011).

Initial economic reforms have focused on identifying quick policy wins that have a rapid impact, in order to build support for further change. This strategy has directed the reformers' attention to macroeconomic reforms and to opening up the economy to trade and investment.

While Myanmar has normalized its economic polices and aligned its macroeconomic development with the trends in comparable Southeast Asian countries, it is still far from achieving a growth miracle. To lift growth above developing country averages and emerge as a star performer, Myanmar must address its remaining weaknesses. These include managing the overvalued exchange rate, which is stifling private sector competitiveness. Still, the country can take advantage of significant economic opportunities in trade and investment as it re-engages with the wider international community. Myanmar is strategically positioned within reach of large emerging markets. The country's future economic opportunities lie in this strategic location close to a large regional and global export market, in its large untapped natural resources, and in improving its prospects for trade, investment, and development aid as it re-engages with the wider international community.

Although Myanmar has accomplished some relatively easy reforms, it must now address the fundamental challenges that present much greater difficulties. A quarter of its citizens live below the poverty line, child mortality is higher than in comparable neighbouring countries, and one-fifth of children in poor families are not enrolled in primary education. While the government has built up expectations for real welfare improvements, little effort has so far been made to meet the population's need for health care and education.

Myanmar's primary challenges are to reduce poverty, particularly in rural areas, through promoting development; to generate employment for its people by encouraging a more dynamic private sector; and to provide improved health care and education services. The country's new political diversity is likely to slow the pace of future economic reforms as a more vocal parliament and civil society seek a stake in policy-making. Myanmar's leaders will need robust political will in order to implement the next wave of reforms focused on public administration.

The impetus to raise the necessary financial resources for the ambitious development plans envisioned by the government will shift attention to mobilizing tax revenue and to better management of revenue. Currently, exports of natural resources, as well as selective taxation of joint ventures and other firms with foreign investment, provide the main contributions to government revenue. Myanmar is also set to begin receiving revenue from natural gas sales to China from the Shwe gas field in 2014. The future of state-owned economic enterprises will be crucial, particularly as the effect of ending their tax-exempt status comes to bear.

Furthermore, Myanmar will have to change its fiscal priorities and reduce the amount of money allocated to the military; so far, however, confronting the privileged budgetary position of the armed forces is something the government has effectively avoided.

How the political scene develops in the lead-up to the 2015 elections will be crucial, as the key players in the Thein Sein administration have to decide if they will address the fundamental challenges of the country's political economy, or start to prepare for an exit. The 2012 cabinet reshuffle, when several key reformers were promoted to the President's Office, was followed by a virtual game of musical chairs that saw a large number of personnel changes at the second layer of the ministries—Directors-General and Directors (the most senior administrators within a ministry). Significantly, civilians with technocratic qualifications have been appointed as minister and deputy ministers in the key Ministry of National Planning and Economic Development. As a result, the number of former military personnel in key positions within ministries has decreased, except in the Ministries of Defence and Border Affairs, which continue to be dominated by the armed forces (in accordance with the provisions of the 2008 Constitution).

In the sub-national governments, however, there has only been limited change, as many Chief Ministers come from a conservative military background and are comfortable surrounding themselves with weak cabinet members. One implication of this tendency is that the states and regions lack the capacity to take on the role of driving development policies. This situation is further aggravated by the lack of fiscal transfers from the central budget to the states and regions. During the transitional period before the

2015 election, there is little scope for the sub-national governments to take on the tasks envisioned by reformers.

According to a speech given by the president on 12 May 2012, and repeated in another speech on 19 June (*NLM* 2012c; Thein Sein 2012), Myanmar is in the second stage of reform. Myanmar's Planning Commission has approved a basic framework for economic and social reforms during this stage that covers public finance, monetary policy, trade and investment, private sector development, food and agricultural development, health and education, mobile communication services and an Internet system, infrastructural development programs, and programs aimed at the emergence of an effective and efficient governing system and transparency.

The government faces difficult challenges in guiding the economy in a situation where the constitution includes many untested provisions, where parliament is in its infancy, and where bureaucrats at both central and local levels have largely unchanged mind-sets. The president seeks to steer a difficult course, having to negotiate and compromise with many interested stake-holders—opposition leader Aung San Suu Kyi, leaders of other political parties, former generals, business groups, ceasefire groups, and the parliament. Overall, future economic reforms are likely to be slowed down as policy-making becomes increasingly complex, with demands for greater involvement from a more vocal parliament and from sub-national governments seeking a stake in policy-making.

Notes

1   Poverty among the rural population is 29 percent, roughly twice the urban poverty incidence of 16 percent, according to the UNDP's Integrated Household Living Conditions Assessment (Ministry of National Planning (Myanmar) and United Nations Development Programme 20011).

2   The Financial Commission was formed in March 2011 and is chaired by the president. Two vice presidents, the Attorney-General, the Auditor-General, chief Ministers of all States and Regions, and the Finance Minister are included in the commission.

3   With the World Bank's engagement with the government of Myanmar, a Public Expenditure and Financial Accountability Assessment (PEFA) was initiated in June 2012 to assess the public finance system of Myanmar (World Bank 2013, Paragraph 355).

4   This figure is different from that in the Budget Law of 2011-12.
5   Naypyitaw Council was formed by the president in accordance with the 2008 Constitution. The chairperson of Naypyitaw Council is one of the members of the Financial Commission.
6   The Large Taxpayers Unit will be an office under the Internal Revenue Department of the Ministry of Finance (Herman 2013).
7   Under EITI, companies must publish payments made, while governments must disclose sums received, and an independent administrator reconciles them (Hindstrom 2012). See also EITI 2013.
8   The Privatization Commission was set up under the Ministry of National Planning and Economic Development in 1995 (Centre for South-South Technical Cooperation 2002).
9   Author's meeting with the Ministry of National Planning and Economic Development in Naypyitaw.
10   MOGE is one of the state-owned economic enterprises under the Ministry of Energy.
11   Myanma Economic Bank is a State Bank under the Ministry of Finance.
12   The seven States, named for the major ethnic groups that comprise their populations, are: Chin, Kachin, Kayah, Kayin, Mon, Shan, and Rakhine States. The seven Regions, formerly known as Divisions, are Ayeyarwady, Bago, Magwe, Mandalay, Sagaing, Tanintharyi, Yangon; the majority of their populations are comprised of ethnic Burmans. Other administrative areas are Naypyidaw Union Territory; Danu, Kokang, Naga, Pa Laung, and Pa-O Self-Administered Zones; Wa Self-Administered Division.
13   For a good explanation of budget-related developments, see UNICEF 2013; World Bank 2013.
14   City Development Committees exist in Yangon, Mandalay, and Naypyitaw only.
15   A fund of one billion *kyat*s for poverty-reduction and rural development has been allocated to all states and regions except Chin State, which received three billion *kyat*s (since the poverty rate there is the highest in Myanmar) (World Bank 2013). Also, information from authors' meeting with officials of the Budget Department of Ministry of Finance.

References

Asian Development Bank. *Myanmar in Transition Opportunities and Challenges*. Mandaluyong City, Philippines: Asian Development Bank, 2012.
Associated Press. "Myanmar democracy group slams military fund". *Washington Post*, 4 March 2011. <http://www.washingtonpost.com/wpdyn/content/article/2011/03/04/AR2011030402820.html>. Accessed 22 November 2013.

Centre for South-South Technical Cooperation. "The Second Expert Meeting on Non-Aligned Movement Reform: Privatisation and Public-Private Partnership". Presentation of Country Report by the Director of Project Appraisal and Progress Reporting Department (PAPRD) of the Ministry of National Planning and Economic Development at the Institut Perkidmatan Awam, Prime Minister's Office, Brunei Darussalam. 16–18 December 2002. <http://www.csstc.org/reports/egm/P4/Presentation_myanmar.htm>. Accessed 5 December 2013.

Constitution of the Republic of the Union of Myanmar (2008). Paragraphs 193, 194, 254, Schedule Five. Naypyitaw: Printing and Publishing Enterprise, Ministry of Information, Union of Myanmar. <http://www.burmalibrary.org/docs5/Myanmar_Constitution-2008-en.pdf>. Accessed 31 October 2013.

Extractive Industries Transparency Initiative (EITI). "Call for tender: EITI Institutional and Regulatory Assessment of Extractive Industries in Myanmar". World Bank, 7 October 2013. <http://eiti.org/news/call-tender-eiti-institutional-and-regulatory-assessment-extractive-industries-myanmar>. Accessed 22 November 2013.

Herman, Cynthia. "Transition to tax self-assessment is initiated with pilot set for 2014". *International Tax Review*, 1 June 2013. <http://www.internationaltaxreview.com/Article/3212600/Myanmar-Transition-to-tax-self-assessment-is-initiated-with-pilot-set-for-2014.html>. Accessed 22 November 2013.

Hindstrom, Hanna. "Burma considers joining transparency drive for extractive industries". *Democratic Voice of Burma*, 17 July 2012. <http://www.dvb.no/news/burma-considers-joining-transparency-drive-for-extractive-industries/22921>. Accessed 22 November 2013.

International Monetary Fund (IMF). *Myanmar: 2103 Article IV Consultation and First Review Under the Staff-Monitored Programme*. Country Report No. 13/250. Washington D.C.: IMF, 2013. <www.imf.org/external/pubs/ft/scr/2013/cr13250.pdf>. Accessed 10 December 2013.

Ministry of National Planning (Myanmar) and the United Nations Development Programme. 2011. Integrated Household Living Conditions Assessment (IHLCA). *Poverty Profile: Integrated Household Living Conditions Survey in Myanmar (2009-2010)*. <http:www.burmalibrary.org/docs14/mya-interim-poverty.pdf>. Accessed 18 November 2013.

New Light of Myanmar (*NLM*). "Success would be achieved only when Union ministries set legal framework and Region/State governments supervise respective departmental personnel". *New Light of Myanmar*, 16 August 2012a, pp. 1, 8. <http://www.burmalibrary.org/docs14/NLM2012-08-16.pdf>. Accessed 20 January 2014.

———. "Job opportunities, income can be increased and triple growth realized only if current volume of financial investments be doubled". *New Light of Myanmar*, 20 June 2012b. <http://www.myanmararchives.com/newspapers/The-New-

Light-of-Myanmar/2012/06_Jun/20-06-2012.pdf>. Accessed 22 November 2013.

————. "Reform, a combination of National Plan approved by Hluttaw and Physical Development Plan, needs to be People-Centred Development Reform which could satisfy demands of people". *New Light of Myanmar*, 14 May 2012c, pp. 1, 8. <http://www.myanmararchives.com/newspapers/The-New-Light-of-Myanmar/2012/05_May/14-05-2012.pdf>. Accessed 26 November 2013.

————. "The government is elected by the people, and it has to respect people's will". Translation of message sent to the Speakers of both houses of parliament by President U Thein Sein on 30 September 2011. *New Light of Myanmar*, 1 October 2011, pp. 1, 7. <http://www.myanmararchives.com/newspapers/The-New-Light-of-Myanmar/2011/10_Oct/01-10-2011.pdf>. Accessed 25 November 2013.

Paris Club. "Myanmar Debt Treatment—January 25, 2013". <http://www.clubdeparis.org/sections/traitements/myanmar-20130125/viewLanguage/en>. Accessed 18 November 2013.

Reuters. "Foreign Investment Jumps Fivefold in Burma". *Irrawaddy*, 13 May 2013. <http://www.irrawaddy.org/business/foreign-investment-jumps-fivefold-in-burma.html>. Accessed 18 November 2013.

Revenue Watch Institute (RWI). *The 2013 Resource Governance Index: A Measure of Transparency and Accountability in the Oil, Gas and Mining Sector*. New York: RWI, 2013. <http://www.revenuewatch.org/sites/default/files/rgi_2013_Eng.pdf>. Accessed 10 December 2013.

Thein Sein. 2012. "President invites successful economists, experts, businessmen doing well overseas to join hands with government for national development". Speech by President Thein Sein, 19 June 2012. Naypyitaw: President's Office, Government of the Union of Myanmar, 2012. <http://www.president-office.gov.mm/en/?q=briefing-room/speeches-and-remarks/2012/06/19/id-522>. Accessed 25 November 2013.

Union Budget Law 2012, (Pyidaungsu Hluttaw Law No. 6, 2012), 28 March 2012. <http://mythogod.com/sites/default/files/2012%20Main%20Law%20(English).pdf>. Accessed 22 November 2013.

United Nation Children's Fund (UNICEF). 2013. *Towards more child-focused social investments: Snapshot of Social Sector Public Budget Allocations and Spending in Myanmar*. Yangon: UNICEF, 2013. <http://www.globalbtap.org/2013/pdf/sanpshot.pdf>. Accessed 24 November 2013.

United Nations Country Team (UNCT) in Myanmar. Thematic Analysis 2011: Achieving the Millenium Development Goals in Myanmar. No date. <http://www.undp.org/content/dam/undp/library/MDG/english/MDG%20Country%20Reports/Myanmar/Thematic-Analysis-2011-for-Myanmar.pdf>. Accessed 22 November 2013.

Wai Moe. "Than Shwe Grants Himself Power to Access 'Special Funds'", *Irrawaddy*, 4 March 2011. <http://www2.irrawaddy.org/article.php?art_id=20878">. Accessed 22 November 2013.

World Bank. *Full report*. Vol. 2 of *Republic of the Union of Myanmar — Public financial management performance report*. Washington DC: World Bank, 2013. <http://documents.worldbank.org/curated/en/2013/05/17718311/republic-union-myanmar-public-financial-management-performance-report-vol-2-2-full-report>. Accessed 22 November 2013.

———. "World Bank Group steps up support for reforms in Myanmar with new interim strategy to improve people's lives". World Bank, Press release, 1 November 2012. <http://www.worldbank.org/en/news/press-release/2012/11/01/world-bank-group-steps-up-support-reforms-myanmar-new-interim-strategy-improve-lives>. Accessed 22 November 2013.

10

THE GLASS HAS WATER: A STOCK-TAKE OF MYANMAR'S ECONOMIC REFORMS

Exchange Rate, Financial System, Investment, and Sectoral Policies

Sean Turnell

The economic reforms set in train in Myanmar in recent times have succeeded in a number of ways, but not least in commanding international attention. Passenger planes flying into Yangon these days are as full as the hotels to which they bring their human cargoes, cargoes that include some of the titans (as well less exalted members) of the global business food-chain. In a world in which investors everywhere imagine themselves as beset by risk and stagnation, Myanmar has emerged as an unlikely field of opportunity for those who are, to use the fashionable phrase of our times, "seeking yield".

Beyond the headlines of the business pages, Myanmar's economic reforms are incomplete, greatly contingent upon shifting alliances, and rather more fragile than supposed. Yet they are authentic and tangible too. As one anonymous contributor to a recent meeting of diplomats put it:

> In Myanmar it is not possible to say yet that the "reform glass" is either full or empty—but we can at least say now there is water in it.

The purpose of this chapter is to undertake a stock-take of Myanmar's economic reforms: to determine the reality behind the rhetoric, to identify the fundamental from the superficial, and to distinguish that which will last from the merely ephemeral. In practical policy terms, the paper will examine Myanmar's new exchange rate regime and its strengths and weaknesses, the ramifications of the country's new *Foreign Investment Law*, mooted changes in banking laws, some changes in agriculture, and some very counterproductive changes to land laws. Highlighted too will be efforts to create institutions for revenue transparency in the extractive and energy sectors, and for fiscal reform generally.

THE FLOATING OF THE *KYAT*

The most important economic reform enacted by the government of Thein Sein was its decision (in April 2012) to reform Myanmar's exchange rate regime by allowing the country's currency, the *kyat*, to be determined via a "managed float" (Reuters 2012). Myanmar's previous dual exchange rate system—under which there was an "official" rate that set the *kyat* at around K6: US$1, compared to an unofficial market rate that mostly fluctuated around K1,000: US$1—had long been the most public symbol of the country's economic oddities. Under the new arrangements, an "auction" is held each morning amongst Myanmar's commercial banks to determine a reference rate for the *kyat* against the U.S. dollar, the Euro and the Singapore dollar. Once set, banks and money changers can then exchange the *kyat* within a band of +/-0.8 percent above or below the reference rate.

The decision to float the *kyat* was an important one, not least in that it brought with it the simultaneous hope that Myanmar's fiscal "anomaly" with respect to the foreign exchange revenues of its state-owned enterprises (SOEs) might be corrected along with it. Prior to the float, Myanmar's military regime had used the dual exchange rate to effectively expropriate the country's earnings from the export of natural gas by recording them in the public accounts at the moribund official exchange rate, rather than according to their true purchasing power as converted at the market rate.[1] With the old fixed rate of the *kyat* now abandoned in favour of the managed float, Myanmar's gas earnings (which flow through the state-owned Myanmar Oil and Gas Enterprise, MOGE) are now convertible at a rate that can make a substantial difference to the country's fiscal circumstances. This has indeed now happened, with Myanmar's budget for 2012-13 (and the projections for 2013-14) including a contribution from MOGE consistent with its earnings being translated at the managed float exchange rate.[2]

The Currency is Overvalued

Given the significance of the fiscal implications noted above, the decision to float the *kyat* must be regarded as a broad success. Nevertheless, it is a qualified success with respect to the exchange rate arrangements themselves. The problem here is that, in practice, the process by which the exchange rate of the *kyat* is determined is not really genuinely representative of true supply and demand for the currency. This is due to two factors: first, the auction process referred to above is one that operates simply for physical cash, rather than for all desired trade and other foreign transactions; second, there is no inter-bank market for foreign exchange (something not yet in place). As a consequence, the exchange rate of the *kyat* derived since flotation has been too high. This fact is sorely felt by Myanmar's small manufacturing sector, and by agricultural producers and exporters generally, who complain loudly that the prevailing value of the *kyat* has made them uncompetitive. Of course, exchange rate regimes everywhere contain anomalies that deliver currency outcomes that diverge from "fundamentals" for extended periods. In Myanmar's case, however, some alleviation from the present difficulties should come from embracing a fully-liberalized foreign exchange market. The reforms to Myanmar's exchange rate regime enacted thus far have been revolutionary. Time now, however, to make them complete.

A NEW FOREIGN INVESTMENT LAW

Next in importance to the exchange rate changes, but eclipsing these reforms in terms of the international coverage it has attracted, is the new *Foreign Investment Law* (FIL) which was finally signed by President Thein Sein on 2 November 2012.[3] Designed initially to attract foreign capital that was hitherto discouraged by Myanmar's economic and political instability, in the process of its drafting the Law took on some more protectionist elements (these are discussed below).

The FIL contains a number of "sweeteners" to attract foreign direct investment. These include:

- An income tax exemption for foreign investors for the first five consecutive years of their business;
- Further income tax exemptions on profits that are re-invested;
- Accelerated depreciation tax deductions;
- Tax relief on profits deriving from exports;
- Relief from customs duties on materials imported during the construction of a business.

Beyond these generous taxation concessions are other enticements, including a necessary guarantee to foreign investors that their businesses will "not be nationalized within the term of contract" (FIL, Chapter 13). Likewise necessary are assurances with respect to access to land, ownership of which in Myanmar has long been prohibited for foreigners. The land ownership prohibition remains, but what is now allowed under the FIL are long leases by foreign investors—for up to fifty years depending on the nature of the business concerned, with two possible ten-year extensions beyond that. Meanwhile, a range of concessions are granted with respect to the movement of funds in and out of Myanmar, including allowing the maintenance of foreign currency accounts in any bank with a foreign exchange licence, and the repatriation of profits and capital contributions (at the expiry of a project) in the original currency in which they were subscribed.

Delays and Controversies

The enticements outlined above survived various drafts of the Foreign Investment Law, the eventual passage of which came about only after prolonged negotiation and controversy. Especially vocal in the debate were cohorts of local businesses who expressed great anxiety that they would not be able to compete against foreign firms with ample capital and modern managerial and technological methods. This protectionist sentiment was made manifest in a draft of the FIL that emerged in August 2012. The draft contained a number of clauses designed to protect local interests, including a minimum capital threshold for foreign investment of US$5 million (a floor that would have removed in one stroke any hope for many diaspora investors wanting to create businesses back "home"), and the sequestering away into "restricted business" of a whole range of economic activities that could only done by locals, or by foreigners in a joint venture with a local enterprise (and within which the foreign ownership stake could not exceed 49 percent).

The outcry against the August draft of the FIL was not long in coming. Potential foreign investors made clear their view that this was a backward step in Myanmar's opening to the world, but it was the objection of local political figures (and some of the more outwardly-focussed business leaders) that proved more decisive. Concerned that this highly protectionist variant of the FIL (which was widely known in Yangon as the "No Foreign Investment Law") was little but an attempt of Myanmar's high profile "cronies" to carve up sectors of the economy for themselves, a countervailing campaign in the parliament (consisting of a broad coalition of forces, including Daw Aung San Suu Kyi and the National League for Democracy (NLD)) steered the Law back in a more open-minded direction (Zaw Win Than 2012).

As finally signed by President Sein Thein on 2 November, the FIL accordingly emerged as a more "liberal" document than it otherwise might have been. The stringent joint-venture percentages in restricted sectors was dispensed with, as was the $5 million threshold. Yet, and notwithstanding the various enticements also detailed above, the FIL continues to trouble international investors and others. Pre-eminent amongst the remaining concerns is the role granted to the Myanmar Investment Commission (MIC), the body which, under the FIL, has responsibility for the approval and oversight of foreign investment in Myanmar. With a powerful mandate that allows great discretion, the MIC alone decides:[4]

- Which sectors of Myanmar's economy are "restricted" to foreign investors;
- The nature of these restrictions, and any exceptions to them;
- The degree of foreign ownership permitted in joint ventures in restricted and other sectors;
- Investment activities that are "not required for taxation exemption and relief";
- Which foreign investments are entitled to long land leases, and any extensions to these;

- What ratios of local labour are mandated for "skilled" activities throughout the life of an investment;[5]
- Whether foreign ownership shares can be sold or transferred to other foreign parties.

The Awkward Role of the MIC

Of course, many of the powers granted to the MIC are not inherently problematic, especially if they are carried out in a non-discriminatory and transparent process that is accompanied by both appeal mechanisms and parliamentary oversight. Such processes and mechanisms are not apparent, however, in the provisions of the FIL related to the MIC, as presently understood. The "riding instructions" for the MIC contained within the Foreign Investment Law are as vague as they are far-reaching. Membership of the MIC is decided solely by the government, and beyond two reports that must be tabled before the parliament each year, the Commission is unaccountable. These governance gaps are important. In a business environment such as Myanmar's, newly emerging from decades of arbitrary and erratic decision-making, periodic nationalization episodes, and macroeconomic instability, bodies such as the MIC face a herculean task of building trust, all in a setting hitherto marked by the profound lack of this virtue.

BANKING AND FINANCIAL SECTOR

Myanmar does not possess a properly functioning financial system. Reforms to the sector are under consideration, including the introduction of new laws to update and upgrade the *Financial Institutions of Myanmar Law* (FIML, promulgated in 1990, under which private banks were first authorized), and the *Central Bank of Myanmar Law* (CBML, likewise 1990). What the modifications might entail is not possible to determine yet, but certainly necessary with respect to the FIML are changes that allow greater freedom for banks against what is, at present, unnecessary and damaging "micro meddling". Such interference in what are, in essence, mostly commercial decisions, includes (in a far from exhaustive list): caps and floors on the interest banks can charge and pay; restrictions on lending to farmers and rural enterprise; unrealistic collateral requirements on lending; and unreasonable (and unfathomable) limitations on branch openings.

Changes to sector-wide laws aside, quite a number of changes (most in the direction of reform) have taken place in Myanmar's banking sector in recent times—some instigated through the relaxation of various rules and regulations, some driven by the banks themselves. Amongst the most prominent of these are:

- The granting of foreign exchange licences to most of Myanmar's private banks. Such permissions are largely manifest in the form of money-changer kiosks in Myanmar's airports and major cities. There has been little development yet of more sophisticated services and instruments for business;
- The expansion of the lending and savings mobilization *potential* of the private banks through the relaxation of their required "capital to deposits" ratio (from 1:10 to 1:25);
- Allowing the private commercial banks to install Automatic Teller Machines (ATMs) and to issue debit cards. At present Myanmar's ATMs are hampered by the volume of notes they have to dispense, even for relatively small transactions, while the use of debit cards is as yet limited, both by consumers and by the small number of outlets that accept them;
- Permitting the entry of global credit cards. These are gradually being accepted by hotels and other tourist sites in Myanmar, and are useable at the ATMs of some of the private banks (*Irrawaddy* 2012*a*). Similarly now operating are the global money transfer firms such as Western Union, likewise in partnership with a handful of the private banks (*Irrawaddy* 2012*b*);
- Expanding allowable collateral beyond land and gold, and to include some agricultural commodities;
- Allowing banks to expand their branch networks, and permitting them to establish branches in buildings they do not own.

Foreign Banks

Under the existing Financial Institutions of Myanmar Law, foreign banks were to be introduced into Myanmar in a three-stage process; first via authorizations to establish representative offices; second by allowing foreign banks to establish "joint venture" banking institutions with local banks; and, finally, allowing foreign banks to establish themselves in their own right in the form of a Burmese subsidiary and/or a local branch able to conduct full banking business. Across the 1990s, representative offices of foreign banks came and went, and a handful of joint venture proposals were put before the Central Bank of Myanmar. None were approved. Meanwhile, against the background of Myanmar's failing economy and the 2003 banking crisis, interest in the country as a banking destination faded, along with its reform prospects. The number of foreign bank representative offices, which at one point in the mid-1990s was over fifty, shrank to little more than a dozen or so hardy survivors.

In the wake of the mooted "new" FIML, and amidst the current general wave of optimism with respect to Myanmar, the interest of foreign banks in the country has once again been awakened. Prominent international banks have again taken up representative offices (Standard Chartered and Australia's ANZ being two of the most notable); more broadly, expectations that foreign banks might at last be allowed to conduct banking operations are running (perhaps unrealistically) high. Not much is known for certain about precisely what the new FIML might say on the issue of foreign banks, but various hints from government and Central Bank of Myanmar officials point to a relaunch of the existing "three step" ladder, albeit with the enticement that foreign entities could be permitted to hold up to 80 percent of any joint venture (Robinson 2013a).

Sanctions Developments

Of course, one of the most significant changes afforded Myanmar's banking sector since the advent of Thein Sein's administration comes from outside the country, through the ending of financial sanctions.[6] These (certain individual lists excepted) were dominated by the sanctions applied by the United States which, under the provisions of the 2003 *Burmese Freedom and Democracy Act* (BFDA) and the *Tom Lantos (JADE) Act* of 2008, banned the export of U.S. financial services to Myanmar. The sanctions, and (more significantly) the deliberate policies of the past State Peace and Development Council (SPDC) regime to wind down much of the banking system following Myanmar's 2003 financial crisis, effectively isolated the country from the global financial system and made difficult the flow of new ideas, methods, and norms that, elsewhere, have become increasingly standard.

In late February 2013, U.S. sanctions on Myanmar's banking sector were further eased when it was announced that four Myanmar banks separately listed on the U.S. Treasury's "Specially Designated Nationals" (SDN) list, could now conduct business with U.S. financial institutions (OFAC 2013). The four banks include the state-owned Myanma Economic Bank (MEB) and the Myanma Investment and Commercial Bank (MICB), as well as two banks founded by a couple of Myanmar's most prominent "cronies", the Asia Green Development Bank (AGD, owned by Tay Za), and the Ayeyarwady Bank (AB, controlled by Zaw Zaw). Being on the SDN list had hitherto excluded these banks from engaging in business with U.S. financial institutions, despite the generalized lifting of the broad financial services ban noted above. With respect to the two private banks, this latest easing is, however, limited to the conduct of transactions business (primarily funds transfer, correspondent relations, and the like). U.S. banks continue to be restricted from investing in either AGD or AB, or from forming joint-venture relations with them.

Central Banking

With respect to the Central Bank of Myanmar (CBM), reform is urgent. According to the International Monetary Fund, in an assessment that followed its annual "Article IV" advisory mission in March 2012, "the CBM does not have a monetary policy framework" (IMF 2012, p. 6). Urging the creation of such a framework to accompany the earlier exchange rate reforms, the IMF recommended that:

> The CBM should be given full operational autonomy and proper accountability, with the clearly defined primary objective of domestic price stability.[7]

Of course, genuine operational autonomy of the CBM will depend not just upon appropriate legislation (which might shortly be forthcoming; see below), but also on the central bank's escape from being the funding vehicle for the government's budget. Put simply, no credible monetary policy can be enacted by the CBM while ever it has to engage in printing money to finance the state. Bringing about fiscal reform, creating a more efficient tax system, creating a viable bond market and, above all, cutting unproductive (primarily military) government spending, will bring many virtues to Myanmar's economy. Just one of these will be the fiscal space within which to grant genuine independence to its central bank.

In January 2013 a revised Central Bank of Myanmar Law was approved by Thein Sein's Cabinet, and was submitted to parliament. Drawn up with the assistance of embedded advisers from Japan, Thailand, the IMF, World Bank, and Asian Development Bank, the new law (as expected) carves the CBM out from the Ministry of Finance and grants it *de jure* independence in the conduct of monetary policy. According to the widely reported comments of Khin Saw Oo (head of CBM's Financial Institutions Regulation and Anti-Money Laundering Department, and seemingly the spokesperson for the Bank), the CBM would also henceforth "stop the direct deficit financing" of the government, while also moving to replace direct monetary controls with open market operations (see Ten Kate and Kyaw Thu 2013). Commenting on the overall program of change at the CBM, the head of the IMF's Asia and Pacific Department noted that the suggested changes were "big for any country—[but] ... particularly big for a country that is emerging from years and years of being a closed economy"(ibid.).

Inflation

The absence of an independent central bank, coupled with high, money-financed budget deficits, has frequently driven inflation in Myanmar into double digits, and to levels that have long stood out against the price stability of its neighbours in Asia. Current IMF estimates suggest that Myanmar's inflation rate is around 6 percent per annum (IMF 2012). This remains above regional norms, although it is lower than in the past. Nevertheless, inflation remains a ever-lurking problem in Myanmar. Since it brings with it certain transaction costs and other inefficiencies, Myanmar's high relative inflation rates also exacerbate the country's falling competitiveness, which is due to a rising real exchange rate for the *kyat*. As previously noted, in nominal terms the *kyat* has appreciated by around 50 percent over the last few years, in the process rendering many Burmese enterprises uncompetitive against cheaper (especially Chinese) imports.[8]

AGRICULTURE

Myanmar's agricultural sector has long been suppressed by poor and intrusive government policy-making, a chronic lack of credit, deficient and degraded infrastructure, and an absence of secure land title and property rights. These woes, which counter Myanmar's bountiful natural endowments, have resulted in the country slipping down the league tables in the trade of foodstuffs and commodities it once dominated, and they determine the dire poverty that characterizes the lives of the country's (majority) rural populace.

Under the Thein Sein administration there has been much talk of reforming Myanmar's agricultural sector. The first of the "national workshops" (on Rural Development and Poverty Alleviation, held in May 2011) that have been such a feature of the economic reform narrative in Myanmar was devoted to agriculture.[9] This came up with a number of recommendations and projected outcomes, mostly concerned with increasing productivity through improvements to rural infrastructure, access to affordable inputs, and expanded credit availability (focussing on microfinance). Other gatherings devoted to agriculture that have been convened since—many sponsored by multilateral institutions, development agencies, and (not least) potential foreign investors—have taken up similar themes.

Reforms have been Slow in Coming

Despite this, and notwithstanding its rhetorical prominence, the record of reforms actually implemented in Myanmar's agricultural sector is, as yet, slim. Extra funding to the sector has been pledged by the government in partnership with the UNDP, but this is more ameliorative than transformational. Meanwhile, great stress is placed on the emergence of private sector agricultural companies to restore input and marketing chains, advance-purchase credit, and other critical soft and hard infrastructure. Over thirty of these "special agricultural development companies" (SADCs)[10] have been formed in recent years, many of which have run into financial difficulties from the credit side of their operations. With regard to the latter issue, the problem has been high credit defaults (bad and doubtful loan ratios of between 30 to 60 percent being reported) amongst Burmese farmers (Dapice and others 2011, pp. 5–6). Of course, all of this is symptomatic of the moribund state of Myanmar's rural credit arrangements, from which a substantial cohort of the remaining SADCs have now withdrawn.

A comprehensive transformation of agriculture in Myanmar is urgently needed, beginning with the removal of the market distortions that continue to bedevil the sector. Prominent in this context are the numerous production controls, export restrictions, and procurement orders that, despite being formally discouraged by the central government, linger from the previous military regime. Myanmar's success as an exporter of beans and pulses in recent years (it is now one of the world's largest exporters of these commodities) demonstrates that its farmers and traders can respond vigorously to market signals. The trade in beans and pulses was liberalized a decade ago, in great contrast to the heavy hand of state intervention in most other commodities.

Agriculture as the Future—Lessons and Voices from Myanmar's Past

Granting Myanmar's farmers greater freedoms over what, when, and how to produce will deliver both immediate livelihood improvements and, likely, greater export volumes, as the beans and pulse example commends. But such a broad policy presumption will also likely yield other improvements to Myanmar's organizational framework—the institutions and infrastructure that, in the long run, will also prepare the way for the country's industrialization, and its *transformational* growth and development. Such development "sequencing" is more or less orthodox in economic advice, and honoured in practice in the experiences of Myanmar's Asian neighbours. It is an idea, however, that was given its earliest and most powerful advocacy in the writings of Myanmar's own and greatest economist, Hla Myint. A figure of genuine global standing in the evolution of economic ideas (but particularly upon the links between openness to trade and economic development), Hla Myint long ago extolled the virtues of farmers as agents of change, in contrast to the then orthodoxy:[11]

> ...[that] the latent entrepreneurial capacity among peasant farmers can be released in a free-market environment offering incentives goes against the once-fashionable sociological stereotype of the traditional farmers, bound by habit and custom in resisting economic change ...[i]t is still worth pointing out that peasant farmers, like the small traders and manufacturers, are self-employed persons who have to make daily economic decisions to allocate their resources to take advantage of market opportunities (Lal and Hla Myint 1996, p. 206).

From the success of small farmers, Hla Myint suggested, could be yielded scale economies and improvements in infrastructure:

Thus the expansion of peasant exports, leading to the development of the market system by drawing the peasant households into the exchange economy, would be a powerful factor in reducing the marketing and organizational costs of the traditional sector. This would pave the way for further economic growth through a greater degree of specialization and division of labour along Adam Smithian lines, by widening the size of the local market through improvements in transport and communications and joining them together into a more articulated market system extending over the whole economy (ibid., p. 194).

Until finally a country's "organizational framework" (what economists would later call its "institutions") were transformed, and its growth path established:

The remarkably rapid expansion of labour-intensive manufactured exports from Taiwan and Korea could not have been possible without the improvements in the organizational framework to support the process, and these improvements spread spontaneously from the agricultural sector. The widening of the domestic market, and the sharing of common facilities such as transport, electricity, and the marketing and credit network, between the small industrialists and the small farmers in a decentralized pattern of industrialization, would then reduce the general level of transactions costs for the whole economy. Last but not least, the close human contacts between the small industrialists and small farmers would help to bring out latent entrepreneurial talent among the latter, stimulating a steady stream of minor technical improvements adapted to local conditions (ibid., p. 342).

LAND REFORM?

One of the most intransigent obstacles to the improvement of Myanmar's agricultural sector is the fact that all rural land is formally owned by the state. Individual farmers have been eligible for 30-year inheritable *use* rights, with such rights determined by village-level land committees, but hitherto land could not be legally *and* voluntarily transferred between unrelated individuals. This also meant that land could not be effectively used as collateral on loans. More broadly, the lack of land title has long denied the Burmese cultivator the incentive, and security, to invest in, or otherwise improve, their holdings.

In late 2011 a new Farmland Bill was introduced, ostensibly designed to rectify some of these problems.[12] Its passage into law thereby revoking the (greatly damaging) *Land Nationalization Act (1953)*, the new legislation asserts a number of rights for farmers and cultivators. These include two especially critical entitlements:

- The right to hold and use farmland;
- The right to "ease, exchange, inherit, donate or permanently transfer" land, but not "without the consent and agreement of the legitimate (sic) owner".

The right to hold and use farmland is unchanged, but is meant to be strengthened through the operations of "Farmland Management Bodies". The second of these rights is, in theory, greatly strengthened under the new law, but at best the law has generated unintended effects. Both will be discussed below.

The Law is Inimical to Security of Tenure

In practice, and in contradiction to its declared aim, the Farmland Bill has done little to improve land tenure security for Myanmar's farmers. The clauses noted above are moves in the right direction, but their efficacy depends upon both a fair starting point, and a process for resolving disputes that is just, transparent, open to public participation, and which recognizes local knowledge as the basis of claims of individuals and families to land. Such a process is lacking in the Farmland Bill.[13] Instead, a centralized process is established, in which extraordinary and highly discretionary powers are assigned in a top-down process to "farmland management bodies", one each at the national (the Central Farmland Management Body), region/state, district, township, and village/tract levels. Authority for these bodies at all levels descends from the Central Body, which is headed by the Minister of Agriculture and Irrigation (currently an anti-reform "hardliner"), and has the Deputy Minister as vice-chairman, the Director General for the Settlement and Land Records Department as Secretary, and "relevant government department officials" as members.

The powers granted to the Farmland Management Bodies (whose internal workings are entirely opaque) include the right to make determinations as to who has work rights over a plot of land; to approve or not approve the transfer of such rights; to resolve any disputes over these rights (and to exclusively hear any appeals against such decisions); and to "revoke the right to work farmland". Should anyone fail to comply with an eviction order issued by the Ministry of Agriculture and Irrigation, or by a farmland management body, the penalty includes a prison term of up to six months. Anyone deemed to be obstructing any member or employee of such bodies "in the performance of … his duties" is likewise liable to six months in prison (Farmland Bill, Chapter 12).

Myanmar's new Farmland Bill likewise does little to reform a system in which government direction to farmers of "what, how, and when" to produce (often at odds with circumstances on the ground) continues to bedevil the creation of a more rational and market-oriented agricultural sector. Chapter 10 of the Farmland Bill consolidates such directions in law, in a seemingly innocuous section (Section 23) that states:

> If it is deemed to be beneficial to the State or to the agriculturalists by cultivating any particular crop in any particular area or by utilizing farmland in the prescribed manner in any particular area, the President may take or cause to be taken such measures by as he deems expedient for the cultivation of such particular crop or for the utilization of farmland…(sic)

Of course, the problems apparent in the above are not simply abstract or theoretical concerns. Since the passage of the Farmland Bill, some 3.6 million hectares of land have allegedly been "re-assigned" from use by cultivators in favour of local and foreign agri-businesses (Mizzima 2012; Kyaw Kyaw 2012). In essence, what the Farmland Bill (and its legislative sibling, the Vacant, Fallow and Virgin Lands Bill which was promulgated at the same time) grants is more or less a Burmese version of the "eminent domain" principle, under which, in the United States and other Western countries, governments can resume land if it can, for social or economic reasons, be better employed otherwise. In the latter countries such powers, however, are greatly restricted in practice by all manner of safeguards, conventions, and appeal processes, none of which yet exist in Myanmar. According to the Asia Legal Resource Centre, the legal framework to provide land security for Myanmar's farmers "has not only failed to keep pace" but, under the laws outlined here, "has in fact gone backwards" (2012; see also AHRC 2011).[14]

EXTRACTIVE SECTOR INITIATIVES

In December 2012 President Thein Sein established the Extractive Industry Transparency Initiative (EITI) Leading Authority.[15] Designed to partially fulfil his earlier promise that Myanmar would sign up to the global EITI framework, and headed by the reform-minded Minister Soe Thane, the Authority was tasked to:

> ... ensure better management for extractive industries of natural resources, develop good investment environment, create opportunity for a frank and transparent discussion between private investors and the people, and join hands with the public-based societies of the private sector so as to be able to effectively deal with the tasks of extractive industry transparency initiative on behalf of the State (*NLM* 2012).[16]

As is apparent from previous discussion in this chapter of the expropriations of gas revenues under the SPDC, extractive sector transparency will be vital to ensure Myanmar has the financial wherewithal to pay for the nation-building ahead. The EITI process is one avenue to assist in achieving this end. A coalition of government, corporations, and civil society groups, EITI was established (at the initiative of the UK government) to ensure that "companies report payments to government (taxes, royalties, etc.) and the government reports what it has received" (EITI website, FAQs). A country becomes EITI "compliant" when governments and companies comprehensively disclose all payments made and received, when these disclosures are reconciled and published by EITI, and when all possible discrepancies are addressed.

Of course, membership of EITI is purely voluntary, and the process levies no legal sanctions. There would be reputational damage to a government that was adjudged "non-compliant" after having signed up for candidacy, but little other censure. Given this and what is at stake, Myanmar should adopt other measures to complement, and make more certain, the revenue transparency sought through EITI.[17] One of these measures, employed in a number of countries around the world (with varying degrees of success), would be to craft legislation that requires all extractive sector revenues to be paid into a special "national account". Such an account, where the balance, as well as flows in and out, would be completely transparent and without government intermediation (the legislation could require that this information be available in real time and online), would allow scrutiny not just of payments made and received, but also of expenditures and disbursements. The most successful example of an "account" of this nature is that established to deal with oil revenues in the African archipelago of Sao Tome and Principe.[18] Created by a bespoke Oil Revenue Law (in 2004), and written with the assistance of the Earth Institute of Columbia University, the World Bank, and the IMF, Sao Tome and Principe's National

Oil Account is meant to guard against corruption, "Dutch disease" effects, as well as the temptations provided to government from revenue windfalls. Accordingly, its emphasis is not just on revenue transparency, but also on expenditure disclosure. Myanmar has similar needs, although the country's very apparent expenditure requirements for health, education, and critical infrastructure would give little room for extravagance on the part of a government that was genuinely concerned with the welfare of the Burmese people. To this end, a law such as that adopted by Sao Tome and Principe might hold more relevance for Myanmar through emphasis on revenue rather than on expenditure (although clearly the latter would be an obvious area for parliamentary scrutiny).

INTERNATIONAL DEBT RELIEF AND NEW IFI LENDING

In late-January 2013 a landmark agreement was reached between the government of Myanmar and a group of countries organized under the "Paris Club" of creditors. The agreement, reached after what were described as "marathon" negotiations, effectively cancelled around 60 percent of Myanmar's external debt. Leading the pack of countries in the mood for debt forgiveness was Japan (some $6.3 billion, including interest arrears), Norway ($534 million, the bulk of which was interest arrears) as well as generous write-offs from smaller creditors such as the United Kingdom, France, Germany, and the Netherlands. Further negotiations with these creditor nations may see further write-offs in the near future, while remaining debts will be "rescheduled" across fifteen years (after a seven-year "grace period" in which no repayments are to be made). The $3 billion or so Myanmar owes to China (from loans made in the last few years, much of it ramped up in the final days of the SPDC regime) are not included in the relief package.

The Paris Club terms granted to Myanmar were generous. Normally debt write-offs are granted to countries designated as "Heavily Indebted Poor Countries" (HIPCs). In order to be counted as an HIPC a country must have must have debts amounting to at least 30 percent of GDP (Myanmar's debt to GDP ratio is about 18 percent), debt to exports ratio of 200 percent (Myanmar's ratio is roughly 115 percent) and debt to government revenues ratio of at least 280 percent (Myanmar's ratio here is about 120 percent) (Robinson 2013b). The Paris Club countries made no detailed justification for Myanmar's favourable treatment, beyond simply acknowledging what the group referred to as the country's "exceptional situation".

Alongside the Paris Club negotiations were similar, if rather more immediately important, negotiations over Myanmar's unpaid arrears to the World Bank and the Asian Development Bank (ADB). The arrears to these two institutions, collectively around $900 million, were a barrier to the granting of future loans and assistance. Against the political import accorded to removing this constraint against international financial institution (IFI) engagement with Myanmar, a "bridging loan" to clear the arrears was provided by the state-owned Japan Bank for International Cooperation (JBIC).

Bridging loan in place, the World Bank and ADB moved with alacrity (or indecent haste, depending upon one's viewpoint). From the World Bank came a loan package (which it labelled "Reengagement and Reform Support Credit to Myanmar") totalling $440 million, and designed to "strengthen macroeconomic stability, improve public financial management and improve the investment climate" (World Bank 2012, 2013). Part of the funds are also ear-marked to repay the arrear-clearing bridge loan provided by the Japan Bank for International Cooperation. Meanwhile, the ADB is allocating $512 million for almost identical purposes, and similarly includes a tranche dedicated to repaying JBIC (ADB 2013).

FRAMEWORK FOR ECONOMIC AND SOCIAL REFORMS

In late 2012, Myanmar's Ministry of National Planning and Economic Development (in conjunction with the country's leading "think tank", the Myanmar Development Resource Institute (MDRI), drafted an important statement of broad policy. This statement, the Framework for Economic and Social Reforms (FESR), was revealed publicly at a coordination meeting of international donors in January 2013, who were requested in turn to conform their own activities with the goals therein set out (Reuters 2013).

Normally documents such as the FESR—broad statements of philosophy and innocuous policy pronouncements—would not amount to much. This may as yet be the case for the FESR too, but in a country in which similar documents in the past have justified and set in train events of enormous significance, it is a document worthy of note.[19] A policy wish-list reliant upon somewhat hopeful assumptions, perhaps the most significant component of the FESR is what it calls the "strategic thrust" of policy, which, in contrast to the past, "emphasizes the importance of moving towards a market-driven economy, the need to move to bottom-up planning and from direct to indirect levers of government policy in nourishing the development of free markets". An obvious appeal to the gallery perhaps, but given Myanmar's history in which the presumptions of the state have long constituted the country's primary economic problem, it is one that might be considered worth making.

CONCLUSION

The first two years of the Thein Sein administration in Myanmar has seen some progress in the reform of Myanmar's economy. Changes to the country's exchange rate arrangements, though incomplete, especially have the potential to be transformative. Other reforms, with respect to trade and foreign investment, agriculture, banking, as well as in more foundational institutional and legal issues, have been touched upon, but as yet incompletely and (sometimes) problematically. The pattern of reform implementation, and its manifestation in legislation, continue to invite concern, especially to the extent this concern coalesces with fears of the possible "cronyization" of Myanmar's economy. The latter outcome, the possibility of which became more visible during the back-and-forth over Myanmar's new Foreign Investment Law, represents a clear threat to the country's progress towards a more prosperous and liberal political economy. Economic reform in Myanmar is a journey that has now commenced, but it is not yet one with an ending in sight.

Notes

1 For background on this issue, see Turnell 2008, pp. 958–76.
2 Budget data here is based upon an official announcement of the Burmese Government on 2 February, 2012. See Aung Hla Tun 2012. For the 2013/14 projections, see Eleven Myanmar/Asia News Network 2013.
3 *Foreign Investment Law* (FIL). *Pyidaungsu Hluttaw Law* No. 21 (2012). <http://www.myanmarlegalservices.com/wp-content/uploads/2012/11/NEW-FILEnglish-from-DICA-2.pdf>. Accessed 15 January 2014.
4 The duties and powers of the MIC are set out in Chapter VII of the FIL.

5   In the earliest and most liberal drafts of the FIL, the ratio of skilled workers in a foreign venture who must be Myanmar citizens was stipulated to be 25, 50, and 75 percent after 5, 10, and 15 years respectively. In the "protectionist" August 2012 draft, the intervals for these benchmarks were shortened to 2, 4, and 6 years. The latter intervals remain in the final version of 2 November 2012. The MIC can waive these requirements, and the FIL makes special note of exemptions for high-technology sectors. Nevertheless, the issue remains one of concern to many potential international investors interviewed by the author.

6   The easing of sanctions became effective on 11 July 2012, when the U.S. Treasury's Office of Foreign Assets Control (OFAC) issued general licences allowing U.S. firms to export financial services to Myanmar, and make investments there. An earlier easing, on 17 April 2012, had allowed U.S. firms to provide financial services to Myanmar for the purposes of religious, humanitarian, and other non-profit activities. See OFAC 2012.

7   Advisory teams from the Bank of Japan and the Bank of Thailand have been in situ in the CBM since early 2012. Their assistance is primarily with respect to operational issues, rather than with policy issues such as the question of central bank independence.

8   The *kyat*/US$ exchange rate is currently around K850: US$1; as recently as 2010 it was over K1,000: US$1. Inflation is seldom less than 8 percent per annum.

9   Details of the workshop are provided at the website of Myanmar's embassy in Geneva; see <http://missions.itu.int/~myanmar/11nlm/jun/n110621.htm> (accessed 28 August 2012).

10 The most prominent SADC is the Myanmar Agri-business Public Corporation Limited (MAPCO), the chairman of which is Chit Khine (whose Eden Group is one of Myanmar's leading "crony" corporations) and whose largest shareholder is Zaw Zaw (owner of the even more prominent Max Myanmar Group); see MAPCO website at: <http://www.mapco.com.mm/.

11 These passages, written solely by Hla Myint, appear in Lal and Hla Myint (1996).

12 For English translations of the Farmland Bill and the Vacant, Fallow and Virgin Lands Bills, see <http://www.Myanmarlibrary.org/docs12/2011_Farmland_Bill(en).pdf> and <http://www.Myanmarlibrary.org/docs13/VFVLM_Law-en.pdf>. For a taste of the discussion around these laws, see AHRC 2011, and Kean 2012.

13 The inequities and other problems in the new land bills have generated much commentary inside and outside Myanmar. For a flavour of the international reaction from highly respected and influential figures in the land rights debate, see Roy Prosterman and Daryl Vhugen 2012.

14 Stung by rising incidences of farmer protests, and other high profile disputes over land, the Thein Sein administration belatedly recognized some of shortcomings of its new agricultural land bills. Promises were made throughout 2012 that the land bills would return to the parliament for modification, but by the first sitting of the parliament in 2013 little progress on this front was apparent. In September 2012 a Land Investigation Committee was formed by the parliament to investigate "land grabs". The Committee reported over three hundred especially egregious examples to the parliament to be taken up in its January 2013 sitting. See Noe Noe Aung 2012.

15 For details of the Extractive Industries Transparency Initiative, see the organization's website at <http://eiti.org/> (accessed 22 December 2012).

16 These events now place Myanmar on the formal track to EITI candidacy. From this point certain "sign up requirements" must be achieved, after which Myanmar has eighteen months to publish its first EITI report, to reconcile what companies have said they have paid with what the government acknowledges it has received. Once a country has met all EITI requirements, it can be recognised as "EITI Compliant". For more on these processes, see the EITI website, <http://eiti.org/eiti>, (accessed 20 December 2012). The official notification about the formation of the EITI Leading Authority was highlighted on the EITI website, <http://eiti.org/news/myanmar-appoints-eiti-lead> (accessed 20 December 2012).

17 For an example of why greater legal force may be necessary when opportunity meets principle, see Ten Kate 2012.

18 For details of the oil revenue laws and institutions for Sao Tome and Principe, and why they are so highly regarded, see Fragile States Unit, AfDB 2011. For a similar positive assessment, see Bel and Faria 2007.

19 "The Burmese Way to Socialism" and the "The System of Correlation of Man and his Environment", two tracts that set the scene for military rule in Myanmar in the early 1960s, come readily to mind).

References

Asia Human Rights Commission (AHRC). "Myanmar: Draft Land Law Denies Basic Rights to Farmers". Statement by the Asia Human Rights Commission, 1 November 2011. <http://www.humanrights.asia/news/ahrc-news/AHRC-STM-163-2011>. Accessed 20 January 2014.

Asian Legal Resource Centre (ALRC). "Myanmar at risk of land-grabbing epidemic". Report, 6 June 2012. Relief Web, United Nations Office for the Coordination of Humanitarian Affairs (OCHA). <http://reliefweb.int/report/myanmar/myanmar-risk-land-grabbing-epidemic>. Accessed 16 January 2014.

Asian Development Bank (ADB). "ADB Returns to Myanmar with First Re-engagement Assistance." Press Release, 28 January 2013. <http://www.adb.org/news/adb-returns-myanmar-first-re-engagement-assistance>. Accessed 9 February 2013.

Aung Hla Tun. "Myanmar plans jump in health, education spending". *Reuters*, 2 February 2012. <http://www.trust.org/item/?map=myanmar-plans-jump-in-health-education-spending/>. Accessed 30 August 2012.

Bell, J.C. and T.M. Faria. "Critical Issues for a Revenue Management Law". In *Escaping the Resource Curse*, edited by M. Humphreys, J.D. Sachs and J.E. Stiglitz. New York: Columbia University Press, 2007.

Dapice, D., T. Vallely, B. Wilkinson and M. McPherson. *Myanmar Agriculture in 2011: Old Problems and New Challenges*. Prepared for Proximity Design, Myanmar. Boston: Ash Center for Democratic Governance and Innovation, Harvard Kennedy School, 2011. <http://www.ash.harvard.edu/extension/ash/docs/myanmar1111.pdf>. Accessed 16 January 2014.

Eleven Myanmar/Asia News Network. "Defense Budget Sparks Debate in Myanmar Parliament". *Asiaone*, 3 March 2013. <http://news.asiaone.com/News/AsiaOne percent2BNews/Asia/Story/A1Story20130303-405886.html>. Accessed 6 March 2013.

Extractive Industries Transparency Initiative (EITI) website. FAQs. <http://eiti.org/faqs#WhatEITI>. Accessed 15 January 2014.

Farmland Bill 2011. Approved by the *Pyithu Hluttaw* on 20 September 2011. Translation available at: <http://www.Myanmarlibrary.org/docs12/2011_Farmland_Bill(en).pdf>. Accessed 15 January 2014.

Foreign Investment Law (FIL). Pyidaungsu Hluttaw Law No. 21 (2012). <http://www.myanmarlegalservices.com/wp-content/uploads/2012/11/NEW-FILEnglish-from-DICA-2.pdf>. Accessed 15 January 2014.

Fragile States Unit (OSFU), African Development Bank. *São Tomé and Príncipe—Maximizing Oil Wealth for Equitable Growth and Sustainable Socio-Economic Development*. Team Leader: Mr. B. Jones. 2011. <http://www.afdb.org/fileadmin/uploads/afdb/Documents/Project-and-Operations/Sao%20Tome%20and%20Principe%20-%20Maximizing%20oil%20wealth%20for%20equitable%20growth%20and%20sustainable%20socio-economic%20development.pdf>. Accessed 22 December 2012.

International Monetary Fund (IMF). *Myanmar—2011 Article IV Consultation: Myanmar—Staff Report for the 2011 Article IV Consultation*. IMF Country Report No. 12/104. Washington DC: IMF, May 2012. <http://www.imf.org/external/pubs/ft/scr/2012/cr12104.pdf>. Accessed 15 January 2014.

Irrawaddy. "Visa Plans to Introduce Credit Cards to Myanmar". *Irrawaddy*, 13 December 2012*a*. <http://www.irrawaddy.org/latest-news/visa-plans-to-introduce-credit-cards-in-burma.html>. Accessed 14 January 2014.

———. "Western Union Begins International Money Transfers in Myanmar". *Irrawaddy*, 13 December 2012b. <http://www.irrawaddy.org/latest-news/21146. html>. Accessed 14 January 2014.

Kean, Thomas. "Expert Cautions on 'Land Grab' Model". *Myanmar Times*, 27 February–4 March 2012. <http://mmtimes.com/2012/news/616/news61612. html>. Accessed 19 March 2012.

Kyaw Kyaw. "Land Reform is Key to Myanmar's Future". *The Diplomat*, 25 August 2012. <http://thediplomat.com/2012/08/25/land-reform-key-to-Myanmars-future/>. Accessed 30 August 2012.

Lal, D. and Hla Myint. *The Political Economy of Poverty, Equity and Growth*. Oxford: Clarendon Press, 1996.

Mizzima News. "Land Confiscation Issue a Major Concern for Myanmar Rights Groups". *Mizzima News*, 23 October 2012. <http://www.mizzima.com/news/inside-Myanmar/8271-land-confiscation-issue-major-concern-Myanmars-rights-groups.html>. Accessed 20 December 2012.

New Light of Myanmar. "Formation of Extractive Industry Transparency Initiative Leading Authority". Republic of the Union of Myanmar, President Office, Notification No 99/2012, 14 December 2012. *New Light of Myanmar*, 15 December 2012. <http://www.burmalibrary.org/docs14/NLM2012-12-15.pdf>. Accessed 15 January 2014.

Noe Noe Aung. "Commission will Report over 300 Land Grabs to Myanmar MPs". *Myanmar Times*, 17 December 2012. <http://www.mmtimes.com/index.php/national-news/3591-commission-will-report-over-300-land-grabs-to-hluttaw. html>. Accessed 22 December 2012.

Office of Foreign Assets Control (OFAC), Department of the Treasury (U.S.). Burmese Sanctions Regulations 31 C.F.R. Part 537, Executive Order 13448 of October 18, 2007, Executive Order 13464 of April 30, 2008. General License No. 19: General License with Respect to Asia Green Development Bank, Ayeyarwady Bank, Myanma Economic Bank, and Myanma Investment and Commercial Bank, 22 February 2013. <http://www.treasury.gov/resource-center/sanctions/Programs/Documents/burmagl19.pdf>. Accessed 15 January 2014.

———. *Burmese Sanctions Regulations*, 31 C.F.R. Part 537, General License No. 16: Authorizing the Exportation or Reexportation of Financial Services to Burma, 11 July 2012. <http://www.treasury.gov/resource-center/sanctions/Programs/Documents/burmagl16.pdf>. Accessed 15 January 2014.

OSFU. *See* Fragile States Unit (OSFU), African Development Bank.

Prosterman, Roy, and Daryl Vhugen. "Land to the Tillers of Myanmar". *New York Times*, 13 June 2012. <http://www.nytimes.com/2012/06/14/opinion/land-to-the-tillers-of-myanmar.html?_r=0>. Accessed 27 December 2012.

Reuters. "Myanmar aims to improve lives, modernise with new reforms". *South China Morning Post*, 19 January 2013. <http://www.scmp.com/news/asia/

article/1131595/myanmar-aims-improve-lives-modernise-new-reforms>. Accessed 16 January 2014.

Reuters. "Central Bank to Strike New Exchange Rate for the *Kyat*". *Bangkok Post,* 21 March 2012. <http://www.bangkokpost.com/lite/topstories/285244/central-bank-to-strike-newexchange-rate-for-the-kyat>. Accessed 21 December 2012.

Robinson, Gwen. "Myanmar Moves to Open Up to Foreign Banks". *Financial Times,* 6 February 2013*a*. <http://www.ft.com/intl/cms/s/0/6c837b0c-707a-11e2-a2cf-00144feab49a.html#axzz2MuPkTwmR>. Accessed 8 March 2013.

————. "Myanmar Signs Deal with Foreign Creditors". *Financial Times,* 28 January 2013*b*. <http://www.ft.com/intl/cms/s/0/9b2d6e4c-68b2-11e2-9a3f-00144feab49a.html#axzz2O7nOpCJk>. Accessed 21 March 2013.

Ten Kate, Daniel. "Myanmar Oil Veteran Rebuffs Suu Kyi as Shell, Chevron Weigh Bids". *Bloomberg,* 18 September 2012. <http://www.bloomberg.com/news/2012-09-18/myanmar-oil-veteran-rebuffs-suu-kyi-as-shell-chevron-weigh-bids.html>. Accessed 13 December 2012.

Ten Kate, Daniel, and Kyaw Thu. "Myanmar Central Bank Revamp to end Army Legacy". *Bloomberg,* 8 February 2013. <http://www.bloomberg.com/news/2013-02-07/myanmar-central-bank-overhaul-to-end-army-legacy-southeast-asia.html. Accessed 9 February 2013.

Turnell, S. "Burma's Insatiable State". *Asian Survey* 48, no. 6 (2008): 958–76.

Vacant, Fallow and Virgin Lands Management Law (Pyidaungsu Hluttaw Law No. 10 of 2012), 30 March 2012. Translation available at: <http://www.Myanmarlibrary.org/docs13/VFVLM_Law-en.pdf>. Accessed 15 January 2014.

World Bank. "Myanmar and World Bank Group now fully engaged to spur growth and create opportunities for all". Press Release, 27 January 2013. <http://www.worldbank.org/en/news/press-release/2013/01/27/myanmar-world-bank-group-now-fully-engaged-spur-growth-and-create-opportunities-for-all>. Accessed 9 February 2013.

————. *Myanmar — Reengagement and Reform Support Credit Program.* Report Number 73899. Washington DC: World Bank, 2012. <http://documents.worldbank.org/curated/en/2012/12/17124707/myanmar-reengagement-reform-support-credit-program. Accessed 10 February 2013.

Zaw Win Than. "NLD To Push For Further Changes to Investment Law". *Myanmar Times,* 15 October 2012. <http://www.mmtimes.com/index.php/national-news/2460-nld-to-push-for-further-changes-to-investment-law.html>. Accessed 16 January 2014.

11

POLICE REFORM IN MYANMAR

Changes "in Essence and Appearance"

Andrew Selth

Since March 2011, President Thein Sein has made several major speeches in which he has acknowledged Myanmar's myriad problems and outlined a plan to introduce a wide range of reforms. His stated aim is to build "a modern, developed democratic nation", in which the work of the central government, and state and region governments, is "transparent, accountable and consistent with the constitution and existing laws" (Thein Sein 2011). In describing this goal, Thein Sein has emphasized "the rule of law". He has not explained precisely what he means by this term, but in 2012 the United Nations General Assembly (UNGA) characterized the principle as a requirement that "all persons, institutions and entities, public and private, including the State itself, are accountable to just, fair and equitable laws and are entitled without any discrimination to equal protection of the law" (UNGA 2012).

At no time during any of these speeches has Thein Sein singled out the Myanmar Police Force (MPF) for particular mention. Nor has opposition leader Daw Aung San Suu Kyi, despite her frequent references to the need for "the rule of law" in Myanmar (Prasse-Freeman 2013a, 2013b). Foreigners interested in this issue have also tended to gloss over the policing dimension. Yet, the reforms envisaged by both the government and the opposition movement will rely in no small measure for their success on the existence of an independent and professional police force that is accountable to the public and commands the respect of the population. Also, if the armed forces (*Tatmadaw*) further loosen their grip on Myanmar society, the MPF can be expected to play a much greater role in maintaining law and order, and safeguarding internal security. Indeed, such a step will be essential if Myanmar is to make an orderly transition to genuine democratic rule.

As other post-authoritarian governments have found, however, the reform of the national police force presents enormous challenges. Structural and procedural changes can be made, new training programmes introduced, modern equipment acquired, proficiency levels raised, and steps taken to improve the force's public image. In some of these areas, foreign governments and international organizations can provide assistance. Such measures, however, will only scratch the surface of the problem. It is imperative that there is also a fundamental shift in the police force's professional culture and a complete transformation of its relationship with the wider community. Both require multi-faceted and sustained campaigns aimed at changing deeply entrenched patterns of thinking and behaviour, at all levels of society.

This chapter summarizes efforts at police reform in Myanmar over the past decade and outlines initiatives currently being pursued under President Thein Sein. It identifies six key obstacles to comprehensive reform of the MPF and suggests that the process will be neither quick nor easy. The chapter also comments on the scope for foreign governments and international organizations to assist in this field and concludes by relating proposed police reforms to wider political and economic developments in Myanmar.

REFORM PROGRAMMES

Even before Thein Sein took office, an effort was being made to expand the police force's capabilities, improve its performance, and reform its culture. This programme appears to have been initiated by former State Peace and Development Council (SPDC) Secretary-1, and later Prime Minister, Lieutenant General Khin Nyunt. In 1994, he became chairman of the Committee for Reform of the People's Police Force Management System (CRPPFMS), the aim of which was:

> ... to assess PPF's present management, intelligence and legal affairs, to analyse PPF training system, to recheck the acts of the police to earn public respect and to do away with corruption and graft, and to promulgate laws, rules and regulations on PPF management and administration and make certain reforms in conformity with the changing situation ... (*NLM* 1994)

In 1995, the military government renamed the People's Police Force (PPF) the Myanmar Police Force and promulgated the MPF Maintenance of Discipline Law. In 1999, the Ministry of Home Affairs issued a code of conduct for police officers (MPF 1999). Colonial-era manuals spelling out the duties, powers, and entitlements of all ranks were amended and reissued in 2000 and 2001.

At the same time, an attempt was made to introduce aspects of "community policing". For example, signs and booklets listing the Buddha's 38 Blessings were distributed to all police stations and prisons, as guides to good behaviour. In 2001, signs were erected at police stations around the country asking "May I help you?" A number of magazines were launched, aimed at boosting police morale and increasing public awareness of police functions. Although Khin Nyunt fell out of favour and was arrested by the SPDC in 2004, the reform programme continued, for a period under the stewardship of Secretary-2 and later Prime Minister—now president—Lieutenant General Thein Sein. Around 2008, the SPDC endorsed a comprehensive thirty-year plan for the expansion and modernization of the MPF (Interview, Naypyitaw, February 2013).

In 2011, the strength of the MPF was around 80,000.[1] This represented an increase of some 8000 men and women over the previous decade, and made the force larger and more powerful than it had been since the colonial era (Selth 2002, p. 309).[2] The total number included 18 battalions of paramilitary police, able to respond to serious outbreaks of civil unrest, such as the so-called "Saffron Revolution", which erupted in 2007. A major recruitment programme is currently under way to increase the MPF's size even further, including by large-scale transfers from the *Tatmadaw*.[3] The goal is a police force of over 100,000, with 34 paramilitary battalions (Interview, Naypyitaw, February 2013).[4] A special effort is being made to boost the number of women in the force, which currently stands at less than two percent of the total.[5] The developed country norm is around 25 percent.

Naypyitaw has also been grappling with other challenges. The MPF's headquarters (HQ) is being upgraded, new functional departments have been created and others expanded, internal coordination has been improved, and more modern technology introduced. For example, the Department Against Transnational Crime was created in 2004, and there are now Maritime and Civil Aviation departments (Eleven Media 2012*a*). A Tourist Police unit is being formed and there have been reports of a new Cyber Crime Division (Interview, Naypyitaw, February 2013; Eleven Media 2013; *Irrawaddy* 2013). In many ways, the MPF's organizational structure now mirrors those of police forces in more developed countries. Efforts have been made to introduce computers into all major police facilities and to upgrade communications links between MPF HQ and state and region-level MPF units. More policemen now carry personal radios.

In addition, officer selection standards have been raised and specialized instruction at all levels has increased. Loyalty to the central government is still valued highly and is reinforced by ideological "refresher" courses to help "keep patriotism alive" (UCSB undated). Internal discipline is strongly enforced. At the same time, the force's doctrine and training programmes have been changed to give greater weight to community policing, which accords a high priority to cooperation with the civil population. Guidance has been given to help MPF officers manage juvenile crime. There is also an increased focus in training courses on personal conduct, in an effort to reduce the level of corruption (BBC 2011; Aye Nai 2011). Steps have been taken to deal with other kinds of abuse, and more reforms have been promised.

One characteristic of the MPF that has not changed is its wider role as a strategic reserve. The CRPPFMS made it clear from its inception that Myanmar's police force was "a trained armed organization in addition to the country's regular armed forces to be able to safeguard the nation in emergency cases" (*Xinhua* 1998). The force's paramilitary arm was singled out for special mention:

The MPF, the reserve force for national defence, is made up of combat as well as security battalions, which are always well trained to carry out national defence duties (*NLM* 2003, p. 9).

The military government repeatedly referred to the MPF as the "younger brother" of the *Tatmadaw* (MPF website). This formula has been invoked less often since 2011, but the MPF is still publicly embraced as an integral part of Myanmar's Defence Services.

OBSTACLES TO REFORM

Looking back over the past fifteen years, the MPF can claim to have achieved a number of successes. The force has become larger, more modern, and, in some respects, more capable. To a degree at least, it has acknowledged corruption and human rights abuses in its ranks and, after a fashion, attempted to address its poor relationship with the wider community. It is clear, however, that the MPF still faces serious problems. These may be easier to tackle now that a new wind is blowing through Naypyitaw. Even so, the transition from a highly-militarized police force used to wielding unbridled power in support of a repressive regime to a more professional and civilianized force observing the rule of law, answerable to an elected government, and respected by the people, is not going to be quick or easy. Six key obstacles to reform can be identified (Selth 2013).

Structural and Resource Pressures

Reflecting both its colonial antecedents and the influence of the *Tatmadaw*, the MPF is a strictly hierarchical organization with a central administration in Naypyitaw and subordinate elements in Myanmar's fourteen states and regions. There are also municipal units in Naypyitaw, Yangon, and Mandalay. At a lower level, there are 1,256 police stations, spread throughout Myanmar's 73 districts, 330 townships, and 16,000 villages (Interview, Naypyitaw, February 2013; Selth 2011; Selth 2012a, pp. 59–63).[6] As the MPF grows, becomes more diverse, and takes on wider responsibilities, it can be expected that the demands on the force's senior and middle management will grow considerably.

Operational control has already been ceded to MPF elements at the state and region level. However, given the government's firm commitment to Myanmar's three "national causes"—summarized as sovereignty, unity, and stability—Naypyitaw has a continued interest in maintaining command of the country's entire coercive apparatus. In these circumstances, there is little chance that the MPF will be further decentralized, let alone broken up into central, regional, and local police forces, as has occurred in other countries. The creation of separate state and region parliaments may give rise to demands from these bodies for increased autonomy and, as a corollary, greater scope to manage the security forces operating within their respective jurisdictions. However, they are unlikely to be granted.

As the MPF expands and assumes a greater role in internal security, including the maintenance of law and order, it will require increased funds. Working and living conditions for police officers badly need to be improved, salaries need to be increased, and operating budgets need to be expanded. Some new technologies sought by the MPF will be very expensive (Interviews, Naypyitaw and Kyauktada, February 2013; Khin Myo Thwe 2013). Given the many demands already being made on the central government, providing these resources will not be easy. Indeed, requests for a greater share of the budget could lead to friction between the armed forces and the police. If increased allocations to the police do not come from the armed forces, they will have to be made at the expense of other sectors, which are also in need of reform and equally desperate for support.

The government is aware that failure to provide the MPF with better facilities and equipment, and increased funding for operational and personnel expenses, will cripple its reform programme. Also, a failure by Thein Sein to keep his promise of higher salaries and allowances for public servants will make it more difficult to tackle the problems of graft and corruption. This is not just a question of increasing efficiency and promoting ethical behaviour in the force. Some of the proceeds of corruption appear to be used to support basic police functions. For example, the sums extorted from the public to conduct investigations are not always to line the pockets of corrupt policemen. They also seem to help maintain police stations, cover the costs of equipment, and facilitate operations not being adequately supported in the official budget.

Police-*Tatmadaw* Relations

As Morris Janowitz once noted, "It is a basic assumption of the democratic model of civilian-military relations that civilian supremacy depends upon a sharp organizational separation between internal and external violence forces" (1964, p. 38). However, if the detachment of Indonesia's national police from the country's armed forces in 1999 is any guide, this is easier said than done. In Myanmar too, there is the potential for serious disagreements to arise between the two institutions over their respective roles and responsibilities, areas of jurisdiction, and budgetary allocations. These problems arose before the 1962 military coup and possibly could do so again (CIA 1981).

Despite the advent of a "disciplined democracy" and the launch of Thein Sein's ambitious reform programme, the *Tatmadaw* retains enormous power and influence. The 2008 Constitution guarantees the armed forces a privileged position in national affairs, and the government includes several former and serving generals. At the parliamentary level, a quarter of the members of all national, state, and region assemblies are serving military officers, and the majority Union Solidarity and Development Party consists largely of former servicemen and their supporters.[7] This is in addition to the fact that the *Tatmadaw* commands substantial military power, which it could exercise in the event that any other institution attempted to usurp its dominant position in Myanmar society.[8]

In administrative terms, the police force falls into the Home Affairs Minister's portfolio. Under current constitutional arrangements, this position is reserved for a military officer recommended to the president by the Commander-in-Chief of the Defence Services (2008 Constitution, Article 232(b)). Quite apart from the *Tatmadaw*'s wish to retain the minister's *ex officio* positions in the cabinet and the powerful National Defence and Security Council, the difficulty of amending the constitution means that the MPF will effectively remain under military control for the foreseeable future. In addition, the Chief of Police (who is also the Deputy Minister for Home Affairs) and many other senior policemen are former military officers.[9] Their primary loyalty, and that of ex-servicemen at more junior levels, probably remains with the *Tatmadaw*. In these circumstances, a direct confrontation between the armed forces and police seems most unlikely.

Myanmar's military leadership appears to have accepted political developments in Naypyitaw and, for the time being at least, seems prepared to let the government and MPF exercise their roles under the constitution (Callahan 2012, pp. 120–31). If the MPF is to develop a distinctive civilian identity, however, then its relationship with the *Tatmadaw* will have to change. This will not be easy, as power and authority in Myanmar are conceived as finite and limited. Alternative centres of influence are seen as threatening and likely to lead to instability (Steinberg 2006, p. 37ff). There is the danger, too, that a more powerful and independent MPF will arouse jealousies in the armed forces, and be seen as a competitor for status and resources. As the MPF grows, the *Tatmadaw* leadership could even become concerned that civilian reformers may use the police force as a counterweight to the army.

If the MPF's institutional autonomy is to mean anything, however, the *Tatmadaw* will need to accept that the force is the national agency with primary responsibility for maintaining law and order. The generals will also need to recognize that the MPF is accountable to the public, through their elected representatives in Naypyitaw, not to the armed forces, as in the past. Similarly, military personnel must be subject to the same laws and restrictions on their behaviour as other citizens. Until now, they have acted almost with impunity. Military bases have effectively offered sanctuary from the civil law. Soldiers responsible for human rights abuses have rarely been charged or prosecuted. If the "rule of law" is to prevail, and the police force is fully to perform its proper role, this situation cannot continue.

If Thein Sein wants to civilianize the MPF and make it more independent, as befits a police force in a democracy, he will have to support efforts by the MPF to develop a separate identity and encourage its own esprit de corps. The MPF will need to open its senior ranks to career police officers. This should not only make the force less subject to military influence, but it would also improve morale by removing a persistent source of complaint from policemen resentful of soldiers being put into positions above them.[10] At the same time, the force will be obliged to take into account the *Tatmadaw*'s continuing power and authority. The MPF's leadership will have to be on good terms with its armed forces counterpart, while finding a workable division of labour, not just legally but also in terms of practical cooperation and responses to security problems.

Investigation and Intelligence

In a democratic Myanmar, it might be expected that responsibility for the investigation of political crimes—those that relate primarily to domestic and external security—would fall to the MPF, or to a dedicated civilian agency. In Myanmar at present, however, such responsibilities seem to be shared between the police and the armed forces. As Thein Sein's wider reform programme unfolds, this arrangement will become increasingly problematic.

Since 2011, Special Branch has been given full responsibility for the collection and assessment of political intelligence. Formally, the Directorate of Military Affairs Security (DMAS) only considers defence-related intelligence (Interview, Naypyitaw, February 2013). However, given the *Tatmadaw*'s self-appointed guardianship role and the enormous power wielded by Myanmar's military intelligence agencies in the past, it is unlikely that the armed forces would give up an independent capacity to monitor domestic developments. Not only do they distrust civilian agencies, but the *Tatmadaw* has always preferred to rely on its own resources when it comes to national security. This will doubtless remain the case while the armed forces hierarchy perceives continuing threats from pro-democracy activists, armed ethnic groups, and narcotics warlords.

Such duplication of functions and responsibilities, however, is likely to exacerbate jurisdictional disputes and jealousies over status and resources. It also risks perpetuating problems like poor coordination and the potential loss of valuable intelligence due to gaps in collection and assessment. Whether or not there is a restructuring of Myanmar's intelligence apparatus, an argument could still be mounted for a rationalization and redistribution of its duties. This would not only increase the levels of cooperation between agencies and better exploit their limited resources, but also provide a clearer delineation of their responsibilities, in particular the separation of military and civilian functions.

Internal Security

There is no question that the *Tatmadaw* will remain responsible for Myanmar's external defence. It will also conduct military campaigns against insurgent groups, such as that being waged against the Kachin Independence Army. The MPF is sometimes directly involved in such operations, as occurs for example when insurgents attack rural police stations (Phaneda 2012). Its strategic reserve function aside, however, the force usually has a non-combat role.

That said, it seems to be envisaged by Naypyitaw that the MPF will assume greater internal security responsibilities. The force already dominates the Central Committee for Drug Abuse Control and takes the lead in efforts to combat narcotics trafficking. It also plays a major part in frontier protection, including in the past through the Border Control Force (*Na Sa Ka*).[11] These days, there are more blue uniforms than green uniforms on city streets, protecting VIPs, providing security for government offices, and guarding diplomatic premises.[12] Myanmar's counter-terrorist unit is drawn from the police force. In addition, the MPF usually takes the lead in quelling outbreaks of civil unrest, with the army only being called in to assist the "civil" power when the problem exceeds the police force's abilities to cope.

The government is intent on building up the MPF's paramilitary capabilities, so that it can respond to major disturbances with modern anti-riot control measures, rather than having always to resort to the blunt instrument of the army. As revealed by the 2007 "Saffron Revolution", there have been some advances in the training of the MPF's battalions since the 1988 uprising, when ill-equipped and ill-disciplined "riot police" (*Lon Htein*) units were guilty of terrible abuses (Lintner 1990; Selth 2008, pp. 281–97). Some battalions used to provide initial responses to civil unrest now wear modern protective clothing and carry more appropriate weapons, offering non-lethal options that range from baton charges, the use of tear gas and water cannon, to the firing of rubber bullets and small-calibre shotgun pellets.[13] Additional training programmes focussing on crowd control are in the pipeline.

The police force's responsibilities for crime prevention, the maintenance of law and order, and the protection of the community place a premium on good relations with the public. Yet these roles are at odds with the military-style training and ethos of the battalions, which are accustomed to exercising violence up to, and including, lethal force. As seen in 2012, when excessive force was used to break up a protest at a mine site near Letpadaung, the battalions are not yet imbued with the more restrained approach now being held up as a model. In that case, more than twenty Buddhist monks were injured, prompting the government and the MPF to make a rare public apology (*NLM* 2012). If the police are to step in before the army, then they cannot act—or be seen to act—like the army. To do so undermines their civilian status and their standing with the population.

The closeness of the MPF battalions and the army poses other problems. Given their overlapping responsibilities for internal security, there is inevitably a crossover of roles and identity. In joint operations it will be the practices and ethos of the more powerful partner—inevitably the army—that sets the tone for the security forces' behaviour. Not being trained or equipped for crowd control, army units tend to resort more quickly to violence, using combat weapons. This leads to a blurring of public perceptions. It is possible that people in Myanmar differentiate between the police and the army during security crackdowns, but this is difficult to confirm. Even if the police act in a more restrained manner, they are still likely to be associated in the popular mind with the more extreme measures taken by the armed forces.

It goes without saying that, in performing these duties, the MPF must act—and be seen to act—impartially in restoring law and order, and upholding the law. Yet, this has rarely been the case. Apart from supporting the government, the force has appeared to side with sectoral interests. During the civil unrest in Rakhine State in 2012, for example, MPF officers were sympathetic to local Buddhists, and some reportedly joined in attacks against Rohingyas (HRW 2012). The action taken at Letpadaung was seen by many as another example of the police force backing wealthy government "cronies" (Wade 2012). After the sectarian unrest in 2013, the MPF was accused of allowing Buddhist mobs to attack Muslims and destroy their property (VOA 2013; Boghani and Winn 2013). Such behaviour not only damages the force's reputation but also undermines the government's rhetoric about fairness, human rights, and the rule of law.

Police Culture and Socialization

For the current reform programme to have any real and lasting effect, the MPF will need to undergo a profound change in its professional culture. There are a number of elements to this, covering the force's view of its place in the "new" Myanmar, its attitude to power, its understanding of proper police roles and responsibilities, and its perceptions of the civil population. Reflecting the president's own "top down" approach to reform, MPF HQ has already issued a number of directives on such matters and implemented a number of practical measures designed to encourage development of a different mindset in the force. However, these will only go so far in achieving the desired end. Real cultural change requires a tectonic shift of consciousness at the psychological and societal levels.

As Nick Cheesman (2009) has pointed out, from the colonial period through to the advent of the Thein Sein government, policing in Myanmar has been conceived of as a regime service rather than a public service. This has encouraged an authoritarian approach to law enforcement. Yet, the new community policing models being considered, and in some cases implemented, will demand a flatter structure in which individual officers and members of civil society can identify problems and find mutually beneficial solutions. Emphasis is given to taking the initiative, rather than waiting for orders from higher up the command chain. Police officers are encouraged to question the effectiveness of ingrained practices and explore new ways of doing things. They are also urged to become familiar with their local neighbourhoods.[14]

While laudable, many of these ideas run counter to generations of police training and socialization. Arguably, some challenge aspects of traditional Myanmar culture, in which respect for status and submission to authority have important places. In Indonesia, it was found that such an approach was very difficult to instill in the police force. Old habits, fear of failure, and loyalty to one's superiors invariably trumped personal initiative. Also, these changes were resisted by many senior officers, who saw them as undermining their own positions, and leading both to a breakdown in internal discipline and a loss of control over police operations and behaviour. Any attempts to introduce such ideas into Myanmar's police force are likely to encounter at least equal levels of resistance.

It may be possible, however, to inculcate more of a service culture through education. New programmes at police training centres can increase levels of awareness about policing methods in democratic societies. Human rights can be given a higher priority in police school curricula. Special courses can raise leadership skills and encourage a more tolerant approach to public participation in democratic processes. Imaginative teaching methods can create a more productive learning atmosphere, in contrast to the rigid learning styles found in most military-style institutions. Provided that such lessons are taught in a way that is relevant to the local political, social, and cultural context, this approach may complement other initiatives by helping change the MPF from below.

Community Relations

Myanmar's police forces have never enjoyed the confidence of the people. Throughout modern history, the police have been seen as the willing servants of repressive and self-serving regimes that have cared little for the welfare and interests of the average citizen. The community's attitude has invariably been one of fear and distrust. There have been exceptions of course, but the common image of the force has been one of remote and poorly-educated authority figures with low personal and professional standards. In these circumstances, it is little wonder that the overwhelming response to the MPF's attempts at reform over the past decade has been one of scepticism, if not disbelief.

There are no reliable surveys of community attitudes, but it is clear that most people in Myanmar see the MPF as a threatening rather than a reassuring presence. The complaints most often heard focus on the brutality of police officers, their capriciousness, lack of responsiveness, greed, and disdain for both the law and professional standards (Cheesman 2012). Other targets for criticism include the perceived tendency for police officers to put their own safety and careers before the public interest, and the lack of redress for complaints about such behaviour. Broader concerns relate to the militaristic character of the force, the MPF's low level of institutional independence, its perceived ineffectiveness, and its collusion with a corrupt and inefficient justice system (ALRC 2009).

A key factor contributing to negative views of the MPF is corruption. The force is not alone in facing this problem. In the view of a senior government official, it is one of the greatest challenges facing Myanmar (Hpyo Wai Tha 2012). By its very nature, the MPF is expected to uphold the highest ethical standards, yet it is reputed that most illegal businesses in the major population centres enjoy some degree of police protection (BBC 2009). Given their position in society, policemen have wide scope to engage in intimidation and extortion. Officers reportedly seek positions that permit them to solicit bribes, commonly referred to as "tea money", or increasingly, "beer money". Also, people who have been arrested are often offered their release on payment of money or sexual favours (Interview, Canberra, December 2012; Kyaw Min San 2012). Such practices suggest that the MPF sees itself as above the laws it is charged to uphold.

Another target for community feeling is the MPF's "riot police". For the battalions have made little distinction between crowd control and combat. During the 1988 uprising, the *Lon Htein* was encouraged to see demonstrators as "the enemy", who were threatening the survival of the Union. In 2007, the regime portrayed the demonstrating Buddhist clergy as "bogus monks", not deserving respect. In such circumstances, it is not surprising that human rights abuses occurred. At present, the battalions constitute only 6 percent of the MPF's manpower, but there are fears that the steady growth in the number of security battalions is a device to strengthen the government's coercive apparatus by stealth. These fears are likely to grow as the MPF creates sixteen more battalions, mainly through transfers from the army.

Due to persistent problems of poor leadership, lax discipline, low educational levels, and an abiding sense of privilege derived from the force's position under successive military regimes, human rights abuses by police officers have been common. Major incidents like the action against protesters at Letpadaung do not occur often, but when they do, they strengthen popular perceptions of the police as thugs, unrestrained either by the law or standards of common decency. In an attempt to recover its reputation from that incident, the government appointed a commission of enquiry led by Aung San Suu Kyi. However, the final report was not as critical of the MPF as many expected, confirming doubts about the force's ability and willingness to reform (Letpadaung Report 2013).

Such attitudes will take a long time to overcome. There has been some progress, but to date modern theories of community policing seem to have had little real impact. Attempts to implement such doctrines may have been successful in some cases, but they will continue to founder on the lack of trust between police and public. Codes of conduct, new uniforms, and welcome signs outside police stations mean little if the officers inside still beat up and molest prisoners, extort money to investigate a complaint, or can be bought off by a wealthy or powerful defendant before or after a case goes to court. Some corrupt practices have become institutionalized, such as the expectation that police station commanders will pay their superiors to remain in comfortable or lucrative postings.

All these problems have not only deepened suspicions of the police force and resentment at its corruption and heavy-handedness, but reinforced public cynicism in Myanmar more broadly. As Errol Mendes (1999, p. 17) has noted, such a situation encourages a lack of respect for the societal institutions that promote the rule of law and the proper functioning of the criminal justice system itself.

THE POLICE AND WIDER REFORMS

It is difficult to envisage the reform of Myanmar's police force being successful if the wider reforms being proposed by President Thein Sein strike significant problems. As is so often the nature of things in Myanmar, political, economic, social, and other factors are all inextricably bound together, so that action—or inaction—in one sector invariably has an impact on others.

In any case, for all the talk of the MPF's future independence, "police forces are the creatures of politics" (Bayley 1971, pp. 91–112). The two cannot be separated. As David Bayley has written, "Government and police cannot be distinguished any more than knife and knife edge can be usefully distinguished in the act of cutting" (1971, p. 102). The new MPF will reflect, and depend on, the transition in Myanmar from a military dictatorship to a "disciplined democracy", and possibly beyond. It is reliant on the *Tatmadaw* stepping back further from the business of government and permitting the evolution of a fairer and more open society. Detailed reform programmes are difficult to implement, however, without a high degree of certainty about the government's political future and direction, and about budget allocations.

Some observers have described Thein Sein's political, economic, and social reforms as "irreversible", but there is still considerable uncertainty about their future. Full democracies and full autocracies are usually the most stable forms of government, but states undertaking the transition from autocracy to democracy are most likely to suffer from instability. In those circumstances, there remains the possibility that the *Tatmadaw* could step back in, to a greater or lesser extent. Should Thein Sein's reform programme falter, systemic weaknesses frustrate popular expectations, or the MPF prove unable to cope with the demands now being made upon it, then the arguments for a return to the old system may become louder, as some members of the armed forces and their supporters hark back to the imagined stability of military rule.

There are currently no signs of such moves but, even should Thein Sein survive his five-year term, reform measures cannot be implemented in isolation from other institutions of state. As the president has stated, the benchmark for public institutions must be the rule of law, administered fairly and impartially. There can be no further tolerance of a system that constantly alluded to such a regime, but enabled practices that contradicted it. For decades, the "rule of law" was conflated with "law and order", as defined by a self-serving military government (Cheesman 2012). For example, a more effective police force will soon be rendered impotent if prosecutors, judges, and prison governors fail in their responsibilities, or if the government's proposed judicial reforms are unsuccessful.

Also, security sector reform is inseparable from economic reform. The MPF is unlikely to succeed in reinventing itself if government revenues are not adequate to pay better salaries and meet the operating costs of the key institutions of government. Corruption, inefficiency, low skill levels, and lack of commitment will remain serious obstacles to change. Besides, political protests in Myanmar have usually been sparked by economic concerns. In theory, political and economic reforms encourage growth and employment, leading to a higher level of economic activity, more opportunities, and greater social stability. Provided the right mechanisms are in place, this should lead in turn to increased government revenues and more resources available for the security sector.

INTERNATIONAL ASSISTANCE

The international community's attitude to Thein Sein's wider reform programme and proposed changes to the security sector is cautiously optimistic. As a result, since March 2011 numerous governments, international institutions, and private foundations have approached Naypyitaw with offers of help. While most of those relating to the security sector refer in broad terms to strengthening the "rule of law" in Myanmar, some envisage direct aid to the MPF.

The force has already received some foreign assistance. For example, since 2005 it has sent over seventy officers to courses at the Jakarta Centre for Law Enforcement and Cooperation (Ludlum 2008). Uniquely among ASEAN countries, Myanmar was excluded from participation in courses at the Bangkok-based International Law Enforcement Academy, but the ban—instigated by the United States—has now been lifted (Interview, Naypyitaw, February 2013). Since 1988, China has provided training for the MPF, mainly to help combat narcotics trafficking. Myanmar police officers have also attended training courses in Australia. The United States and the United Kingdom are now considering ways to strengthen the rule of law in Myanmar. These measures will probably include assistance to the MPF.

Some international organizations are already involved in MPF reform programmes. UNICEF has helped it prepare a guide for the treatment of children caught up in the criminal justice system. For some years, the United Nations Office on Drugs and Crime (UNODC) has provided training for the MPF, related primarily to transnational crime. Help in areas like human rights training, community policing, and crowd management is likely to be provided by the European Union in 2013.[15] Myanmar's Chief of Police has told the International Bar Association that he would welcome advice on how best to implement civilian oversight procedures, and he has "expressed a particular interest in learning about good international practice in the matter of state security laws" (IBAHRI 2012, p. 30). The US Institute of Peace is also examining the "rule of law" in Myanmar.

Probably with all these initiatives in mind, Naypyitaw has asked the UNODC to conduct a comprehensive review of the MPF to identify issues requiring attention, not only to help formulate additional reform programmes but also to assist in the coordination of foreign assistance. The UNODC's report was expected in mid-2013 (Interview, Yangon, February 2013).

The scope for foreigners to change Myanmar's police force, however, is limited. They can provide specialized advice, technical assistance, and modern equipment. This can lift the MPF's ability to perform its basic functions and "enhance the capacity of local police to control crime and disorder, and to develop 'democratic policing'" (Bayley 2005, p. 206). However, "international assistance cannot determine but can only facilitate changes in the character of local policing" (Bayley 2005, p. 209). Fundamental reform of the MPF will depend heavily on a new power dynamic in Myanmar, a paradigm shift in the force's professional culture, and the development of a genuine relationship of trust with the community. These matters will ultimately depend on the Myanmar government and people themselves.

CONCLUSION

A broad consensus has developed about what democratic policing looks like. Analysts have identified seven basic principles: that the police force operates in accordance with the law, is regulated by a professional code of conduct, protects life by minimizing the use of force, is accountable to the public, protects life and property through proactive crime prevention, safeguards human rights and dignity, and acts in non-discriminatory manner (Bayley 2005, p. 207). These principles can be condensed to just three: the police force must adhere to international standards of human rights; it must maintain effective internal and external accountability; and it must develop a partnership with local communities to achieve public safety (Bayley 2005, p. 207). Measured against all these benchmarks, Myanmar has made some progress, but it still has a very long way to go.

Given the widespread optimism that has followed in the wake of Thein Sein's wider reform programme, it is worth noting that in every country where security sector reform has been attempted, it has taken a long time. Inevitably, there will be setbacks. Some observers have suggested, for example, that the excessive use of force by the MPF at Letpadaung meant that the wider reform process—and thus the reform of the MPF— is stalling (Ponnudurai 2010). Certainly, that incident demonstrated that old ways of thinking about political dissent in Myanmar die hard. Yet, it can be argued that the public apology and parliamentary enquiry that followed indicate that the government is aware of the need for change, is trying to be responsive to public concerns, and wishes to make the MPF more accountable for its actions (Selth 2012b).

Police reform in Myanmar will depend on a high level of public trust, which is sorely lacking. Symbolic measures are a start, but substantial and sustained changes are required, notably in the force's professional culture and observable behaviour. This is particularly important at the local level. For, as Indonesia has shown, "it is in the performance of mundane duties that the role of the police can have the greatest impact in either strengthening or undermining democracy" (Greenlees 2011, p. 18). No one can doubt the benefits of more open lines of communication, and the need to leave behind the confrontational relationship between the police and public, but at present the prospect of "fostering collaborative police- community partnerships that ... respond to the public safety needs and expectations of the community" (Asia Foundation 2007), as recommended in the textbooks, must be considered slight.

In 1994, the CRPPFMS set out to change the police force "in both essence and appearance" (NLM 2002). Its problems appear to have been recognized, a range of corrective measures has been explored and, in some cases, implemented. There is the prospect of international assistance in some areas. The final outcome, however, will depend on factors that are out of the police force's direct control. These relate mainly to developments in Naypyitaw, in particular the success of Thein Sein's wider reform programme and the willingness of the Tatmadaw to relinquish its tight control over Myanmar society. Ultimately, the police force will reflect the political system and society in which it operates. The future of the MPF, and indeed of Myanmar itself, will depend on the success or otherwise of the president's bold attempt to change "mindsets and behaviours" and "foster a new political culture of patience and dialogue" (Thein Sein 2012*a*, Thein Sein 2012*b*).

Notes

1   Personal communication from Yangon, July 2011.
2   INTERPOL's website states that the MPF's strength is over 93,000, and other estimates range as high as 110,000. However, these claims are difficult to sustain. See INTERPOL undated, and Eleven Media 2012b.
3   In addition to transfers from the Myanmar Army, 4000 men have been taken from the Myanmar Navy to help create the new Maritime Police, and another 4000 have been drawn from the Myanmar Air Force to help establish the Civil Aviation Police.
4   Another source states that the aim is 33 battalions. See MPF 2012, p. 24.
5   Personal communication from Yangon, November 2011.
6   A number of armed separatist groups, notably the Kachin and the Wa, have formed their own police forces, but these are not officially recognised.
7   The UN has estimated that 89 percent of the members of Myanmar's parliament have some affiliation to the former military regime (IBAHRI 2012, pp. 52–53).
8   For a discussion of the *Tatmadaw*'s strengths and weaknesses, and the difficulty of discovering them, see Selth 2009, pp. 272–95.
9   About 10 percent of the MPF are former members of the *Tatmadaw*. Interview, Naypyitaw, February 2013.
10 Personal communication, Canberra, December 2012.
11 Both "Border Control Force" and "*Na Sa Ka*" are commonly-used abbreviations. A more precise translation of the agency's Burmese name, *Nezat detha luwinhmu Sitseye Kutkehmu tunachok* is "Border Area Immigration Scrutinization and Supervision Bureau".
12 This is not to overlook Myanmar's traffic policemen and women, who wear white tunics.
13 This equipment is still in short supply. See *Japan Times* 2013.
14 See Asia Foundation 2007 for a description of community policing in a comparable Indonesian context.
15 Personal communication from Brussels, March 2013. The report on the 2012 Letpadaung incident recommended that the MPF's "riot police" be given training in crowd control in Myanmar and, if possible, overseas. Letpadaung Report 2013.

References

Asia Foundation. *Community Policing in Indonesia*. Jakarta: The Asia Foundation, 2007. <http://asiafoundation.org/resources/pdfs/indocommpolicingeng.pdf>. Accessed 9 January 2014.

Asian Legal Resource Centre (ALRC). "Burma's Cheap Muscle". *Article 2*, 8, no. 1 (2009). <http://www.article2.org/mainfile.php/0801/343/>. Accessed 9 January 2014.

Aye Nai. "Corruption Charges Hit Police Chiefs". *Democratic Voice of Burma*, 26 January 2011. <http://www.dvb.no/news/corruption-charges-hit-police-chiefs/13894>. Accessed 9 January 2014.

Bayley, David. "Police Reform as Foreign Policy". *Australian and New Zealand Journal of Criminology* 38, no. 2 (2005): 206–15.

———. "The Police and Political Change in Comparative Perspective". *Law and Society Review* 6, no. 1 (1971): 91–112.

Boghani, Priyanka, and Patrick Winn. "Myanmar: Security Forces Stood by while Anti-Muslims Raged Says Rights Group". *Global Post*, 2 April 2013. <http://www.globalpost.com/dispatch/news/regions/asia-pacific/myanmar/130402/myanmar-security-forces-stood-by-anti-muslim-riots>. Accessed 9 January 2014.

British Broadcasting Corporation (BBC). "Burma Dismisses Five Division, State Police Commissioners on Graft Charges". BBC Monitoring Service, East Asia and the Pacific, 27 January 2011.

———. "Burma Said to Dismiss Rangoon Police Chief". BBC Monitoring Service, East Asia and the Pacific, 7 October 2009.

Burma Partnership. "Letpadaung Report Does Not Address Concerns, Places Security Forces Above The Law". *Burma Partnership*, 18 March 2013. <http://www.burmapartnership.org/2013/03/letpadaung-report-does-not-address-concerns-places-security-forces-above-the-law>. Accessed 9 January 2014.

Callahan, Mary P. "The Generals Loosen Their Grip". *Journal of Democracy* 23, no. 4 (2012): 120–31.

Cheesman, Nick. "The Politics of Law and Order in Myanmar". PhD dissertation, Department of Political and Social Change, Australian National University, 2012.

———. "Policing Burma". Unpublished background research paper No. 2, Department of Political and Social Change, Australian National University, Canberra, 24 February 2009.

Central Intelligence Agency (CIA). "Memorandum for the Secretary of Defense: Report on Trip to Burma, February-March", by General G.B. Erskine USMC, 16 April 1957. Released by the Central Intelligence Agency under the Freedom of Information Act, 13 February 1981.

Constitution of the Republic of the Union of Myanmar (2008). Naypyitaw: Printing and Publishing Enterprise, Ministry of Information, Union of Myanmar. <http://

www.burmalibrary.org/docs5/Myanmar_Constitution-2008-en.pdf>. Accessed 31 October 2013.

Eleven Media. "Myanmar Police to Receive Assistance in Setting Up Cyber-Crime Division". *Eleven*, 27 March 2013. <http://elevenmyanmar.com/national/science-tech/2938-myanmar-police-to-receive-assistance-in-setting-up-cyber-crime-division>.

———. "Marine Police Established in Myanmar". *Eleven*, 9 August 2012*a*. <http://www.thedailyeleven.com/national/471-marine-police-established-in-myanmar>. Accessed 8 January 2014.

———. "Myanmar Police Needs Modern Equipments [sic]". *Eleven*, 21 November 2012b. <http://www.elevenmyanmar.com/national/1403-myanmar-police-needs-modern-equipments>.

Greenlees, Donald. "Unfinished Business: Reform of the Security Sector in Democratic Indonesia". *Security Challenges* 7, no. 3 (2011): 5–22.

Hpyo Wai Tha. "Corruption is Burma's Biggest Problem: Upper House Speaker". *Irrawaddy*, 26 March 2012. <http://www2.irrawaddy.org/article.php?art_id=23286>. Accessed 8 January 2014.

Human Rights Watch (HRW). *"The Government Could Have Stopped This": Sectarian Violence and Ensuing Abuses in Burma's Arakan State*. New York: Human Rights Watch, 2012. <http://www.hrw.org/reports/2012/08/01/government-could-have-stopped>. Accessed 8 January 2014.

International Bar Association's Human Rights Institute (IBAHRI). *The Rule of Law in Myanmar: Challenges and Prospects*. Report of the International Bar Association's Human Rights Institute, December 2012. London: International Bar Association, 2012. <http://www.ibanet.org/Article/Detail.aspx?ArticleUid=c68828b3-9c10-48a7-a1c7-f5d394b63cc9>. Accessed 8 January 2014.

INTERPOL. "Myanmar". Undated. <http://www.interpol.int/Member-countries/Asia-South-Pacific/Myanmar>. Accessed 8 January 2014.

Irrawaddy. "Burma to Launch Tourist Police Force". *Irrawaddy*, 26 March 2013. <http://www.irrawaddy.org/archives/30513>. Accessed 8 January 2014.

Khin Myo Thwe. "Myanmar Police Go Hi Tech". *Mizzima News*, 8 March 2013. <http://www.mizzima.com/news/inside-burma/9022-myanmar-police-go-high-tech.html>.

Kyaw Min San. "Critical Issues for the Rule of Law in Myanmar". In *Myanmar's Transition: Openings, Obstacles and Opportunities*, edited by Nick Cheesman, Monique Skidmore and Trevor Wilson. Singapore: Institute of South East Asian Studies, 2012.

Kyi Wai. "Policeman's Life Isn't Easy, Say Officers". *Irrawaddy*, 12 July 2010. <http://www.irrawaddy.org/article.php?art_id=18949>. Accessed 8 January 2014.

Janowitz, Morris. *The Military in the Political Development of New Nations: An Essay in Comparative Analysis*. Chicago: University of Chicago Press, 1964.

Japan Times. "Myanmar Police Slow to Adjust to Unfamiliar Role of Peacekeepers". *Japan Times*, 12 April 2013. <http://www.japantimes.co.jp/news/2013/04/12/asia-pacific/myanmar-police-slow-to-adjust-to-unfamiliar-role-of-peacekeepers/>. Accessed 8 January 2014.

Letpadaung Report. Final Report of the Investigation Commission, 11 March 2013. Unofficial translation in the author's possession.

Lintner, Bertil. *Outrage: Burma's Struggle for Democracy.* London: White Lotus, 1990.

Ludlum, Scott. "Question to AFP regarding Burma". 5 December 2008. <http://scott-ludlum.greensmps.org.au/content/estimates/question-afp-regarding-burma>. Accessed 8 January 2014.

Mendes, Errol P. "Raising the Social Capital of Policing and Nations: How Can Professional Policing and Civilian Oversight Weaken the Circle of Violence?". In *Democratic Policing and Accountability: Global Perspectives*, edited by E.P. Mendes and others. Aldershot: Ashgate, 1999.

Myanmar Police Force (MPF). *Myanmar Police Force.* Naypyitaw: Ministry of Home Affairs, 2012.

———. *Manual for Members of the Police Force.* Yangon: Myanmar Police Force Headquarters, Ministry of Home Affairs, 1 October 1999 (in Burmese).

New Light of Myanmar (NLM). "It is time for all to carry out purification and propagation of Sasana Ceremony to apologize to State Sangha Maha Nayaka Sayadaws for incidents stemming from protest in Letpadaungtaung Copper Mining Project". *New Light of Myanmar*, 8 December 2012, pp. 1, 10. <http://www.networkmyanmar.org/images/stories/PDF13/nlm081212.pdf>. Accessed 8 January 2014.

———. "Myanmar Police Force Management System Reform Committee meets". *New Light of Myanmar*, 8 September 2003. <http://www.burmalibrary.org/docs6/NLM2003-09-08.pdf>. Accessed 9 January 2014.

———. "Myanmar Police Force Management System Reform Committee Meets". *New Light of Myanmar*, 3 August 2002. <http://www.myanmars.net/myanmar-news-2002/myanmar-news-n020803.htm>.

———. "Lt-Gen Khin Nyunt Accuses Police". *New Light of Myanmar*, 14 March 1994. <http://www.ibiblio.org/obl/docs3/BPS94-03.pdf>.

Phaneda. "KIA Raids Police Station, Three Killed". *Mizzima News*, 18 December 2012. <http://www.mizzima.com/special/kachin-battle-report/8590-kia-raids-police-station-3-killed.html>.

Ponnudurai, Parameswaran. "Is Reform Stalling in Burma?" Radio Free Asia, 4 December 2012. <http://www.rfa.org/english/east-asia-beat/mine-12042012121852.html>. Accessed 8 January 2014.

Prasse-Freeman, Elliott. "The Rule of Law Will Not Save Burma". *Democratic Voice of Burma*, 15 March 2013a. <http://www.dvb.no/analysis/the-rule-of-law-will-not-save-burma/27000>. Accessed 8 January 2014.

———. "What Does Rule of Law Actually Mean for Burma?" *Democratic Voice of Burma*, 18 March 2013*b*. <http://www.dvb.no/analysis/what-does-rule-of-law-actually-mean-for-burma/27051>. Accessed 8 January 2014.

Selth, Andrew. *Police Reform in Burma (Myanmar): Aims, Obstacles and Outcomes*. Regional Outlook Paper No. 44, Griffith Asia Institute. Brisbane: Griffith Asia Institute, Griffith University, 2013.

———. "Myanmar's Police Forces: Coercion, Continuity and Change". *Contemporary Southeast Asia* 34, no. 1 (2012*a*): 281–97.

———. "Burma's Police: The Long Road to Reform". *Interpreter*, 13 December 2012*b*. <http://www.lowyinterpreter.org/post/2012/12/13/Burmas-police-The-long-road-to-reform.aspx>.

———. *Burma's Police Forces: Continuities and Contradictions*, Griffith Asia Institute, Regional Outlook No. 32. Brisbane: Griffith University, 2011.

———. "Known Knowns and Known Unknowns: Measuring Myanmar's Military Capabilities". *Contemporary Southeast Asia* 31, no. 2 (2009): 272–95.

———. "Burma's 'Saffron Revolution' and the Limits of International Influence". *Australian Journal of International Affairs* 62, no. 3 (2008): 281–97.

———. *Burma's Armed Forces: Power Without Glory*. Norwalk: EastBridge 2002.

Steinberg, David. *Turmoil in Burma: Contested Legitimacies in Myanmar*. Norwalk: EastBridge, 2006.

Thein Sein. "All Must Try to See National Race Youths Who Brandished Guns Using Laptops; Government Not Divided into Hard-liners and Soft-liners". Republic of the Union of Myanmar, President Office, Naypyitaw, 1 March 2012*a*. <http://www.president-office.gov.mm/en/?q=briefing-room/speeches-and-remarks/2012/03/01/id-218>. Accessed 8 January 2014.

———. "Text of Thein Sein's UN Speech". *Mizzima News*, 28 September 2012*b*. <http://www.mizzima.com/research/8126-text-of-thein-seins-un-speech.html>.

———. "Members of Union and Region/State Governments Will Not Enjoy Salaries in Full in Consideration of Objective and Financial Conditions of the Nation and in Public Interests; President Thein Sein Speaks to Members of Union Government, Heads of Union Level Organizations". Republic of the Union of Myanmar, President Office, Naypyitaw, 31 March 2011. <http://www.president-office.gov.mm/en/?q=briefing-room/speeches-and-remarks/2011/03/31/id-196>. Accessed 8 January 2014.

Union Civil Service Board (UCSB). "Training Activities". Union Civil Service Board, Central Institute of Civil Service (Phaunggyi), undated. <http://www.ucsb.gov.mm/about%20ucsb/Central%20Institute%20of%20Civil%20Service%20(Phaung%20Gyi)/details.asp?submenuid=33&id=502>. Accessed 8 January 2014.

United Nations General Assembly (UNGA). Resolution 66/102 on the Rule of Law at the National and International Levels. UN General Assembly, A/RES/66/102, 13 January 2012. <http://unrol.org/files/GA%20Resolution%202012.pdf>. Accessed 8 January 2014.

Voice of America (VOA) News. "Burma Urged to Prosecute Perpetrators of Sectarian Unrest". 1 April 2013. *Voice of America (VOA) News*, <http://www.voanews.com/content/rights-group-urges-burma-to-investigate-sectarian-violence/1632277.html>. Accessed 8 January 2014.

Wade, Francis. "Progress Stops at the Myanmar Elite's Door". *Al Jazeera*, 4 December 2012. <http://www.aljazeera.com/indepth/opinion/2012/12/201212484532708930.html>. Accessed 8 January 2014.

Xinhua. "Myanmar Police Urged to Implement Three Main Tasks". *Xinhua*, 20 June 1998. <http://www.burmalibrary.org/reg.burma/archives/199806/msg00343.html>. Accessed 8 January 2014.

12

ELECTORAL SYSTEM CHOICE IN MYANMAR'S DEMOCRATIZATION DEBATE

Kyle Lemargie, Andrew Reynolds, Peter Erben, and David Ennis[*]

EXECUTIVE SUMMARY

For stakeholders in Myanmar, the 2012 by-elections revealed the potential of the National League for Democracy (NLD) to dominate, once again, winner-take-all elections in Myanmar that are held under credible electoral conditions. Looking towards the 2015 general election, when 75 percent of parliament's seats should be contested, the NLD's landslide victory in 2012 significantly raises the political stakes.

Political actors in Myanmar are now looking ahead to 2015 to assess their prospects under the prevailing electoral system. Assuming the NLD can maintain its levels of popularity, it is possible the first-past-the-post (FPTP) system will deliver the NLD a single-party parliamentary majority in 2015, even if the 25 percent of seats set aside for the military are taken into account. As other analysts have observed, "the ruling USDP [Union Solidarity and Development Party] won only one seat in the by-election even though it garnered [close to] 30 per cent of the vote, and leaders are said to be concerned that the party could be wiped out by an NLD landslide in the elections in 2015 unless proportional representation is introduced" (Bower and others 2012). In this light, the tendency of Myanmar's FPTP system to amplify wins and losses can also be seen as a political liability, potentially undermining the fragile political calculus that since 2011 has given the reformers licence to shape Myanmar's politics positively. The NLD may, in fact, have much to gain by changing the electoral system to one that increases the likelihood that powerful political forces in the transition process still feel represented in the future parliament. The debate about electoral systems takes on another important dimension with the legitimate concerns of ethnic minorities about their representation in Myanmar's new political system. An FPTP system with a resurgent NLD poses significant challenges for ethnic minority parties. While the 2012 by-elections included few constituencies in the ethnic states, in those constituencies where ethnic minority parties did compete they only gained political ground in one seat, winning by a narrow margin over the NLD. The 2015 elections are already looming, and both the NLD and USDP are seeking to lead the nation down a path towards peace and national reconciliation. In this context it will be increasingly difficult for the NLD and USDP to ignore the calls for political accommodation by the ethnic minority parties.

Discussion of electoral system reform in Myanmar has been initiated by an alliance of small democratic parties and ethnic minority parties. Despite major public speeches on the need for peace and reconciliation, the NLD has avoided or dismissed the near-term importance of electoral system reform. Many national and international contacts have noted that in their meetings with NLD party officials the topic of electoral system reform is not really open for discussion. This caution is not surprising, as the NLD has the biggest system advantage to lose if there is a shift away from FPTP. Sensitivity on the issue may be intensified if the NLD leadership is considering the problem only in the black-and-white terms of a full parliamentary shift from FPTP to proportional representation, which has been the dominant narrative in much of the media reporting on the topic to date.

The USDP has much to gain from shifting to a system that delivers a more proportional allocation of seats. Consequently, the USDP is at risk of appearing self-serving if it initiates the discussion on electoral system reform or uses its current majority in parliament to legislate a new system without the NLD's agreement. The latter move, even taken in the name of national reconciliation, would potentially undermine the credibility of the 2015 election result. In an interview with the *Myanmar Times* in December 2012, USDP vice-chairman U Htay Oo said that the USDP was still studying proportional representation. Indicating that his party had no immediate plans to call for proportional representation, he did not rule out introducing the changes at some point, or supporting a motion from other parties to change the voting system (Win Ko Ko Latt 2012).

The decision to reform the electoral system in Myanmar is deeply political and one that can only be taken by national stakeholders. The current, early phase of the 2015 electoral process should be seen as a critical window for the electoral systems discussion. An electoral system reform discussion that is too long delayed runs the risk of becoming increasingly politicized as elections draw near. Parties will have less time to react to changes in the underlying rules of electoral competition, and the likely impact of such changes on results will be more apparent. It should also be noted that changes to the electoral legal framework late in the electoral cycle could undermine the effective management of the elections. Such changes would come as a significant new hurdle to an election management body already challenged with improving the basic electoral process by 2015.

It is likely that as the national peace and reconciliation process moves forward and the electoral calendar narrows, calls for electoral system reform will increase. Waiting for such pressure to build risks delayed resolution of the electoral system debate until late in the electoral cycle, which could undermine the 2015 election in the ways described above. A proactive approach that includes key stakeholder discussion of a wider spectrum of electoral system reform options may serve the interests of all stakeholders in defusing a dangerous political situation before preparations for the 2015 elections begin in earnest.

Given the multiple objectives of small group representation for peace and national reconciliation, and of maintaining geographic representation in parliament, the discussion on electoral systems could constructively expand to explore the following four compromise system configurations. These system configurations include features to mitigate the disadvantages of both FPTP and pure proportional representation.

Each of these compromise system configurations strikes a different balance between proportionality and geographical representation, and thus has different cost implications in terms of the NLD's electoral system advantage (see Fig. 12.1). A "parallel system", which would divide the seats in parliament between FPTP and proportional representation seats, presents the NLD with the strongest option of holding onto some of its FPTP seat bonus. Some of the advantages of a parallel system might alternatively be produced by using different systems for each chamber of parliament; for example, maintaining FPTP for the House of Representatives while adopting a proportional system for the House of Nationalities. This "incongruous bicameral" configuration could have additional effects on the function of parliament.

A preliminary examination of electoral system clauses in the constitution suggests that parts of the current FPTP system are embedded in the document. In particular, the constitution appears to require that members of the House of Representatives be elected in single-member township-based districts. This may limit electoral system reform alternatives to the incongruous bicameral configuration unless there is a constitutional amendment. For changes to the relevant provisions, constitutional amendment must be approved by a two-thirds majority in parliament, then by a majority of voters in a national referendum.

Finally, it is important to examine electoral system reform not only in terms of its implications for the NLD, but also in terms of the costs and benefits to other key stakeholders. Even if the NLD accepts a compromise system, especially one that maintains a portion of its FPTP systems advantage, will this be enough to satisfy ethnic demands for accommodation in the formal political process? Will it be enough to convince former regime power-holders that their interests will be sufficiently protected? These

FIGURE 12.1

Compromise Systems Alternatives by Non-proportional vs. Proportional Result

First-past-the-post (FPTP)	Four potential compromise models				Proportional representation (PR system)
	Parallel system	Incongruous bicameralism	Proportional representation with multi-member districts	Mixed-member proportional (MMP)	
	Maintains some FPTP seat bonus, a system advantage favoring NLD		Delivers proportional results offering no system advantage to NLD		

thresholds are not clearly established, so "defusing" a tense political situation is by no means formulaic. Given these concerns, the best that Myanmar's international friends can do is to highlight the problems and risks in the current system, inform stakeholders about the strengths and weaknesses of various alternatives, and stress how important it is for the long-term prospects for peace and reconciliation that a consensus emerge in this area.

BACKGROUND

By-elections were held on 1 April 2012 to fill a limited number of legislative seats, following the appointment of previously-elected representatives to the new government of President Thein Sein. For the first time since being denied its overwhelming electoral mandate to govern in 1990, the NLD sought to contest seats in the by-elections. These elections also marked the first time that NLD leader Daw Aung San Suu Kyi was a candidate and was elected for political office. Decisions by the NLD and Aung San Suu Kyi to contest the elections were pragmatic responses to the new government's top-down reforms that have opened limited, but significant, democratic political space in Myanmar.

Analysts predicted the NLD would fare well under credible conditions, but the extent of the NLD's electoral success was a surprise to most. The party captured a landslide victory, winning 43 of the 45 seats in the by-elections. One of the remaining two seats went to the USDP (the party most closely associated with the former regime) in a constituency in which the NLD candidate was disqualified. The other seat went to the Shan Nationalities Democratic Party (SNDP) by a narrow margin over the NLD's candidate. The NLD's successes even included victories in four constituencies in the capital city and military stronghold of Naypyitaw. Overall, the NLD captured 66 percent of the vote and the USDP captured 27 percent; however, due to the FPTP system, this resulted in the NLD winning approximately 96 percent of the seats and the USDP 2 percent. This was similar to the 1990 general election results in which the NLD won over 80 percent of the parliamentary seats with less than 60 percent of the national votes. In 2012, however, President Thein Sein publicly accepted the by-election results and thus continued his apparent commitment to reform. As all sides anticipated, this was a key factor in several countries deciding to lift or suspend economic sanctions.

For stakeholders in Myanmar, the 2012 by-elections revealed the NLD's potential to dominate once again winner-take-all elections under credible electoral conditions. Looking towards the 2015 general election, when 75 percent of parliament's seats should be contested, the NLD's landslide victory in 2012 significantly raises the political stakes. As one respected analyst said, "the scene may be set for a more polarized political space in the lead-up to 2015, and possibly for more confrontational politics, as key sectors of Myanmar society—the conservative political elite, ethnic parties, and non-NLD democrats—see the risk of marginalization" (Horsey 2012). Perhaps most importantly, the commitment of Myanmar's leaders to competitive elections (which was critical to the conduct of credible elections in 2012), may be more challenging to maintain unless the current electoral system's amplification of wins and losses is addressed.

Currently, as the party with a comfortable majority of seats in parliament, the USDP must play a key role in any near-term efforts for electoral systems reform. Despite its much smaller share of seats, the NLD is also a key stakeholder, with considerable leverage in any process of electoral system reform.[1] As the 2012 elections revealed, the first-past-the-post (FPTP) system is a real political asset for the NLD. If the party can maintain its level of popularity with the public, the FPTP system stands to deliver the NLD a single-party parliamentary majority in 2015, even if the number of seats set aside for the military is taken into account. However, the political aftermath of Myanmar's general election in 1990 is a reminder that the FPTP system's amplification of wins and losses can also be a political liability, potentially undermining the fragile political calculus that since 2011 has given the reformers licence to positively shape Myanmar's politics.[2]

Assuming the NLD fails to negotiate an arrangement with ethnic minority parties to avoid vote-splitting, the FPTP system may be a liability in another important sense: it runs at cross-purposes with several ethnic minority parties' expectations to have significant representation in national-level legislative institutions as part of an historic process of national reconciliation. In her initial address to parliament as an elected member of parliament (MP) in May 2012, Aung San Suu Kyi stressed the centrality of issues of ethnic inclusion, stating: "to become a truly democratic union with a spirit of the union, equal rights and mutual respect, I urge all members of parliament to discuss the enactment of the laws needed to protect equal rights of ethnicities" (Hla Hla Htay 2012). Similarly, in her

June acceptance speech for the Nobel Peace Prize in Oslo, Aung San Suu Kyi said that she and her party "stand ready and willing to play any role in the process of national reconciliation" (ibid.).[3]

Shortly after the by-elections on 1 April 2012, a group of non-NLD democratic parties and ethnic minority parties, collectively known as the Democratic and Ethnic Alliance (DEA),[4] began advocating for a shift to a more proportional electoral system. In July 2012 they held meetings with President Thein Sein; with *Pyithu Hluttaw* (House of Representatives) Speaker Thura U Shwe Mann, Committee Chairpersons, and *Hluttaw* officials; and with the Union Election Commission (UEC) and the Constitutional Tribunal. At the coordination meeting between the UEC and representatives of the DEA, both sides discussed points made in the DEA's paper "Suggestions on Improvement to the Electoral System". The group proposed to replace the current FPTP system with a proportional voting system, which would allow independents and minority parties to win seats in parliament more easily (*NLM* 2012).

With then Constitutional Tribunal member Tin Aung Aye in attendance, UEC Chairman Tin Aye said that the question of whether the proportional representation system recommended by the political parties conforms to the concepts of the constitution must be assessed, so the suggestion was sent to the Constitutional Tribunal to seek the Tribunal's opinion. Chairman Tin Aye also indicated that the UEC would submit "the outcome from the meeting to the *Pyidaungsu Hluttaw* [combined houses of parliament] after reviewing it so as to made [*sic*] decisions necessarily" (*NLM* 2012). The understanding of the DEA participants, reported in other articles, confirmed that the UEC had expressed plans to forward DEA's proposal to the full parliament for review and consideration.[5]

None of the media reporting on the meeting addresses the timing or sequence of action between the submission of the paper to the Constitutional Tribunal and its subsequent submission to parliament. On 6 September 2012 all nine Constitutional Tribunal judges resigned after more than two-thirds of the House of Representatives called for their impeachment.[6] On 8 April 2013, the UEC held a meeting with fifty-six political parties during which seven parties, including the National Unity Party and National Democratic Force, again raised the issue of proportional representation. The NLD and three other parties spoke against the proposal (Win Ko Ko Latt 2013*a*). The Chairman of the UEC informed the parties that the UEC was not in a position to decide whether to change to a proportional representation system and that a proposal would have to be submitted to parliament and would be subject to its approval (Chan Myae Khine 2013).

RESEARCH APPROACH

Within the families of electoral systems under discussion in Myanmar (plurality/majority, proportional representation, and "mixed" systems), this chapter focuses on four electoral system configurations that would maintain a degree of geographic representation while also responding to the demands of some ethnic groups, small democratic parties, and various other stakeholders for more proportional representation (see Fig. 12.2).

The authors assume that the dominant narratives of national reconciliation and strong arguments for continued geographic representation will likely place increased emphasis on these "compromise" electoral system configurations in future stakeholder and academic discussions. Using a fictional electoral scenario, the chapter examines the impact of each of the four systems on election results. The reader is cautioned that such modelling is not an attempt to forecast 2015 election results in Myanmar, but rather an effort to illustrate the impact of system selection using an illustrative set of election results. To further emphasize this point, the number of parliamentary seats and names of parties have been purposefully set to be relevant to (but not match) the situation in Myanmar. Showing the variety of compromise system outcomes possible, the chapter attempts to examine briefly the likely advantages and disadvantages of these systems for key stakeholder groups, including the NLD, USDP, ethnic minority parties, other small parties, and citizens.

FIGURE 12.2

Compromise System Alternatives Between FPTP and Proportional Representation

First-past-the-post (FPTP)	Four potential compromise models				Proportional representation
	Parallel system	Incongruous bicameralism	Proportional representation with multi-member districts	Mixed-member proportional (MMP)	

APPROACHES TO ACHIEVING GEOGRAPHIC AND PROPORTIONAL REPRESENTATION

During a July 2012 visit to Myanmar, democracy scholar Larry Diamond noted that proportional representation:

> ... may be more effective at giving a stake in the political system to a variety of forces, including the current ruling party, if those forces don't do very well in the next election. At the same there is a need in country [sic] like Burma that is still overwhelmingly rural to have geographically-based representation, in which there are representatives that people can identify, each in their own constituency, to represent them and speak for them, that they can have access to express grievances and interests (Roughneen 2012).

There are generally four ways of moving towards a model that combines elements of proportional representation with geographic representation. Three of these uniform system approaches are presented in Table 12.1 below. The fourth, incongruous bicameralism, will be addressed separately.

Making similar observations to other electoral systems scholars,[7] Diamond noted that an answer for Myanmar might be found in the consideration of one of the mixed systems "in which there is a substantial if not full proportionality in the distribution of votes into seats, but at the same time that people can identify individual representatives that speak for them" (Roughneen 2012).

In meetings held in early August 2012 with Burmese political analysts, election officials, and a number of political party and civil society representatives, the authors noted high levels of awareness and interest about proportional representation. There was less awareness of "mixed systems" that combine features of FPTP and proportional representation. Where discussants were aware of mixed systems, Thailand, which uses a parallel system for their lower house, was a constant reference point. The authors found that few discussants understood which mixed systems would deliver semi-proportional as opposed to proportional distribution of votes into seats. If the electoral system discussion expands to include a discussion of mixed systems, it will be critical for stakeholders to examine in greater detail the difference between a *parallel system* and a *mixed-member proportional (MMP) system* for Myanmar. While both achieve a compromise between geographic and proportional representation, each has distinct implications for structuring stakeholder advantages and disadvantages in

TABLE 12.1
System Options and Constitutional Considerations

System	Features	Constitutional considerations
From proportional representation (PR) family of electoral systems		
List PR with multi-member constituencies	Generally in list PR elections, parties compete with lists of candidates and seats are distributed among the lists in proportion to their share of the votes. By opting to run this system in several multi-member constituencies rather than a single national constituency, a degree of geographic representation would be achieved. Depending on the district magnitude (number of members representing a district) the results would be more or less proportional. An example of a country using this system that policy makers in Myanmar may find relevant is Indonesia.	House of Nationalities: It seems that a PR system for elections to the House of Nationalities under which each state or region is a multi-member constituency with 12 members per state/region would be consistent with the existing Constitution. While it would retain the (constitutionally mandated) disproportionality between states/regions, that approach would allow PR within states/regions. House of Representatives: Article 109(a) of the Constitution appears to call for election of members of the House of Representatives in separate single member districts based on townships, which would seem to rule out any form of PR.*

*Note: It has been suggested to us by some interlocutors that the Constitution might allow townships to be combined to form multi-member constituencies. However, it is hard to see why, if the drafters of the Constitution did not intend for the townships to form the basis of separate districts, they would have included a provision for the combination of townships in case the number of townships exceeds 330. Unfortunately, given the ambiguity of the wording of Article 109(a) both in the original Burmese and in the available English translations, it is difficult to predict with any confidence what the Constitutional Tribunal would make of that issue.

System	Features	Constitutional considerations
From mixed systems family of electoral systems		
Mixed-member proportional (MMP)	Generally MMP delivers a result consistent with overall list PR systems. Under MMP candidates compete to win single member districts, however a separate pool of PR seats are considered "compensatory seats". These PR seats would be awarded to parties in quantities meant to achieve proportionality in the overall results.	House of Nationalities: A mixed member proportional or parallel system could work for House of Nationalities elections, provided that the twelve member rule is respected (for example, nine single member districts with three compensatory seats in each state/region).
Parallel system	Generally under a parallel system candidates compete to win single member districts and parties also enter lists of candidates to compete for separate PR seats. There is no compensatory link when allocating the seats for the list PR election as is the case with MMP above: the result of one contest is independent of the other. Because there is no compensatory mechanism, it is unlikely that a parallel system would provide fully proportional results. Parallel systems would offer a degree of minority party inclusion, and the proportionality of the system would increase as the ratio of PR to FPTP seats in the mixed system increases.	House of Representatives: Article 109(a) of the Constitution appears to require that members of the House of Representatives be elected in single-member township-based districts, which would seem to rule out the PR component of a parallel system and the compensatory seats under MMP.**

]**Note: There may be an argument that a mixed-member proportional or parallel system for House of Representatives elections would be constitutional, since they would retain single-member districts based on townships for some seats. While we are sceptical about this argument, the ambiguity of the wording of Article 109(a) of the constitution, both in the original Burmese and in the available English translations, makes it difficult to predict with any confidence how the Constitutional Tribunal would respond to that issue.

the 2015 race, as outlined in the choice diagrams and illustrative electoral systems model that follow.

Choice Between Mixed Systems

The following table, Table 12.2 further explores the potential advantages and disadvantages of mixed-member proportional and parallel systems.

If the decision between mixed systems is to adopt a parallel system, then stakeholders face an additional choice within the parallel system, a choice that concerns the ratio of FPTP to proportional representation seats (see Fig. 12.3).

TABLE 12.2
Comparative Strengths and Weaknesses of MMP and Parallel Systems

Mixed-Member Proportional (MMP)		OR	Parallel System	
Potential Advantage	Potential Disadvantage		Potential Advantage	Potential Disadvantage
Minority parties are fairly included (in proportion to votes received)	The legislature may be fragmented		Minority parties can gain representation	Minority parties are unlikely to win as many seats as their vote share would predict
Majorities are less likely to dominate	Coalitions are more likely		Majority parties are more likely to be able to rule alone	Majorities may be unrestrained in government
Voters have both a district and a party representative	The vote may be confusing to some		Voters have both a district and a party representative	The vote may be confusing to some
It does not matter if a party's voters are concentrated or dispersed				Parties with concentrated pockets of support will do better than those with dispersed support

FIGURE 12.3
Possible Effects When Adjusting the Mix of Seats in a Parallel System

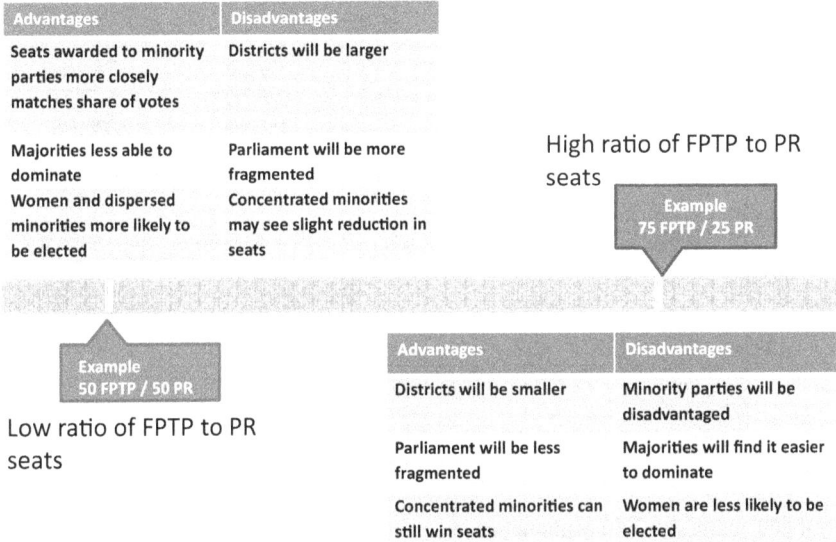

Advantages	Disadvantages
Seats awarded to minority parties more closely matches share of votes	Districts will be larger
Majorities less able to dominate	Parliament will be more fragmented
Women and dispersed minorities more likely to be elected	Concentrated minorities may see slight reduction in seats

High ratio of FPTP to PR seats

Example
75 FPTP / 25 PR

Example
50 FPTP / 50 PR

Low ratio of FPTP to PR seats

Advantages	Disadvantages
Districts will be smaller	Minority parties will be disadvantaged
Parliament will be less fragmented	Majorities will find it easier to dominate
Concentrated minorities can still win seats	Women are less likely to be elected

Model To Illustrate the Importance of System Choices in Myanmar

The significance that these systems have in shaping the playing field and their impact on final results can be illustrated through a simple model that has reasonable "distortion" figures entered for the FPTP results (see Table 12.3). This model represents a fictional country with a 600-seat legislature, 150 of which are seats set aside for a non-party special interest group. This leaves 450 seats to be decided by election. There is no parliamentary threshold.

As this simple model illustrates, even with seats set aside for a special interest group, Party A will win a majority in the legislature under FPTP and both parallel systems. The margin shrinks in the parallel system as the ratio of FPTP seats to proportional representation seats is reduced. It is important to stress that these models are purely simulations based on reasonable guesses about how votes for large and small parties are likely to be translated into seats under varying systems.

TABLE 12.3
Election Results Under Different Systems and System Configurations

A: If 450 seats

	Percentage of vote received	FPTP	PR or MMP	Parallel 300 FPTP + 150 PR	Parallel 225 FPTP + 225 PR
Party A	60%	363 (81%)	270 (60%)	240 + 90 = 330 (73%)	179 + 135 = 314 (70%)
Party B	30%	66 (14%)	135 (30%)	43 + 45 = 88 (20%)	34 + 68 = 102 (23%)
Party C	4%	9 (2.5%)	18 (4.5%)	7 + 6 = 13 (3%)	5 + 9 = 14 (3%)
Others	6%	12 (3%)	27 (6%)	10 + 9 = 19 (4%)	7 + 13 = 20 (4%)
Total	100%	450 (100%)	450 (100%)	450 (100%)	450 (100%)

B: If 600 seats, with 150 seats set aside

	Percentage of vote received	FPTP	PR or MMP	Parallel 300 FPTP + 150 PR	Parallel 225 FPTP + 225 PR
Party A	60%	363 (61%)	270 (45%)	330 (55%)	314 (52%)
Party B	30%	66 (11%)	135 (23%)	88 (15%)	102 (17%)
Party C	4%	9 (1%)	18 (3%)	13 (2%)	14 (3%)
Others	6%	12 (2%)	27 (4%)	19 (3%)	20 (3%)
Set-Aside		150 (25%)	150 (25%)	150 (25%)	150 (25%)
Total		600 (100%)	600 (100%)	600 (100%)	600 (100%)

In the "Background" section above, we have explored arguments that the NLD may face a stark choice—whether to stick to the current FPTP system that will likely deliver the NLD an electoral advantage, or whether to support a change to a proportional representation system in order to strengthen the prospects for peace and stability in Myanmar. Looking at the compromise options discussed in this chapter, switching to list proportional representation with multi-member constituencies or to a mixed-member proportional system would also involve the same high-cost trade-off for the NLD. The introduction of a parallel system, however, could create other scenarios under which the NLD would preserve some of its advantage. That is, a compromise in types of representation would likely be matched by a compromise in total seat results. If it supported the introduction of proportional seats through a parallel system, the NLD could still be seen as taking conciliatory steps to include the USDP, small party, and minority representation in parliament, although not to the same extent as with MMP or proportional representation system choices.

It is also important to note that some of the advantages of a parallel system might be produced by using different systems for each chamber of parliament—for example, by maintaining the FPTP system for the House of Representatives while adopting a proportional or semi-proportional system for the House of Nationalities (hereinafter this configuration is called an "incongruous bicameralism" option). The House of Nationalities is a body with real legislative power: a system likely to deliver high levels of minority representation in the House of Nationalities might go some way towards addressing minority concerns. The constitutionally-mandated allocation of House of Nationalities seats already provides disproportionate representation to the less populous states and regions where most ethnic-minority voters live. A switch from FPTP to a system that yields more proportional results within states and regions could further strengthen minority representation in the House of Nationalities. As long as elections remain based on regional or state constituencies having twelve representatives each, with self-administered zones and divisions retaining their separate individual representatives, the incorporation of proportional representation with multi-member constituencies, MMP, or parallel systems for the House of Nationalities election does not appear to present constitutional difficulties.

Table 12.4 below outlines the implications of the different systems for key stakeholders. The first four columns assume that the voting system for both houses of parliament will be the same, while the last column assumes that different systems will be applied to each house.

ELECTORAL SYSTEM CHOICES IN THE CONTEXT OF NATIONAL RECONCILIATION

On 27 July 2012, the same day that the Democratic and Ethnic Alliance met with the Union Election Commission to advocate for a shift to proportional

TABLE 12.4

Comparison of Compromise Systems by Implications for Stakeholders

	Current System	Compromise Systems			
	First-past-the-post	*List PR with multi-member districts*	*Mixed member proportional (MMP)*	*Parallel system*	*Incongruous bicameralism*
NLD	• Highest system advantage, positioning NLD to achieve single party majority even with military set aside seats; • Possible landslide victory risks alienating other groups; • Could appear insensitive to historic grievances of ethnic groups.	• NLD less likely to receive a seat bonus under this system than under FPTP; • NLD will win roughly as many seats as their national vote share would predict; • Would be a major concession to the historical grievances of ethnic groups.	• NLD less likely to receive a seat bonus under this system as it uses compensatory seats to deliver proportional results; • Would be a major concession to the historical grievances of ethnic groups.	• Offers NLD option of keeping a portion of its FPTP seat bonus advantage; • Offers NLD chance to appear sensitive to historical grievances of ethnic groups.	• NLD may dominate House of Representatives but lack a single party majority of seats in the House of Nationalities; • Offers NLD chance to appear sensitive to historical grievances of ethnic groups.
USDP	• Highest systems risk; • Winner-take-all result risks not rewarding incremental improvements achieved in transforming the party; • Strong possibility USDP + military not able to achieve parliamentary majority on issues of common concern.	• As a minority party that is geographically dispersed, the USDP will benefit from proportional result; • Possibility USDP + military could achieve parliamentary majority on issues of common concern.	• As a minority party that is geographically dispersed, the USDP will benefit from proportional result; • Possibility USDP + military able to achieve parliamentary majority on issues of common concern.	• USDP is likely to gain representation through proportional seats but may struggle in the FPTP seats. • Benefits for USDP will increase with the ratio of PR to FPTP seats in the parallel system.	• USDP will struggle to win seats in House of Representatives but should gain seats in a proportional or semi-proportional House of Nationalities.

Military	• Highest systems risk as USDP seats are drastically reduced; • With limited USDP seats, strong possibility USDP + military not able to achieve parliamentary majority on issues of common concern.	• Possibility that USDP + military could achieve parliamentary majority on issues of common concern; • Military block's parliamentary importance potentially enhanced as others lack numbers to form single party majority.	• Possibility that USDP + military could achieve parliamentary majority on issues of common concern; • Military block's parliamentary importance potentially enhanced as others lack numbers to form single-party majority,	• Very limited possibility USDP + military able to achieve parliamentary majority on issues of common concern; • USDP + military may be able to form a significant opposition block on these issues.	• USDP + military likely unable to achieve a majority on issues of common concern in House of Representatives but may be able to do so in the House of Nationalities.
Ethnic minority parties	• If no pre-election pact, many ethnic-minority parties may lose national seats to NLD; • If ethnic parties are small or geographically concentrated, could create incentives for some to merge so as to compete against large parties for single-member seats; • In some cases ethnic minority parties benefit in state parliaments from maintaining FPTP.	• Ethnic minority parties would likely benefit from proportional result when facing NLD challenge; • Ethnic groups with geographically dispersed pockets of support particularly likely to see benefit over FPTP; • Some ethnic minority parties will face a loss of seats in state legislatures.	• Ethnic minority parties would likely benefit from proportional result when facing NLD challenge; • Ethnic groups with geographically-dispersed support particularly likely to see benefit over FPTP; • Some ethnic minority parties will face a loss of seats in state legislatures.	• Against strong NLD challenge most ethnic minority parties would benefit from addition of proportional seats at national level. Would share an interest with USDP and other non-NLD parties in having high ratio of PR to FPTP seats in parallel system; • Possible exceptions at state level where ethnic minority parties enjoy FPTP advantages.	• Many will struggle to win a significant number of seats in House of Representatives (unless highly geographically concentrated and popular), but will do better in House of Nationalities under a proportional or semi-proportional system.

continued on next page

TABLE 12.4 – cont'd

	Current System	Compromise Systems			
	First-past-the-post	List PR with multi-member districts	Mixed member proportional (MMP)	Parallel system	Incongruous bicameralism
Other small parties	• Highest electoral system risk; • Small parties' support likely eclipsed by NLD, resulting in few (if any) seats in winner-take-all race.	• High electoral systems advantage with near proportional result; • Some risk of losing out to big parties if there is a low district magnitude or a parliamentary threshold applied.	• Highest electoral systems advantage; • Proportional result further ensured by compensatory seats; • Some risk of losing out to big parties if a parliamentary threshold is applied.	• Other small parties would benefit from the addition of proportional seats at national level, although to a lesser degree than PR or MMP. They would share an interest with USDP and some ethnic-minority parties in calling for high ratio of PR to FPTP seats in a parallel system.	• For lower house, small parties' support likely eclipsed by NLD, resulting in few (if any) seats in winner-take-all race; • May only win seats in House of Nationalities under proportional or semi-proportional system.
Citizens	• Offers geographic representation; • Potential accountability between citizen and individual representative; • If a voter's political views are not reflected by major parties, less likelihood they will be represented in parliament; • Ease of voting.	• Offers a degree of geographic representation; • If a voter's political views are not reflected by major parties, less likelihood they will be represented in parliament; • Ease of voting.	• Offers substantial geographic representation; • If a voter's political views are not reflected by major parties, less likelihood they will be represented in parliament; • Voting more complex if two votes used.	• Offers substantial geographic representation; • If a voter's political views are not reflected by major parties, less likelihood they will be represented in parliament; • Voting more complex if two votes used.	• Offers strong geographic representation in lower house plus representation of minority parties and ethnic groups in upper house; • Having two systems may seem more intuitive if used for two different houses of parliament.

representation, the International Crisis Group (ICG) released a report that recommended consideration be given to "the possibility that Myanmar would be better served during the transition by a system with greater proportional representation" (ICG 2012). The ICG pointed out that:

> The deal that is being presented to the ethnic armed groups is to give up armed struggle in return for the possibility to pursue their objectives through the political system. If an NLD landslide comes at the expense of minority ethnic representation—as the results of the recent by-elections and the 1990 elections suggest it well might—those deals might start to unravel. In the post-independence parliamentary era, prior to General Ne Win's 1962 coup d'état, there had been considerable ethnic disaffection that the plurality voting system favoured large Burman parties at the expense of minority ethnic parties (ICG 2012).

In post-authoritarian and post-conflict environments, the possibility for representation in the legislature and executive serves as a critical reassurance to historically marginalized groups that their rights will be protected and that they will have a voice in the new state arrangement. In a country like Myanmar, where ethnic minorities have been marginalized from the state for the entirety of the independence era, the need for adequate representation is even more pronounced. Many ethnic minority members are worried that democratic elections would hand power from a Burman-led military to a Burman-led NLD. The NLD may be viewed as more sympathetic to their needs but it is still not regarded as being sufficiently committed to working to advance ethnic issues and rights.

The Thein Sein government has largely pursued a peace-building strategy that has encouraged the formation of political movements that operate within the political system rather than against it. Because most of the ethnic minorities in Myanmar are geographically concentrated, it is possible for them to elect representatives in FPTP districts.[8] However, the elections in 1990 and 2012 demonstrated that simple FPTP systems may not accurately reflect the diversity of opinion in ethnic areas or be able to counter the dominant popularity of the NLD or the advantages of the former regime. Not all ethnic groups have homogeneous opinions, and using an election system that allows one party to win all, or nearly all, of the seats in a region is unlikely to provide the foundation for democratization and peace.

The historical and political realities of Myanmar suggest that the views of domestic stakeholders about the most appropriate election system are complex. The motivations and incentives associated with various systems pull both the government and the NLD opposition in different directions, complicating national reconciliation. The NLD should expect a seat-bonus advantage under FPTP, but this may be counter-productive in the NLD's efforts to negotiate with the government.

The USDP and the military have reason to be apprehensive about maintaining FPTP: the precedents of the 1990 election and the 2012 by-election show that the USDP (and its regime-associated predecessors) were dramatically disadvantaged by winner-take-all elections. Under a free multi-party election, the USDP may win very few FPTP seats with their minority share of the vote, far fewer than they would win under proportional representation. The USDP has established networks in villages and townships and may believe these can be exploited to gain local votes; however, the results of the 2012 by-elections appear to have significantly shaken this belief. In an interview with the *Myanmar Times* in December 2012, USDP vice chairman U Htay Oo said that the USDP was still studying proportional representation. Indicating that his party had no immediate plans to call for proportional representation, he did not rule out introducing the changes at some point, or supporting a motion from other parties to change the voting system (Win Ko Ko Latt 2012). Speaking at a press conference in late June 2013, just before parliament's seventh session, Htay Oo left the USDP's options open, saying that the policy decisions on proportional representation would be made at a later date by the USDP central committee in the "interest of the nation and the citizens" (Win Ko Ko Latt 2013a).

Opposition parties outside the NLD, such as the National Democratic Force (NDF), should be heavily in favor of some form of proportional representation, based on their election performance in 2010 and 2012. Ethnic minority parties may well be courted by these various interests and encouraged to include electoral system reform as one item in their advocacy for national reconciliation.

Perhaps sensing other political agendas at play, in early 2013 many ethnic-minority parties have expressed concerns about proportional representation, and have actively reached out for additional information on the likely trade-offs associated with the system. Some have called for pilot testing of proportional representation in limited areas outside their own constituencies. Some have also expressed concerns about what new parties or interests might choose to contest elections if proportional representation increases small party prospects for parliamentary representation. Adding further levels of complexity, some ethnic minority parties face divergent national and local incentives—they may favour proportional representation or MMP for national elections but fear the impact of similar reforms for state-level elections. In a few reported cases, this has prevented ethnic-minority party leaders from advocating strongly for a shift to a more proportional system.

POSSIBLE TRAJECTORIES FOR THE ELECTORAL SYSTEMS DISCUSSION

The dominant political dialogue in Myanmar points towards national reconciliation, with both Thein Sein and Aung San Suu Kyi using their respective political offices to call for change in the spirit of Panglong. In their speeches on national reconciliation, both leaders have avoided direct statements about electoral system reform; however, it is unlikely that a broader, consultative reconciliation process can move forward without addressing this issue, especially given the historic grievances many ethnic minority groups hold against the current FPTP system.

There are political and administrative advantages to addressing electoral system reform as early as possible in the electoral cycle. Reform taken two years before elections will structure the incentives of different political stakeholders while there is still time for them to develop their strategies and political support. In this case, the rules of the game are negotiated before the players start playing in earnest. Reform initiated too close to elections risks becoming highly politicized, with the rules changing as the game is being played, and the impact of these changes on electoral outcomes becomes much more evident.

The 2012 by-elections highlighted weaknesses in Myanmar's election management, and the Union Election Commission has much ground to cover between 2013 and 2015 to put in place the resources, training, and systems necessary to deliver credible elections. These efforts would be negatively impacted by electoral system changes happening late in the electoral cycle. At a meeting with political parties on 8 April 2013, UEC Chairman U Tin Aye stated that, "if [changes to the electoral system] cannot be approved during 2013, the electoral system will remain unchanged. This is because [change] takes time. It cannot be reformed of my own volition. Free and fair elections will have to be held on the basis of an approved system" (*Eleven Myanmar* 2013).

The national reconciliation narrative will be increasingly impacted by the 2015 general elections as Myanmar moves towards that critical milestone.

This overlap of national reconciliation and electoral timelines stands to highlight the role that electoral competition plays in empowering—or failing to empower—ethnic minority voices. Advocacy by the Democratic and Ethnic Alliance in 2012 put the issue of electoral system reform on the national stage, and developments in 2013 appear likely to keep it there. At the time of writing, discussions between several ethnic-minority parties about the formation of a new, national, Federated Union Party (FUP), as well as parliament's plans to form a committee to evaluate the 2008 Constitution, have renewed focus on the electoral system question.

As parliament proceeds with plans to form an evaluating committee for amending the 2008 Constitution, the position of the ethnic parties may be critical in determining whether or not the electoral system debate becomes part of this process. In early strategy coordination discussions with some of the ethnic minority parties, the NLD seems to be encouraging the ethnic-minority parties' pursuit of federalism (another key topic in national reconciliation) while trying to dissuade them from proportional representation. Immediately after a meeting on 18 June 2013 between Aung San Suu Kyi and representatives from five ethnic parties, one senior SNLD official noted: "we do not think the PR system is intended to make the [needed] changes for the country … Daw Suu also does not think it is an honest plan" (Nyein Nyein 2013).

Through early 2013 the NLD leadership has been very cautious about engaging in formal or informal discussion on electoral system reform. In an April 2013 interview with the *Irrawaddy*, NLD spokesperson Nyan Win sought to clarify the NLD's position, stating, "our stand is that the PR system is not fit at the present time, for the next election. We have to educate the Burmese people about any new system, and that will take time" (Roughneen 2013). So far the national discussion has largely focused on shifting from an FPTP system to proportional representation. It is understandable that senior NLD officials might rigidly oppose such a shift: party strategists likely see it as giving up a major political asset for 2015.

The discussion of "mixed systems" is just surfacing in Myanmar. Among the mixed systems (parallel system and mixed-member proportional system), it could be expected that the NLD would also object to MMP. Like a proportional representation system, it delivers fully proportional outcomes (see Fig. 12.1, p.3). If the seats set aside for the military are taken into account, asking the NLD to agree to a change to a mixed-member proportional system may be asking it to give up its opportunity to win a single-party parliamentary majority.

The parallel system and incongruous bicameralism, however, represent interesting compromise options. A parallel system would maintain some of the NLD's FPTP seat bonus while allowing for the introduction of proportional representation seats, a direct (if limited) response to the national reconciliation concerns of the ethnic-minority parties and the political apprehensions of the USDP and smaller democratic parties. Incongruous bicameralism would achieve this as well, only with the effects of each system concentrated in each house of parliament. The NLD's advantage under a parallel system would be affected by the agreed-upon ratio of FPTP to proportional representation seats in the parallel system.

Electoral system reform would require changes to the political parties law, and to one or both of the laws governing elections for the House of Representatives and the House of Nationalities. However, as presented above in Table 12.1, there are also critical components of the current electoral system found in the 2008 Constitution that likely preclude the adoption of many electoral system reform options. In particular, the constitution appears to require that members of the House of Representatives be elected in single-member township-based districts. This requirement may narrow the field of possible electoral system reforms for the 2015 general elections to the House of Nationalities election, which would entail an incongruous bicameral electoral structure for parliament unless stakeholders pursue a near-term constitutional amendment to open additional options. Amendment of the relevant articles would require approval by 75 percent of the combined members of both houses of parliament, followed by approval by at least 50 percent of eligible voters in a referendum.

The parallel system and incongruous bicameralism appear to be options that would maximize the NLD's utility under the range of compromise system options discussed in this chapter. However, an equally important question may be to ask which electoral system option best guards against the former regime's interests being critically threatened in 2015. Maintaining the current FPTP system is clearly a challenge in this regard. Would the compromise offered through a parallel system or incongruous bicameralism be enough to quell these concerns, or would it be necessary to have a system that offered full proportionality and a clear shot at maintaining a USDP and military parliamentary majority on issues of common concern? This is an area that deserves additional research and monitoring as the electoral systems discussion moves forward.

CONCLUSIONS

1. Any decision to reform the electoral system is a deeply political decision, and one that can only be taken by national stakeholders. The discussion of system options, however, could benefit from information about international comparative experience and technical expertise. Informed stakeholder discussion of alternatives should be a precursor to electoral system reform.

2. The NLD's leadership on electoral system reform is critical. Reform pushed through against the NLD's will, even in the name of national reconciliation, would threaten to delegitimize the results of the 2015 general elections.

3. Electoral system reform that is too long delayed runs the risk of becoming highly politicized as actors have less time to react to changes in the underlying rules of the competition. To avoid a polarized view of the choices available (from FPTP to a proportional representation system), stakeholders may need to be encouraged to discuss this topic while being presented with information on the wider range of options available.

4. If a consensus on electoral system reform is reached between key political leaders, voter education should be conducted to inform public expectations about the function and impact of a new system. Publicizing key stakeholder agreement with the new system would form an important element of this voter education.

5. The electoral reform debate is best finalized early in the electoral calendar. A shift in electoral systems, especially a late shift, would pose substantial administrative challenges for the UEC and may distract from other high-priority reform efforts. To the extent possible, the UEC needs to develop contingency plans for switching to a new system.

6. The international community should coordinate support for electoral system reform in order to deliver timely and consistent analysis to key stakeholders. If consensus cannot be reached among experts, different conclusions should be well documented and produced in a format where the differences are clearly explained to increasingly well-informed local stakeholders.

7. Additional research should be conducted on the views and concerns of all key stakeholders. This may be particularly relevant for answering questions about the potential peace and stability dividend of each

system. It is also important to better understand the region and state-level implications of electoral system reform for key stakeholders.

8. Additional research should be conducted on the option of applying a different electoral system for elections to each house of parliament (incongruous bicameralism), including the legislative implications of creating a more asymmetric seat result between the chambers.

Notes

*   The views expressed in this chapter are those of the authors and do not necessarily reflect those of the institutions for which they work.

1   In discussions held in August 2012, interlocutors recognized that the governing party has sufficient seats to pass legislation to reform the electoral system without the acquiescence of the NLD, and may even be able to couch the move in terms of "national reconciliation". However, they point out that doing so would risk the NLD's saying that the 2015 elections had been stolen from the start. Given the broad public support that exists for the NLD and Aung San Suu Kyi, such statements could be politically destabilizing. Thus it becomes important that Suu Kyi and her party are seen as endorsing, or even leading, the move to reform the country's electoral system. This has led to quiet speculation about the potential political concessions that could be requested in exchange for the NLD giving up a clear opportunity to win a parliamentary majority in 2015.

2   Several election analysts have noted the example that South Africa might provide for Myanmar, especially for the NLD. In this case Nelson Mandela's African National Congress (ANC) stood to be clearly advantaged in the 1994 National Assembly Elections if the country's FPTP system were maintained. Early in the peace negotiations the ANC offered a PR system to the National Party as a sign of good faith and a foundation for power sharing. The guarantee that they would not be wiped out electorally gave the ruling National Party the confidence to concede on other issues of multi-party democracy (Reynolds, Reilly and Ellis 2005).

3   On 7 August 2012 Aung San Suu Kyi was approved by Myanmar's parliament to chair the newly-formed Committee for Rule of Law and Peace and Stability. Three NLD parliamentarians are listed also as members of the committee, which is comprised of fifteen members, including MPs representing the Chin, Kachin, Karenni, Arakanese, Mon, and Shan ethnic minorities (Nyein Nyein 2012). Amongst its responsibilities the Committee oversees the amendment and promulgation of laws and by-laws being implemented by central-level organizations. According to a *Xinhua* news report, the committee "is effective

for one year, will render help to and coordination with MPs, the government's judicial bodies, government staff and the media to stay under law and take action if necessary through presentation to the house's speaker [Speaker of the lower house of parliament], monitoring of implementation of rule of law and coordinating for revoking, amendment and promulgation of laws and by-laws being practised by central-level organizations" (*Xinhua* 2012).

4   The Democratic and Ethnic Alliance is composed of the National Democratic Force, the Democracy and Peace Party, the Democratic Party, the Shan Nationalities Democratic Party, the Rakhine Nationalities Development Party, the Chin National Party, Phalon-Sawal Democratic Party, the All Mon Regions Democracy Party, the Union Democracy Party, and the Union and Peace Party (Ingjin Naing 2012). In much of the media reporting, this group is also referred to as the Friends of Democracy Parties, or Group of Friends of Democracy Parties. This name is usually used to refer to the six ethnic minority parties in the DEA.

5   Meeting participant Thu Wai, chairman of the Democratic Party, stated: "The Election Commission Chairman said he will submit the proposal to parliament to be discussed and approved. But we have to work harder [on it]." (Ingjin Naing 2012).

6   The calls for impeachment and subsequent resignations were the result of a controversial ruling that limited the power of parliamentary committees and commissions to overrule the work of government.

7   After meeting NLD and ethnic leaders in 2000, Reynolds, Stepan, Zaw Oo and Levine outlined the potential advantages of a system which combined single member districts with proportionality (see Reynolds and others 2001).

8   For example, the Shan Nationalities Democratic Party's narrow win in Shan State constituency 3 in the 2012 by-election.

References

Bower, Ernest, Michael Green, Christopher Johnson, and Murray Hiebert. *State of the Nation and Recommendations for U.S. Foreign Policy.* CSIS Myanmar Trip Report. Washington DC: Center for Strategic and International Studies (CSIS), 2012.

Chan Myae Khine. "Burma Parties Divided over Proportional Electoral System". *Asian Correspondent,* 16 April 2013. <http://asiancorrespondent.com/105411/burma-myanmar-proportional-representation/>. Accessed 12 December 2013.

Eleven Media. "Time running out to introduce proportional electoral system". *Eleven Media,* 9 April 2013.

Hla Hla Htay. "Suu Kyi urges Myanmar MPs to back minority rights". *Agence France Presse (AFP),* 25 July 2012. <http://www.google.com/hostednews/afp/article/ALeqM5h4ri23R0gASfR_6CNun-5jIkAEBg?docId=CNG.007421df9b1fa45b01208882a65fff0b.4d1>. Accessed 12 December 2013.

Horsey, Richard. *The Results of the Myanmar By-elections*. Paper prepared for the Conflict Prevention and Peace Forum, Social Sciences Research Council (SSRC), 17 November 2010. <http://www.networkmyanmar.org/images/stories/PDF5/rhout.pdf>. Accessed 12 December 2013.

International Crisis Group. *Myanmar: The Politics of Economic Reform*, Asia Report No. 231, 27 July 2012. <http://www.crisisgroup.org/en/regions/asia/south-east-asia/myanmar/231-myanmar-the-politics-of-economic-reform.aspx>. Accessed 12 December 2013.

McCartan, Brian. "Ethnic peace key to Myanmar reform". *Asia Times Online*, 28 July 2012. <http://www.atimes.com/atimes/Southeast_Asia/NG28Ae01.html>. Accessed 12 December 2013.

Ingjin Naing. "Burma Eyes Proportional Representation". Radio Free Asia, 27 July 2012. <http://www.rfa.org/english/news/myanmar/proportional-representation-07272012173300.html>. Accessed 12 December 2013.

New Light of Myanmar (*NLM*). "Consequences of election system rest on basic causes regarding principles, religion, ethnic affairs, race, language and social standing of the people of the country". *New Light of Myanmar*, 28 July 2012, p. 16, 9. <http://www.burmalibrary.org/docs13/NLM2012-07-28.pdf>. Accessed 12 December 2013.

Nyein Nyein. "Suu Kyi, Ethnic Leaders to Work toward Federal Union". *Irrawaddy*, 18 June 2013. <http://www.irrawaddy.org/constitution/suu-kyi-ethnic-leaders-to-work-toward-federal-union.html>. Accessed 12 December 2013.

———. "Suu Kyi to Head 'Rule of Law' Committee". *Irrawaddy*, 7 August 2012. <http://www.irrawaddy.org/suu-kyi/suu-kyi-to-head-rule-of-law-committee.html>. Accessed 12 December 2013.

Reynolds, Andrew, Alfred Stepan, Zaw Oo, and Stephen Levine. "How Burma Could Democratize". *Journal of Democracy* 12, no. 4 (October 2001): 95–108. <http://muse.jhu.edu/login?auth=0&type=summary&url=/journals/journal_of_democracy/v012/12.4reynolds.html>. Accessed 12 December 2013.

Reynolds, Andrew, Ben Reilly, and Andrew Ellis. *Electoral System Design: The New International IDEA Handbook*. Stockholm: International Institute for Democracy and Electoral Assistance (International IDEA), 2005.

Roughneen, Simon. "Ahead of 2015, Voting Systems Debate Heats Up in Burma". *Irrawaddy*, 22 April 2013. <http://www.irrawaddy.org/parliament/ahead-of-2015-voting-system-debate-heats-up-in-burma.html>. Accessed 12 December 2013.

———. "Burma's Emerging Democracy". *Irrawaddy*, 24 July 2012. <http://www.irrawaddy.org/interview/burmas-emerging-democracy.html>. Accessed 12 December 2013.

Win Ko Ko Latt. "Bill on voting system slated for June". *Myanmar Times*, 22 April 2013*a*. <http://www.mmtimes.com/index.php/national-news/6471-bill-on-voting-system-to-be-submitted-in-june-uec>. Accessed 12 December 2013.

Win Ko Ko Latt. "No change to USDP policy at meeting". *Myanmar Times*, 1 July 2013*b*. <http://www.mmtimes.com/index.php/national-news/7317-no-change-to-usdp-policy-at-meeting.html>. Accessed 12 December 2013.

———. "USDP Has No Plans to Change Voting System: Official". *Myanmar Times*, 17 December 2012. <http://www.mmtimes.com/index.php/national-news/3594-usdp-has-no-plans-to-change-voting-system-official.html>. Accessed 12 December 2013.

Xinhua. "Myanmar President Meets Aung San Suu Kyi for a Second Time". *Xinhua*, 12 August 2012. <http://news.xinhuanet.com/english/world/2012-08/12/c_131779848.htm>. Accessed 12 December 2013.

V

Enduring Concerns

13

THE CONTINUING POLITICAL SALIENCE OF THE MILITARY IN POST-SPDC MYANMAR

Renaud Egreteau[*]

For a long time, analysts and commentators have labelled the various army-dominated types of government that Myanmar[1] has experienced since General Ne Win first seized power in 1958 as "military dictatorships", without making much of a distinction between them. Little effort has been made to differentiate the various forms of political intervention the Burmese armed forces (or *Tatmadaw*) and its successive leaderships have favoured over the past six decades. To better grasp the diverse realities of the *Tatmadaw*'s enduring interventionism—and, more particularly, the landscape shaped by the transition that began in 2011—this chapter rediscovers old theoretical models of the "praetorian state". The literature on praetorianism highlights the patterns and drivers behind the military's intrusion into state policy-making, and examines plausible paths towards military disengagement. Above all, it distinguishes different forms of political intervention by armed forces (from direct rule to indirect forms of influence and policy control) and evaluates their impact on political stability, governance, and democratization.

I argue hereafter that Myanmar has long been a "praetorian state", with its armed forces enjoying various degrees of policy control. All the requisites of a praetorian state can be identified in the country since its independence in 1948: an unruly political and civilian scene; a fragmented, if not polarized, post-colonial society constantly at war with itself; and extensive perceptions of domestic and external threats, all clearly formulated by a leviathan-type army institution able to deal with its internal differences and appear as a unified, cohesive, and disciplined organization with vested interests.

These praetorian patterns did not vanish with the startling transformations initiated by President Thein Sein's administration after 2011. Therefore, drawing on classical categorizations of praetorian regimes may help us better to construe the militarization of Burmese political affairs, and understand in particular the implications of the military-civil transition observed after the disbanding of the State Peace and Development Council (SPDC) in March 2011.

The passage from direct military rule to a quasi-civilian government is a classic example of "praetorian transition". Over time, military institutions move up, or down, the scale of praetorianism, according to their interests and ability in seeking more or less control over policy-making. In the post-SPDC landscape—which had been foreshadowed since the adoption in 2003 of a "Road Map" towards a "discipline-flourishing democracy"—the Burmese military institution has transferred to civilians much of the power it had monopolized during the years since 1988. Yet the military retains a good deal of its policy influence, albeit through more indirect and subtle means than it used before. It appears that the military has decided to take a back seat, although without fully disengaging, and therefore can be said to have moved down the spectrum of praetorian intervention. Despite the civilianization of the highest structures of the post-SPDC state, the acceptance of a plurality of voices by the military leadership, and the welcomed return of Daw Aung San Suu Kyi, the *Tatmadaw* remains a key policy actor, especially under the terms of the constitution that was controversially adopted in 2008.

A few scholars of Burmese affairs have offered tentative interpretations of the civil-military transition that has occurred since 2011 (Kyaw Yin Hlaing 2012; Callahan 2012; Taylor 2012; Skidmore and Wilson 2012). I propose to move beyond these explanations to see *how*, and not only *why*, the *Tatmadaw* is reshaping its praetorian intrusion into Myanmar's political and public affairs in the years after 2010. This chapter highlights the continuing political salience of the *Tatmadaw* in the post-SPDC context, and demonstrates how the Burmese army still retains the instruments, networks, and political leverage that would allow it to intervene in Myanmar's affairs. Consequently, the Burmese army continues to be in position to impose its own political, legislative, strategic, and corporate agenda on the current post-junta polity; however, it can only do this in ways that are far less direct and absolute than was possible during the SLORC-SPDC era (1988–2011).

In particular, I examine three features of indirect intervention by an army acting as a praetorian "guardian" or "arbitrator", and no longer as an absolute praetorian "ruler", following classical models offered by the literature on praetorianism: first, the indirect influence of retired senior military officers, who have moved into post-SPDC civilian and bureaucratic politics; second, the channels through which high-ranking and active-duty *Tatmadaw* officers have retained policy influence in the executive branch; and third, the participation of *Tatmadaw* representatives in the new legislative bodies shaped by the 2008 Constitution and brought into being after the 2010 elections. I conclude by examining the implications these continuing praetorian behaviours will have for the post-SPDC transitional venture and the country's long-term democratization prospects.

ON PRAETORIANISM AND THE PRAETORIAN STATE

In the midst of the Cold War, social scientists and policy-makers discussed praetorian state behaviours.[2] Between the 1950s and 1970s a lively literature conceptualizing the place and role of the military in modern political systems flourished. It identified the patterns of political interventionism of various armed forces in post-independence Asia, Africa, and Latin America, evaluating their performances, especially in terms of modernization and governance. The succession of military *coups d'état* in Karachi, Bangkok, Lagos, Rangoon, and Cairo served as illustrative cases of what was then a popular concept: "praetorianism". Samuel Huntington appeared as a pioneer in the study of modern praetorianism (Huntington 1957, 1968). His aristocratic interpretation of the politicized role of an army was thereafter critically reviewed by, among others, Morris Janowitz (1960), Samuel Finer (1975), Amos Perlmutter (1969, 1974), Alfred Stepan (1971), Edward Feit (1972), Eric Nordlinger (1977), and more recently Muthiah Alagappa (2001).

"Praetorianism" is a term taken from the political history of ancient Rome. It refers to decisive action taken by the Praetorian Guard, a military contingent directly assigned to the protection of the emperor or, during the later Roman Republican era, the *praetor*, an elected magistrate. Consisting of a number of elitist military units, the praetorians became a potent political force and directly intervened in Rome's public affairs. Nordlinger (1977, p. 3) writes that, in modern polities, their intrusions into the civilian sphere used to convey an implicit message that an army officer corps was to be considered a major political actor by virtue of its expertise in violence and mighty force.

A modern praetorian system is therefore construed as a political configuration in which the armed forces tend to intervene in politics and civilian affairs to the point of being able to control the whole political system. An army can always play a foremost, if not exclusive, role in policy-making—and this as the result of its use (or threat of use) of its military might. The military institution can move beyond its traditional function of acting as a security apparatus to become a governing body that shapes state policies. Perlmutter (1969, p. 383) argues that, to this end, the military institution usually manipulates the concept of legitimacy by asserting itself as the "protector" or "saviour" of the state.

Many reasons exist for why a society degenerates into praetorianism. The lack of institutionalized political practices and participatory norms, the impotence and corruption of civilian authorities, and the shared perceptions of a wide range of external or internal threats to the state or its people are all factors that have encouraged political interventionism by praetorian armies. In contrast to civilians, praetorian armies appear as a more capable and effective form of organized, cohesive, and bureaucratized force, expert in management of violence, with a professional ethic, a high moral position, and a potential for self-sufficiency. In the post-1945 world, national armed forces have also often stepped in to take up the challenges of modernization (Nordlinger 1970, Lissak 1976).

Scholars of civil-military relations have identified several forms of political involvement by armed forces, according to the depth and breadth of military participation in policy-making and governance. Perlmutter (1969) and Nordlinger (1977) identified Weberian ideal-types of praetorian intrusion into politics. Perlmutter initially defined two types of praetorian "regime", according to the extent of the army's control of governmental power: the "arbitrator" (the army "arbitrates" the political scene but does not directly participate in policy-making; it dominates through indirect means and "blackmails" civilians by threatening them with further interference); and the "ruler" (the army steps in, seizes power and takes control over the institutions of state and policy-making). Nordlinger extended this typology, adding one ideal-type (the "guardian") in between the praetorian "ruler" and the "arbitrator"—which he names "moderator". Praetorian "guardians" commonly control a sizeable share of governmental power, but for a limited period of time and with limited policy objectives—for instance, so as to swiftly restore political order or to correct the deficiencies of previous civilian administration (Nordlinger 1977, pp. 22–27). More recently, Alagappa (2001, p. 34) has revisited this typology and added one more category, describing four levels of political participation by military institutions: the "referee" (the army is strong enough to choose which civilian group governs, but does not necessarily exert this power); the "guardian" (the army more regularly displaces civilian governments as it has acquired the constitutional immunity and legitimacy to do so); the "participant-ruler" (the army has legally secured direct political and legislative instruments to participate in policy-making along with civilians); and the ultimate "praetorian ruler" in which a junta controls the whole political system and state structures.

VIEWING THE 2011 TRANSITION THROUGH THE PRAETORIAN LENS

Military Regimes Do Change

The form taken by military regimes is not static. Political regimes constantly evolve, and so do regimes overtly dominated by armed forces. Over time, it is common for one type of military regime to transform into another, according to the evolving policy objectives of the army and the extent of its control over governmental power, but without necessarily going so far as to democratize the polity. It is, therefore, not unusual to find sequences of types of military regime, from direct rule by armed forces (the praetorian rulers of the literature) to indirect and more limited intervention (whether guardians, moderators/arbitrators, or referees), and back again.

Huntington (1957) and Finer (1975, 1985) in particular have emphasized that political interventionism by praetorian armies covers a wide spectrum, and have discussed how praetorian armies move up or down the spectrum. Alagappa (2001, p. 34) further promoted the value of this sequencing as a good indicator of whether praetorianism is declining or increasing in a specific society. There are many reasons why a military regime changes over time and goes up or down the scale of praetorianism. Direct military rule can develop when the armed forces consider their core interests are threatened, even despite existing forms of military control over policy and legal domination by the army of key state institutions. Alternatively, a military regime can choose to disengage and seek to lessen its political power for fear of external intervention, or because of a lack of competence, or because of internal dissensions that have weakened its continuing direct rule. As Samuel Finer (1975, p. 252) puts it, the military in power always faces a dilemma: "they can neither go nor stay". This leads them, therefore, to transform into a "transit regime", epitomizing this dilemma and highlighting any hesitancies of the army leadership.

With the dismantling of the SPDC in March 2011, what has emerged in Myanmar is in fact a "transit regime". This regime, led by ex-general Thein Sein, who was sworn in as President of the Union on the same day the SPDC was dissolved, succeeded the direct and absolute praetorian rule that had been imposed by the army since the 1988 *coup d'état*. The regime of Senior General Than Shwe suffered no opposition from the civilian sphere: military men populated all state structures, and the *Tatmadaw* leadership imposed its own political views, strategic perceptions, and economic ideologies onto the Burmese polity, society, and economy. The policy-making process was entirely in the hands of active-duty members of the armed forces under the aegis of their commander-in-chief. What is more, the junta could be regularly rejuvenated through internal purges, as in 1992, 1997, and 2004, but these purges did not alter direct military rule. Quite to the contrary, they reinforced it.

When the government of President Thein Sein was established in early 2011, the *Tatmadaw* did not retreat fully to its barracks nor did it leave the entire policy-making process and state structure to civilians. The new regime evolved to some degree, into a form approaching Alagappa's "participant-ruler" model or, to some extent, Nordlinger's "guardian" model. The *Tatmadaw* has secured constitutional prerogatives and immunity; it has rapidly populated post-2011 governing bodies and law-making institutions, but has accepted a certain level of policy control and influence by civilians—unlike before 2011.

For a junta acting as a "praetorian ruler", the returning of power to civilians, who are often perceived as unruly and ill disciplined, can be seen as a perilous venture. Pakistan has over the years offered one of the best illustrations in the Asian region of a powerful military institution regularly transferring policy control back to civilians, only to seize it again just a few years later (Sattar 2001, Siddiqa 2007). It is common, therefore, for a military institution to take steps to ensure a gradual transition down the spectrum of praetorianism, either by legal provision or through constitutional restructuring. With the 2003 Road Map and the 2008 Constitution, the SPDC has secured the instruments to control its succession and has shaped what Finer calls a "transit" or "successor regime", asserting itself as the guardian or protector of the new institutions while showing willingness to team up with civilians.

Praetorian Provisions of the 2008 Constitution

The constitution that was passed in 2008 has given the Burmese armed forces a powerful policy and legal instrument for implementing the first steps of the transition and moving down the praetorian scale. Its provisions essentially sanction political interventionism by, and the legal immunity of, the *Tatmadaw*, but not absolute rule and policy control by it (Myint Zan 2008, Williams 2009, Nyein 2009). The constitution has nonetheless prompted strong criticism from the international community and Burmese opposition groups—including from Aung San Suu Kyi. The latter eventually agreed to play by its rules after 2011, in order to participate in the by-elections held in April 2012. Yet she (like most of the Burmese opposition forces) still aims to amend the text of the constitution (RFA 2013).

The prominent political role taken by the army is endorsed in the constitution. Article 6(f) states that one of the consistent objectives of the Union of Myanmar is to facilitate its Defence Services "to be able to participate in the National political leadership role of the State". Article 20(e) further widens the leading policy role of the army, which is recognised as "mainly responsible for safeguarding the non-disintegration of the Union, the non-disintegration of national solidarity and the perpetuation of sovereignty". In short, the *Tatmadaw* is expected to continue to intervene in national politics for the good of the nation, as its natural and legitimate saviour, or "moderator" and "guardian" (Selth 2002, Steinberg 2006, Maung Aung Myoe 2009). This arrangement is much in accordance with how a praetorian army thinks of itself—especially when it decides to relinquish power gradually, attempting to run down the scale of interventionism toward more indirect rule while still seeking to legitimize its continuing political intrusion as arbitrator or guardian.

Furthermore, the constitution guarantees the non-accountability of the *Tatmadaw* and the immunity of the military on all matters deemed military-related (Article 20(b)). The Supreme Court has no jurisdiction over the *Tatmadaw* and its personnel but *ad hoc* martial courts do (Articles 293, 319, and 343). Besides these provisions, the dominance by the armed forces of the new legislative power is constitutionally secured (Chapter 4). Lastly, the constitution confers on the Commander-in-Chief of the Army—with conditions—"the right to take over and exercise State sovereign power" if a state of national emergency arises (Article 40(c)).

It would seem therefore, that the *Tatmadaw* has secured enough policy instruments to remain relevant to the overall policy decisions in a post-SPDC era, thanks to a constitutional framework carefully drafted by its own strategic thinkers during the two National Conventions (1993–1996 and 2004–2007) and whose basic principles had, in fact, been much thought-about since the early 1990s. (Guyot 1994, Kyaw Yin Hlaing 2009, Win Min 2010). But the *Tatmadaw* strategists have not shaped the new constitution in order to take over the whole political system and state institutions after the dismantling of the SPDC. The "transit regime" led by ex-general Thein Sein in 2011 thus fits into the ideal-type of the army as a moderator, arbitrator, or guardian.

MILITARY PRESERVES: HOW THE *TATMADAW* MAINTAINS ITS POLITICAL INFLUENCE IN A POST-SPDC ERA

We turn now to examining three classic patterns of the subtle and indirect intervention of an army acting as a praetorian "guardian" that are manifest in the post-SPDC political and institutional landscape, in order to evaluate the *Tatmadaw*'s new policy role. The first pattern is the influence of ex-military men and former senior army officers who, once retired, have taken government positions and moved into civilian politics or the state bureaucracy. Influential and charismatic, they continue to impose a military style on policy-making, and keep close connections with the new generation of army leaders, although disagreements may soon appear between, and among them. The second pattern is found in the channels that active-duty members of the armed forces have secured for holding on to policy influence, by retaining key executive and government positions for serving army generals and high-ranking officers. The third is the participation of army representatives in the new legislatures shaped by the 2008 Constitution.

Former Soldiers in Post-Junta Bureaucratic Politics

Beyond constitutional prerogatives, the Burmese military has ensured that the wider "military family" plays a significant role in the post-junta polity and captures key policymaking positions. Besides active military officers (whose role we explore in the next sections), former soldiers-turned-politicians and bureaucrats have been prepared to populate the state's most critical post-junta institutions.[3] A military "family" institution is construed by the literature as including not only the active armed forces, but also an array of military-linked interest groups, including former military officers who have moved into civilian politics, veterans associations, army-funded lobbies, and business managers of military-run conglomerates. However, this does not imply that former generals systematically formulate and conduct pro-army policies once in office (Finer 1975, pp. 258–59). Power struggles often abound between soldiers still on active duty and former army officers who are leading the "transit regime", to the point that these power games become a key determinant of the success of the whole transition—as in the Philippines in the late 1980s or Indonesia under the presidency of former general Susilo Bambang Yudhoyono in the 2000s.

The post-SPDC political and legislative institutions are peppered with co opted ex-military men or former senior officials of the SPDC. The new quasi-civilian government was formed on 30 March 2011 under the former SPDC Secretary 1, Thein Sein. Former *Tatmadaw* Joint Chief-of-Staff Thura Shwe Mann became Speaker of the lower house after the November 2010 elections. He is now the *de facto* second-most important civilian statesman in the country. Former *Tatmadaw* Quartermaster-General Lt Gen. Thiha Thura Tin Aung Myint Oo was elected in February 2011 by the military representatives of the national parliament (*Pyidaungsu Hluttaw*) to one of the two vice-presidencies (*NLM* 2011g).[4] The "lock" on the two crucial positions of president and vice-president-2 seemingly held by the armed forces comes as no surprise. It is aimed at securing the highest governing posts for the military institution, which feels that if one of its own (even if retired) is co-opted as the head of the post-transition civilian state structure, the army's core interests will be secured and the incentives for staging another coup far less (Callahan 2012, p. 123).

President Thein Sein's civilian government has otherwise proved to be chiefly dominated by former senior military officers or SPDC officials with a military background, including 85 percent of the ministerial cabinet appointed in March 2011 (Tin Maung Maung Than 2012, p. 90). The proportion of civilians was subsequently increased to one quarter (nine ministers) of the 36-member cabinet after two reshuffles arranged by Thein Sein himself, in August 2011 and again in August 2012. Notably, in the 2012 reshuffle, for the first time in decades a civilian woman was appointed as a full cabinet minister (Mrs Myat Myat Ohn Khin, Minister for Social Welfare, Relief and Resettlement) (Fuller 2012). Civilian technocrats and non-military experts were also progressively brought in, while SPDC old hands (such as the long-standing Minister for Information Kyaw Hsan, a former Brigadier General and regional commander allegedly close to Senior General Than Shwe) were demoted to more obscure ministerial positions or simply encouraged to resign. The 2012 reshuffle seemed to signal a consolidation of Thein Sein's influence over the post-SPDC executive civilian administration just a year after he was sworn in as President.

Another indication of the preponderance of the military is that, after the 2010 elections, thirteen of the fourteen nominated Chief Ministers of the country's decentralized states and regions were retired senior army officers. The fourteenth, Brigadier General Zaw Min, did not even resign from active duty when he was appointed Chief Minister of Kayin (Karen) State (NLM 2011e). Other key policy-makers and office-holders of influence in the post-SPDC polity are also ex-military officers. For instance, U Tin Aye, a retired (and decorated) lieutenant general and former chair of one of the Tatmadaw's two conglomerates (Union of Myanmar Economic Holdings Ltd) was appointed in February 2011 as head of the Union Election Commission (Shwe Yinn Mar Oo 2011). The new Chief Justice (U Tun Tun Oo) as well as the Chair (U Thein Soe) and senior members of the Constitutional Tribunal (until its collective forced resignation in September 2012) were all promoted from the military-run Judge Advocate General's office in 2011 (NLM 2011c; Ko Wild 2011). The chairman of the Union Civil Services Board (U Kyaw Thu) and the Auditor-General (U Lun Maung), both also nominated in early 2011, are two former army generals (NLM

2012*a*).[5] Lastly, many members of the Union Solidarity and Development Party (USDP), which overwhelmingly won the controversial elections in November 2010, also boast a military background.

The Burmese military sphere has long been the only matrix for producing would-be Burmese state leaders and political figures, and these appointments follow the logic of that arrangement. After the 2010 elections and the convening of the national and provincial assemblies, the armed forces initiated a gradual (yet not total) withdrawal from the forefront of the state political administration and governance. Meanwhile, many former senior officers, born and bred in the military institution, have stepped forward to play a more active role in the new mode of governance since the disbanding of the SPDC. This arrangement echoes events in the late 1980s when former army officers close to Ne Win rallied the opposition or chose to form their own political movements. All certainly take into account their own military background and know perfectly where lie the interests of the (active) armed forces they have come from.

Yet, political struggles between retired military leaders-turned-politicians (or bureaucrats) and younger disgruntled army officers still on active service are inevitable in a post-transitional polity, although infighting may be based more on undercurrents of internecine power struggles and factional tensions within the army than on severe ideological fractures (as with non-military civilian opposition groups for instance). Rising army officers are often former subordinates of retired generals who are now running Myanmar's new civilian, political, and legislative institutions. Conflicts of interest routinely emerge, yet loyalties seem to prevail.

In May 2011, Mandalay's Chief Minister, Lieutenant General (retired) Ye Myint, was rumoured to be engaged in a local dispute with the military commander of the Central Region, Lt Gen. Ye Aung over the granting of vehicle licenses (Wai Moe 2011). Yet it was the civilian chief minister who was said to have soon secured his own agenda over that of the active-duty military commander, the latter having in the end complied with his former (but retired) superior. With the exception of Kachin State, where conflict erupted again in June 2011, all regional commanders (who under the SPDC hierarchy used to hold considerable power) seem so far to have deferred to their relevant civilian chief ministers (Tin Maung Maung Than 2012, p. 91).

Likewise, former army chief Shwe Mann is said to have made the most of his former position as Joint Chief-of-Staff of the *Tatmadaw*, now that he sits as Speaker of the lower house of the national parliament. He has frequently used his moral authority and shrewdly engaged with military appointees during parliamentary debates, especially to guide their votes on specific bills.[6] As long as he maintains a cordial relationship with the current head of the *Tatmadaw*, Vice-Senior General Min Aung Hlaing, who nominates the military representatives in local and national assemblies, Shwe Mann can expect to hold sway over the parliament. Nonetheless, to avoid being bypassed by former officers turned rogue (as has often been observed in Thailand, Indonesia, and the Philippines), the *Tatmadaw*'s active hierarchy has secured legal political and legislative instruments— and constitutional immunity with them—for direct intervention, and is therefore in a position to keep a close eye on law and policy-making.

Soldiers in the Post-Junta Executive

Active-duty army officers have populated key policy-making positions in the post-junta state structure. Despite being confident enough to initiate the transition after the 2010 elections, the Burmese army leadership clearly still does not feel secure enough to completely (and promptly) withdraw from politics. Historical legacies and decades of propaganda praising the *Tatmadaw*'s traditional role as guardian and protector of the nation since independence in 1948 explain much of the reluctance to disengage.

Praetorian armies retain political power as long as they consider it to be their historical and legitimate duty. Vice-Senior General Min Aung Hlaing confirmed this position to the letter in his inaugural speech during the 67th Armed Forces Day in 2012 (*NLM* 2012c; Ba Kaung 2012a). President Thein Sein too declared a year after he was sworn in that the *Tatmadaw*, along with the people and the government, was the country's "fifth estate", after the media (the "fourth estate") and the classic legislature-executive-judiciary trinity (*NLM* 2012d). The *Tatmadaw* therefore could not but keep its hands on policy after the junta was dissolved.

According to the 2008 Constitution, three ministries are left under the sole authority of the armed forces in the civilian-dominated cabinet: Home Affairs, Defence, and Border Affairs (Nyein 2009, p. 639). Under Article 232(b) of the constitution, in order to appoint ministers to these three ministries the president is first required to obtain the names of suitable armed forces personnel nominated by the Commander-in-Chief. This requirement is also stipulated for all the Home, Defence, and Border

Affairs deputy ministers (Article 234(b)), as well as for the Security and Border Affairs regional ministers to be nominated in each of the fourteen states and regions (Article 262(a)). These ministers and their deputies do not have to resign from active duty when taking these posts, as specified under Article 232(j) of the constitution—unlike the president or other high-ranking state civil servants, who must officially retire from the armed services and abandon their uniforms for the traditional *longyis* of Burmese politicians.

In March 2011, Lieutenant General Ko Ko (a former chief of the Bureau of Special Operations-3 (BSO-3) during SPDC rule) was appointed Minister for Home Affairs. He has since been assisted by a deputy minister, Brigadier General Kyaw Zan Myint, and a second deputy, Major-General Kyaw Kyaw Tun, a senior officer from the Myanmar Police Force, was assigned to him in August 2012 (*NLM* 2011d; *Eleven Media* 2012). Major-General Hla Min (also a former Chief of BSO-3) was likewise appointed as Minister of Defence in March 2011. His deputies were a navy commander (Aung Thaw) and an army major-general (Kyaw Nyunt); however, he was re-assigned in August 2012 and Lieutenant General Wai Lwin, who had earlier succeeded General Tin Aung Myint Oo as *Tatmadaw* Quartermaster-General and was a former regional commander of Naypyitaw, took up his post. Lastly, the newly appointed Minister for Border Affairs, U Thein Htay, was an army lieutenant general. He was previously a Deputy Minister for Defence during the SPDC rule, and has been seconded by Major-General Zaw Win since March 2011 (*NLM* 2011d). Besides the above appointments, all the fourteen states and regions have also seen army colonels appointed by the Commander-in-Chief as Ministers for Security and Border Affairs (NLM 2011f).

Finally, Article 201 of the 2008 Constitution created a crucial decision-making body, the National Defence and Security Council (NDSC).[7] Headed by the Union president, the Council is dominated by active senior army officers and includes eleven members, including the commander-in-chief and his deputy, and the three decisive "army-ministers" mentioned above. A great deal has been speculatively written about the strategic functions of the NDSC, yet neither the constitution nor any other laws have precisely defined its role. Since its formation in 2011, it has met at least three times a week, with Shwe Mann and Min Aung Hlaing reportedly being particularly active; but its impact over the future strategic direction remains opaque (Kyaw Yin Hlaing 2012, p. 211).

Nevertheless, even through these three Union-level ministries and the NDSC, the *Tatmadaw* cannot retain absolute control over the overall policy decision-making of the sort that it had during the SLORC-SPDC administration (Callahan 2012, p. 128). The military hierarchy has thus shown its willingness to relinquish most of the power it once enjoyed, keeping only key policy-making positions and leaving the rest of the governance and day-to-day politics to a civilian leadership. Indeed, since March 2011 the power of the three armed forces ministers in the post-SPDC governmental structure has been quite disputed by other civilian ministers and even by parliamentarians.[8] For instance, when Defence Minister Lieutenant General Hla Min in February 2012 submitted his budget proposal for the defence services (along with that of his own ministry), he seemed to receive much opposition from the national parliament, albeit via the backdoor (AFP 2012). With time, civilian political leaders and members of parliament might prove more confident to engage, and even openly challenge, their military counterparts in the cabinet or parliament.[9]

Soldiers in the Post-Junta Legislatures

Securing a "Veto Force" in the New Legislative Assemblies

Under authoritarian rulers, parliaments are frequently construed as rubber-stamp legislatures, and are expected to act according to the wishes of the powerful executive. This was very much the case in General Ne Win's unicameral People's Assembly between 1974 and 1988, when elections were rigged and parliamentary debates were controlled by Ne Win himself.

In transitional periods, the significance of newly-formed legislatures increases considerably. Newly-elected parliaments can either be obstructionist bodies, stoutly defending the interests of the old ruling group and resisting the transition, or can foster democratization and expand political participation. In post-junta regimes, the military commonly seeks a constitutionally-sanctioned presence in these parliaments—but not always, as in the post-1986 civil-military transition in the Philippines, for instance. The legislative participation of the military is usually secured through having reserved seats in national and/or local assemblies. Through this presence in law-making bodies, praetorian armies keep an eye on the legislative process and safeguard their own interests—a means additional to the other channels of influence they have captured in the state bureaucracy and transitional executive and other policy-making structures.

Indonesia has long offered a model in the *Orde Baru* of General Suharto (1965–1998). The Indonesian military managed to institutionalize the secondment of army officers to non-military positions and policy functions—the *kekaryaan* system. In this system, not only were army officers specifically commissioned to legislative bodies but they were also expected to take up key civilian posts in various parts of the state administration at one point or another during their careers. Active generals and colonels thus populated Indonesia's embassies, ministries, and local parliaments. Even in departments under civilian control, military officers were commonly assigned as secretaries-general (Chandra and Kammen 2002). It is only in the early 1990s that the mandated presence of the armed forces in the national parliament in Jakarta began to be seriously debated. Military parliamentarians were eventually withdrawn from national and local legislatures in 2004 (Ziegenhain 2008; Mietzner 2011).

The 2008 Constitution provided a significant opportunity for the *Tatmadaw* to follow this rather resourceful Indonesian model—although the practice has to some extent been observed in Myanmar since the 1950s, with the posting of army officers in various Burmese embassies worldwide, for instance (Egreteau and Jagan 2013, pp. 51–52), as well as across ministries. According to the new constitutional order, Burmese army delegates represent a quarter of each local and national assembly formed after the 2010 elections. They can therefore boast 110 seats in the lower house (*Pyithu Hluttaw*) of the national parliament (see Article 109(b) of the constitution), 56 seats in its upper house (*Amyotha Hluttaw*; see Article 141(b)), and a total of 222 seats in the fourteen state and region legislatures (see Article161(d)).

The Commander-in-Chief of the *Tatmadaw* nominates all military appointees. The appointment of military representatives was one of the last decisions taken by Senior General Than Shwe, on 20 January 2011, two months before his official retirement (NLM 2011*h*). Out of 388 first-time delegates appointed by Than Shwe, there were only three army colonels in the *Pyithu Hluttaw*, and two in the *Amyotha Hluttaw*, while one army colonel led each military delegation in the fourteen decentralized local assemblies, except for Kayin (Karen) State, where a brigadier-general was posted (he would thereafter be nominated chief minister). All other military appointees were of lower ranks—majors, captains, and navy lieutenant-commanders—apparently to ensure that their groups remained cohesive within their respective assemblies.

Since their first appearance in January 2011, military representatives have always attended in uniform, tainting the national and local legislatures with khaki. For many observers, their core objective in the parliament has been to ensure the army has a non-negotiable veto on any potential constitutional amendments; indeed 75 percent of members of parliament are required to pass any amendment of the constitution (Williams 2009, p. 1669).

Towards a New Legislative Role for the Tatmadaw?

If the presence of the military in the post-SPDC national and local assemblies seems secure, and negotiable only "on army terms", the *Tatmadaw's* legislative power appears to be not as unlimited and unchecked as sometimes claimed by pro-democracy activists (ICG 2013). As in Indonesia in the 1990s, the reservation of 25 percent of seats for the armed forces has been increasingly criticized.[10] Criticism has come even from the ranks of the party that dominates the post-2010 legislature, the USDP (Ba Kaung 2012*b*).

Initially, many an observer thought the military appointees would only have to resist potential amendments to the constitution that were prepared by leading opposition members of parliament, secure the nomination of the president and one of the two vice-presidents (both of whom had substantial military backgrounds), and deal with military-related affairs. Yet, constitutional amendments apart, military MPs cannot oppose a decisive veto on any other legislative activities. The political significance of the army representatives in the national parliament (far more than in the local legislatures) has thus gradually evolved. During the first parliamentary sessions after the 2010 election, newly-appointed army delegates tended to keep a low profile in all assemblies. None of them were nominated to key parliamentary committees such as the Public Accounts Committee or the Bill Committee in 2011. But once the charismatic Aung San Suu Kyi and her National League for Democracy entered both houses after the by-elections held on 1 April 2012, the parliament's prestige was somewhat redeemed. The assertion of Shwe Mann's political authority as Speaker of the lower house has, since early 2011, strengthened the assembly's importance.[11] This situation was further sharpened by rumours of his emerging political rivalry with the executive, and with President Thein Sein in particular (Kyaw Yin Hlaing 2012, p. 205).

Above all, military representatives have progressively shown skills at participating in parliamentary debates, discussing legal propositions, and arranging for the movement of bills between the two houses (*Bangkok Post* 2012). Special training sessions have been provided for them, and political science is now a compulsory subject at the prestigious Defence Services Academy (DSA) based in Pyin Oo Lwin (Sandar Lwin 2012). When in 2013 I conducted interviews in Naypyitaw and Yangon with civilian parliamentarians, some recalled how they have attempted to establish some sort of friendly dialogue with their military colleagues, especially the middle-ranked officers.[12] Discussions within the premises of the national assemblies in Naypyitaw appeared far more productive than initially expected (ICG 2012, p. 10).[13] After all, legislative mechanisms were also quite unfamiliar to civilian members of parliament. Both military and civilian members of parliament have had to improvise and learn.

Furthermore, three weeks after the historic election of Aung San Suu Kyi in April 2012, the substitution of fifty-nine majors and captains with brigadier generals and colonels as new military appointees in both the Upper and Lower Houses underscored an evident policy change from the armed forces (*NLM* 2012b; Min Zin 2012). From then on, higher-ranking military officers were to get thoroughly involved in legislative debates (Marshall 2012). This change indicated the increasing importance the *Tatmadaw*—and, more particularly, its commander-in-chief, Min Aung Hlaing—has given to the legislative branch attempting to strengthen its mandate *vis-à-vis* the powerful presidential executive (Callahan 2012, p. 128).

Military appointees have increasingly proved ready to vote not as a bloc on draft bills prepared by opposition members.[14] A local member of parliament from the Democratic Party (Myanmar) recalled how she offered flowers to the four majors who voted in favour of (while their colleagues in uniform abstained or voted against) her draft bill on licensed trishaws at the Yangon regional assembly in early 2013.[15] On some issues once considered matters of "national security", military delegates have proved willing to listen, and sometimes align with the civilian MPs. When a National Democratic Front-turned-independent member from Yangon proposed a general amnesty for prisoners in August 2011, military appointees acquiesced altogether (*NLM* 2011a, 2011b). According to civilian parliamentarians themselves, the new legislature—although far from perfect—in no way resembles the tightly controlled National Convention that drafted the constitution between 2004 and 2007.[16]

If the post-SPDC national and local parliaments can prove they are not rubber-stamping legislatures, and if military delegates can continue to act cooperatively with the dominant party as well as with the opposition, then the prospects for consolidation of the post-SPDC transition through parliamentarian activism would appear brighter. Encouragingly, since 2011 the military delegates have not opposed the formulation of the most significant reform-minded laws—especially at the Union level. A further positive sign would require that the military move beyond its primary veto function as sanctioned by the constitution to participate actively in law-making (Egreteau 2013). This is where the transition appears to remain extremely fragile, and expectations too idealistic. Tensions might loom soon. Opposition members, and particularly Aung San Suu Kyi, have repeatedly claimed that the presence of men in uniform in the legislative assemblies is an anomaly that has to be corrected. They are pushing for a constitutional amendment before 2015. As in Indonesia in the 1990s, how the issue is dealt with will prove critical to the consolidation (or otherwise) of a peaceful relationship between the civilians and the still-dominant military, both within and beyond the premises of the parliament.

THE SALIENCE OF PRAETORIAN POLITICS IN MYANMAR

In early 2011, the commanding heights of the *Tatmadaw* were rejuvenated after the old guard, represented by the septuagenarian generals Than Shwe and Maung Aye, retired. At the same time, former generals-turned-politicians began to populate most key government, bureaucratic, and legislative positions of the post-SPDC polity. Predictably, and despite a welcome post-junta transition and startling reforms initiated by President Thein Sein, both groups share the same vision of the *Tatmadaw* perpetuating its monitoring of state policy for the good of the nation. Echoing the resentment and disappointment already observed among army ranks in the late 1980s—best illustrated by Aung Gyi's letters to Ne Win in 1987—many a senior *Tatmadaw* officer has been appalled by the enduring inefficiency showed by his own home institution in the 1990s and 2000s. Finding themselves acting like the "unsavoury" politicians they once criticized, unable to govern appropriately or lead Myanmar towards worthwhile development, many leaders of the armed forces now openly deplore the fact that the self-image of the *Tatmadaw* has been badly soiled. But far from fully withdrawing from politics, a new generation of officers seems now to be willing to work on the restoration of the prestige and public reputation of the armed forces. For them, the post-SPDC transition has to be well thought-out and peaceful, while ensuring the continuing yet evolving intervention into politics by the military institution.

Rather than being a straightforward transition from military rule to civilian rule, the current political transformation in Myanmar illustrates how a military regime can move down the scale of praetorianism. Unlike popular transition and democratization studies (Huntington 1991), the scholarship on praetorianism draws attention to the dynamics of a military regime, and attempts to interpret an army's evolution down, or up, the scale of political interventionism. Post-SPDC politics in Myanmar offers a case study of an army carefully moving down the praetorian scale—but still not fully retreating to its barracks and disengaging from politics. The post-SPDC government—a "transit regime"—now sits somewhere between the traditional command-and-control approach described by Eric Nordlinger or Amos Perlmutter's absolute "praetorian rulers", and a more sophisticated and indirectly participating "guardian" or "arbitrator" army institution. Despite its record of failure in government, and doubts about the prospects for behavioural change among Burmese army officers, the *Tatmadaw* persists in its insistence on "leading the way" and protecting the nation. Praetorian politics has a good chance of continuing in Myanmar over the coming years, albeit with a lesser depth to military interventionism.

The outside world has begun to recognize that beyond Aung San Suu Kyi's iconic figure it will have to deal with an enduring Burmese praetorian machine that might now include fewer active army officers at the forefront of politics and tolerate more civilian opposition and bureaucracy, but which is still reliant on an array of ex-military circles, army ideologues, and military-backed business conglomerates—all more or less directly involved in the post-junta state decision-making process. The post-Than Shwe transition has allowed some positive evolution. It has become far less a torment for Western statesmen to shake hands with Burmese top leaders, now that they more commonly wear *longyis* than military uniforms.[17] Nevertheless, Myanmar's new civilian leaders for the most part still have an obvious army background, and consequently particular strategic, economic, and policy interests are as yet very much linked to those of the active armed forces.

Observers therefore need to further decipher the Burmese military man's views of the world today, his perceptions and core concerns, as well as try to understand his cultural and historical background. The focus of the international community has to include the military, not only Aung San Suu Kyi, Myanmar's civil society, or its economy, so as to integrate more of the praetorian institution into regional and international networks, to expose its members to the outside world after decades of isolation, and to train them to face modern administration, management, and governance imperatives. In that respect, one can hope that in the foreseeable future the *Tatmadaw* will move further down the scale of praetorianism in order to prepare for full disengagement from politics.

Sceptics, however, continue to stress the continual failures of the Burmese army leadership to fully and permanently disengage ever since the first withdrawal of Ne Win's caretaker military government in April 1960, noting that it seems to be in the *Tatmadaw's* genes to continuously and decisively intervene in state politics. Whether the military is "moderating", "arbitrating" or "ruling", praetorian politics will remain a salient feature of Myanmar's landscape in the coming years.

Notes

*   I wish to thank the organizers of the 2013 ANU Myanmar/Burma Update for their invitation and for funding to attend the conference. Marcus Mietzner and Nick Cheesman gave insightful comments on drafts of the paper, as did fellow panelists and the audience during the Update, which was much appreciated.
1   For simplicity, this article uses the vernacular and official name of the country "Myanmar", but the English adjective "Burmese".
2   I offer a more detailed review of the concept and its usefulness for the Myanmar case in the first chapter of a recently published co-authored book (Egreteau and Jagan 2013, pp. 19–45).
3   Mary Callahan (2012, p. 123), however, argues that the distribution of senior ministerial and executive posts (the "who's who and who's doing what") of the post-Than Shwe landscape might have been decided *ad hoc*.
4   Tin Aung Myint Oo resigned in July 2012 and was replaced by Admiral Nyan Tun.
5   U Lun Maung resigned in August 2012.
6   Author's interviews with opposition members of parliament from the *Amyotha Hluttaw* and the *Pyithu Hluttaw*, Naypyitaw, February 2013, and Yangon, May 2013.
7   The 1974 Constitution (Article 54) also envisioned a "National Defence and Security Committee".

8   See Thomas Kean's contribution in this volume.
9   Author's interviews with party leaders from various opposition parties, Yangon, May 2013.
10 Author's interviews with opposition members of parliament from the *Amyotha Hluttaw* and *Pyithu Hluttaw*, Naypyitaw, February 2013, and Yangon, May 2013.
11 Soe Than Lynn 2012. See also Kean's contribution in this volume.
12 Author's interviews with members of parliament from the USDP, NLD, Shan Nationalities League for Democracy, National Democratic Front, All Mon Region Democracy Party, and Rakhine Nationalities Development Party, Naypyitaw and Yangon, February, May and August 2013.
13 One has to note that members of parliament from the opposition reside in a separate compound in Naypyitaw, and therefore cannot freely mingle with military delegates (who go back to their barracks after each working day) outside the parliament or during special events.
14 Author's interviews with opposition members of parliament from the *Amyotha Hluttaw* and *Pyithu Hluttaw*, Naypyitaw, February and August 2013, and in Yangon, May 2013.
15 Author's interview, Yangon, May 2013.
16 Author's interviews with opposition members of parliament from the *Amyotha Hluttaw* and *Pyithu Hluttaw*, Naypyitaw, February 2013, and in Yangon, May 2013.
17 Author's discussions with several foreign diplomats, Yangon, November 2012 and May 2013.

References

Agence France-Presse (AFP). "Myanmar MPs Tackle First Budget in Decades". NDTV (New Delhi Television), 12 February 2012. <http://www.ndtv.com/article/world/myanmar-mps-tackle-first-budget-in-decades-175549>. Accessed 1 January 2014.

Alagappa, Muthiah, ed. *Coercion and Governance: The Declining Political Role of the Military in Asia*. Stanford CA: Stanford University Press, 2001.

Ba Kaung. "Burma Army Chief Defends Political Role". *Irrawaddy*, 27 March 2012a. <http://www2.irrawaddy.org/article.php?art_id=23290>. Accessed 3 January 2014.

————."Opposition MPs Take Aim at Army Influence". *Irrawaddy*, 15 February 2012b. <http://www2.irrawaddy.org/article.php?art_id=23041>. Accessed 3 January 2014.

Bangkok Post. "Burma Old Guard Adapt to New Life as Lawmakers". 18 January 2012. <http://www.bangkokpost.com/news/asia/275722/burma-old-guard-adapt-to-new-life-as-lawmakers>. Accessed 3 January 2014.

Callahan, Mary P. "The Generals Loosen their Grip". *Journal of Democracy* 23, no. 4 (2012): 120–31.

Chandra, Siddharth and Douglas Kammen. "Generating Reforms and Reforming Generations: Military Politics in Indonesia's Democratic Transition and Consolidation". *World Politics* 55, no. 1 (2002): 96–136.

Eleven Media. "Myanmar Reshuffles Cabinet Ministers, Deputy Ministers". *Nation* (Bangkok), 28 August 2012. <http://www.nationmultimedia.com/aec/Myanmar-reshuffles-cabinet-ministers-deputy-minist-30189227.html>. Accessed 3 January 2014.

Egreteau, Renaud. *Patterns of Military Behavior in Myanmar's New Legislature.* Washington DC: East-West Center Asia-Pacific Bulletin No. 233, 2013.

Egreteau, Renaud and Larry Jagan. *Soldiers and Diplomacy in Burma: Understanding the Foreign Relations of the Burmese Praetorian State.* Singapore: NUS Press, 2013.

Feit, Edward. *The Armed Bureaucrats: Military-Administrative Regimes and Political Development.* New York: Houghton Mifflin, 1972.

Finer, Samuel E. "The Retreat to the Barracks. Notes on the Practice and the Theory of Military Withdrawal from the Seats of Power". *Third World Quarterly* 7, no. 1 (1985): 16–30.

———. *The Man on Horseback: The Role of the Military in Politics.* Revised and enlarged edition. Harmondsworth: Penguin Books, 1975.

Fuller, Thomas. "President of Myanmar Reshuffles Its Cabinet". *New York Times,* 27 August 2012. <http://www.nytimes.com/2012/08/28/world/asia/myanmar-leader-thein-sein-reshuffles-his-cabinet.html?_r=0>. Accessed 3 January 2014.

Guyot, James F. "Burmese Praetorianism". In *Tradition and Modernity in Myanmar,* edited by Uta Gartner and Jens Lorenz. Berlin: LIT Verlag, 1994.

Huntington, Samuel P. *The Third Wave: Democratization in the Late Twentieth Century.* Norman: University of Oklahoma Press, 1991.

———. *Political Order in Changing Societies.* New Haven: Yale University Press, 1968.

———. *The Soldier and the State.* Cambridge MA: Belknap, 1957.

International Crisis Group (ICG). *Not a Rubber Stamp: Myanmar's Legislature in a Time of Transition.* Asia Briefing No. 142, 13 December 2013. http://www.crisisgroup.org/en/regions/asia/south-east-asia/myanmar/b142-not-a-rubber-stamp-myanmar-s-legislature-in-a-time-of-transition.aspx. Accessed 6 January 2014.

———. *Reform in Myanmar: One Year On.* Asia Briefing No. 136, 11 April 2012. <http://www.crisisgroup.org/en/regions/asia/south-east-asia/myanmar/b136-reform-in-myanmar-one-year-on.aspx>. Accessed 3 January 2014.

Janowitz, Morris. *The Professional Soldier: A Social and Political Portrait.* Glencoe: The Free Press, 1960.

Ko Wild. "Tin Aye to be EC Chairman; Tun Tun Oo Appointed Chief Justice". *Mizzima News*, 17 February 2011. <http://archive.is/JY78Q>. Accessed 3 January 2014.

Kyaw Yin Hlaing. "Understanding Recent Political Changes in Myanmar". *Contemporary Southeast Asia* 34, no. 2 (2012): 197–216.

———. "Setting the Rules for Survival: Why the Burmese Military Regime Survives in an Age of Democratization". *Pacific Review* 22, no. 3 (2009): 271–91.

Lissak, Moshe. *Military Roles in Modernization: Civil-Military Relations in Thailand and Burma*. London: Sage Publications, 1976.

Maung Aung Myoe. *Building the Tatmadaw: Myanmar Armed Forces since 1948*. Singapore: ISEAS Publications, 2009.

Mietzner, Marcus. "The Political Marginalization of the Military in Indonesia". In *The Political Resurgence of the Military in Southeast Asia: Conflict and Leadership*, edited by Marcus Mietzner. London: Routledge, 2011.

Marshall, Andrew R.C. "Myanmar's Military Moves Amid Suu Kyi No-show". *Reuters*, 25 April 2012. <http://www.reuters.com/article/2012/04/25/us-myanmar-suukyi-idUSBRE83O0BA20120425>. Accessed 3 January 2014.

Min Zin. "Military Maneuvers (in Burma's Parliament)". Transitions, *Foreign Policy*, 30 April 2012. <http://minzin.blogspot.com.au/2012_05_01_archive. html>; also <http://transitions.foreignpolicy.com/posts/2012/04/30/military_maneuvers_in_burmas_parliament#sthash.bw33zJMO.dpbs>. Accessed 3 January 2014.

Myint Zan. "Myanmar (Burma): From Parliamentary System to Constitutionless and Constitutionalized One-Party and Military Rule". In *Constitutionalism in Southeast Asia*, edited by Clauspeter Hill and Jorg Menzel. Singapore: KAS, 2008.

New Light of Myanmar (NLM). "Permission granted to resign from the post of Union Auditor-General". President Office, Order No. 24/2012. *New Light of Myanmar*, 29 August 2012*a*, p. 1. <http://www.burmalibrary.org/docs14/NLM2012-08-29.pdf>. Accessed 2 January 2014.

———. "39 Defence Services Personnel Pyithu Hluttaw Representatives substituted" and "20 Defence Services Personnel Amyotha Hluttaw Representatives substituted". Union Election Commission, Notifications No. 22/2012 and 23/2012. *New Light of Myanmar*, 23 April 2012*b*, p. 1. <http://www.burmalibrary. org/docs13/NLM2012-04-23.pdf>. Accessed 2 January 2014.

———. "To possess high defence power, State, people & *Tatmadaw* will have to join hands". *New Light of Myanmar*, 28 March 2012*c*, p. 7. <http://www.burmalibrary. org/docs13/NLM2012-03-28.pdf>. Accessed 2 January 2014.

———. "Three powers have been equally shared" (Excerpt from address delivered by President U Thein Sein at the regular session of the Pyidaungsu Hluttaw on 1 March 2012). *New Light of Myanmar*, 26 March 2012*d*, p. 1. <http://www.burmalibrary.org/docs13/NLM2012-03-26.pdf>. Accessed 2 January 2014.

———. "Second regular session of First Pyithu Hluttaw continues for fifth day: Questioning, answering, and submitting proposals at the session". *New Light of Myanmar*, 27 August 2011*a*, p. 7. <http://www.burmalibrary.org/docs11/NLM2011-08-27.pdf>. Accessed 2 January 2014.

———. "Fourth-day second regular session of First Pyithu Hluttaw takes place: Questioning, replying, discussing and submitting proposals". *New Light of Myanmar*, 26 August 2011*b*, p. 9. <http://www.burmalibrary.org/docs11/NLM2011-08-26.pdf>. Accessed 2 January 2014;

———. "Appointment of Union Chief Justice". President Office, Order No. 1/2011; "Appointment of Chairperson of Constitutional Tribunal of the Union". President Office, Order No. 2/2011; "Appointment of members of Constitutional Tribunal of the Union". President Office, Order No. 11/2011. *New Light of Myanmar*, 31 March 2011*c*, pp 8, 10. <http://www.burmalibrary.org/docs11/NLM2011-03-31.pdf>. Accessed 2 January 2014.

———. "Appointment of Union Ministers". President Office, Order No. 4/2011. *New Light of Myanmar*, 31 March 2011*d*, p. 10. <http://www.burmalibrary.org/docs11/NLM2011-03-31.pdf>. Accessed 2 January 2014.

———. "Appointment of Chief Minister of Regions or States". President Office, Order No. 9/2011. *New Light of Myanmar*, 31 March 2011*e*, p. 10. <http://www.burmalibrary.org/docs11/NLM2011-03-31.pdf>. Accessed 2 January 2014.

———. "Appointment of Region/State Ministers". President Office, Order No. 19/2011. *New Light of Myanmar*, 31 March 2011*f*, pp. 11–12. <http://www.burmalibrary.org/docs11/NLM2011-03-31.pdf>. Accessed 2 January 2014.

———. "Group of Defence Services Personnel Representatives elects Thiha Thura U Tin Aung Myint Oo as Vice-President". *New Light of Myanmar*, 4 February 2011*g*, p. 1. <http://www.burmalibrary.org/docs11/NLM2011-02-04.pdf>. Accessed 2 January 2014.

———. "The Union Election Commission announces the Defence Services Personnel Hluttaw Representatives under Notification No. 1/2011, Notification No. 2/2011 and Notification No. 3/2011". *New Light of Myanmar*, 21 January 2011*h*, pp. 7–9. <http://www.burmalibrary.org/docs11/NLM2011-01-21.pdf>. Accessed 2 January 2014.

Nordlinger, Eric A. *Soldiers in Politics: Military Coups and Governments*. London: Prentice Hall, 1977.

———. "Soldiers in Mufti: The Impact of Military Rule upon Economic and Social Change in the Non-Western States". *American Political Science Review* 64, no. 4 (1970): 1131–48.

Perlmutter, Amos. *Egypt: The Praetorian State*. New Brunswick NJ: Transaction Publishers, 1974.

————. "The Praetorian State and the Praetorian Army: Toward a Taxonomy of Civil-Military Relations in Developing Countries". *Comparative Politics* 1, no. 3 (1969): 382–404.

Prager Nyein, Susanne. "Expanding Military, Shrinking Citizenry and the New Constitution in Burma". *Journal of Contemporary Asia* 39, no. 4 (2009): 638–48.

Radio Free Asia (RFA). "Suu Kyi Pushes Constitutional Change before 2015". Radio Free Asia, 10 May 2013. <http://www.rfa.org/english/news/myanmar/charter-05102013184110.html>. Accessed 3 January 2014.

Sandar Lwin. "In the Hluttaws, More Green Shoots". *Myanmar Times*, 2–8 January 2012. <http://www.mmtimes.com/2012/news/608/news60802.html>. Accessed 3 January 2014.

Sattar, Babar. "Pakistan: Return to Praetorianism". In *Coercion and Governance: The Declining Political Role of the Military in Asia,* edited by Muthiah Alagappa. Stanford CA: Stanford University Press, 2001.

Selth, Andrew. *Burma's Armed Forces: Power without Glory.* Norwalk: EastBridge, 2002.

Shwe Yinn Mar Oo. "Former MP to Lead Commission". *Myanmar Times*, 21–27 February 2011. <http://www.mmtimes.com/2011/news/563/news56301.html>. Accessed 3 January 2014.

Siddiqa, Ayesha. *Military Inc.: Inside Pakistan's Military Economy*. Oxford: Oxford University Press, 2007.

Skidmore, Monique and Trevor Wilson. "Interpreting the Transition in Myanmar". In *Myanmar's Transition: Openings, Obstacles and Opportunities*, edited by Nick Cheesman, Monique Skidmore and Trevor Wilson. Singapore: ISEAS Publications, 2012.

Soe Than Lynn. "The Hluttaw Flexes its Muscles". *Myanmar Times*, 21–27 May 2012. <http://www.mmtimes.com/2012/news/627/news13.html>. Accessed 3 January 2014.

Steinberg, David. *Turmoil in Burma: Contested Legitimacies in Myanmar*. Norwalk: EastBridge, 2006.

Stepan, Alfred C. *The Military in Politics: Changing Patterns in Brazil*. Princeton NJ: Princeton University Press, 1971.

Taylor, Robert H. "Myanmar: From Army Rule to Constitutional Rule?". *Asian Affairs* 43, no. 2 (2012): 221–36.

Tin Maung Maung Than. "Myanmar's Security Outlook and the Myanmar Defence Services". In *Security Outlook of the Asia-Pacific Countries and its Implications for the Defence Sector*, NIDS Joint Research Series No. 7. Tokyo: National Institute for Defence Studies (NIDS) 2012. <http://www.nids.go.jp/english/publication/joint_research/series7/pdf/07.pdf>. Accessed 3 January 2014.

Wai Moe. "Changes within Burmese Military Take Shape". *Irrawaddy*, 3 August 2011. <http://www2.irrawaddy.org/article.php?art_id=21825>. Accessed 3 January 2014.

Williams, David. "Constitutionalism before Constitutions: Burma's Struggle to Build a New Order". *Texas Law Review* 87 (2009): 1657–93.

Win Min. "Looking Inside the Burmese Military". In *Burma or Myanmar? The Struggle for National Identity*, edited by Lowell Dittmer. Singapore: World Scientific, 2010.

Ziegenhain, Patrick. *The Indonesian Parliament and Democratization*. Singapore: ISEAS Publications, 2008.

14

STATE TERRORISM AND INTERNATIONAL COMPLIANCE

The Kachin Armed Struggle for Political Self-Determination

Seng Maw Lahpai

In March 2011 ex-General and former State Peace and Development Council (SPDC) Prime Minister Thein Sein became President of Myanmar, under the banner of reform and transition to democracy. The international community hailed this news as fundamentally positive after decades of military rule. However, the response of the people inside Myanmar was more sceptical, as was the response of Daw Aung San Suu Kyi, leader of the National League for Democracy (NLD), who initially advocated a response of "cautious optimism". On 9 June 2011, three months into the presidency of Thein Sein's quasi-civilian government, what has been described as the largest military offensive in modern-day Myanmar (KWAT 2013, pp. 11–12) was launched against the Kachin Independence Organization (KIO), breaking a seventeen-year ceasefire.[1] Within the first year of Thein Sein's presidency the country saw the forced displacement of over 200,000 civilians in Kachin and Shan States in the north and Rakhine State in the west.

This chapter explores the on-going use of violence and terror as a means to force the objectives of the Myanmar government and its army on the Kachin people. It highlights the continuing historical patterns of the Myanmar government and military or both acting simultaneously, and their attempt to exert centralized power and control over ethnic areas through the use of violence and terror. In the case of the Kachin there are two processes at work: the first is the Myanmar state's systematic use of terror against its citizens, based on enduring ethnocentric ideologies; and second, the Kachin struggle for political self-determination and equality. In tracking the future trajectories of Myanmar's stated reform, it is essential to address the Myanmar government's systematic and institutionalized culture, mentality, and tactics of state terrorism.

THE INSTITUTIONALIZATION OF STATE TERRORISM

Every legal order or every order of explicit normativeness has to rely on a complex network of informal rules which tells us how we are to relate to explicit norms: how we are to apply them; to what extent we are to take them literally; and how and when we are allowed, even solicited, to disregard them....One of the strategies of totalitarian regimes is to have legal regulations (criminal laws) so severe that, if taken literally, everyone is guilty of something. But then their full enforcement is withdrawn. In this way, the regime can appear merciful: "You see, if we wanted, we could have all of you arrested and condemned, but do not be afraid, we are lenient..." (Zizek 2008, pp. 134–35).

Since the arrival of the British in Burma the state has been continuously at war with its population (Callahan 2003, p. 13). During the years of army rule after the 1962 coup, the military attempted to reassert the power of the central government through the sustained use of force. State terrorism has been a common feature of the country's political history.

The term "terrorism" is commonly applied in a very narrow context to denote acts of violence perpetrated by non-state actors. This chapter expands the definition and use of the term to encompass the actions and behaviors, direct and indirect, of the state carried out against its own citizens. State terrorism thus constitutes a systematic use of violence, intimidation, and fear to bring about and maintain specific political objectives of the state (Jackson and others 2010).

Even in times of war, domestic and foreign, there are rules and accepted forms of action that prohibit the use of certain types of weapons and prohibit attacks on specific categories of targets. It is the deliberate targeting of civilians that highlights the illegality of state terrorism, as states have a fundamental responsibility to protect their populations. Accordingly, state terrorism can be seen as the intentional, deliberate, and planned use or threat of violence by any state agent or institution perpetrated against individuals or groups, based on their ethnic or religious background, to achieve political, economic, and ideological dominance over the wider population (Grosscup, in Jackson and others 2010).

A counter argument to the use of the term "state terrorism" follows the position that the state has the legitimate right to use violence. But as Wilkinson (cited in Blakeley 2010) explains, the difference between state terrorism and repression is the instrumentality of the state's actions to harm or terrorize its citizens to achieve its political objectives. Blakeley (2009) shows that in order to understand the difference and, in turn, the level of complicity of the state in acts of terrorism, it is necessary to rule out the possibility that a terrorist act was simply an isolated act without state sanction. Blakeley argues that the state "still holds a degree of responsibility for the actions of its representatives … if the State fails to prosecute the individual to the full extent of the law and fails to compensate the victims, and if the State attempts to excuse the actions in some way, the State is, to some extent the condoning the actions of the individual" (2009, p. 12).

THE THREAT OF ANNIHILATION: WAR AGAINST THE KACHIN

Fundamentally, since 2011 the Myanmar state's human rights abuses, attacks on civilian populations, forced displacement of hundreds of thousand of civilians, and other atrocities such as sexual violence, torture, and extrajudicial killings against the Kachin, conform to the general definitions of terrorism. Violence is used to promote and maintain political objectives.

State campaigns of terror in Kachin State are not new, and have been well documented by international organizations and local people alike.[2] Since Burma gained independence from the British, not only have the Kachin been deprived of promised ethnic and political rights, but they have also been subjected to ethnocentric state policies. A widely used expression that has long had a place in the Kachin vocabulary is *Myen hprawng ai*, which means "fleeing from the Burmese". The use of this term in Kachin is indicative of the history of violence faced by the Kachin at the hands of successive Myanmar governments under different political systems. The U.S. Central Intelligence Agency's declassified reports from the 1970s, for instance, identified a core grievance that has consistently fuelled recruitment to the Kachin Independence Army (KIA): "Ruthless and poorly focused GUB [Burmese government] suppression operations such as the burning of an entire village ... the forced transfer of the entire population of Kachin villagers from insurgent infested areas ... [and] enough instances of rape, knifing and chicken-stealing to foster bitter resentment among the Kachin" (quoted in Mathieson 2012). Military offensives accompanied by human rights abuses (employing the Myanmar army's standard strategy against ethnic populations of "four cuts"[3]) have cost countless innocent lives, destroyed numerous villages thus wiping out whole communities, and ruined livelihoods.

The latest violence began on 9 June 2011, when Myanmar Army battalions 437 and 348 entered and began firing into a KIA base in Sang Gang village, near Ta Pein Chinese hydropower project site, abducting the KIO liaison officer Lance Corporal Chang Ying from his office (KNG 2011). The KIO demanded his release; however, his severely tortured body was returned several days later, while Myanmar troops deployed eleven additional battalions and gave the KIA a deadline to move their long-established base from the area. The killing was the final straw. After years of putting up with killings of its soldiers, liaison officers, and civilian staff (Ba Kaung 2011) in the hope of political dialogue, settlement, and inclusion after seventeen years of ceasefire, the KIO announced that it would defend itself.

During the ceasefire period from 1994 to 2011, the Myanmar army increased its troop numbers in Kachin State fourfold, to a total of eighty battalions. Since the offensive began in June 2011 a total of 142 Myanmar army battalions have been deployed from lower Myanmar (KWAT 2013, p. 3). In the same period, more than 100,000 Kachin have become internally displaced persons (IDPs) and refugees. A total of 364 villages have been wholly or partially abandoned (KWAT 2013), including 66 churches (KBC 2013), and in some cases churches have been used by the Myanmar army as sites to commit sexual violence. Bombing attacks with fighter jets and helicopter gunships on areas surrounding IDP camps and the KIO headquarters in Laiza on the border of China, which started from Christmas Eve 2012, indicate a deliberate strategy to signal to the predominantly Christian Kachin that the Myanmar army will stop at nothing to enforce the government's political agenda in ethnic areas.

Three months into the offensive, President Thein Sein said in a statement to media groups at an Association of Southeast Asian Nations summit in Bali, Indonesia, "… that if the Burmese armed forces truly wanted to annihilate the KIA, they could do so 'within a day'" (Sai Zom Hseng, 2011). Such threats are not empty, as the following months saw the intensification of military operations against the Kachin.

The government's use of the word "annihilate" when referring to the KIO serves the state's twin purposes of perpetrating violence against one group in order to intimidate other armed ethnic groups, and at the same time to achieve political and economic control and authority in the resource-rich Kachin State. As a political strategy, the Myanmar army's attacks against the Kachin send a clear warning to the entire country, and constitute a warning for continued strategies of engagement by the international community (TNI/BCN 2013). The fact that these attacks took place under the nominally-democratic administration of President Thein Sein, that was "promising peace and reform with the NLD and other opposition parties in the country" (TNI/BCN 2013, p. 4), suggests major contradictions in Myanmar government policies and the actions of the military.

WIDESPREAD HUMAN RIGHTS ABUSES IN KACHIN AREAS

The United Nation's Special Rapporteur on human rights in Myanmar has listed a series of human rights abuses committed during the current period that could constitute war crimes and crimes against humanity. These abuses include "grave violations of international human rights and humanitarian law, including attacks against the civilian population, extrajudicial killings, internal displacement, the use of human shields and forced labour, confiscation and destruction of property, and conflict-related sexual violence" (OHCHR 2013). The following case is indicative of how violence perpetrated by the Myanmar army against Kachin people symbolizes not only the power that soldiers have but also the sense that they enjoy impunity for their actions. On 17 October 2011 two young women from Myitkyina were abducted along with some young Kachin men. The women were gang-raped nightly for several weeks as they accompanied a military patrol of several hundred troops in the hills south of the state capital. A male Kachin porter who was lucky enough to escape recalled the following:

> On the third night, the senior officers started to rape the two girls. They were raped for the whole night and were passed on from place to place among them. I saw they could hardly walk the next morning. One girl cried and came out from the army barracks and another girl looked very weak and leaned over the tree.

> We had to stay together with the soldiers, not very close to where the officers were staying, but I could see everything clearly. On the next morning, the captain took one of the girls and forced her to take a bath with him. I know he was from a Meiktila-based battalion because of his insignia. All the porters were asked to collect water for his shower. He bathed naked and forced the girl to clean his whole body. She also had to rub him with a towel. After this he forced the girl to take a shower naked, threatening that he would kill her if she didn't. She had to bathe in the open space where everyone could see.

> On another morning I saw the other girl rush out from an army officer's hut. While she was crying and saying her prayers on her knees, she was slapped on the head and told, "Don't pray! It will not help you. Where is your God? You think he can do anything? So where is he now?" Then he slapped her on her face again and I saw she had lost one of her teeth and her face was swollen.

> During lunchtime, when we (porters) could have time together, the girls told us that the officers took methamphetamines and raped them like animals. (KWAT 2012a, b).

Since June 2011 at least sixty-four women and girls in seventeen townships across Kachin State have been the victims of rape and sexual violence by Myanmar troops from fourteen different battalions. On 1 November 2012 a mother of four was gang-raped by Myanmar army soldiers from Light Infantry Battalion 13 in her home in Hkasan village on the Kamaing-Mogaung road (KWAT 2013, p. 9). Furthermore, women like those witnessed in the case described above have been openly kept as sex slaves by military units, showing the military's complete confidence of impunity from punishment for their actions.

Instances of unlawful arrest and forced labour were also endemic in Kachin State. The Asian Human Rights Commission (2013) documented that by the end of 2011 alone at least thirty-six Kachin people had been detained and tortured under a colonial-era law, the *Unlawful Association Act 1908*. Other groups have documented similar instances:

> At least eight men were unlawfully arrested, detained and forced to serve as porters for the Burma Army. Of these eight men, one escaped from captivity and later confirmed the testimony of a witness whose husband was arrested. The fate and whereabouts of the remaining seven men are unknown. An additional 35 porters were alleged to have been called from villages neighbouring Nam Lim Pa on 16 October 2011. The villages and the numbers called are as follows: Je Hkam village - 10 men; Gawng Run village - 10 men; Tan Dadar village - 10 men; Je U village - 5 men.

> Witness: I was outside the Roman Catholic church (approximately 11 a.m. on 8 October 2011) cutting the grass with my husband when I saw about 200 Burmese soldiers coming up the street. No one was shooting at that time. One of the soldiers yelled to my husband, 'Come with us, brother.' My husband walked toward them and asked when they would let him return. The soldier said, 'When the war is over' and laughed. I saw him walk away and that was the last time I saw him. (PRD 2011, p. 25).

On 12 February 2013 a meeting was held between Kachin residents and lower house Speaker Thura Shwe Mann during his first official visit to Kachin State. At this meeting the Kachin community urged the Speaker to take action against the perpetrators of human rights abuses.

> The government usually denies that cases of rape have taken place against Kachin women. So some local community leaders collected letters written by the family members of rape victims and submitted the letters to the Kachin State Chief Minister with instructions to forward the letters to Naypyitaw authorities. The Lower House Speaker told us that blaming each other would not solve the problems. (*Mizzima News* 2013)

By entwining military aggression and domestic legal frameworks as forms of violence and control, the Myanmar government has eliminated potential political rivalry and civil protest through the use of sweeping laws which guarantee that the institutions that do exist are dependent on the state (Jackson and others 2010). As Zizek (2008, p. 135) argues, one strategy of totalitarian regimes is to have a multitude of interrelated criminal laws that if enacted ensure that everyone is guilty of something. Through intimidation and fear reinforced by such laws, state institutions have the power to arbitrarily arrest and detain citizens and render excessive sentences (Department of State 2012). These laws are combined with ineffective judicial powers, depriving citizens of their rights to due process and a fair trial.

The institutionalization of such broad laws and the targeting of a specific group, Kachin people in this case, illustrate the interconnections between terror and mercy. As Zizek (2010, p. 99) points out, only a power that exerts a "terroristic right and capacity to destroy anything and anyone it wants can symmetrically universalize mercy—since this power could have destroyed everyone, those who survive do so thanks to the mercy of those in power". In the case of Myanmar, although the entire population is subjected to these laws, their implementation is selective.

ARMY AND GOVERNMENT: AN AMBIGUIOUS SEPARATION

The government has already ordered the army not to destroy or seize Laiza [KIA Headquarters]. This proves that our army loves peace. (President Thein Sein 2013 cited in Weng 2013).

Since the start of the renewed conflict, the KIA has met Burmese government delegations ten times to discuss the terms of a peace agreement. The KIA has demanded withdrawal of Burmese troops and political negotiations. However, the Burmese army has continued its troop build-up and offensive operations (KWAT 2013, p. 3).

Since the war in Kachin State began, President Thein Sein has ordered a halt to the war three times: first on 10 December 2011; second on 13 January 2012; and the most recent announcement of a unilateral ceasefire was on 19 January 2013, after the Myanmar parliament unanimously approved a call for a ceasefire to end the offensive in Kachin State on 18 January 2013. Each time the Myanmar army has continued its assault, until May 2013 when a tentative ceasefire was agreed and following this there have been several subsequent negotiations.

The double game of "talking peace and waging war" is indicative of the Burmese government's strategy. As president, Thein Sein has the power to bring international statutes before the parliament for ratification, including the Geneva Convention on Protection of Civilian Persons in Time of War, the Rome Statute of the International Criminal Court, and the General Assembly

Resolution on Human Rights.[4] To date he has not done this, and has also continued to declare to the international community that the government and military are constitutionally detached, while simultaneously failing to rectify the worsening humanitarian crisis in Kachin State.

According to Blakeley's analysis (2009, p. 12), the state is ultimately responsible for the actions of its army, and by not prosecuting those responsible, the state is in fact condoning the actions of its institutions. So far as Myanmar is concerned, little emphasis is placed on the fact that many of the current government members and parliamentarians, including the president himself, are former military personnel. This situation raises the question: how could the Myanmar military launch prolonged military operations on such a massive scale without approval from the president and his administration?

When the offensive against the Kachin began, the Myanmar army transported a range of aircraft and helicopter gunships, along with heavy weapons, from central Myanmar to Kachin State. Combined with the exponential increases in troop and battalion numbers, the movement of equipment is a clear indication that these attacks were centrally planned, organized, and in some way endorsed by the government. As Myanmar's military hierarchy consists of a chain of command from the top down, a military operation that includes air force and infantry troops from 142 battalions in Kachin State indicates that at a certain level the objectives and actors of the government and army are deeply intertwined. Propaganda from the President's Office claiming the Myanmar army had to take military action in self-defence, while at the same time the army was launching offensives that covered most of Kachin State all the way to the Myanmar-China border, does not reduce the culpability of the government and the army.

The current war against the Kachin has in fact revitalized the long-standing "four cuts" tactics as part of a sophisticated new strategy that involves the government: (1) launching a well-orchestrated "charm offensive" targeting the international community, by announcing presidential orders to stop the offensive in Kachin State; (2) effectively blocking much-needed international humanitarian aid from reaching 66,000 out of 100,000 IDPs in KIO-controlled areas, citing "security reasons"; (3) using state media and interconnected media networks to engage in what the United Nationalities Federal Council (UNFC), an alliance of armed ethnic minority groups, has called a "Nazi-like propaganda" (*Kachinland*

News 2013) against the KIO/KIA; and (4) carrying out a brutal offensive
and heinous human rights abuses against the Kachin people.

According to Bertil Lintner (2012) a long-time observer of Burmese
politics, not only are the Myanmar army and government following
similar objectives, but they are also actors working together to implement
measures in accord with a specific "master plan", which one long-time
observer claims was circulated in 2004, and which outlined detailed "ways
and means to deal with both the international community, especially the
US, and domestic opposition".[5]

> Entitled "A Study of Myanmar-US Relations", the main thesis of the 346-page
> dossier is that ... Myanmar must normalize relations with the West after
> implementing the roadmap and electing a government so that the regime can
> deal with the outside world on more acceptable terms ... normalization with
> the West would not be possible as long as Myanmar was ruled by military
> juntas ... If bilateral relations with the US were improved, the master plan
> suggests, Myanmar would also get access to badly needed funds from the
> World Bank, the International Monetary Fund and other global financial
> institutions. The country would then emerge from "regionalism", where it
> currently depends on the goodwill and trade of its immediate neighbors,
> including China, and enter a new era of "globalization". (Lintner 2012)

Central to this document was the recognition of specific problems
that needed to be addressed by the Myanmar government to increase the
West's level of trust. The main issue, according to Lintner, was the fact that
Aung San Suu Kyi, who was under house arrest at the time of writing,
was considered a key "focal point": "Whenever she is under detention
pressure increases but when she is not there is less pressure" (Lintner 2012).

INTERNATIONAL COMPLACENCY

> ... *it takes both specific enabling structures—internal and external structures,
> and social/discursive and material structures—and the involvement of active
> agents—political elites and their agents and supporters—to turn the latent
> possibility of state terrorism into a form of political practice in a given situation*
> (Jackson 2010, p. 232).

Embedded in analysis of institutionalized violence and state terrorism is
the level of international compliance and acceptance of the reform rhetoric
portrayed by the Myanmar government to the international community.
To a great extent the international community has supported Myanmar
reformist rhetoric while grave human rights abuses are not accorded the
same priority as direct engagement with the Myanmar government.

On 21 February 2013 the Australian Foreign Minister Senator Bob Carr announced that the Australian government would donate AUD$750,000 to be used in Kachin State to support access to clean water and sanitation (Australian Minister for Foreign Affairs 2013). This type of aid is welcome news for the long-suffering IDPs in Kachin State; however, it was the first direct support from Australia to Kachin war victims during the twenty months of state-induced forced displacement. In fact, US$2 million is needed each month just for food for the IDPs in the KIO-controlled areas, and currently international aid groups, including the United Nations, have met only 4 percent of these food needs (KWAT 2012a). The Myanmar government has also blocked international non-governmental organizations based in the country from providing emergency relief.

While the plight of the Kachin has been ignored, the international community has been quick to embrace Myanmar government reforms, offering full financial and political support. For instance, Australia has rushed to promise considerable amounts of government aid to Myanmar totalling $100 million by 2015. Australia is also openly campaigning to change the language of the UN General Assembly's annual resolution on Myanmar (Sheridan 2012).

Such lobbying may also be aimed at gaining greater access to Myanmar for foreign investors. Myanmar is a last frontier for resource extraction in Southeast Asia. Since President Thein Sein came to power, the country has been receiving a long line of foreign dignitaries. Engagement with the Myanmar government and access to the country's vast natural resources has become increasingly competitive. A number of international governments are understood to be matching each other in terms of aid and political support. One advocacy group has accused the German government of pushing privately for a change in the status of Myanmar in its dealings with the European Union, noting that, "Germany has a long track record within the European Union of opposing international pressure against the government of Myanmar to promote human rights and democracy. Germany consistently worked to either attempt to block increased pressure, or to push for relaxing pressure" (Burma Campaign UK 2013).

The Paris Club, a group of the world's largest lenders, announced that it was "aware of Myanmar's 'exceptional situation' and had agreed to a 50 percent cancellation of arrears and a seven-year grace period for the remainder" (Biron 2013). This agreement came on top of separate agreements by the World Bank and the Asian Development Bank to restructure close to a billion dollars of Myanmar debt, a move that effectively altered the debt repayment regulations of these institutions.

The Yangon-based Myanmar Peace Center was initiated with a start-up grant of EUR€700,000 in funding from the European Commission on 3 November 2012, to be followed by a total of EUR€30 million for Myanmar's ethnic peace process and development. Similarly, the Myanmar Peace Support Initiative (MPSI) established in January 2012 has the support of Norway, Australia, the United Kingdom, European Union, United Nations, and World Bank. The MPSI's approach of supporting ceasefires through development grants has been heavily criticized, including by Karen community-based organizations, as it pressured only the ethnic armed groups. It was accused of causing an internal rift in the Karen National Union within the first year of a ceasefire, resulting in the need to publicly clarify, and temporarily scale back, its involvement (RFA 2012).

Blakeley's analysis (2009), that by not condemning acts of terror that occur within its borders the state is in essence condoning these actions, can be expanded to encompass the actions of the international community placing reform, development, and investment before human rights violations occurring in the country. Given the Myanmar government's war with various ethnic groups over many decades, external international actors need to acknowledge that conflict resolution should not be focused on the political dynamics of one stakeholder. Such unilateral endorsement not only disadvantages the other parties but also does nothing to improve the situation, when the supported side is the one who has been instigating the violence and who is the perpetrator of a campaign of terror against its own citizens.

"REFORM" FOR WHOM?

The nature and character of these reforms are subject to much controversy, but it is likely that they are not the consequence of a newly discovered love for democracy among the men who have tyrannized Burma for five decades. Perhaps, the Italian writer Giuseppe Tomassi de Lampedusa said it best in his novel Il Gattopardo: *"If we want things to stay as they are, things will have to change"* (Galache 2013).

In October 2012, President Thein Sein was under consideration to receive the Nobel Peace Prize. Subsequently, he was awarded the International Crisis Group's annual In Pursuit of Peace Award, for being one of the "inspirational figures from government, diplomacy and public policy whose visionary leadership has transformed the lives of millions and brought forth the promise of a world free of conflict" (ICG 2012). Many in the international community have described Thein Sein as a reformer who is pulling the country towards democratic transition. Although unsuccessful with the Nobel Peace Prize, the very fact that he was a possible candidate is indicative of the international community's acceptance of the image of reform, while ignoring ever-increasing human rights abuses committed by the Myanmar army under the government's reform campaign.

The level of complacency of the international community through its engagement with, and support of, the Myanmar government cannot be underestimated as a determining factor in the continuing campaign of terror in Kachin State. On the domestic front, neither can the failure of the ethnic majority opposition to speak out and act more forcefully on the violence be ignored. One year into the military offensive, a Kachin participant at a seminar at the London School of Economics asked Aung San Suu Kyi why she has been reluctant to condemn the Myanmar military offensive against the Kachin. She responded that "resolving conflict is not about condemnation, it is about finding out the root, the cause of the conflict" (*Kachinland News* 2012). However, by not condemning acts of violence and terror, Aung San Suu Kyi shows a certain level of acceptance of the acts themselves. The failure of the leader of the NLD to recognize and understand the specifics of the struggles faced by ethnic populations contributes to the reinforcement of Burman-centered privilege (Walton 2013, p. 11). Such uninformed and belated talk of "finding the root cause" after more than six decades of civil war and political turmoil will only lead to a widening gap in ethnic relations.

Aung San Suu Kyi's position can be analyzed as an ethnocentric view of "Burman-ness" where she openly questions the ethnicity of others because her own ethnicity is unproblematic in the eyes of the dominant Burman society (Walton 2013). She has long ignored or downplayed the historical, as well as the contemporary, causes of ethnic grievances and armed conflict, and has asked ethnic minority groups to put aside their own experiences of injustice and suffering for the sake of the Union. Her priority unambiguously lies in creating a Burman-led democratic government, and only after this goal is achieved will she address ethnic issues. Under these circumstances, Walton (2013, p. 2) shows that non-Burmans are not in a position to enjoy the benefits of political reform, to a point where it seems that the government is implementing separate but intimately interconnected policies of increased openness on the one hand—where the Burman majority are the primary beneficiaries—and violent repression of non-Burmans on the other.

CENTERING THE PERIPHERY: THE KACHIN ARMED STRUGGLE FOR SELF-DETERMINATION

As a KIO youth leader put it, "if there is a ceasefire without ethnic rights, it is better to have no ceasefire". This is a widely-held view not only in KIO areas but also in the Kachin State capital of Myitkyina. The head of a local organization that works extensively with Kachin State areas said, "at this moment, when you speak about peace, it's like you are a traitor to the Kachin cause".... A Kachin humanitarian worker said that many members of the community felt that "to get peace, we must fight" (ICG 2011, p. 11).

The very existence of Myanmar as a "union" is thanks to the Panglong Agreement of 1947 between General Aung San and leaders of the Kachin Hills, Chin Hills, and Shan Federated States, who sought political autonomy and equality. If we take the Panglong Agreement as a starting point for understanding the current conflict, then it is essential that we put ethnic-minority political rights and struggles for self-determination at the centre of our analysis. Such analysis must move past static geo-political, statist, and elitist narratives of minority/majority relations to instead recognize the Kachin people's role as co-founders of the Union of Burma.

Self-determination connotes that the Kachin and all ethnic groups are not subjected to institutionalized forms of violence or discrimination that exclude them from a place as equals, having shared rights in the formation of a federated union. Self-determination allows for ethnic groups to have the right to maintain their culture, religion, identity, and traditional autonomous territories.

Decades of political exclusion and failed ceasefires with multiple ethnic groups are representative of ongoing and deliberate political strategies by the Myanmar government, initiated for resource and political exploitation, as well as militarization of ethnic areas. Ceasefire talks are a prominent part of the Myanmar government's reformist rhetoric, regardless of sustainability or success. Ceasefires can also themselves serve strategic purposes for the military, allowing it to increase its presence in ethnic areas on the pretext of political settlement. The essence of ceasefire agreements also varies considerably from one case to the next.

From the start of the recent conflict up to June 2013, there have been fifteen rounds of talks between the KIO and the Myanmar government; however, no concrete solution has so far been reached, with the KIO insisting on a political settlement, not just another ceasefire. In June 2013 alone, twenty-one clashes followed the latest round of "peace talks". KIO spokesperson La Nan said that "the agreement to de-escalate fighting had given the government a chance to redeploy troops, send reinforcements and ammunition and get closer to KIA camps" (AP 2013). No definite timeframe has been reached for the withdrawal of government troops from areas of combat.

Growing international news coverage of the violence in Kachin State in early 2013 prompted the first preliminary meeting between the UNFC and the Union Peacemaking Working Committee (UPWC) in Chiang Mai, Thailand. A UPWC representative said that convening a national conference of ethnic nationalities is a possibility. However, the outcomes of such meeting would have to be decided in parliament, where to make any constitutional changes would need the approval of 75 percent of representatives—of whom the great majority are members of the army-established Union Solidarity and Development Party, not to mention those in the 25 percent of seats reserved for the military.

Even with immense international support thrown behind calls for national reconciliation and peace, the establishment of a rights-respecting democracy and promised federated union is only feasible with genuine political will from the new government. Unless the rightful place of ethnic minorities is recognized, and ethnic parties are permitted to take part in ratifying a free and fair democratic constitution, transition towards democratic reform will remain superficial.

CONCLUSION: KACHIN CAUGHT IN THE CROSSFIRE

The Myanmar government's current talk of reform, while opening the country to foreign investment, will not end decades of political conflict, violation of human rights, and uneven development in ethnic areas. The continuing disregard and violation of human rights in ethnic areas cannot be dismissed in pursuit of the illusion of reform in central Myanmar.

Multiple factors and complex issues exist in the historical relationship between the Myanmar government and the Kachin people. These issues cannot be addressed in isolation. They are interconnected with the struggle for recognition, political legitimacy, increased autonomy, development, and human rights.

This chapter has shown that, regardless of the level of international acceptance for the government's reform rhetoric, there remains a culture of impunity and a sustained campaign of violence and terror perpetrated by the Myanmar government and its army against the Kachin. Such tactics of terror have been deeply institutionalized through governmental agencies and reinforced by the complacency of the international community. There are continuing historical precedents for the actions of the Myanmar state and its attempt to exert centralized power and control over ethnic areas through violence. Conceptualizing the Kachin conflict through the lens of state terrorism leads to a better understanding of its dynamics, and of the interests of various stakeholders.

Notes

1   The ceasefire negotiated between the KIO and SPDC in 1994 ended an earlier period of civil war which had ravaged Kachin State, but the ceasefire was never followed up with a peace agreement.
2   See reports regarding human rights abuses by Myanmar troops during the current offensive, such as HRW 2012; KWAT 2012a, 2012b, 2013; PRD 2011; also, PHR 2011.
3   A strategy implemented by the Myanmar army to cut off food, recruits, finance, and information from the enemy by attacking local ethnic populations.
4   Geneva Convention (IV) relative to the Protection of Civilian Persons in Time of War states in Article 27 that "protected persons are entitled, in all circumstances, to respect for their persons, their honour, their family rights, their religious convictions and practices, and their manners and customs. They shall at all times be humanely treated, and shall be protected especially against all acts of violence or threats". Article 8 of the Rome Statute of the International Criminal Court states that the following constitute war crimes: willful killing, intentionally directing attacks against the civilian population as such or against individual civilians not taking direct part in hostilities and attacking or bombarding, by whatever means, towns, villages, dwellings or buildings which are undefended and which are not military objectives. The General Assembly Resolution on Human Rights of 19 December 1968 states

that distinction must be made at all times between persons taking part in the hostilities and members of the civilian population, and that it is prohibited to launch attacks against the civilian population.

5 Bertil Lintner (2012) writes that the "authors of that plan are not known but an internal military document written by Lt Col. Aung Kyaw Hla, who is identified as a researcher at the country's prestigious Defense Services Academy, was completed and circulated in 2004."

References

Asian Human Rights Commission (AHRC), ed. *Cases under the* Unlawful Associations Act 1908 *Brought Against People Accused of Contact with Kachin Independence Army.* AHRC-PRL-002-2013. Hong Kong: Asian Human Rights Commission and Asian Legal Resource Centre, January 2013. <http://www.burmalibrary.org/docs14/AHRC-Unlawful_Assoc_Act-Kachin.pdf>. Accessed 5 January 2014.

Associated Press (AP). "Myanmar Rebel Clashes Continue Despite Agreement". Associated Press, 23 June 2013. <http://abcnews.go.com/International/wireStory/myanmar-rebel-clashes-continue-agreement-19466397>. Accessed 24 June 2013.

Australian Minister for Foreign Affairs. "Assistance for Myanmar". Media release, Office of the Australian Minister for Foreign Affairs, 21 February 2013. <http://foreignminister.gov.au/releases /2013/bc_mr_130221c.html>. Accessed 5 March 2013.

Ba Kaung. "Burma's Vice-President Implicated in Kachin Massacres". *Irrawaddy*, 15 July 2011. <http://www2.irrawaddy.org/print_article.php?art_id=21705>. Accessed 5 January 2014.

Biron, Carey. "Debt Relief Package for Myanmar Unusually Generous". Inter Press Service News Agency, 28 January 2013 <http://www.ipsnews.net/2013/01/debt-relief-package-for-myanmar-unusually-generous>. Accessed 25 February 2013.

Blakeley, Ruth. "State terrorism in the social sciences: Theories, methods and concepts". In *Contemporary State Terrorism: Theory and Practice,* edited by Richard Jackson, Eamon Murphy and Scott Poynting. Routledge Critical Terrorism Studies series. London and New York: Routledge, 2010.

———. *State Terrorism and Neoliberalism: The North in the South.* Routledge Critical Terrorism Studies. Abingdon: Routledge, 2009.

Burma Campaign UK. "Is Germany Siding with Burma to Downplay Human Rights Abuses?". News release, Burma Campaign UK, 20 February 2013. <http://www.burmacampaign.org.uk/index.php/news-and-reports/news-stories/

is-germany-siding-with-burma-to-downplay-human-rights-abuses/142>. Accessed 5 January 2014.

Callahan, Mary P. *Making Enemies: War and State Building in Burma*. Ithaca and London: Cornell University Press, 2003.

Department of State (U.S.), Bureau of Democracy, Human Rights and Labor. 2012. *Country Reports on Human Rights Practices for 2011: Burma*. Washington DC: Bureau of Democracy, Human Rights and Labor, Department of State, 2012. <http://www.state.gov/j/drl/rls/hrrpt/2011humanrightsreport/index. htm#wrapper>. Accessed 5 January 2014.

Galache, Carlos. "Democracy, Suu Kyi and Ethnic Rights in Burma". *Democratic Voice of Burma*, 28 January 2013. <http://www.dvb.no/analysis/democracy-suu-kyi-and-ethnic-rights-in-burma/26044>. Accessed 12 February 2013.

Human Rights Watch (HRW). *Untold Miseries: Wartime Abuses and Forced Displacement in Kachin State*. Washington DC: Human Rights Watch, 2012.

International Crisis Group (ICG). 2012. "In Pursuit of Peace Award Dinner: Peace, Prosperity and the Presidency". International Crisis Group, 6 November 2012. <http://www.crisisgroup.org/en/publication-type/media-releases/2012/ general/in-pursuit-of-peace-award-dinner.aspx>. Accessed 14 January 2013.

———. 2011. "Myanmar: A New Peace Initiative". International Crisis Group, 30 November 2011. <http://www.crisisgroup.org/en/publication-type/ media-releases/2011/asia/myanmar-a-new-peace-initiative.aspx>. Accessed 25 January 2013.

Jackson, Richard. "Conclusion: Contemporary state terrorism—towards a new research agenda". In *Contemporary State Terrorism: Theory and Practice*, edited by Richard Jackson, Eamon Murphy and Scott Poynting. Routledge Critical Terrorism Studies series. London and New York: Routledge, 2010.

Jackson, Richard, Eamon Murphy and Scott Poynting, eds. *Contemporary State Terrorism: Theory and Practice*. Routledge Critical Terrorism Studies series. London and New York: Routledge, 2010.

Kachin Baptist Convention (KBC). "66 Churches and Over 200 Member Villages Destroyed". *Kachinland News*, 9 March 2013. <http://kachinlandnews. com/?p=23047>. Accessed 12 March 2013.

Kachinland News. "UNFC says government's press release is nothing but a Nazi-like propaganda". 21 January 2013. <http://kachinlandnews.com/?p=22986>. Accessed 20 January 2014.

Kachin News Group (KNG). "KIA Denies Starting War with Burmese Army". *Kachin News Group*, 24 June 2011. <http://www.kachinnews.com/news/1957-kia-denies-starting-war-with-burmese-army.html>. Accessed 24 June 2013.

Kachin Women's Association Thailand (KWAT). *State Terror in the Kachin Hills: Burma Army Attacks Against Civilians in Northern Burma*. Chiang Mai: KWAT,

February 2013. <http://www.kachinwomen.com/images/stories/publication/state_terror.pdf>. Accessed 5 January 2014.

―――. *From Persecution to Deprivation: International Donors Neglect 60,000 Displaced Kachin on China-Burma Border*. Chiang Mai: KWAT, October 2012*a*. <http://www.burmalibrary.org/docs14/from_persecution_to_deprivation.pdf>. Accessed 5 January 2014.

―――. *Ongoing Impunity: Continued Burma Army Atrocities Against the Kachin People*. Chiang Mai: KWAT. June 2012*b*. <http://www.kachinwomen.com/images/stories/publication/ongoing_iimpunity%20.pdf>. Accessed 5 January 2014.

Kachinland News. "The Root, the Cause of the Kachin Situation". *Kachinland News*, 25 June 2012. <http://kachinlandnews.com/?p=21965>. Accessed 11 February 2013.

Lintner, Bertil. "The Master Plan for Myanmar". *Asia Times Online*, 10 February 2012. <http://www.atimes.com/atimes/Southeast_Asia/NB10Ae01.html>. Accessed 5 March 2013.

Mathieson, David S. "Burma's Military Reform Gap". Human Rights Watch, 12 June 2012. <http://www.hrw.org/news/2012/06/12/burmas-military-reform-gap>. Accessed 26 January 2013.

Mizzima News. "No By-elections in Kachin State". 12 February 2013. <http://www.mizzima.com/news/by-election-2012.html>. Accessed 18 February 2013.

Office of the High Commissioner for Human Rights (OHCHR). "Report of the Special Rapporteur on the situation of human rights in Myanmar, Tomás Ojea Quintana". United Nations Human Rights Council A/HRC/22/58, 6 March 2013. New York: Office of the High Commissioner for Human Rights (OHCHR), 2013. <http://www.ohchr.org/Documents/Countries/MM/A-HRC-22-58.pdf>. Accessed 5 January 2014.

Partners Relief & Development (PRD). 2011. *Crimes in Northern Burma: Results From a Fact-Finding Mission to Kachin State*. Partners Relief & Development, November 2011. <http://www.burmapartnership.org/wp-content/uploads/2011/11/Crimes in Northern-Burma.pdf>. Accessed 5 January 2014.

Physicians for Human Rights (PHR). *Under Siege in Kachin State, Burma*. Report written by Bill Davis. Cambridge MA and Washington DC: Physicians for Human Rights, November 2011.

Radio Free Asia (RFA). "Three Karen Officials Removed". Radio Free Asia, 4 October 2012. <http://www.rfa.org/english/news/myanmar/karen-10042012152054.html>. Accessed 20 January 2014.

Sheridan, Greg. "Carr Playing Honest Broker in Burma". *Australian*, 28 June 2012. <http://www.theaustralian.com.au/opinion/columnists/carr-playing-honest-broker-in-burma/story-e6frg76f-1226410414580>. Accessed 10 January 2013.

Transnational Institute, Burma Centrum Netherlands (TNI/BCN). *The Kachin Crisis: Peace Must Prevail*. Burma Policy Briefing No. 10, March 2013. Amsterdam:

Transnational Institute, Burma Centrum Netherlands, 2013. <http://www.tni.
org/sites/www.tni.org/files/download/bpb10.pdf>. Accessed 5 January 2014.

Walton, Matthew J. "The 'Wages of Burman-ness': Ethnicity and Burman Privilege
in Contemporary Myanmar". *Journal of Contemporary Asia* 43, no. 1 (2013): 1–27.

Weng, Lawi. "Amid Ongoing Kachin Clashes, President Urged to Stop the Army".
Irrawaddy, 20 January 2013. <http://www.irrawaddy.org/archives/24699>.
Accessed 1 February 2013.

Zizek, Slavoj. 2010. *Living in the End of Times*. London: Verso, 2010.

———. 2008. *Violence: Six Sideways Reflections*. London: Profile Books, 2008.

15

ENGENDERING DEVELOPMENT IN MYANMAR

Women's Struggle for *San, Si, Sa*

Ma Khin Mar Mar Kyi

On every available index, Myanmar is still one of the poorest and least developed countries in the world, and it has been one of the most conflict-ridden countries in modern times. Women represent more than half the population of approximately of 59.13 million.[1] This means the active participation of womenfolk in social, economic, and political life is crucial for the country's sustainable economic development and peace initiatives—and, inevitably, that gender is an important matter, particularly in the current historical transformative reforms under the current President U Thein Sein. Yet to date the prospects for peace and alleviation of poverty in Myanmar have not often been analysed from a gender perspective.

Whilst women are overrepresented among the poorest of the poor, they are underrepresented in political administration, privileged positions, and decision-making, and have unequal access to power and resources. Like women in many other countries, they are the sole bearers of gender-specific responsibilities as the primary producers of food and caretakers of the family. They also have an extra burden due to lack of infrastructure and modern technologies, such as domestic equipment or a regular supply of electricity. What is more, over half a century of militarization has created a gender hierarchy, and patriarchal ideologies create structural inequality between women and men.

This ethnographically-informed paper is drawn from multi-sited fieldwork carried out from 2009 to 2012 in Myanmar, Thailand, and Australia, and includes interviews, life stories, and surveys. It will focus on how militarization has affected the power and status of women, and how women suffer in their everyday lives from gendered discrimination and widespread poverty. I discuss how women in Myanmar struggle daily for subsistence—*san*, *si* and *sa*, which is to say, rice, oil and salt. I associate their dire poverty with both gender inequality and failed development, and discuss how patriarchal ideologies, policies, inflation, lack of modern technology, collapsing infrastructure, and inadequate health care impact on the lives of women.

MILITARIZATION, POVERTY AND GENDER

Militarization since 1962 has made Myanmar into one of the world's biggest producers of refugees, trafficked persons, forced migrants, and child labourers. It is among the poorest nations, even by regional standards (Lintner 1990; Fink 2001). In 1988, under the pressure of nation-wide protests led by students, and after twenty-six years in power, General Ne Win was forced to admit that his "Burmese way to socialism" was a failure (Lintner 1990). The successor regime took the name of the State Law and Order Restoration Council (SLORC) in 1988, then later, in 1997, changed its name to the State Peace and Development Council (SPDC). Yet Myanmar was neither peaceful nor developed. Instead, Burma increasingly became a militarized, masculinized nation filled with poor and hungry people.

In Myanmar militarization is directly linked to dire poverty. Many researchers have shown how militarization creates structural violence which results in poverty, social breakdowns, structural inequality, and gender-based violence, all of which are associated with the intensification of gender ideologies (Bourgois 2003; Farmer and others 2006; Galtung 1969;

Scheper-Hughes and Wacquant 1992; Sen 1999). Militarization, by its nature, lacks respect for human rights, freedom, and liberty. It prevails through deprivation, destitution, and oppression. The unequal and hierarchical nature of relationships between the rulers and the ruled in militarized societies is extreme, with widespread exploitation of power, persistence of poverty, violations of elementary political freedoms and basic liberties, as well as extensive neglect of the interests and agency of ordinary people.

Freedom is a central element in development, as it provides the individual with agency—that is, the capacity of individuals to act independently and to make their own free choices, which is, ultimately, the link for the individual to maximize her potential (Sen 1989). Individual agency is how a person can make voluntary choices to achieve the best outcomes for her interests and needs without any restraint or obstruction. People can be active agents to change their society through both collective and individual action. Freedom minimizes constraints on social, political, and economic behaviour that can otherwise handicap progress.[2] There is also strong evidence that economic and political freedoms reinforce one another.

By contrast, militarization encourages extreme nationalism, egoism, conservatism, authoritarianism, and anti-democratic attitudes. Violence and repression used in militarized settings as means to control the behaviour of people constrain human capacities. Political dominance creates structural inequality and imbalances of power, which lead indirectly to corruption and other negative consequences. Dysfunctional political and economic circumstances mean that "[t]he burden of petty corruption falls disproportionately on poor people ... without money and connections ... [which has] 'debilitating consequences' on social sectors such as education, infrastructure and health clinics" (World Bank 2001, p. 103).

Many researchers have indicated the linkage between militarization and food shortages in Myanmar (Hudson-Rodd 2004; Turnell 2006; Messer and others 1998). The People's Tribunal on Food Scarcity and Militarization in Burma found significant evidence of "a causal nexus [that] links militarization to food scarcity" (1999). Attesting to this linkage is the correspondence between areas in which the worst food shortages have occurred and the most militarized zones (HRW 2005).

The majority of Burmese are subsistence farmers and landless labourers. The Agricultural Census of Myanmar (1993) indicated that more than 80 percent of Burmese held less than five acres of land each—just enough for subsistence farming (FAO 2004, p. 15). In 1997, the Human Development Index Baseline Survey revealed that one-third of households had no land, 40 percent owned no livestock, and 25 percent owned neither land nor livestock. By 2004, almost 50 percent of Burmese had no access to land, and one in three rural households was landless (Hudson-Rodd 2004, p. 14).

Other research has shown that land rights, poverty, and food security are gendered. Agarwal's research in South Asia on the relationship between land, property, and gender is relevant. She argues that lack of land rights is a "social obstacle" for women and "[t]he gender gap in the ownership and control of property is the single most critical contributor to the gender gap in economic well-being, social status, and empowerment." (1994, p. 1455). Agarwal points out that the substantial proportion of women within landless rural households, generally considered the poorest section of the population, cannot benefit from any intra-family or intra-household land redistribution (2003, p. 195). Women in agricultural sectors bear the larger burden of farm activities, receive lower agricultural wages for their labour, and own a smaller distribution of land holdings, if any. Landowners prefer to hire men who are considered to possess greater physical strength than women. Women without lands are unable to engage in land-related economic activities such as selling fish or vegetables from the farm. Hudson-Rodd, a long term researcher on the Myanmar agricultural sector, argued that in Myanmar female-headed rural households tend to have less land and be poorer, less educated, with few or no economic skills or training (2004).

GENDER MATTERS IN MYANMAR

There is historical evidence that in Burma women have traditionally had high status, although since the colonial era, and particularly in the military era, this status has been diminished through political and patriarchal power (Khin Mar Mar Kyi 2013). Yet many Burmese continue to claim that gender relations are equal. For example, many officials, as well as ordinary men and women, still argue that the lack of patrilineal surnames is a sign of women's autonomy from their husbands or fathers. Women's role as financial manager of the household is also considered an indicator of gender equality in Burmese culture: men hand over their income to their wives, which is taken to show the woman's dominant position in the family. The irony of this observation is that today household income is often lower than the household's cost of living, so this practice transforms traditional rights of a women to a structural burden and gender-based responsibility on the woman in managing household financial matters (ibid.).

As Daw Mi Mi Khaing stated in her book, *The World of Burmese Women*:

> Spiritually, he [the husband] is her senior and tradition tells her to give recognition to this fact.... A man has this, but a woman has more worldly satisfactions: management of house, control of budget and diversion of savings to jewellery, closeness to children, awareness of details ... [but] if money does not stretch enough from the man's regular earning, the wife-cashier must do something to mend the whole (1984, p. 179).

According to the United Nations, a major factor underlying the feminization of poverty is lack of power of women (UNIFEM 2002, p. 60). The marginalization of women from positions of influence and power in society under the former military regime in Myanmar is demonstrated by the absence of women from the SLORC and SPDC, and the lack of any high-ranking women in either the police force or the Union Solidarity and Development Association (now the Union Solidarity and Development Party). The 2006 National Convention[3] included only 67 women among its 1,013 representatives, and only 20 women were among the 659 members "elected" to parliament in 2010. Government is almost exclusively a male club. In the most privileged and powerful profession, the military, women are in the lowest ranks, and fill less than one percent of positions (Mills 2000, p. 285).

Under military rule, women lost much of the power they used to have in certain areas, particularly in commerce, which in the past was traditionally and particularly dominated by female traders. Famous businesswomen of the past included Daw Myint (cheroots), Hajji Daw Pu, Ah-Yee-Taung (tea leaf salad), Naga Daw Oo (cigar business), Daw Thi (*thanakha* business), Hla Galay Sein (Burmese cakes), Daw Thet Yee (leather-ware), and Tin Tin Aye (Htoo Moq) (Khin Mar Mar Kyi 2013). Today, however, military men or their male friends own most major businesses and enterprises in imports and exports, tourism, banking, mining, logging, construction, hotels, bars, and clubs (including soccer and golf). All business permits and licenses require connections, capital, "friendships", "gifts" and "presents", and deals are often decided over a friendly drink and "treat" (such as an evening of karaoke, or a gift of time with a sex worker). Without power, capital, or membership of gentlemen's golf clubs or bars, women were left out.

Education is expensive in today's Myanmar. If parents can afford to educate only one child, they will send their son to school in preference to their daughter, still believing that he has to provide for his family when he marries. This creates structural inequalities that hinder a girl's capacity to maximize her potential.

Notwithstanding this factor, the teaching profession is still dominated by women, but once-highly-respected professors and teachers no longer enjoy the same power, prestige, respect, and status in Burmese society as they formerly did. Previously revered on a par with Buddha, monks, and parents, their status has been undermined for fear they will foment trouble among the young people and students.

The Myanmar government has had one of the lowest levels of public spending on education in the world (UNDP 2010). Most teachers are employed by the government. Because of low pay, however, teachers are obliged to seek additional income such as providing extra tuition to their students for a fee, and favouring rich students.

Furthermore, in accord with government policy, new teachers are assigned to schools in locations other than their home town. A pre-school teacher in Myanmar will earn 60,000 *kyats* (about US$60 per month) but travelling costs can take up to half her salary. In order to save the daily expense of transportation costs, teachers seek for an alternative ways to travel.

One rainy day in May 2013, I was in a car driving back from Hlawga, about 35 kilometres north of Yangon, where we had been to donate and distribute books, raincoats, and schoolbags to poor students studying at three monastic schools. It was about 4:30 or 5pm when we reached the main road to Yangon. As we drove, we saw a group of teachers along the way, stopping our car to get a lift. As we had a van to carry supplies to the schools, we stopped. In no time the van was filled with teachers, all females. Then we saw two more teachers on the road, reluctantly stopping our car. The driver told me, "Sorry, we can't, there is no space left in the car".

Seeing them soaking wet, I told him to stop and let them sit in the front seat with me. As three of us squeezed in we started a conversation. They were young women, recently-graduated teachers who had been working for more than a year. The two of them lived in Hmawbi, approximately 46 kilometres northwest of Yangon. They earned only 60,000 *kyats* (at the time about US$60) a month. As it is a long and expensive daily trip to school, they simply cannot afford to pay the bus fees. In order to save the fees, they ask cars to take them from Hlawga to Yangon (more than an hour away). One of the teachers with a shy smile said:

> We have graduated. We want to teach. We love teaching. But we can't afford all the travelling costs. If we have to pay all the transportation costs, it will leave no money to eat. In Myanmar, if you are appointed as a teacher, the government will send you to distant places. We will not get jobs near our hometown unless we pay a lot of bribes to the senior officials. We can't. So we have to take these jobs. Many have to travel like us. But it is hard for us to stop these cars. We are afraid because we don't know the drivers. We don't know whether they are kind or nasty. It is scary. It is also embarrassing for us to stop the cars driven by unknown men, strangers. But we have no other options. Thank god, we are two travelling together. If I were alone by myself, I don't know what to do. May be I would give up this job and go and work in a factory. (Interview 2013.)

The teachers are very grateful to the drivers who stop their cars. The driver told me after hearing my conversation with them:

> In Myanmar we respect teachers. For me, I will stop my car if there is space to take them. I sympathize with their struggle. But not all the drivers are nice, genuine or trustworthy. It could be dangerous for them. I would be worried if my sister were working as a teacher like them. (Interview 2013.)

It was interesting to overhear the conversations between the teachers and the driver. The teachers spoke to the driver humbly and with gratitude. I could not help but think how the situation they are in has forced them to reduce their traditionally high status in society just to get a free ride. It is one of the indicators of how women's status, given that most teachers are women, is being reduced by the government lack of support for education.

COST OF LIVING AND THE GENDER STRUGGLE

The Burmese proverb *"uma-saung-hma thila-saung-naing"* ("Only if the stomach is full can one practice morality") indicates how food plays a crucial role in Burmese culture and links an individual's existence in this life to the next. In August 2007 when the government removed fuel subsidies, causing the prices of petrol and basic commodities to soar, it led to a nationwide protest, joined by monks. The monks chanted the *Metta Sutta*, calling for loving kindness to ease the people's struggle with the cost of living. The monks, who have daily access to the lives of ordinary Burmese people, sympathized with the call to reduce commodity prices and make ends meet. Yet this only ended in a violent military crackdown. In 2009 the World Food Programme warned that Burmese were facing serious food shortages and that six million people were in need of food aid (World Food Programme 2009).

Myanmar has in recent years had the highest cost of living in the Southeast Asian region (IMF 2007). Although there are many and varied theories about the causes of this hyperinflation, clearly contributing factors include unstable government; civil unrest; a lack of fiscal discipline (Capie 1986); corruption (World Bank 2001, p. 103; Turnell 2006); and, formerly, the double exchange rate (IMF 2007; Turnell 2006). The inflation rate in Myanmar not long ago was so extreme that it overtook other countries in the region and was ranked third-highest in the world in 2003 (CIA 2010). From 2005 to 2009 inflation increased from 17.2 percent to 35 percent, but fell in 2010 when the election was held (to 7.7 percent). Even so, it still exceeded global trends in the same year (CIA 2010).

In 1961, just a year before the military first took power, the average urban Burmese spent 48 percent of his or her income on food (Steinberg 1981, p. 78). By the early 2000s, expenditure on food was the largest single item as a proportion of average incomes, with the main staples being rice and cooking oil (IMF 2007)). According to one 1990 report, 90 percent of the population have to spend 75 percent of their income on food, that nine out of ten Burmese who struggle for food live on less than 65 cents per day, and that three out of four do not meet basic nutritional requirements (Dalpino 2009, p. 2). Another researcher reported that one in two Burmese were living below subsistence level, while yet another reported that one in five Burmese lived in "acute poverty" (Pedersen 2009, p. 5).

Researchers have shown there is a higher incidence of poverty among women than among men around the world (Davids and van Driel 2005; Wennerholm 2002, cited in Chant 2007, p. 1). It is hard to measure poverty, but estimates are that between 60 to 70 percent of the world's poor are females, and this number is increasing (Chant 2007, p. 5; DFID 2000, p. 13; UNDP 1995, p. 4). The "feminization of poverty" has been popularized as an indicator of the notion that poverty affects women more than men.[4]

Rising consumer prices hit everyone in Burma, but as managers of family finances, women are affected differently from men, particularly in providing food and basic necessities. Ma Ma San, a 60-year-old mother of seven children who lives in Kyimyindine, Yangon, explained Burmese women's values as follows:

See, Burmese say if you cook chicken then breast would be for your husband, thigh and leg would be for sons and daughters, and you would eat left over curry sauces. By seeing how much they enjoyed the meal you satisfy your inner hunger (Interview 2012).

One of the most common findings in my investigation of the effect of inflation among Burmese women is their anxiety about the imbalance between income and cost of living, and consequent anxiety about not being able to provide food for their families, which is a constant source of stress. Aye Aye Win, a 34-year-old mother of two who lives in Hlaing Township in Yangon, said:

Cost of living! It is killing all of us alive. We live in fear of not being able to bring food on the table for our family. We have to get food. It is our duty and I am a woman, I will do anything for my family (Interview 2009).

Ma Myint, a shop owner in her fifties with a clothing stall in Malamyaing market in Yangon, who supports her 84-year-old father and 30-year-old sister, told my research team how she feels about inflation in food prices:

We eat just for the day, just to live, NOTHING ELSE. I have to starve for my dad to give him his better and bigger portion. He is old, his time is getting shorter! (Interview 2009).

Daw Daw Than, in her late fifties, a housewife in Hlaing, explained about inflation as a life crisis:

We are fighting and being beaten by inflation. Under inflation we cannot breathe peacefully. See for yourself. Go to the market. You will see hell. We all beg, moan, scream, fight and bargain even for a cent or a piece of bean to make our food just a little bit better (Interview 2009).

According my data, more and more women and men are marrying late because they are struggling day to day with poverty. Many Burmese, particularly in city areas, are also having fewer children and planning only for affordable numbers. My data indicate that whereas once families had five to seven children, now they are having two to three children only because they can afford no more. If a family consists of five members in total, an adult would eat at least one tin or approximately 212 grams of rice per meal, while a child will consume half a tin per meal. If a family of five consisting of two parents, one teenager, and two young children eat only lunch and dinner (without breakfast or snacks) the family needs eight tins (one *pyi*) of rice per day. Even the worst-quality rice, rough rice (*san-gyan*) such as *ngasein* is 700 *kyat* for one *pyi*, so the cost of rice alone will be 21,000 *kyat* per month for the family (around US$20). If everyone in the family eats half an egg with the rice, they will have to buy five eggs per day, which will come to at least another 1500 *kyat* a day, or 45,000 *kyat* for a month, without adding any other ingredients. As against these numbers, if a husband and wife are manual labourers they might earn as little as 24,000 *kyat* per month, an income lower than the cost even of the most basic meals.

When people struggle for daily food, education and health care are out of the question, which is one of the reasons why Myanmar is today one of the few countries where the older generation is better educated than young people.

One of the most direct beneficial outcomes for ordinary Burmese from the current political reforms under President U Thein Sein is the steadying of the cost of living, as well as creation of work for many Burmese. Ma Myint, the stallholder who in 2009 complained about the cost of living (above), sees the political development in these terms:

> Well. Thank god that it seems there is no inflation at the moment and the price of food is steady. But still we cannot afford to eat what we want to eat or how much we want to eat. I focus on food for my dad to have proper meals and we all have to ration curry. We still cannot afford what or how much we want to eat or how often. So what do you call this? Lack of human rights. Yeah … if I can eat what I want and how much I want then I can say I have rights as a human. That's how I see human rights (Interview 2013).

Cost of living-related stress also impacts on the physical and psychological well-being of women. Burmese women often joke that their hearts beat fast going to the markets. Many women whom I have interviewed say that their major health concerns are weakness (*a-nè*), dizziness (*gaung-mu*), headache, shaking, fatigue, and breathlessness. Many of these problems are related to concerns for their own and their family's economic security. For example Aunty Ti Ti, a widow in her fifties, told me by phone that:

> I have headaches, dizziness, and anxiety. I feel sick before I go to the market, thinking and counting how much money I have and what can I buy with that money so it will be enough food for the family. In the market

I go dizzy. I just circle and circle and memorize the price of food. I will go back to a shop that I find something 10 *kyat* cheaper, even if I have to circle the whole market again. Then I get exhausted. I have to cook but there is nothing in my stomach the whole day. I just drink water (Interview 2009).

Women frequently attribute weakness to lack of food, lack of rest, overwork, sleepless nights, stress, and exhaustion caused by financial strain. As Belton (2007, p. 93) says, weakness is "a socially mediated expression of distress, when life has become unbearably hard" (see also Kleinman 1995; Scheper-Hughes 1992).

World Health Organization figures indicate that the government of Myanmar has had the lowest per capita spending on health in Asia, even when compared to countries like Laos and Cambodia (WHO 2006*b*), and that in the mid-2000s, there was only one doctor for every 2772 patients (WHO 2006*a*). Consequently, health care is inaccessible to many Burmese, which again places an onerous burden on women. As women are considered caretakers of their families, they are often obliged to take care of sick family members by themselves.

Although development aid from the international agencies has recently poured into Myanmar in response to changed political conditions, so far such projects have had little effect on the lives of most people. A new NGO elite class is now emerging, with relatively high salaries and other privileges. However, most ordinary people have not yet seen new opportunities as a result of these groups' interventions. It is crucial for the development of Myanmar that the transformation that is under way be felt widely. The millions of women who are the country's traditional financial managers should be provided with opportunities to maximize their potential, so as to help Myanmar's economic and social development, lest Myanmar become another case-study of development aid failure. Considering the socio-political economy of Myanmar, we should take into consideration the negative experiences of other countries that are similarly positioned, and learn from them in order to avoid replication of the same mistakes.

Increasing women's potential and capacity will in the long run help not only the well-being of their families but also their communities, and the nation overall. Conditions will improve only if women are freed from the obstacles associated with poverty, discrimination, marginalization, masculinization of business, and a culture of patriarchy.

GENDERING BASIC INFRASTRUCTURE

Historians and social scientists agree that technology has helped reduce the burden of household duties through devices that save time and physical effort. However, this technological revolution has not affected the lives of most women in Myanmar. The lack of adequate infrastructure has enormous impact on the everyday life of Burmese women: for example, the lack of reliable power and running water mean that women and girls have to spend a great deal of time and energy carrying water, and spend time at home and in the kitchen rather than studying or engaging in income-generating activities. Nyo Nyo, an economics graduate from Yangon University, who is in her thirties and a single woman supporting her parents and siblings, described the situation as follows:

> There are many jobs that we have to do at home. Everything and anything are women's jobs—cooking, cleaning and caring. Without water, how can we carry out these jobs? If we don't do them who will? If there is no electricity we have to do it manually. We have to go to the well to get some water. Because we don't want to spend extra money to buy water from the water seller, we have to do it ourselves. We have to carry water all the way. We have to use water for cooking, cleaning, and washing (Interview 2009).

Most Burmese cannot afford luxury items such as dishwashers, washing machines, fridges, or microwaves. Even people who have these things do not have a reliable source of power to run them; in practice, they do not offer an easier life for the women responsible for the households in which they are located. Lack of electricity also adds to household expenses. Ma Ma, in her late forties and a housewife from a reasonably wealthy background who lives in Dagon, on the outskirts of Yangon, explained:

> When we do not get electricity regularly I have to buy charcoal or sometimes firewood to cook with. This is extra money I have to find from my shopping money, so I have to spend less money on food. How else? (Interview 2010.)

The shortage of electricity increases the difficulties of small business owners. Mya Mya, in her late forties, who owns a photocopy shop on the outskirts of Yangon, explained:

> Well, I charge two prices. If there is mains electricity I will charge 20 *kyat* per page, if there is no mains electricity and I have to use the generator it costs 50 *kyat*. If I have to pay more, I have to charge more. If they have time and can wait for mains power then they pay less (Interview 2009).

These increased costs have caused some small businesses to close. Nu Nu, in her early thirties, owned a small photographic shop but, as she could not afford to buy a generator, she decided to close the business:

> Well I cannot afford a generator, and it is expensive to run as well because diesel is expensive. If you have a car, you can use the oil to run a generator. But if you don't, you must buy petrol. It is a cycle of expenses. So I had to stop my business (Interview 2009).

The intermittent and unreliable electricity supply increases poverty. Gyi Gyi Kywe, in her late seventies, a widow with three grown-up children, told me how many fires had broken out in recent years because of the lack of electricity:

> In our neighbourhood there have been so many fires in recent years. People cook with all kinds of dangerous fuel. While parents go to work, children are left to cook. If fire breaks out it burns everything, because our houses are made of thatch, bamboo and wood. We all have had so many experiences when we had to run away from fire. Only if we have electricity can we cook with an electric stove. This will be clean and tidy as well as less dangerous (Interview 2010).

Inadequate infrastructure and housing also impact on the health of women. After 1990, the government allowed the building of new housing apartments in Yangon as part of a modernization plan. They are six or seven stories high, with lifts, air-conditioning and ventilation, which rely on electricity for their operation. Although these modern apartments initially attracted Burmese who had grown up in houses, they have not improved women's lives. As Thi Thi, a woman in her twenties, explained to my research team in Yangon:

> We used to live in a house. So it had a window and a door. Burmese never close the door. We knew our neighbours. Since we moved to an apartment where there's no electricity, there is no elevator and we live on the sixth floor. Without electricity nothing works in this flat. No water, no air conditioner or fan. We become steamed vegetables. The conditions have become worse and worse since the government moved to Naypyitaw (Interview 2009).

Khaing Khaing, who is in her thirties and also from Yangon, explained how solving one problem leads to the creation of another:

> I live in the city, on 33rd Street. I develop regular headaches. We have to use a generator to get electricity. The smell is so strong. We have to breathe

it in. The house is full of smoke and noise. My husband works in an office so he does not have to deal with it as much as I do. I, on the other hand, have to stay at home, cook, clean, and wash. If I go without electricity there is no air-conditioning or fan. I cannot even breathe in peacefully. So I breathe the fumes in and listen to the noise. That is a stressful life. I am always sick. There's no peace and quiet even at home. It just causes me unnecessary stress. I know many do not have any electrical light and I am lucky (Interview 2009).

All the above examples illustrate how the failure of the Burmese regime to invest in infrastructure affects the everyday lives of ordinary citizens, and in particular, of women. Sound infrastructure in a country demonstrates good governance and a state's ability to manage economic development; lack of infrastructure shows the opposite.

Since 2012, thanks to the new government led by U Thein Sein and his positive approach to democracy and opening-up of the country, people are seeing some improvements in living conditions. Now they are getting more regular electricity, and yet it will still take longer to increase the living standard of people with the help of modern technology. However, not all the developments are positive. Since the government reduced the restrictions on imports and sales of cars, massive numbers of cars have been brought in, but the roads have not been upgraded, leading to major traffic problems. Many more women than men rely on buses, and women are spending longer hours in crowded buses because of traffic jams, so they have less time to spend cooking or buying food, or resting at home.

SOCIETY, SEX EDUCATION, AND SEXUAL HEALTH

Women suffer because of inadequate reproductive health care and education. Lack of accessibility to, and affordability of, contraceptive pills also causes health problems. Maternal mortality rates among Burmese women are staggering. In 2005 the maternal mortality rates per 100,000 Singaporean, Malaysian, and Burmese women were estimated at 6, 44, and 380 respectively (UNICEF 2012). Most maternal deaths in Burma are due to induced abortions, unsanitary conditions, and/or lack of basic reproductive knowledge (that is, sex education, and birth spacing and contraceptive methods).

In 2008 Johns Hopkins University and the Burmese Medical Association carried out a survey of 3000 pregnant Burmese women in the Shan, Mon,

Karen, and Karenni regions of eastern Burma. Although this survey was focussed on a specific area, it noted that "Coverage of basic maternal health interventions is woefully inadequate (Mullany and others 2008, p. 1689).

Delivering babies at home is the preferred, and/or most affordable, method for most Burmese women. In 2008, approximately 90 percent of Burmese women delivered babies at home, but only 5 percent were helped by a traditional midwife, and only one in three had any antenatal or postnatal care (ibid., p. 1690). According to a United Nations Population Fund report, by 2010 the figures had changed somewhat: 76.4 percent still delivered babies at home, but 16.6 percent delivered their babies at government hospitals or private clinics. The report noted that the majority of maternal deaths (62 percent) occurred at home, and went on to say: "bringing maternal mortality down ... by the year 2015 remains an on-going challenge" (UNFPA Myanmar 2010).

Given the growing sex industry in cities such as Yangon and Mandalay on the one hand, and changes of lifestyle as well as lack of sex education and access to family planning on the other, abortion among adolescents presents a challenge. Again according to the UNFPA report, the abortion rate was "highest in 15-19 years age group and university-educated youth, with 11.39% and 9.07%" (ibid. 2010).

This is although abortion is illegal in Burma. Abortion is punishable by law, condemned and stigmatized by society and religion as "killing one's own blood", and is permitted only if a woman's life is in danger. Sexually-transmitted diseases like HIV/AIDS also continue to be a challenge for young women of Myanmar. HIV/AIDS is no longer limited to high-risk groups, but is spreading to heterosexual married women. Nevertheless, reproductive health is still considered to be the woman's responsibility.

Today, condoms can be bought on the streets of cities in Myanmar, and yet sex education for young women is still a major problem because of cultural considerations. The restrictive beliefs about how Burmese women should behave, which were revived and reinforced over decades of military government, deter women from learning about sexual health and sexuality. They are ashamed to discuss such matters openly, and this shame encourages a lack of sexual knowledge. For example, Ma Lay, a 25-year-old woman of Sanchaung, Yangon, told my research team:

> Now today in Myanmar we have some NGOs and I would like to learn about "these things". But I am embarrassed, and my mother thinks I am up to something. She said, I will learn when I am married; this is the only

way and the proper way. Why do I need knowledge like that? I must be up to something (Interview 2009).

Another girl, 28-year-old Thet Thet, explained shyly:

I just got married a few months ago. I know about condoms. I want to ask my husband whether he has that disease or not. Because you know we cannot trust them nowadays. I also want to ask him to wear a condom, as I am not ready to have children. But I am afraid he might think I am experienced (Interview 2009).

WOMEN WORKERS IN THE INDUSTRIAL SECTOR

The industrial sector employs predominantly women. This feminizing of labour began with the growth of the textiles industry under military rule. In 1995, the SPDC converted 8463 acres of land into industrial zones (Ministry of Information 2006, p. 32). Although exploitative, the industries in these zones provided jobs for women who would otherwise have been unemployed. However, after the United States led the imposition of trade sanctions in response to the regime's brutal attack on Daw Aung San Suu Kyi in 2003, as many as sixty-four factories were closed down, which left 180,000 young women jobless. Some observers argue that that unemployment forced women to work at brothels as the only alternative means of survival. Those businesses that remained open generally had investors from China, Korea, Hong Kong, and Singapore (Kudo 2005).

The socio-economic background, wages, and working conditions of women are all indicators of the structurally-gendered nature of employment in Myanmar. Women are mostly employed in labour-intensive, low-paid, exploitative industries, among which the manufacture of ready-made garments is the most prominent, followed by shoes or seafood factories. The garment industry currently employs around 1.5 million workers, the overwhelming majority of whom are women. Garment factories are typically joint ventures with foreign companies, attracted by low labour costs and favourable government incentives. These factories attract young, poor, and desperate women, who come from the countryside and have little or no education.

The owners' intention to exploit these workers is shown by their systematic and strategic use of multiple categories of payment methods, such as bonuses for dutifulness, obedience, snack fees, regular attendance, service, skills, position, Sunday allowances, transport, and living allowances, ranking from 1000 *kyat* (around US$1.20) to 22,000 *kyat* (around US$27) for each category. Most workers in factories are uniformly given a very minimum basic salary from 10,000 to 15,000 *kyat* (around US$12–20) per month, which covers only rent in a small dormitory, forcing them to earn money from other sub-categories to cover food, clothing, transportation, and to send money home. Even if they do succeed in earning money in all these multiple categories, a maximum payment would be less than 50,000 *kyat* (around US$62) per month. For this amount of money young female workers work long hours, tolerate abuse, and compromise their basic human and labour rights, such as by denial of proper lunch and toilet breaks.

To take an example, a South Korean-owned hat factory in Bago, north of Yangon, has 260 employees, of whom approximately 92 percent are women. These workers are not allowed to use the toilets according to their bodily needs; they are only allowed to use the toilet between 8 and 9am or 3 and 4pm. According to the rules of the factory owners, if anyone uses the toilet out of these hours they are fined for "wasting time". If the worker can pay cash because they go to toilet outside these hours, they are charged 200 *kyat* on the spot. Otherwise, 500 *kyat* is deducted from their salary (Kyaw Kha 2011).

One factory official told me that, "Burmese do not work hard. These women will be sitting on the toilet in order to avoid working hard. So sometimes that is fair [to restrict toilet breaks] for the foreign companies. In their countries, workers have to work hard" (Interview 2012). Coming from masculine assumptions and without understanding the nature of women's bodies and their needs, particularly those needs associated with reproductive health, men in decision-making positions seem to have have concluded that female workers sit on the toilet unnecessarily. One official explained that the lack of toilet facilities in these factories is not accidental but is purposeful, so as to prevent workers from "wasting time" in the toilets.

Conditions for workers in Myanmar have improved in recent times with the support of labour rights activists, civil society groups, political groups, the Federation of Trade Unions-Burma, and others. In March 2012 the new government enacted the *Settlement of Labour Dispute Law (2012)*. It also passed the *Labour Organization Law (2011)*. The enactment of labour rights laws is a significant step for workers' rights in Myanmar, after many decades of heavy repression. According to the Ministry of Labour, 236 basic labour associations had registered as of September 2012. Freedom of speech, sharing of knowledge, and networking among workers in the industrial sector means they are learning that across the board that their basic salaries are not acceptable, even in Myanmar's economic situation. Burmese workers receive far below the wages set down in international labour standards. However, workers who are now able to exercise their rights have not necessarily yet enjoyed pay rises or other improved conditions.

CONCLUSION

Myanmar is currently undergoing a historic process of economic adjustment, political reform, and social transformation on its path of economic development, peace, and social harmony. Nonetheless, women continue to face structural inequality, violence, and discrimination, so that many desperately seek alternative strategies in order to carry out gender-specific duties for the survival of their families, including going into prostitution. Although there has been progress, and further political and economic reforms are expected, these will not succeed without addressing the specific development needs of women. Economic and political development should go hand-in-hand with a concern for gender issues, to alleviate poverty and empower women so as to maximize their full potential. This empowerment will in turn help the overall development of the Myanmar economy, as well as contributing to social harmony, well-being, and prevention of gender-based violence.

Notes

1   Estimates of population for Myanmar vary. UNFPA, the United Nations Population Fund, reports the population as being 59.13 million in 2009–2010. See UNFPA Myanmar 2013. The last official census was held on 31 March 1983. A nation-wide census scheduled to take place between 30 March and 10 April 2014.
2   These ideas were developed by Mahbub ul Haq and Amartya Sen, who launched the first *Human Development Report* (published for UNDP) in 1990, with an explicit focus "to shift the focus of development economics from national income accounting to people-centred policies" (Mahbub ul Haq 1995). In their new

paradigm, human development was seen as a process of enlarging a person's "functionings and capabilities to function, the range of things that a person could do and be in her life" (Sen 1989).

3   The National Convention was Step 3 out of 7 on the "Roadmap" for democracy drawn up by the then Prime Minister, General Khin Nyunt, for "Drafting of a new constitution in accordance with basic principles to lay down at the National Convention".

4   For example, the idea of the "feminization of poverty" informs one of the key policy goals of the Beijing Platform for Action of the Fourth World Conference on Women.

References

Agarwal, B. "Gender and Land Rights Revisited: Exploring New Prospects via the State, Family and Market". *Journal of Agrarian Change* 3, no. 1–2 (2003): 184–224.

———. "Gender and Command over Property: A Critical Gap in Economic Analysis and Policy in South Asia". *World Development*, 22 (1994): 1455–78.

Ba-Thike, K. "Abortion: A Public Health Problem in Myanmar". *Reproductive Health Matters* 5, no. 9 (May 1997): 94–100.

Belton, S. "Borders of Fertility: Unplanned Pregnancy and Unsafe Abortion in Burmese Women Migrating to Thailand". *Health Care for Women International* 28, no. 4 (May 2007): 419–33.

Bourgois, P.I. *In Search of Respect: Selling Crack in El Barrio*. Cambridge and New York: Cambridge University Press, 2003.

Capie, F. "Conditions in Which Very Rapid Inflation Has Appeared". *Carnegie-Rochester Conference Series on Public Policy*, 24 (1986), pp. 115–68.

Central Intelligence Agency (CIA). *World Factbook*, Central Intelligence Agency, United States of America, 2010.

Chant, S. *Gender, Generation, and Poverty: Exploitation the 'Feminisation of Poverty' in Africa, Asia, and Latin America*. Cheltenham (UK): Edward Elgar Publishing Limited, 2007.

Dalpino, C. *Burma/Myanmar: Views from the Ground and the International Community*. Report to conference sponsored by the Atlantic Council of the United States, the National Bureau of Asian Research (NBR) and the US-ASEAN Business Council and Refugees International, held on 8 May 2009. <http://www.nbr.org/Downloads/pdfs/ETA/BMY_Conf09_PR.pdf>. Accessed 7 January 2014.

Davids, Tine, and Francien van Driel. *The Gender Question in Globalization: Changing Perspectives and Practice*. Aldershot: Ashgate, 2005.

Department for International Development (DFID) (UK). *Poverty Elimination and the Empowerment of Women*. Written for DFID by Linda Mayoux. London:

Department for International Development, 2000. <http://www.sed.man.ac.uk/research/iarc/ediais/pdf/PovElimEmpowerWomen.pdf>. Accessed 6 January 2014.

Fanon, F. *Black Skin, White Masks*. New York: Grove Press, 1967*a*.

———. *The Wretched of the Earth*. Harmondsworth: Penguin, 1967*b*.

Farmer, P., Margaret Connors and Janie Simmons, eds. *Women, Poverty and AIDS: Sex, Drugs and Structural Violence*. Series in Health and Social Justice. Monroe ME: Common Courage Press, 1996.

Farmer, P., B. Nizeye, S. Stulac and S. Keshavjee. "Structural Violence and Clinical Medicine." *PLOS Medicine* 3, no. 10 (2006): 1686–91. <http://www.plosmedicine.org/article/fetchObject.action?uri=info%3Adoi%2F10.1371%2Fjournal.pmed.0030449&representation=PDF>. Accessed 7 January 2014.

Fink, Christina. *Living Silence: Burma under Military Rule*. Bangkok: White Lotus, 2001.

Food and Agriculture Organization (FAO). *Myanmar: Agricultural Sector Review and Investment Strategy. Volume 1 – Sector Review*. Rome: Food and Agriculture Organization, 2004.

Galtung, Johan. "Violence, Peace and Peace Research". *Journal of Peace Research* 6, no. 3 (1969): 167–91.

ul Haq, Mahbub. *Reflections on Human Development*. New York: Oxford University Press, 1995.

Hudson-Rodd, Nancy. *Housing, Land, and Property Rights in Burma*. Centre for Housing Rights and Evictions (COHRE), COHRE Asia & Pacific Programme, Collingwood (Vic.), October 2004. <http://www.ibiblio.org/obl/docs4/Housing_and_Property_Rights_in_Burma.pdf>. Accessed 14 January 2014.

Human Rights Watch (HRW), Human Rights Documentation Unit. *They Came and Destroyed Our Village Again: The Plight of Internally Displaced Persons in Karen State*. Vol. 17, No. 4(C), June 2005. New York: Human Rights Watch, 2005.

International Monetary Fund (IMF). *World Economic Outlook Database October 2007: Myanmar*. <http://www.imf.org/external/pubs/ft/weo/2007/02/weodata/index.aspx>. Accessed 6 January 2014.

Khin Mar Mar Kyi. "Race, Gender and Sexuality in the Reconstruction of Politics in 20th Century Burma/Myanmar". In *The Illusion of Progress: The Political Economy of Reform in Burma/Myanmar*, edited by David Mathieson and R.J. May. Adelaide: Crawford House Publishing, 2004.

———. "In Pursuit of Power: Politic, Patriarchy, Poverty and Gender Relations in New Order Myanmar/ Burma". PhD dissertation, Anthropology Department, School of Culture, History and Language, Australian National University.

Kleinman, A. *Writing at the Margin: Discourse between Anthropology and Medicine*. Berkeley: University of California Press, 1995.

Kudo, T. "The Impact of United States Sanctions on the Myanmar Garment Industry". IDE Discussion Paper Series No.42. Tokyo: Institute of Developing Economies (IDE), JETRO. December 2005.

Kyaw Kha. "Striking Factory Workers in Pegu Win Demands". *Mizzima News*, 8 June 2011.

Lintner, Bertil. *Outrage: Burma's Struggle for Democracy*. London and Bangkok: White Lotus, 1990.

Messer, Ellen, Marc J. Cohen, and Jashinta D'Costa. *Food from Peace: Breaking the Links between Conflict and Hunger*. Washington DC: International Food Policy Research Institute, 1998.

Mills, J. "Militarism, Civil War and Women's Status: A Burma Case Study". In *Women in Asia*, edited by L. Edwards and M. Roces. Ann Arbor: University of Michigan Press, 2000.

Mi Mi Khaing, Daw. *The World of Burmese Women*. London: Zed Books, 1984.

Ministry of Information. *Sustainable Development in the Sectors of Border Areas, Communication, Industry, Mining, and Energy*. Yangon: Printing and Publishing Enterprise, Ministry of Information, 2006.

Mullany L.C., Lee C.I., Yone L., Paw P., Oo E.K.S., and others. "Access to Essential Maternal Health Interventions and Human Rights Violations among Vulnerable Communities in Eastern Burma". *PLOS Medicine* 5, no. 12 (December 2008): 1689–97. <http://www.plosmedicine.org/article/fetchObject.action?uri=info%3Adoi%2F10.1371%2Fjournal.pmed.0050242&representation=PDF>. Accessed 7 January 2014.

Pedersen, Morten. *Burma/Myanmar: Aid, State Fragility and the Emerging Principles for Aid to Fragile States*. AusAid Policy Study. Canberra: December 2009.

People's Tribunal on Food Scarcity and Militarization in Burma. *The Voice of the Hungry Nation*. Hong Kong: Asian Human Rights Commission, 1999. <http://www.humanrights.asia/resources/journals-magazines/article2/0202/the-permanent-peoples-tribunal-on-the-right-to-food-and-the-rule-of-law-in-asia>. Accessed 6 January 2014.

Scheper-Hughes, Nancy. *Death without Weeping: The Violence of Everyday Life in Brazil*. Berkeley: University of California Press, 1992.

Scheper-Hughes, Nancy, and L. Wacquant. *Commodifying Bodies*. London: Sage Publications, 2002.

Sen, Amartya. "Development as Capability Expansion". *Journal of Development Planning* 19 (1989): 41–58.

———. *Development as Freedom*. Oxford: Oxford University Press, 1999.

———. "Foreword". In *Human Development, Essential Readings*, edited by Sakiko Fukuda-Parr and A.K. Shiva Kumar. New Delhi: Oxford University Press. 2002.

Steinberg, David. *Burma's Road Toward Development: Growth and Ideology Under Military Rule*. Boulder, Colorado: Westview Press, 1981.

Turnell, Sean. *Burma's Economic Prospects.* Testimony before the U.S. Senate Foreign Relations Subcommittee on East Asian and Pacific Affairs, 29 March 2006. <http://www.globalsecurity.org/military/library/congress/2006_hr/060329-turnell.pdf>. Accessed 6 January 2014.

United Nations Children's Fund (UNICEF). ChildInfo: Monitoring the Situation of Children and Women. *Trends in estimates of maternal mortality ratio (MMR, maternal deaths per 100 000 live births) by 5-year intervals, 1990–2010, by country.* June 2012. (Source: UN Maternal Mortality Estimation Group (MMEIG) WHO, UNICEF, UNFPA, WB). <http://www.childinfo.org/maternal_mortality_ratio.php>.

United Nations Development Fund for Women (UNIFEM). *Progress of the World's Women 2002, Volume 2: Gender Equality and the Millennium Development Goals.* Written by Diane Elson and Hanke Keklik. New York: UNIFEM, 2002.

United Nations Development Programme (UNDP). *Human Development Report 1990.* Published for UNDP by Oxford University Press. New York: UNDP, 1990. <http://hdr.undp.org/sites/default/files/reports/219/hdr_1990_en_complete_nostats.pdf>. Accessed 11 January 2014.

———. *Human Development Report 1995: Gender and Human Development.* Published for UNDP by Oxford University Press. New York: UNDP, 1995. <http://hdr.undp.org/sites/default/files/reports/256/hdr_1995_en_complete_nostats.pdf>. Accessed 6 January 2014.

———. *Human Development Report 2010: The Real Wealth of Nations: Pathways to Human Development.* New York: UNDP, 2010. <http://hdr.undp.org/en/content/human-development-report-2010>. Accessed 6 January 2014.

United Nations Population Fund (UNFPA) Myanmar. *Country Profile.* 26 February 2013. <http://countryoffice.unfpa.org/myanmar/2009/11/11/1545/country_profile/>. Accessed 6 January 2014.

———. *Report on Situation Analysis of Population and Development, Reproductive Health and Gender in Myanmar.* 16 July 2010. <http://countryoffice.unfpa.org/myanmar/2010/08/03/2561/executive_summary>. Accessed 11 January 2013.

Wennerholm, C.J. *The 'Feminisation of Poverty': The Use of a Concept.* Stockholm: Swedish International Development Cooperation Agency, 2002.

World Bank. *World Development Report 2000/2001: Attacking Poverty.* Written by Christina Malmberg Calvo, Monica Das Gupta and others, for the World Bank. Published by Oxford University Press, New York, for the World Bank, Washington. Washington DC: World Bank, 2001. <http://documents.worldbank.org/curated/en/2000/09/17408018/world-development-report-20002001-attacking-poverty>. Accessed 6 January 2014.

World Food Programme (WFP). "Hunger in the news: Many in Burma hungry despite food surplus". World Food Programme, 5 February 2009. <http://www.wfp.org/news/hunger-in-the-news?page=5&tid=257>. Accessed 11 January 2014.

World Health Organization (WHO). Regional Office for South-East Asia. *Report on Global Health Professional Survey in Myanmar*. New Delhi: WHO Regional Office for South-East Asia, 2006*a*.

————. *World Health Statistics 2006*. Geneva: World Health Organization, 2006*b*. <http://www.who.int/gho/publications/world_health_statistics/whostat2006_erratareduce.pdf>. Accessed 6 January 2014.

VI

Conclusion

People's lives in the transition period

People's lives in the transition period...

Man: I'll have to march with all my energy

Cost of living: Really?

The first encounter...

Crony: Where to, fella?

After that...

Land-grabbing company: Hey guy, where you going?

And now...

Conflict: Where you off to all worked up, huh?

Man: Whatever the times, Myanmar people always have to cultivate forbearance...

Distant figure: They'll come thump you if you don't stop bawling.

Cartoon by Soe San Win, *The Voice Daily*, 2 April 2013, p. 7

16

DEMOCRATIZATION, VIOLENCE AND MYANMAR

Nick Cheesman

I propose to conclude this book by reexamining the current debate about democratization in Myanmar in terms of violence, by which I mean political violence. I have three reasons for concentrating on violence. First, most of the chapters in the book explicitly or implicitly raise questions that intersect with the problem of violence. What types of political violence are common in Myanmar today? Do they threaten democratization? How do they matter, and why?

Second, while the contents of the book raise questions about some types of political violence in Myanmar today, they omit, or pass lightly over, other types. Notably, no chapter is dedicated to communal violence, whether the violence in Rakhine State, or the growing incidence of anti-Muslim violence in other parts of the country.[1] By concentrating on violence in this concluding chapter, I will attempt briefly to address this omission.

Third, by rethinking democratization in relation to violence I hope to obtain some new perspectives on the stories and analyses offered by the book's contributors. Some of these perspectives sharpen and enhance the authors' views. Others cast doubt on their findings. All of them speak to problems of violence as "the decisive means for politics" (Weber 2009, p. 121) in Myanmar.

The two broad categories of violence that I will use for this purpose, drawn from Johan Galtung's influential schema, are personal violence and structural violence (1969, p. 170). The categories are convenient, because they encompass a wide range of political phenomena. They also permit rudimentary analysis of these phenomena as described in the preceding chapters, and invite possibilities for further research. I begin with personal violence, and then turn to its structural counterpart.

PERSONAL VIOLENCE

Personal violence is direct. A person (or persons) commits it against another person or persons. It is visible as action, and instrumental in character (Arendt 1969, p. 46; Weber 2009). Targeted at individuals, personal violence takes the form of killing, torture, rape, and abduction, among other practices. As a collective political phenomenon it is found in war, terrorism, communal violence, pogroms, riots, and genocide, just to name a few of its most pronounced forms. I will concentrate here on collective personal violence, because the media and experts tend to point towards this sort of violence when warning of dangers to the future of democratization in Myanmar.[2]

Personal violence is in this volume most apparent in the chapter by Seng Maw Lahpai, who characterizes the massive levels of personal violence suffered by people living in areas of Kachin State and neighbouring parts of Shan State affected by fighting between government troops and the Kachin Independence Army as state terrorism. Her assertion rests on observations about the widespread and apparently calculated manner in which government soldiers kill, rape, torture, and abduct civilians, as well as state agencies' use of a tranche of repressive laws to imprison alleged insurgents without adequate evidence or fair trial.

To situate her narrative, Lahpai cites a classic monograph on war and state building in Myanmar in which Mary Callahan traces protracted military rule to "discrete historical circumstances that established a state predicated on, constructed around, and ultimately held hostage to organized violence" (2003, p. 2). Drawing upon Charles Tilly's work on coercion-intensive states, Callahan argued in her study that the unusually direct manner in which the British colonized Myanmar, then Burma, followed by world war and post-colonial disarray, enabled the emergence of a highly militarized state, one in which politics has failed to extricate itself from the warfare entailed in its formation.

Looked at from this angle, the fighting in the country's north suggests that the state in Myanmar is still very much a state being built. Yet, in Lahpai's analysis it is not a state being held hostage to organized violence at all. Rather, the state is a hostage-taker, a duplicate entity consisting of a quasi-civilian government and an unapologetic army, working together to achieve "a specific 'master plan'" (Lahpai this volume, p. 294). Under these conditions, she insists, political reform is illusory. A country whose army systematically attacks a large segment of its population cannot simultaneously democratize.

To scholars of Myanmar, Lahpai's arguments are familiar in their tone. Likewise, sadly, are her descriptions of the violence in Kachin State. Reports documenting human rights abuses by rapacious army battalions in frontier zones are legion. Specialist organizations have for years collected narratives of violence from these areas, investing them with their own meanings. Consequently, the personal violence associated with insurgency has a peculiar coherence. So do the groups engaged in insurgency. Military forces like the KIA and its political wing act out the state in miniature, replete with flags, uniforms, and calendars to celebrate their existence, alongside soldiers, spies, and spokesmen. Their collective project requires that they make themselves knowable, or rather, that they invest in practices which encourage particular types of knowledge about who they are, what they do, and why.

Most of these features are absent from communal violence. It lacks the same familiarity. Despite its recurrence, it has a seeming unpredictability. It is not so readily researched and interpreted. And although its advocates rally around symbols and laud martyrs to their cause, producing stickers and Facebook pages, no state in miniature stands behind or alongside them. They have an inherent ambiguity that defies the methods of documentation and analysis that students of Myanmar have brought to the study of its civil war. The ideas and practices of communal violence seem to require of us a more emic analysis than those of insurgency: one necessarily more contingent, less generalizable — more locally grounded, less able to travel.

To illustrate this point, take the fascinating study of "small town wars" after the fall of Suharto in which Gerry van Klinken attributes communal violence in late-1990s Indonesia to an "open opportunity structure" (2007, p. 23). Through careful empirical analysis, he identifies four important short-term developments that enabled violence there: a fragmented political elite; the inability of the military and police force to repress protest; aspirants to leadership positions who had lost faith in the incumbent leadership; and economic decline.

Although Myanmar's opportunity structure is today more open than it was a few years ago, and some features of the communal violence there have superficial likenesses with events in Indonesia, Van Klinken's account of the causes for violence in Indonesia lacks explanatory power when applied to the events described in this book.

Most obviously, the political changes in Myanmar are occurring under management of what Renaud Egreteau describes as a praetorian "transit regime" (p. 264), rather than amid the collapse of a defiantly personalistic regime. The military in Myanmar has so far maintained corporate cohesion and protected its core interests. It continues to command a large percentage of national resources with "little or no civilian oversight" (Maung Aung Myoe forthcoming) of its affairs. At the same time, it has offset criticism by making more room for civilian aspirants to senior positions in government who had hitherto been locked out, and by doing so faster than most analysts had expected. The sense that Myanmar is now on the path to a viable "transition pact" (Diamond 2012) has encouraged a generally cooperative atmosphere in key political institutions and among important personalities. Whether or not these conditions continue as the anticipated 2015 election approaches remains to be seen, and in part depends upon how, if at all, the current electoral system is reformed (Kean; Lemargie and Reynolds; Pedersen this volume). In any event, to the present time domestic responses to communal violence have been marked more by consensus than by dissent.

Nor has the repertoire of state responses to violence in Myanmar shifted considerably. The police force is still effectively under military control, as Andrew Selth explains in his chapter, and has to date undergone relatively little change to its organizational culture and behaviour. The president has been ready to enact emergency regulations and mobilize the army and paramilitary police quickly in response to conflict, consistent with established procedures for the management of large-scale public violence in earlier periods. Although the burgeoning private print media and other forms of modern communication—including rapidly growing Internet access—put some new limits on the extent to which the police and army can use coercive force, in areas where emergency powers are in effect, these limits are of relatively little consequence.

A further difference between Myanmar during the current period and late-1990s Indonesia relates to how the violence is produced. In Indonesia, most of the violence emerged out of specific localities and remained situated in them, as episodes of "local politics by other means" (Van Klinken 2007, p. 138). The violence in Rakhine State, by contrast, from the beginning had qualities that entwined it with the politics of indigenous identity and the post-colonial utility of the "national races" taxonomy, whereby persons classed as belonging to one or another of the national races are imbued with a sense of common ancestry and a shared obligation to guard the nation against external and internal dangers (Cheesman 2002*b*, p. 217). These qualities have motivated normative citizens—ethnically Burman Buddhists (Cheesman 2002*a*, pp. 226-228; Walton 2013, pp. 5-6)—to mobilize in response to the violence in western Myanmar, and to encourage people of other ethnicities to invest in the conflict, enabling its spread.[3] As in Sri Lanka, where attacks on Tamils were re-cast as "an expression of an inevitable and explicable response by the Sinhala community as a whole" (Spencer 1997, p. 123) to the agitation of some Tamils against the state, in Myanmar attackers have situated localized violence on the national register, enacting claims of national identity in the local (Das 2007, pp. 158–60). Consequently, violence that may have very particular characteristics in each individual site is reinterpreted as part of a shared response—and a shared responsibility—to the supposed threat posed by the steady infiltration of so-called illegal Bengalis, or more generally, *kala*.[4]

In its production, communal violence relies on a wide variety of agencies and agents. These people constitute what Paul Brass has described as rehearsal, enactment, and interpretation specialists (2010, pp. 48–53). Specialists develop skills to produce violence that effectively institutionalizes it. Rehearsal specialists create the enabling environment for communal violence, preparing for, and sometimes hastening, its eventuality; enactment specialists initiate and supervise the performance of communal violence, and interpretation specialists narrate and analyze it afterwards, ensuring that it remains a feature of public discourse.

The qualities of the specialists and features of institutionalization vary from one place to the next. In Myanmar, rehearsal and production specialists learned their techniques under successive periods of military rule. Therefore, we should not be surprised that the violence has followed similar patterns from one region to the next.[5] In some towns, local officials have allegedly formed attack gangs from among thugs whom they had previously used to police, detain, and disperse demonstrators in the 2000s.[6] The gangs are linked to 969, a Buddhist movement with rabidly anti-Muslim ideology that some commentators have labeled neo-Nazi (Ghosh 2013; Zarni 2013; Kyaw Zwa Moe 2013), although monks closely associated with the movement insist disingenuously that whatever its ideology, it is non-violent in its methods.[7]

Where the production of communal violence has perhaps changed the most over the last couple of years is in its interpretation. The belated but now rapid spread of new communications technology and emergence of private print media in Myanmar have had a large part in shifting this specialization away from the previously monopolistic state-run media.[8] Facebook pages with names like "969 Golden Myanmar" and "Myanmar National Mobilization Committee" have sprung up to decry acts of violence against their own community and celebrate it when directed against their opponents.[9] Dogmatic historians have seized new opportunities to spread xenophobia dressed up as scholarship.[10]

A presidential commission to investigate events in Rakhine State has also played a part. After eight months on the job, the commission delivered a report in April 2013 that not only elided a half-century of violence through military rule and ethnic chauvinism via schooling and the media, but invited more of the same by recommending that the "security forces" increase operations, target alleged "Bengalis" posing as members of national races, scrutinize identification records, close border crossings, and enforce the 1982 Citizenship Law (ICSVRS 2013, executive summary), an odious statute which elevated the subsidiary concept of indigenousness contained in an earlier law that it superseded, making it the primary criterion for citizenship.[11]

One of the intriguing outcomes of the commission's work as an interpretation specialist is that, rather than encouraging healthy democratic debate about events in Rakhine State during 2012, it shut out alternative views on what happened and why. It achieved this outcome in part by bringing key people among returning exiles and activists, who are the subject of Kerstin Duell's chapter in this book, into the formal report-writing process. Whereas associations like the 88 Generation Students group declined to join an inquiry into a copper mining operation and attack on protestors at the Letpadaung Hills that was chaired by Myanmar's democracy icon and leader of the National League for Democracy, Daw Aung San Suu Kyi, they agreed to participate in the Rakhine State investigation.[12] In the Letpadaung case, the 88 Generation Students group joined with a newly-established group of lawyers to publish a report that offered an interpretation very different from the official one (LN-UM and 88GS 2013; ICLHCMP 2013).[13] The alternative report is valuable not only as a record of events, but also because it invites debate about democratic rights. No equivalent report exists against which the contents of the official Rakhine State report can be compared and argued locally.

In the absence of a comparable domestically-researched and published alternative report on communal violence, agencies based abroad have led the effort to document and publicize alternative accounts of the violence in Rakhine State, criticizing the government over its response to the attacks and pointing to the inaction or complicity of the police and other state institutions (HRW 2013; PHR 2013; ALTSEAN 2013). The effect has been to further polarize interpretations of the communal violence, with international groups and experts talking about crimes against humanity, which erstwhile allies in the country forcefully reject.[14] The effect has also been to cower groups or individuals who might otherwise have offered support to people affected by the violence—irrespective of religion or ethnicity—because they fear being ostracized, and possibly threatened, if they challenge the consensus position of locally influential interpretation specialists.[15]

In short, the production of personal violence in Myanmar today is in many respects contiguous with its production prior to the beginning of the country's nascent democratization. The field of personal violence is marked out by the appearance of some new specialists, especially those concerned with interpreting violence, and by some new opportunities for action. However, the producers of violence for the most part continue to draw from the same repertoire of context-specific inherited ideas and practices, and, if anything, the production of collective personal violence in the current period has endorsed and consolidated certain types of political thought inculcated over decades of military rule—political thought that also has a close, dynamic relationship with the structural violence that is the subject of the next section.

STRUCTURAL VIOLENCE

Structural violence is indirect. It relates to political and economic institutions that cause misery, degradation, and death, without necessarily having those results as their objectives. It is understood as violence specifically because it enables the continuance of a social order in which suffering is, as Akhil Gupta has written, "not only tolerated but also taken as normal" (2012, p. 21). Structural violence is at once collective and political, inasmuch as it concerns the general arrangements of people brought together by chance or choice (Oakeshott 1991, p. 44). It can be extremely resilient, because once embedded in institutions and practices it subverts and frustrates the attempts of individuals—including well-meaning bureaucrats and other people in positions of authority—to effect real change in people's lives (Gupta 2012, p. 23).

Khin Mar Mar Kyi is the one author in this book who refers directly to literature on structural violence, linking it in her discussion to militarization and patriarchy. In her analysis, women are more acutely affected by structural violence than men, since they suffer disproportionately from its manifold forms, and for decades have been systematically excluded from positions of authority. Through ethnographic research she illustrates how such violence manifests itself in physical symptoms among women in Myanmar, including dizziness, headaches, and weakness. This violence is visceral: it affects lives deeply, if not visibly.

Other authors address structural violence indirectly. That "millions of deeply impoverished households have yet to see significant material benefits" (Pedersen this volume) from the country's change of political course is a major concern addressed across a number of chapters. The overall mood is circumspect. Anders Engvall and Soe Nandar Linn (this volume, pp. 173–74) think that the "country's new political diversity is likely to slow the pace of future economic reforms as a more vocal parliament and civil society seek a stake in policy-making". Sean Turnell (this volume, p. 199) also warns that the record of implementing changes that might improve people's lives has so far been patchy, and that "the possible 'cronyization' of Myanmar's economy ... represents a clear threat to the country's progress". Restated as a problem of structural violence, this possibility represents a clear threat not only to the country's progress but also to the lives of many millions of its people.

Larry Diamond (2012, p. 144) proposes that one way to deal with cronies would be to give legal security over corruptly-acquired property in exchange for commitments to democratization. Whether or not this strategy might advance democratization, it is unlikely to do anything to diminish the structural violence that cronyism engenders. Cronies—and here I join with Turnell and Diamond in using the term because it is now firmly a part of the Burmese lexicon—adapt to new political circumstances, including electoral democracy (Winters 2011, p. 180). The parallel modes of legality, administration, taxation, and profiteering through which they organize their businesses can weather political transitions. Where parallel modes not only persist but also rival their formal counterparts in scale and scope, as in Myanmar—how else are we to account for an official tax-to-GDP ratio of less than five percent (Engvall and Soe Nandar Linn this volume)—structural violence pervades transactions. Under these circumstances, public commitments "to improving governance, cleaning up corruption, and instituting economic policies that truly benefit the general population" (Pedersen this volume, p. 37) may not amount to much, even if made sincerely.

A number of chapters speak to the nexus between structural and personal violence. One of the ways in which frustration at structural violence in Myanmar is giving rise to politically disruptive personal violence is via labour disputes. Kyaw Soe Lwin in his chapter discusses labour unrest at factories—which predominantly employ women—and violence. He tracks strikes at two factories that turned physically violent, suggesting that the violence in these cases emerged out of long-standing grievances, highly concentrated workforces, changing political and economic conditions, and the improved organization of workers seeking to make rights claims.

Another way that violence imposed structurally gives rise to personal violence is via disputes over land. Tamas Wells and Kyaw Thu Aung in this volume present an encouraging case study of how farmers' networks in the Ayeyarwady Delta established after Cyclone Nargis have been able to organize and take advantage of new opportunities to advocate for laws and policies on agricultural land. However, the scale of discontent over land in Myanmar is enormous—a fact now widely acknowledged in the public debate—and the measures taken to address that discontent have so far been extremely limited. As these two authors note, although farmers have succeeded in increasing their voice, they have not necessarily succeeded in obtaining a greater level of government responsiveness to their demands. Indeed, new laws that have been passed, far from offering farmers greater guarantees for the future, are inimical to security of tenure (Turnell this volume).

Just how much land the army and its business partners have grabbed over the last couple of decades remains anyone's guess, but with increased official openness and new institutions of government, as well as the efforts of Myanmar-based research and advocacy groups and reporting by growing numbers of active and interested journalists, we are getting more information than in the past. At the end of January 2013, a commission established to investigate cases of land-grabbing announced that it had so far received complaints concerning almost a quarter of a million acres of land seized by the armed forces alone (Nyan Hlaing Lin 2013). The figure is likely to be only a small fraction of the total amount of land grabbed by the army, given the penetration of battalions into practically all parts of the country and policies to encourage battalions to self-fund—and given that not many complaints have yet come in from those parts of the country where the army presence has been most intrusive, areas remote from urban centres, many of which have suffered protracted civil war.

The official response to land-grabbing so far has been to pay off those people whose claims administrators—not the courts—deem genuine. At the start of 2013, an army officer reported that the year before the military had "resolved" complaints regarding the seizure of a little less than two thousand acres of land, via payment of compensation equalling a little over a million dollars (Thiha and Htun Khaing 2013). Leaving aside the vast disparity between the amount of land for which compensation has been paid and the total amount of land grabbed by the military, and whether or not compensation is paid at a fair market price, by reducing land disputes to a question of payment administrators deny the structural character of the violence committed on those whose land has been grabbed. This approach is inconsistent with democratic values, since it treats the problem as one of the economic value of a commodity, rather than as one of political and legal rights.[16]

The Letpadaung Hills copper mine dispute is a well-known example of the disjuncture between land claims made as demands for political rights in response to structural violence and "solutions" to land claims provided through financial compensation. Like its counterpart that investigated the Rakhine State conflict, the official inquiry into the copper mine project (which was headed by Aung San Suu Kyi) interpreted violence in such a way as to ensure its continuance. The commission recommended compensation and some other measures aimed at limiting environmental damage, but failed to address grievances caused by dispossession and suffering that go back to the 1970s (ICLHCMP 2013). It also neglected to recommend criminal inquiries and the prosecution of police officers who fired incendiary weapons into demonstrators, which led close allies of the National League for Democracy to issue strong objections to the report's contents (Lawyers Network 2013). By failing to challenge the police force's established impunity and non-accountability to the public (Selth this volume), the commission left the door wide open for police and other authorities to continue operations against opponents of the mine. By June 2013 seven people whom police had detained without warrants had been imprisoned, following trials in which they were allegedly unable to defend themselves (Eleven Media 2013).

The Letpadaung mine dispute is only one among hundreds, perhaps thousands, of similar conflicts over land around the country that have the potential for structural violence to be realized as personal violence. As Wells and Kyaw Thu Aung observe, land rights are a longstanding cause of tension in Myanmar, and one that in some areas—like the Delta region—has reached a critical point. Thus, during February 2013 hundreds of farmers in the Delta township of Ma-ubin fought a pitched battle with police that left one constable dead and over forty people injured (Aung Soe and Kyaw Oo Naing 2013).[17] The farmers were occupying parts of around 550 acres of land that had first been confiscated from them without compensation in 1996 for a fisheries project, which had reportedly left them with inadequate, brackish water with which to sow rice crops in their remaining paddies.

After the melee in Ma-ubin, a farmer from the locality precisely captured the structural causes of the personal violence when she asked, "How can you dare blame us who are facing starvation and have no choice but to act to save our lives if we no longer respect so-called law?"[18] The proximity between structural violence and the juridical instruments for the use of violence by the state classed as law, which exists to one degree or another everywhere, is most obvious in places where it "results in the premature and untimely deaths of people" (Gupta 2012, p. 21). Law tolerates death by malnutrition, illness, and infirmity. It does not tolerate resistance to structural violence that challenges its own authority.

Poverty as a statistical problem is being addressed through programmes that aim at its reduction and eradication but which also act to obfuscate violence and deny the epistemology of the hungry farmer who has been forced off his or her land to make way for the (often badly-designed and badly-implemented) project of a crony—even when, as in Ma-ubin, the land has been seized unlawfully (Kyaw Kyaw Oo 2013). Because structural violence is impersonal, officials can deny that they are the ones to blame when people suffer. Insofar as governments form pacts with international agencies for the delivery of programmes to alleviate poverty, they can even displace blame onto others (*Irrawaddy* 2012). Underdevelopment is, after all, nobody's fault in particular.

CONCLUSION

My goal in this chapter has been to draw together some strands of the debate about democratization in Myanmar by concentrating on political violence. I have used two broad categories to demarcate and describe violence—one personal, the other, structural. I have also tried to show that events of collective, personal violence cannot be isolated from one another or from other types of violence. Rather, they are closely related to one another and to a range of ideas and practices that are structurally integrated into Myanmar's administrative and political institutions.

In a militarized regime, violence is a compulsory and unavoidable means for achieving ends. The military is, after all, as Nancy Scheper-Hughes has pointed out, "not an educational, charitable, or social welfare institution; violence is intrinsic to its nature and logic" (1992, p. 223). As democratization leads away from militarization, we can infer that it will also diminish violence. But democracy does not guarantee this outcome—it only allows for more alternatives. Therefore, whereas much of the concern about violence in Myanmar today has been about whether or not it might significantly disrupt the country's nascent democratization, I think we should worry more about the extent to which violence, both personal and structural, has the capacity to insinuate itself into whatever nominally-democratic institutions emerge over the next few years.

If this conclusion sounds unduly pessimistic at a time when the trend is to be optimistic, then I should add to it my earnest hope (which, I believe, is a hope shared by my fellow authors), that the people of Myanmar may succeed in building a robust and lasting democracy in which political violence of all types is minimized. As the contents of this book make plain, a lot of goodwill exists for realizing that hope. Yet, goodwill obviously is not enough, and success is far from certain. Violence is as yet the decisive means for Myanmar's politics.

Perhaps in this respect Myanmar is not different from anywhere else. Still, the path to democracy that diminishes violence is not at all the same as the path through violence that diminishes democracy. Between the two lies all the difference in the world.

Notes

1   The 2013 Myanmar/Burma Update Conference at which the authors of chapters in this book participated did include a paper on Rakhine State from U Oo Hla Saw, Secretary General, Rakhine Nationalities Development Party, as well as a rejoinder from Mohammed Anwar, President, Burmese Rohingya Community in Australia. Podcasts of papers given at the conference are available online at http://asiapacific.anu.edu.au/news-events/podcasts/series/2013-myanmarburma-update. Most of the anti-Muslim violence in other parts of the country began during and after the conference.

2   See for instance: UN News Centre 2013; Kurlantzick 2013; Editorial board 2013.

3   Witness the speed with which the domestic media in June 2012 jumped atop of a pro-Rakhine anti-Rohingya platform.

4   *Kala* is a generic term that is used to designate people of South Asian origin and their descendants, and in general use it has a pejorative connotation. Here I refer to "so-called" illegal Bengalis in response to the narrative in domestic media on "so-called Rohingya" (*Yohingya-amigan...* or *Yohingya-hu-sothaw...*). As every act of naming is in a sense an act of "so-calling", the usage is in every instance redundant. See further, fn. 11.

5   Apart from Rakhine State, other areas where, up to time of writing, mobs had attacked and killed Muslims and burned down mosques, madrassas, and homes, include Meikhtila, Mandalay Region, and parts of Magway and Bago Regions in March and April 2013; Okkan in Yangon Region and surrounds at the end of April 2013; and Lashio, in Shan State, at the end of May 2013. Following events in Lashio, the violence took on a regional dimension, when a series of attacks occurred in Kuala Lumpur, Malaysia, leaving at least four people dead and others hospitalized (Malaysian Insider 2013).

6   Personal communications, April–June 2013.

7   Some media reports describe the Mandalay-based monk U Wirathu—whom *Time* magazine featured on its 1 July 2013 cover—as the founder of 969; however, he and other sources attribute its origins to a religious affairs bureaucrat, U Kyaw Lwin (Bookbinder 2013; Marshall 2013; Voice 2013, p. 13). In videos on

YouTube U Wirathu has described the 969-boycott campaign as having its origins in Mon State.

8   On the growth of private periodicals in Myanmar after 2008, see Pe Myint 2012.

9   *969 Shwe Myanma* and *Myanma Naingngan-lôn-saingya Amyothaye Hlutsha-hmu Kawmati.*

10 See, for instance, Nan Su Nin Htwe, Than Htaik Aung, and Kaung Than 2013. In mid-2012 in the immediate aftermath of the first round of violence in Rakhine State, photocopy shops in Yangon were doing a roaring trade running off copies of papers, articles, and books by local scholars as well as those based abroad arguing against the historical existence of Rohingya.

11 The report declines to recognize the term Rohingya because the group is not listed among the 135 official ethnic groups designated members of the "national races" (ICSVRS 2013, p. 7). By way of a contrasting example that also speaks to the politics of naming, the president of the United Nations Human Rights Council, in a statement condemning the violence read out in Geneva, pointedly referred to "Rohingya Muslims in Rakhine State and other Muslims in Myanmar", whereas the written draft text had only referred loosely to "Muslims in Myanmar" (Human Rights Council 2013).

12 The Rakhine State inquiry commission included Ko Ko Kyi of the 88 Generation Students Group, which has been active since the initial releases from prison of its members in the mid-2000s; famous writers and artistes like Maung Wuntha and Zarganar; and political party leaders and former dissidents like U Hkun Htun Oo of the Shan Nationalities League for Democracy, Daw Than Than Nu of the Democratic Party (Myanmar) (who does not offer any insights into the commission's work in her chapter of this book), U Khin Maung Swe, from the National Democratic Front, and returned academic, Kyaw Yin Hlaing (Thein Sein 2012a). Ko Ko Kyi and Min Ko Naing from the 88 Generation Students group were both named in the original presidential notification for the Letpadaung inquiry, but did not participate (Thein Sein 2012b).

13 On lawyers as activists, a topic not covered in Duell's chapter, see Cheesman and Kyaw Min San (forthcoming).

14 On 3 May 2013, for instance, one of the Rakhine State inquiry commissioners, Daw Yin Yin Nwei, went on the Voice of America Burmese Service to reject outright the contents of the Human Rights Watch report. She also vaguely criticized the BBC and United Nations Special Rapporteur on Human Rights in Myanmar for their responses to the violence.

15 Human rights lawyers have cited perceived threats from political groups as reasons for not taking up the cases of Muslims accused of involvement in the violence in Rakhine State (Personal communication, 1 May 2013). Not only villagers and townsfolk but also at least one prominent and hitherto respected

community leader has been convicted of serious criminal offences without having legal representation (AHRC 2013).

16 On the relationship between democratization, land, and rights claims, see Cheesman forthcoming.

17 For another example, in Kanma Township, Magway Region, see Cheesman and Kyaw Min San forthcoming.

18 Cited in personal communication, 28 February 2013.

References

Asian Human Rights Commission (AHRC). "Burma: Islamic Community Leader Unfairly Tried and Imprisoned Over Communal Violence". Asian Human Rights Commission, 1 February 2013. <http://www.humanrights.asia/news/urgent-appeals/AHRC-UAC-013-2013>. Accessed 5 June 2013.

Alternative ASEAN Network on Burma (ALTSEAN). "Anti-Muslim Violence in Central Burma". Bangkok: Alternative ASEAN Network on Burma, 2013. <http://www.altsean.org/Reports/Anti-Muslimviolence.php>. Accessed 8 December 2013.

Arendt, Hannah. *On Violence*. New York: Harcourt, Brace & World, Inc., 1969.

Aung Soe and Kyaw Oo Naing. *"Ma-ubin Myonè Ma-letto kye-ywa ôksu Ye hnin Taungthu Patipekka Ye Tat-pwè-win tit-u The-zôn* [Police Officer Dies in Conflict Between Police and Peasants in Maleto Village Tract, Ma-ubin Township]". *Voice*, 4–10 March 2013, p. 23.

Bookbinder, Alex. "969: The Strange Numerological Basis for Burma's Religious Violence". *Atlantic*, 9 April 2013. <http://www.theatlantic.com>. Accessed 10 April 2013.

Brass, Paul R. "Forms of Collective and State Violence in South Asia". In *Political Violence in South and Southeast Asia: Critical Perspectives*, edited by Itty Abraham, Edward Newman, and Meredith L. Weiss. Tokyo, New York and Paris: United Nations University Press, 2010.

Callahan, Mary P. *Making Enemies: War and State Building in Burma*. Ithaca and London: Cornell University Press, 2003.

Cheesman, Nick. "Legitimising the Union of Myanmar Through Primary School Textbooks". MEd dissertation, Graduate School of Education, University of Western Australia, Perth, 2002a.

———. "Seeing 'Karen' in the Union of Myanmar". *Asian Ethnicity* 3, no. 2 (2002b): 199–220.

———. Forthcoming. "What Does the Rule of Law Have To Do with Democratisation (in Myanmar)?". *South East Asia Research*.

Cheesman, Nick, and Kyaw Min San. Forthcoming. "Not Just Defending: Advocating for Law in Myanmar". *Wisconsin International Law Journal*.

Das, Veena. *Life and Words: Violence and the Descent into the Ordinary*. Berkeley, Los Angeles and London: University of California Press, 2007.

Diamond, Larry. "The Need for a Political Pact". *Journal of Democracy* 23, no. 4 (2012): 138–49.

Editorial Board, *New York Times*. "Attacks on Muslims in Myanmar". Editorial, *New York Times*, 30 May 2013. <http://www.nytimes.com/2013/05/31/opinion/attacks-on-myanmars-muslims.html?_r=0>. Accessed 3 June 2013.

Eleven Media. "*Thangadaw-mya-a Mi-laungze-thaw-pôn A-thônbyu Hnein-hningyin-adwet Ayeyugyin Ma-shi-zegamu Letpandaung Taung Kyeni Simankein Ayedwin Ubade-gyaung-aya Tugyegwin Ma-shebè Taungdan-gyagan-gèyathu Kunit-u-ati Shi-la* [Although No Action Taken Over Use of Incendiary Bombs In Suppression of Monks, Number of Persons Imprisoned Without Legal Right to Defence in Letpadaung Hills Copper Project Affair Reaches Seven]". Eleven Media, 9 June 2013. <http://www.news-eleven.com>. Accessed 11 June 2013.

Engvall, Anders, and Soe Nandar Linn. "Myanmar Economic Update: Macro-economy, Fiscal Reform, and Development Options". In *Debating Democratization in Myanmar*, edited by Nick Cheesman, Nicholas Farrelly, and Trevor Wilson. Singapore: Institute of Southeast Asian Studies, 2014.

Galtung, Johan. "Violence, Peace, and Peace Research". *Journal of Peace Research* 6, no. 3 (1969): 167–91.

Ghosh, Nirmal. "Myanmar Govt Targets 'Neo-Nazi' Buddhist Group". Asia News Net, 8 April 2013. <http://www.asianewsnet.net>. Accessed 18 June 2013.

Gupta, Akhil. *Red Tape: Bureaucracy, Structural Violence, and Poverty in India*. Durham and London: Duke University Press, 2012.

Human Rights Watch (HRW). "'All You Can Do is Pray': Crimes Against Humanity and Ethnic Cleansing of Rohingya Muslims in Burma's Arakan State". Washington DC: Human Rights Watch, 2013.

Human Rights Council. *Situation of Human Rights in Myanmar as Regards Rohingya Muslims in Rakhine State and other Muslims*. In *A/HRC/23/L.26*, United Nations General Assembly, 2013.

Inquiry Commission on the Letpadaung Hills Copper Mine Project (ICLHCMP). "*Sitkaing Taing-dethagyi, Mônywa Khayaing, Salingyi Myonè Letpandaung Taung Kyeni Simankein Sônzanzitseye Kawmashin-e Abyithat Aziyinkanza* [Final Report of the Inquiry Commission on the Letpadaung Hills Copper Mine Project, Salingyi Township, Monywa District, Sagaing Region]". *Myanma Alin*, 12 March 2013, 3–12.

Inquiry Commission on the Sectarian Violence in Rakhine State (ICSVRS). "*Rakhaing Pyinè Patibetka-mya Sônzanzitseye Kawmashin Aziyinkanza* [Report of the Inquiry

Commission on the Sectarian Violence in Rakhine State]". Yangon: Republic of the Union of Myanmar, 2013.

Irrawaddy. "'Underdevelopment' Caused Arakan Violence, Government Says". 9 December 2012. <http://www.irrawaddy.org>. Accessed 10 December 2012.

Kean, Thomas. "Myanmar's Parliament: From Scorn to Significance". In *Debating Democratization in Myanmar*, edited by Nick Cheesman, Nicholas Farrelly, and Trevor Wilson. Singapore: Institute of Southeast Asian Studies, 2014.

Kurlantzick, Joshua. *Myanmar: Listen to the Warnings.* Council on Foreign Relations, 2013.

Kyaw Kyaw Oo. "*Ma-ubin Myonè Maletto naik Pôkma 144 Yôk-thein* [Section 144 Retracted in Maleto, Ma-ubin Township]". *People's Age*, 7 March 2013, p. 36.

Kyaw Zwa Moe. "Fascism is Back in Fashion in Burma". *Irrawaddy*, 23 April 2013. <http://www.irrawaddy.org>. Accessed 18 June 2013.

Lahpai, Seng Maw. "State Terrorism and International Compliance: The Kachin Armed Struggle for Political Self-determination". In *Debating Democratisation in Myanmar*, edited by Nick Cheesman, Nicholas Farrelly, and Trevor Wilson. Singapore: Institute of Southeast Asian Studies, 2014.

Lawyers Network. *Letpadaung Taung Simankein Kawmashin Aziyinkanza abaw Shene-mya Kunyet-e Thabawta-tôkpyan-chet* [Lawyers Network Position on the Letpadaung Hills Project Commission Report]. 2013.

Lawyers Network (Upper Myanmar) (LN-UM) and 88 Generation Students Group (88GS). *Letpandaung Taung Kyeni Simankein-ko Nyeinchan-zwa Sandabya-negya-thudo-a Yè Tat-pwè-hma Hnein-hnin-hmu-abaw Sônzanzitse-twe-shi-hmu Aziyinkanza* [Report of Investigation into Police Battalion Suppression of Peaceful Demonstrators against the Letpadaung Hills Copper Project]. Edited by Lawyers Network (Upper Myanmar) and 88 Generation Students Group. Yangon: LN-UM and 88GS, 2013.

Lemargie, Kyle, Andrew Reynolds and others. "Electoral System Choice in Myanmar's Democratization Debate". In *Debating Democratization in Myanmar*, edited by Nick Cheesman, Nicholas Farrelly, and Trevor Wilson. Singapore: Institute of Southeast Asian Studies, 2014.

Malaysian Insider. "Four Dead as Myanmar Religious Clashes Bleed into KL". 5 June 2013. <http://www.themalaysianinsider.com/malaysia/article/four-dead-as-myanmar-religious-clashes-bleed-into-kl/>. Accessed 6 June 2013.

Marshall, Andrew R. C. "Myanmar Gives Official Blessing to Anti-Muslim Monks". Reuters, 27 June 2013. <http://www.reuters.com>. Accessed 11 July 2013.

Maung Aung Myoe. Forthcoming. "The Soldier and the State: The Tatmadaw and Political Liberalization in Myanmar since 2011". *South East Asia Research*.

Nan Su Nin Htwe, Than Htaik Aung, and Kaung Than. "*Yohingya-thi Taingyintha Ma-hôk-thi-hma Thamaing Adauk-ada Khainglônzwa-shi hu Daukda Aye Chan Yangôn-*

myo naik Pyaw-kya [Historical Evidence Solid that Rohingya Not A National Race, Dr Aye Chan Says in Yangon]". *Weekly Eleven*, 20 March 2013, p. 4.

Nyan Hlaing Lin. "*Tatmadaw Thein-yu thi Myeya-mya a-ye Amyanzôn Pyeshin-pe yan Sônzanye Kawmashin Taiktun* [Investigation Commission Urges Speediest Resolution of Matter of Defence Services Confiscated Lands]". *People's Age*, 7 March 2013, 19.

Oakeshott, Michael. "Political Education". In *Rationalism in Politics and Other Essays* by Michael Oakeshott. Indianapolis: Liberty Fund. 1991. Original edition, 1962.

Pe Myint. "The Emergence of Myanmar Weekly News Journals and Their Development in Recent Years". In *Myanmar's Transition: Openings, Obstacles and Opportunities*, edited by Nick Cheesman, Monique Skidmore, and Trevor Wilson. Singapore: Institute of South East Asian Studies, 2012.

Pedersen, Morten. "Myanmar's Democratic Opening: The Process and Prospect of Reform". In *Debating Democratization in Myanmar*, edited by Nick Cheesman, Nicholas Farrelly and Trevor Wilson. Singapore: Institute of Southeast Asian Studies, 2014.

Physicians for Human Rights (PHR). *Massacre in Central Burma: Muslim Students Terrorized and Killed in Meiktila*. Cambridge MA and Washington DC: Physicians for Human Rights, 2013.

Scheper-Hughes, Nancy. *Death without Weeping: The Violence of Everyday Life in Brazil*. Berkeley, Los Angeles and Oxford: University of California Press, 1992.

Selth, Andrew. "Police Reform in Myanmar: Changes 'in Essence and Appearance'". In *Debating Democratization in Myanmar*, edited by Nick Cheesman, Nicholas Farrelly and Trevor Wilson. Singapore: Institute of Southeast Asian Studies, 2014.

Spencer, Jonathan. "On Not Becoming a 'Terrorist': Problems of Memory, Agency, and Community in the Sri Lankan Conflict". In *Violence and Subjectivity*, edited by Veena Das, Arthur Kleinman, Mamphela Ramphele, and Pamela Reynolds. Berkeley, Los Angeles and London: University of California Press, 1997.

Thein Sein. *Ahmein Kyaw-nyaza Ahmat* 58/2012 [Notification No. 58/2012]. Naypyitaw: President's Office, Government of the Union of Myanmar, 2012*a*.

———. *Ahmein Kyaw-nyaza Ahmat* 92/2012 [Notification No. 92/2012]. Naypyitaw: President's Office, Government of the Union of Myanmar, 2012*b*.

Thiha, and Htun Khaing. "*Tatmadaw ka Mye-thein-hmu Tainggyachet 430 kyaw-htè-hma 41 hmu ko Pye-shinbyi* [41 of 430 Complaints of Armed Forces Land Seizure Resolved]". *7 Day News*, 28 January 2013. <http://www.7daynewsjournal.com>. Accessed 4 June 2013.

Turnell, Sean. "The Glass Has Water: A Stock-take of Myanmar's Economic Reforms". In *Debating Democratization in Myanmar*, edited by Nick Cheesman, Nicholas Farrelly, and Trevor Wilson. Singapore: Institute of Southeast Asian Studies, 2014.

UN News Centre. "Myanmar: UN Warns of Humanitarian Crisis Amid Continued Inter-communal Tensions". United Nations, 28 March 2013. <http://www.un.org>. Accessed 28 March 2013.

Van Klinken, Gerry. *Communal Violence and Democratization in Indonesia: Small Town Wars*. Routledge Contemporary Southeast Asia Series. London and New York: Routledge, 2007.

Voice. "*969 abaw Sayadaw-mya-e Thônthatchet* [Abbots' Reading of 969]". 2 April 2013, 13.

Walton, Matthew J. "The 'Wages of Burman-ness': Ethnicity and Burman Privilege in Contemporary Myanmar". *Journal of Contemporary Asia* 43, no. 1 (2013): 1–27.

Weber, Max. "Politics as a Vocation". In *From Max Weber: Essays in Sociology*, edited by H.H. Gerth and C. Wright Mills. London and New York: Routledge, 2009.

Winters, Jeffrey A. *Oligarchy*. New York: Cambridge University Press, 2011.

Zarni, Maung. "Neo-Nazi Denial in Myanmar". *Asia Times*, 24 May 2013. <http://www.atimes.com>. Accessed 18 June 2013.

LIST OF ABBREVIATIONS

AB	Ayeyarwady Bank
ABFSU	All Burma Federation of Student Unions
ABSDF	All Burma Students' Democratic Front
ADB	Asian Development Bank
AEC	ASEAN Economic Community
AFPFL	Anti-Fascist People's Freedom League
AGD	Asia Green Development Bank
AHRC	Asia Human Rights Commission
ALRC	Asian Legal Resource Centre
ASEAN	Association of South East Asian Nations
ATM(s)	Automatic Teller Machine(s)
BCP	Burma Communist Party
BDF	Burma Donors Forum
BOT	Build–Operate–Transfer
BSO-3	Bureau of Special Operations-3
BSPP	Burma Socialist Program Party
CBM	Central Bank of Myanmar
CBML	*Central Bank of Myanmar Law*
CDD	Community Driven Development (World Bank programme)
CIA	Central Intelligence Agency (U.S.)
CIDA	Canadian International Development Agency
CNF	Chin National Front
CRPPFMS	Committee for Reform of the People's Police Force Management System
CSO	civil society organization
DANIDA	Danish International Development Agency
DEA	Democratic and Ethnic Alliance
DFID	Department for International Development

DMAS	Directorate of Military Affairs Security
DP(M)	Democratic Party (Myanmar)
DPNS	Democratic Party for a New Society
DSA	Defence Services Academy
EITI	Extractive Industries Transparency Initiative
ENC	Ethnic Nationalities Council
EU	European Union
FAO	Food and Agriculture Organization
FDI	Foreign Direct Investment
FESR	Framework for Economic and Social Reforms
FIL	*Foreign Investment Law*
FIML	*Financial Institutions of Myanmar Law*
FPTP	first-past-the-post (voting system)
FTUB	Federation of Trade Unions-Burma
FUP	Federated Union Party
FY	fiscal year
GDP	gross domestic product
GIGA	German Institute of Global and Area Studies
GIZ	The German Society for International Cooperation (Deutsche Gesellschaft für Internationale Zusammenarbeit)
HIPCs	Heavily Indebted Poor Countries
HQ	headquarters
HRDU	Human Rights Documentation Unit
HRW	Human Rights Watch
ICG	International Crisis Group
IDEA	International Institute for Democracy and Electoral Assistance
IDP(s)	internally displaced person(s)
IDP(s)	internationally displaced person(s)
IFI	international financial institution
ILO	International Labour Organization
IMF	International Monetary Fund
INGO(s)	international non-government organization(s)
IRI	International Republican Institute
ITUC	International Trade Union Confederation
JBIC	Japan Bank for International Cooperation
JETRO	Japan External Trade Organization
KIA	Kachin Independence Army

KIO	Kachin Independence Organization
KNU	Karen National Union
MADB	Myanma Agricultural Development Bank
MAPCO	Myanmar Agri-business Public Corporation Limited
MCPT	Ministry of Communications, Posts and Telegraph
MDGs	Millennium Development Goals
MDRI	Myanmar Development Resource Institute
MEB	Myanma Economic Bank
MIC	Myanmar Investment Commission
MICB	Myanma Investment and Commercial Bank
MMP	mixed-member proportional (voting system)
MOFA	Ministry of Foreign Affairs
MOGE	Myanmar Oil and Gas Enterprise
MP(s)	Member(s) of Parliament
MPF	Myanmar Police Force
MPSI	Myanmar Peace Support Initiative
MPU	Members of Parliament Union
NCDO	National Committee for International Cooperation and Sustainable Development (Netherlands)
NCDP	National Comprehensive Development Plan
NCGUB	National Coalition Government of the Union of Burma
NCUB	National Coalition of the Union of Burma
NDF	National Democratic Force
NDSC	National Defence and Security Council
NED	National Endowment for Democracy
NGO(s)	non-government organization(s)
NIAS	Nordic Institute of Asian Studies
NLD	National League for Democracy
NLM	*New Light of Myanmar*
NORAD	Norwegian Agency for Development Cooperation
NUP	National Unity Party
OFAC	Office of Foreign Assets Control
OSFU	Fragile States Unit
OSI	Open Society Institute
PPF	People's Police Force
RNDP	Rakhine Nationalities Democratic Party
SADCs	special agricultural development companies
SDN	Specially Designated Nationals

SEE(s)	state-owned economic enterprise(s)
SIDA	Swedish International Development Cooperation Agency
SLORC	State Law and Order Restoration Council
SMO(s)	Social movement organization(s)
SNDP	Shan Nationalities Democratic Party
SNLD	Shan Nationalities League for Democracy
SPDC	State Peace and Development Council
SSA	Shan State Army
TAN(s)	Transnational advocacy network(s)
UEC	Union Election Commission
UNDP	United Nations Development Programme
UNESCAP	United Nations Economic and Social Commission for Asia and the Pacific
UNFC	United Nationalities Federal Council
UNFPA	United Nations Population Fund
UNGA	United Nations General Assembly
UNHCR	United Nations High Commission for Refugees
UNICEF	United Nations Children's Fund
UNIDO	United Nations Industrial Development Organization
UNIFEM	United Nations Development Fund for Women
UNODC	United Nations Office on Drugs and Crime
UPWC	Union Peacemaking Working Committee
USAID	United States
USDA	Union Solidarity and Development Association
USDP	Union Solidarity and Development Party
VOA	Voice of America
WFP	World Food Programme
WHO	World Health Organization

INDEX